Zoraida
A Romance of the Harem
and the Great Sahara

by

William Le Queux

Zoraida
A Romance of the Harem and the Great Sahara
by William Le Queux

ISBN: 978-93-59950-91-4

Published by

DOUBLE 9 BOOKS

2/13-B, Ansari Road
Daryaganj, New Delhi – 110002
info@double9books.com
www.double9books.com
Tel. 011-40042856

ABOUT THE AUTHOR

Anglo-French journalist and author William Tufnell Le Queux was born on July 2, 1864, and died on October 13, 1927. He was also a diplomat (honorary consul for San Marino), a traveler (in Europe, the Balkans, and North Africa), a fan of flying (he presided over the first British air meeting at Doncaster in 1909), and a wireless pioneer who played music on his own station long before radio was widely available. However, he often exaggerated his own skills and accomplishments. The Great War in England in 1897 (1894), a fantasy about an invasion by France and Russia, and The Invasion of 1910 (1906), a fantasy about an invasion by Germany, are his best-known works. Le Queux was born in the city. The man who raised him was English, and his father was French. He went to school in Europe and learned art in Paris from Ignazio (or Ignace) Spiridon. As a young man, he walked across Europe and then made a living by writing for French newspapers. He moved back to London in the late 1880s and managed the magazines Gossip and Piccadilly. In 1891, he became a parliamentary reporter for The Globe. He stopped working as a reporter in 1893 to focus on writing and traveling.

CONTENTS

Chapter One
Ali Ben Hafiz

The adventure was strange, the mystery inexplicable.

A blazing noontide in the month of Moharram. Away across the barren desert to the distant horizon nothing met the aching eye but a dreary waste of burning red-brown sand under a cloudless sky shining like burnished copper. Not an object relieved the wearying monotony of the waterless region forsaken by nature, not a palm, not a rock, not a knoll, not a vestige of herbage; nothing but the boundless silent expanse of that wild and wonderful wilderness, the Great Sahara, across which the sand-laden wind swept ever and anon in short stifling gusts hot as the breath from an oven.

Far beyond the Atlas mountains, under the fiery rays of the African sun, I was riding with all speed in order to overtake a caravan which I had been informed by the cadi at Wargla had started for Noum-en-Nas, the small town in the Touat Oasis, two days before my arrival. The caravan, I learned, was composed of camels, therefore, mounted as I was on a fleet Arab stallion, and guiding myself by my pocket compass and the very inadequate map of the Dépôt de la Guerre, I expected to come upon them ere two suns had set.

Four long breathless days had now passed, yet I could detect no living thing.

In the far south of Algeria the intense dry heat of summer always affects Europeans, and although clad lightly in haick and burnouse, with my feet thrust into rough slippers, I was no exception. Alone in that trackless, arid desert, with my food and water nearly consumed and my brain aflame with fever, I was bound to admit my position decidedly unenviable. I was afflicted by a hundred miseries. Into my face the glaring noonday heat was reflected by the sand; I was hungry, my throat was parched, the racking pain of fatigue cramped my bones, and my horse, weary and jaded, stumbled now and then as he plodded slowly onward under the fierce, pitiless rays.

The two Chasseurs d'Afrique who had been sent with me for protection by my friend the General of Division, had foolishly partaken of melons soon after leaving Tuggurt, and had been stricken down with illness in consequence; therefore I had been compelled to set out upon my journey into the Areg alone.

Suddenly, about an hour after noon, my eager eyes were rewarded by a sight in the far distance of a cloud of dust. Spurring my horse, I galloped onward, and in half an hour the bells of the camels and the jingle of the horses' trappings fell upon my ears. The dense whirling cloud of sand preceded the cavalcade, and whenever a gust of wind parted it, slow-plodding camels heavily laden with merchandise, glittering arms, and flowing scarlet and white burnouses could be seen. In this way the caravan presented itself as I pressed on towards its flank.

Within fifty paces of the vanguard I dug my heels into the horse's sides and bounded across to the head of the convoy of a dozen Spahis. A solitary rider journeying across the desert is such an unusual spectacle that the ferocious-looking advance guard, fearing attack, shouted and lowered their rifles.

"*Phtaris*! Peace be upon thee!" I cried in Arabic, seeing myself received in such a hostile manner. "Cowards! Thou seemest afraid that a single Englishman will attack thy caravan!"

The guards, thus reproached, muttering that they were pressing through the turbulent country of the Beni Zougs, raised their weapons with a look of shame upon their dark-bearded faces, while their chief reined his horse to interrogate me.

"Whose is this caravan?" I asked, disregarding his string of rapidly-uttered inquiries.

"It belongeth to Ali Ben Hafiz, the merchant of Biskra," he replied.

"And thou art on thy way to Noum-en-Nas?"

"True," he answered, with a puzzled look. "But how dost thou know? What dost thou want with us?"

"Conduct me to thy master," I said. "It is imperative that I should speak with him."

As I uttered these words, an elderly grave-faced man, with a long white beard flowing over his spotless burnouse, rode up, and, judging him to be the merchant for whom I had been searching, I greeted him and gave him peace.

"*Aish ism arrajol di?*" ("What is the name of this man?") he asked suspiciously of the chief of the convoy.

"My name," I exclaimed, "is Cecil Holcombe, an Englishman who desireth to travel to the Touat Oasis. The Director of Fate turned the bridle of my horse towards thee and allowed me to hear the bells of thy camels from afar; the Guide of the Reins of Destiny moved my intention so that I came hither to meet thee. Behold! I bear unto thee a letter from our mutual friend, General Malezieux, Chief of Division."

The name of that high official caused him to open his keen dark eyes wider, and, taking the letter from me, he quickly read it. In Arabic my friend the General greeted his brother Ali Ben Hafiz with strings of salutations and references to the Prophet, and implored him to take under his protection the adventurous Englishman.

When the old merchant had read it through twice, he slowly stroked his patriarchal beard. Then, looking up, he said in his own language—

"M'sieur Holcombe, be welcome to our shade. Allah, the One Merciful, is mighty: Allah, Lord of the Three Worlds, is wise. He ordaineth that although thou art an unbeliever, we should nevertheless be companions. It giveth me pleasure to succour thee—but before all take salt with us."

The order was given to halt, a tent was quickly pitched, and we took salt and ate our kousskouss together, afterwards smoking our long haschish pipes until the noon was far spent. About five o'clock we resumed our journey again over the barren plain, the venerable-looking old Arab, in whom I found a most prayerful, pious, and entertaining host, riding by my side. The convoy of dark-faced Spahis, who, picturesque in their scarlet burnouses, had viewed me with such distrust, now regarded me as a distinguished guest, and were ready at every moment to do my bidding. To those who, like myself, have learned in the desert to regard life steadily, nothing temporal seems of moment when travelling by caravan, and our civilisation, of which we in Western Europe pride ourselves, seems but a frivolous thing of yesterday. Desert life to-day is the same as it was ten centuries ago; the same as it will ever be. Free and charming in its simplicity, yet with certain terrors ever-present, it offers many attractions to those in search of change and excitement. Thus, with the fiery sunset flooding the boundless wilderness, we wended our way due westward in the blood-red track of the departing day.

When the last rays were fading, another halt was made, the mats were spread, and Ali Ben Hafiz with his convoy and camel-drivers knelt, and, turning their faces towards Mecca, repeated their evening prayer, afterwards reciting with fervent devotion the Fâtiha: "Praise be to Allah, Lord of all creatures; the most merciful, King of the day of Judgment, Thee do we worship, and of Thee do we beg assistance. Direct us in the Right

Way, in the way of those to whom Thou hast been gracious; not of those against whom Thou art incensed, nor of those who go astray."

Then in the falling gloom we again moved on. Slowly our camels plodded, the rhythmic movement of their heads causing their bells to jingle, and now and then an Arab would chant a weird Bedouin song, or goad on his animals, administering heavy blows emphasised by sundry forcible imprecations with frequent references to Eblis.

Old Ali—who was a native of Morocco and still acknowledged Mulai Hassan as his ruler, although he lived under the French flag—asked me to relate my history, and tell him of England and the Great White Queen; therefore, as we rode together, I entertained him with descriptions of my distant home, explaining to him our insular manners and customs, until the bright moon rose and the stars twinkled like diamonds in the cloudless vault of blue. At last, having entered a wild ravine, where some prickly acacias, dusty aloes, and patches of coarse hulfa grass grew, under the shadow of the rocks we encamped for the night. Our kousskouss was cooked and eaten, our horses fed and watered at the well, and while the Spahis were posted as sentinels to raise the alarm in the event of a raid by any of the fierce marauding bands that constantly prowl about that region, we wrapped ourselves in the ample folds of our burnouses and rested our weary heads upon our saddles.

Chapter Two
The Omen of the Camel's Hoof

On over the barren sand-hills, always in the track of the setting sun, each day passed much as its predecessor. I was no stranger to Northern Africa, for the wild, free life, unshackled by conventionalities, had a fascination for me, and consequently I had accompanied caravans through Tunis and Tripoli, and had wandered a good deal in Morocco. In the course of these journeys I had learned to love the Arabs, and had formed the acquaintance of many powerful Sheikhs, several of whom I now counted among my most faithful and devoted friends. Indeed, it was to join one of them, the head of the Tédjéhé-N'ou-Sidi, that I was now on my way south to Zamlen, in the Afelèle region.

After three years among the True Believers, I had at last overcome most of the difficulties of language, and could converse with them in their own tongue. It may have been this which commended itself to pious old Ali Ben Hafiz, for throughout our journey he was particularly gracious, though he bored me sometimes with his constant objurgatory remarks regarding Infidels in general and myself in particular. Once in exuberance of spirits I so far forgot myself as to whistle a popular English air, and although we were excellent friends, he reprimanded me so severely that I am not likely to forget that among the followers of the Prophet whistling is forbidden.

One morning, while riding together soon after dawn, he surprised me by suddenly observing in a grave tone—

"Thou art young and of good stature. It surpriseth me that thou dost not return to thine own people and take a wife from among them."

"Why should I marry?" I asked, laughing. "While I am alone, I wander at my own inclination; if I married, my actions would be ruled by another."

"Because ere the sun had risen this morning a camel had placed its hoof upon thy spittle," he answered, looking at me with his keen serious eyes that age had not dimmed. "It is an omen. 'Ty-ib bi'chire Allah yosallimak!'"

"An omen! Of what?" I asked.

"Of impending evil."

"But we English believe not in superstition; neither have we witches nor sorcerers," I replied, smiling.

"Infidels have no need of them," he retorted, angrily. "Only True Believers will behold the great lote tree, or quench their thirst at Salsabil, Allah be thanked!"

"But this strange omen—what particular misfortune is it supposed to presage?" I inquired eagerly, astonished at the vehemence of his denunciation.

"Hearken, and take heed," he said, earnestly. "Thou art young, and as yet no woman hath captivated thee. Do I give utterance to the truth?"

"Yes," I answered. "As yet I have never been enmeshed."

"Then beware! There will be a day when thy life will be lightened by the rays of a woman's face, rivalled only by the sun. Her eyes will be brilliant as the gazelle's, her cheeks will bear the bloom of the peach, and her lips will be sweet as the fresh-blown rose. In those eyes the love-light will flash, those cheeks will blush at thine approach, and those lips will meet with passion thy caress. Then remember the words of Ali Ben Hafiz. Remember the Omen of the Camel's Hoof!" We rode on together in silence for some minutes. I was pondering over his strange words.

"On the auspicious day when I meet this paragon of beauty which you prophesy, how am I to act?" I asked presently.

"Act?" he cried. "Do nothing. Return not her caresses. Cast her from thee even though she be one of the houris of Paradise, and—"

"Will she be a Moor, an Arab, or one of mine own people?" I inquired, interrupting him.

"Ask me not. I am no prophet, though this is not the first time I have seen similar cases to thine. The Omen of the Camel's Hoof hath been revealed—and it is fatal."

"Fatal?" I cried in alarm. "What dost thou mean? Am I to die?"

"It resulteth in death—sometimes. It is always fatal to love."

"Have others succumbed, then?" I asked.

"Yes, alas!" he said, with knit brows and a curiously thoughtful expression. "One case occurred in mine own family. My nephew, who was of about the same age as thou art, had the distinctive mark between the eyes, the same as thou hast upon thy countenance. After the last Fast of Ramadân, he took the caravan of his father and journeyed for one moon west to Duera, in Morocco. Before the sun had risen on the last day of Doul

Hadja, the camel he was riding, alas! stepped upon his spittle. His tent-man, a Biskri well versed in anthroposcopy, told him of the ominous warning, but he ridiculed it, saying that Kamra Fathma, the daughter of the cadi at Bona, was already betrothed unto him, and that he could never look with admiration upon another woman's face. The Omen had been revealed; its warning was, alas! disregarded."

"What was the result?" I inquired, rather alarmed at my friend's extraordinary prophetic demeanour.

"Ah, the result? It was fatal! A week later he who scoffed at the humble tent-man's words crossed the Figuig into the land of our lord the Sultan. There, at Sidi Mumen, he chanced to pass the daughter of the Basha on foot. An ill wind blew aside her veil, and he gazed for a second upon her uncovered face. The lines of her fatal beauty were in that instant graven deeply upon his heart, and he loved her violently, casting aside the pretty Kamra, his betrothed at Bona. Tarrying long near the woman who had fascinated him, he succeeded in earning the good graces of the Basha, and at length married her."

He paused, and, drawing a long breath, pulled his burnouse more tightly around his shoulders.

"Well, if he succeeded in marrying her, the Omen of the Camel's Hoof could not have been fatal to love," I argued.

"But it was!" he replied quickly. "After his marriage, he remained in Sidi Mumen, and set up a large house, and his wife had many slaves."

"Was he not happy?"

"For three moons, and then—"

"And then?"

"The prophecy was fulfilled. He took a cup of tea too much. (An expression used by the Moors, poison being invariably administered in tea.) The woman who had entranced him and obtained his money was verily a daughter of Eblis. She poisoned him!"

"Horrible!" I said. "I hope mine will not be a similar fate."

The old man, who, before setting out on his journey, had without doubt promised a feast to his favourite marabout in return for the latter's all-powerful prayers for his safety, shrugged his shoulders, but answered nothing.

Chapter Three
Entrapped

The curiously prophetic utterances of Ali Ben Hafiz caused me to reflect. I knew much of Moslem superstition,—in fact, I had collected many of the strange beliefs of the Arabs, Moors, and Koulouglis, with the intention of including them in a book I was writing,—but this extraordinary *avant-coureur* of evil was new to me. During the blazing day, as we toiled on over the sun-baked plain, again and again I recalled his ominous words. The prophecy made me feel uncomfortable. Somehow, try how I would, I could not rid myself of the thought that some untoward event would ere long occur.

In this record of facts I am compelled to speak briefly of myself. Life had indeed been a strange series of ups and downs. Being left an orphan, I had early in life imbibed the reckless Bohemianism of the Quartier Latin, and my later years had been almost equally divided between the conventionalities of London and Paris and the wild, free life of the Bedouins of Northern Africa. Truth to tell, civilisation, with its hollow shams and its *décolleté* and frock-coated *beau monde*, had no charm for me. The leaden skies of London and the glitter and artificiality of Paris were alike hateful. I only enjoyed happiness when, attired in haick and slippers, I sat cross-legged with the people of Al-Islâm, studying their grave, interesting characteristics, and perfecting my knowledge of that most wonderful of languages, Arabic.

Fettered no longer by the shackles of Society, I wandered, explored, and studied, the reason of this restlessness being most likely due to the fact that I had never gazed upon a woman with thoughts of love. The Bohemianism of the Seine-bank had distorted my views of life, so that I regarded woman as a heartless coquette, and perhaps had become cynical, even misanthropic. Therefore, on thinking over old Ali's warning, I grew at length to regard it as a mere superstition of the mystic Moslem, and succeeded at last in dismissing it from my mind.

The blazing day wore on, and was succeeded by a glorious evening. We were in that wild, inhospitable region known as the Adjemor, about midway between the little Arab settlement of El Biodh and the palms of Aïn-el-Redjem. Away on the misty horizon the rising ground of the great plateau of Tademait was tinged with orange and gold, but as my fellow wanderers knelt upon their carpets, cast dust over their feet, and, salaaming, droned forth passages of the Saba in a monotone, the deep well of the west was still ablaze with crimson and silver. It was a bad sign, for the thin haze which hung upon the ground warned us that ere long we should be overwhelmed by one of the terrors of the desert—the sandstorm. Its stifling clouds of whirling sand might sweep down upon us immediately, or might not reach us for twelve or fourteen hours; but we were all aware that assuredly it must come, therefore, before throwing ourselves down to rest, we took necessary precautions to ensure our safety.

Alone in my tent, I lay unable to sleep, for before the sirocco the heat always becomes unbearable. The dead silence of the wilderness was only broken by the champing of the camels and the jingle of the single Spahi, who, mounting guard over us, marched slowly up and down, his footsteps sounding muffled in the sand. Through the open door of the tent I could see how clear and bright was the night, how brilliantly the big moon of the East shone white over the desert, and for a long time I lay thinking of home and of the strange words of Ali, until sleep at length came to my aching eyes.

Loud shouting and rifle-shots rapidly exchanged awakened me. For a moment I was dazed by the weird, exciting scene. White-robed figures on horseback tearing past my tent were firing their long-barrelled guns, and our men were repelling the assault vigorously with their Winchesters.

We were being attacked by a band of marauders; I knew it would be a fight to the death!

Grasping my revolver, I sprang to my feet and rushed forth. As I did so, a gigantic Arab barred my passage. The fierce, dark-faced fellow had just swung himself from his horse, and in his sinewy hand there gleamed a long curved knife.

In a second we had closed in deadly embrace. Clutching me by the throat, he forced me backwards, at the same moment uttering a curse and raising the keen blade above his head. For a second it was poised in mid air, but quick as thought I managed to wrench away my right hand, and, bringing it across my breast, fired my revolver full into his dark, sinister face.

With a cry he staggered. The knife fell, but I evaded it, and, gradually loosening his hold upon my throat, he stumbled backwards, and, tottering, sank heavily to the ground.

Leaving him, I rushed out to assist my companions, for the rattle of musketry was incessant, and bullets were singing about us in a manner that was particularly disconcerting. Dashing forward, I saw our Spahis had apparently been taken completely by surprise, four of them having fallen dead, and two were lying near, writhing under the agony of their wounds.

The shouting and firing were deafening, the flashing of guns shedding a lurid glare, while, to add to the horror of those moments, the storm had burst upon us, choking clouds of sand enveloping both enemy and friend.

Once only, amid the whirling cloud of dust and smoke, I caught sight of the hospitable old merchant. Two of the robbers had seized him, and were securing his arms and legs with cords, when suddenly he turned upon them with the ferocity of a tiger, and, drawing a knife from his crimson sash, plunged it into the heart of one of his captors.

The man staggered and fell backwards dead, like a stone.

A second later there was a bright flash from a rifle fired by a man near me, and Ali Ben Hafiz, throwing up his arms with a cry, fell forward over the corpse of the man he had killed. Just at that moment I felt myself seized from behind. Turning quickly, intending to use my revolver, the weapon was snatched from my hand, and a cord with a noose passed quickly over my head. I fought hard; but how long can one fight against a score? The flash of the guns illumined for a second the faces of the fierce bandits into whose power I had unfortunately fallen. All were big, desperate-looking Bedouins of the tribe of the Ennitra, who live away south in the Ahaggar region, and whose men, reputed to be the worst of desperadoes, were the terror of the caravans.

While they forced my hands behind me and secured them, my brave companions, the Spahis and camel-drivers, after making a most desperate resistance, were one after another shot down before my eyes. The band outnumbered us by six to one, and already the camels, with Ali's valuable packs of textile fabrics, arms and ammunition, had been captured and driven off.

"Devils!" I cried, as I watched the sickening slaughter. "Why not complete thine hideous work and shoot me also?"

"Behold! he hath a pale face!" cried one of my captors, peering into my eyes and showing his white teeth as he grinned viciously. "See! he is not an Arab! He is a dog of an Infidel!"

"Kill him! kill him!" cried one of the others, excitedly brandishing a knife. "His touch will contaminate. The Roumi will bring the curse of Sajin upon us!"

His words and threatening attitude alarmed me, for, remembering that these men were of the sect of the Aïssáwà, the wildest of the fanatics of Al-Islâm, I knew they were not likely to show much mercy to one who had not embraced their religion or gone through their hideous rites. Whoever Sidi ben Aïssa, the patron saint of this strange sect, might have been, he certainly numbers among his followers some of the worst malefactors of Algeria. Any Mohammedan may be initiated into the Aïssáwà. He makes a pilgrimage to Mequinez, in Morocco, calls upon the representative of Sidi ben Aïssa's family, to whom he offers prayers and money. This over, the priest blows upon him, and the devotee arises and departs, firmly believing that however many venomous snakes may bite him, no harm will befall him.

Although in a frenzy of excitement over their terrible work of slaughter, they seemed in no mood to kill me. As the sandstorm abated, and dawn spread, the scene was awful. The whole of our men had, I saw, been ruthlessly massacred, and I alone remained the sole survivor.

Breathlessly I stood, my arms bound so tightly as to cause me pain, awaiting my fate. How, I wondered, would it end? Presently, when the contents of our camels' packs had been cursorily inspected, I was tied to a mule, and dragged on over the desert in the direction of the rising sun. Through the long hot day I was forced to trudge wearily onward into that region of the Ahaggar where no Bedouins dare penetrate. Jeering, they refused my request for water to moisten my parched throat, and it was not until long after noon that they tossed me a handful of dates to satisfy my hunger.

Just before sundown we came upon an oasis where the palms grew high, and there came out to meet us a dirty, ferocious rabble, shouting, gesticulating, and rejoicing that the raid had been successful. My captors were cheered again and again, while I, as an unbeliever, was cuffed and spat upon. Between two tall bronzed ruffians I was led straightway among the scattered tents to the Sheikh of the marauders, whom I afterwards learned was Hadj Absalam, the notorious outlaw upon whose head a price had long been set by the French Government.

He was a sinister-looking old man, with a pair of black, gleaming eyes, a long grey beard, and an ugly cicatrix across his tawny forehead. As his name denoted, he had made the pilgrimage earlier in life, but the criminal was stamped in every line of his face, and I could quite believe him capable of the many barbarous cruelties attributed to him.

The marauders explained how they had attacked and captured our caravan, and, finding that I was an Englishman, they had spared my life and brought me to him.

The robber Sheikh of the Ennitra heard all without removing his long pipe from his lips or betraying the least excitement. Suddenly turning his piercing eyes upon me, he exclaimed—

"Thou art an unbeliever that Allah hath delivered into our hands for punishment. Verily, Allah hath cursed the Infidels, and hath prepared for them in Al-Hâwiyat a fierce fire wherein they shall remain for ever. They shall find no patron or defender. Death by the knife is too merciful an end for dogs of thy mongrel breed."

"But, my father," I exclaimed, "I have not offended against thee. I am merely journeying here to study thy tongue."

"Silence, Infidel!" he roared. "Speak not to Allah's chosen. Thine accursed body shall be racked by the torture ere thou goest unto the Kingdom of Shades."

Then, turning to the men who held me, he said, "Take him out among the rocks and let the punishment commence."

Heedless of my vigorous protests, I was hurried along, followed by the ragged crowd of excited fanatics, who still jeered and spat upon me, until we reached the edge of the oasis, which, as I afterwards learned, was named the Igharghar. It was die game, or die coward. I remembered the strange Omen of the Camel's Hoof!

At a spot where great grey rocks cropped out of the sand, my captors halted, and, forcing me to the ground, lashed me to the trunk of a date palm. The rope was passed under my arms and fastened to the base of the trunk, leaving about four feet of slack rope between my head and the tree. Then, my feet being bound, they drove a stake into the ground and tied them to it. Thus I lay stretched upon the ground, and, struggle as I would, I was unable to move. The cords sank into my flesh, and the crowd around me laughed and shouted when they saw my face distorted by pain.

I knew no mercy would be shown me by Hadj Absalam's band, who delighted in cruelty to their victims, and whose religious rites were practised amid scenes of horror and bloodshed. Yet if they meant to simply leave me there to starve and die under the blazing sun, why did they secure me in this fashion? They could have maimed my feet and hands, and there would have been no need of this elaborate preparation.

A sudden shout caused me to try and look up. Several men were running towards me, their white burnouses flowing behind them. One of them carried in his hand a little stick with a noose on the end, and in the noose there writhed a large black asp, one of the deadly denizens of the rocks.

The sight froze my blood. I knew that they meant to kill me.

Amid the wild excitement of the crowd, who had now gone half mad at the prospect of seeing an Infidel done to death, two long thin thongs of mule-skin were placed through the skin and muscles of the snake, close to its tail. The serpent squirmed under the pain, but his head was held fast in the loop.

Within four feet of my face another stake was driven into the ground, and to this the loose ends of the thongs were fastened. The Arabs sprang back. The snake was free from the noose, but bound fast by the thong through its tail.

My face was directly before it; yet I could not move! In an instant the snake was in a half coil, with its bead-like eyes fixed upon mine.

As I held my breath in that brief second, the warning of Ali Ben Hafiz again flashed through my mind. The sweat stood upon my brow. The crowd pressing around me became hushed in expectancy. To have been murdered with my fellow-travellers would have been far preferable to this torture.

The horror of that moment was awful.

The serpent, enraged by pain, raised its flat head ready to strike. I set my teeth and closed my eyes, waiting to feel its deadly fangs upon my cheek.

Another instant, and its venom would be coursing through my veins!

Chapter Four
A Veiled Face

But my cruel captors intended to torture me; to delay my death as long as possible.

Like a flash the head of the gliding serpent shot out. The thong withstood its spring. It fell two inches short of my face. A tiny drop of liquid spurted upon my temple and ran down my cheek. It was the venom from the fangs that failed to reach! The Arabs roared with laughter.

But they were wasting time. From their conversation I gathered that a squadron of Spahis were in search of them to punish them for the many robberies and murders they had committed, and that they were moving at dawn towards the Tanezrouft, a waterless desert that has never been wholly explored by Europeans. They had to examine the packs of Ali Ben Hafiz's camels, so, after laughing and jeering at me for some time, they teased the asp, and then returned to their encampment.

Through the long brilliant evening I lay there alone, the snake's head playing before my eyes, more of the venom being spat into my face.

The sun at last disappeared in a blaze of crimson, and the clouds covered the heavens.

The snake had learned that it could not reach my face. It lay coiled at the foot of the stake watching. For a while longer it struck each time I moved my head, but presently it lay again in its sullen coil. The strain of holding my head back, back, until the cords fairly cracked, was awful. How long, I wondered, would it be before my mind would give way and madness relieve me from this deadly terror?

Darkness crept on. Above the low Iraouen hills the moon rose, and shone full upon my face. The beating of *derboukas*, the playing of *kánoons*, and sounds of singing and dancing made it plain that the marauders had discovered the great value of the merchandise they had stolen, and were making merry. Slowly the moments dragged. Time after time I struggled to get free, but in vain. The outlaws had bound me in such a manner that the more I struggled the deeper sank the cords into my flesh. Presently I heard shuffling footsteps, and, looking up, saw approaching two of the villainous men who had assisted to bind me. One of them carried a pitcher of water he had procured from the well.

"Take thy knife and kill me," I cried. "Death is better than this horrible torment."

They both laughed derisively, and, bending, poured water upon the rope that held me and upon the serpent's thongs.

"Thou wilt be claimed by Eblis soon enough," one of the men replied, grimly.

"My throat is dry. Give me a drop of water—one mouthful—that I may quench this terrible thirst consuming me," I implored.

But again they only laughed, and, flinging the water from the battered copper pitcher upon the sand, the man said, "Thou art accursed of Allah, and our father hath decreed that thou shalt die."

"Then kill me! kill me!" I cried in agony. "I am going mad."

"That is part of thy punishment," replied the other man, unconcernedly shrugging his shoulders and walking away, followed by his laughing companion. My heart sank within me.

The cool wind that had sprung up revived me, and I felt the pangs of hunger. Still before me I saw those coils and that flat head. In the white moonlight I could distinguish the snake's tongue darting out; he was preparing for another spring.

He struck, but still he could not reach. An inch more, and his venomous fangs would have buried themselves in my cheek!

I rubbed my face in the sand to clear it of the horrible poison now thickening upon it.

I must have lapsed into unconsciousness for a long time, but on awaking, all was silent as the grave. The nomads of the Ennitra, who had long been hunted in vain by the Algerian soldiers, were asleep. I felt the strain of the rope growing more painful. I had been pulling back on it with all my force, but now I felt a counter-pull that was slowly drawing me towards the asp and death.

Why did I not push my face towards the serpent and end the torture? I had a presentiment that I should die from the moment I had fallen into the hands of these robbers. I knew that I must succumb to hunger and thirst, even if the asp did not reach me. But life is always sweet. I could not bring myself to die. My mad brain refused to order the muscles to meet the reptile.

The rope pulled harder. Then I knew. The water those brutes had poured upon it was shrinking it! The distance between my face and the fangs of my black enemy was gradually being lessened. An inch more would mean death!

I dug my toes into the ground. I pulled back until the rope cut deeply into my flesh and the blood flowed. The cords that bound me were shortening!

Water had also been poured upon the thongs that held the snake. The mule-hide swelled and stretched, while the hempen rope shrank.

The snake tried to crawl away. The strings in its flesh held it back. The pain enraged it, and its head shot forth once again. Its tongue came within half an inch of my forehead!

Closing my eyes, I must have once more lapsed into a state of half-consciousness, knowing that the thongs which held the reptile were stretching, and that in a few minutes death would release me from the torture.

Suddenly the *frou-frou* of silk greeted my ears, and a second later I became aware of someone leaning over me.

"Hist! Peace be upon thee!" exclaimed a soft voice in tuneful Arabic. "*Lissa fih wákt!*" ("There is yet time.") The face bending over me was closely veiled, but above the *adjar* a pair of bright sparkling eyes peered into mine, while across the white forehead hung rows of golden sequins. I was amazed. Whether my strange visitant were young or old I could not tell, but her splendid eyes had a curious fascination in them such as I had never before experienced.

Her arm, bare to the shoulder, was white and well rounded; on her slim wrists were heavy Arab bracelets of gold and silver, studded with jacinths and turquoises, and in her hand was a long thin knife, the blade of which flashed in the moonlight.

"What art thou?" I gasped. "Who art thou?"

"Thy friend," she replied, quietly. "Make not a sound, for my life as well as thine is at stake. See! I cut the cords that bind thee!" and so saying, she severed my bonds quickly and deftly with her curved dagger, the jewelled scabbard of which hung upon her girdle.

Half dazed, but finding both hands and feet free, I jumped up, and, stepping aside from the spot where the serpent darted forth, stood before my mysterious deliverer.

She was of medium height, slim and graceful. The hideous haick and baggy white trousers which always shroud the women of the Arabs when out of doors were absent, for apparently she had stolen from her tent, and, with the exception of the flimsy veil across her face, she was still in her harem dress. Set jauntily upon her head she wore the usual dainty little skull-cap of velvet thick with gold and seed pearls, her *serroual* of pale blue China silk were drawn tight midway between the knee and ankle, her rich velvet zouave was heavily trimmed with gold, and her bare feet were thrust into tiny velvet slippers. A wide sash of silk encircled her waist, and the profusion of gold bangles on her ankles had been tied together so that they should not jingle as she walked.

"*Al'hamdu lillâh dâki lakom!*" she exclaimed solemnly, which translated meant, "Praise be unto Allah, praying for thee."

"Allah be praised!" I responded fervently. "Thou art my deliverer. How can I ever sufficiently thank thee?"

Shrugging her shoulders with infinite grace, she replied, "Thanks are not necessary. The knowledge that thou hast escaped a horrible death is all the reward I require." She spoke in low musical tones, and her accents were those of a town-dweller rather than of a nomad of the Sahara.

"But why dost thou run such risks in order to deliver me—an Infidel?" I asked, recollecting that if detected, little mercy would be shown her by that barbarous fanatical band.

"I watched thee brought before the Sheikh, and I heard him condemn thee to the torture. For hours I have been awake thinking, and at last determined to save thee. Come, make no noise, but follow."

Cautiously she moved away, taking care to keep in the shadow of the rocks. So graceful was her carriage, so supple was her figure, that, as I walked behind her, I felt convinced that she must be young. Once she halted, and, turning her splendid eyes upon me, said—

"Thou wilt forgive my people, wilt thou not? I make no excuse for their barbarities, I only ask thee to forgive."

"Thou hast saved my life," I replied. "How can I refuse any request thou makest?"

She laughed a short, silvery laugh, and, turning, sped on again, her little slippers coming to sad grief over the rough stones. Presently I stopped her, and, placing my hand lightly on her shoulder, said—

"May I not gaze upon thy face for one brief moment?"

"I cannot permit," she cried, shrinking from me. "Remember, thou art an Infidel!"

Her answer was a stinging rebuff.

"None of thy people are here to witness," I urged. "Let me for one second unclasp thy *adjar* and gaze upon thy countenance;" and at the same time I made a movement as if to tear away the tantalising veil that concealed her features.

"No! no!" she cried in alarm, stepping back and covering her face with both hands. "Thou must not! Thou shalt not! This, then, is thy reward to one who has risked so much to save thee?" she said reproachfully.

"Forgive me," I exclaimed quickly, dropping upon my knee and raising her soft, delicate hand to my lips. But she drew it away firmly, as if my touch stung her.

"Rise," she said, rather harshly. "I forgive thee, of course, but there is no time for courtesies. Come."

Passing round to the other side of the rock, I found tethered in the centre of a patch of tamarisk a splendid Arab horse with handsome trappings.

When she approached, the animal pawed, rubbing its nose upon her hand.

"It is mine," she said, "and I give it to thee in the hope that Allah may guard thee, and that thou wilt get away to the Atlas in safety. I saddled it with mine own hands, so in the bags thou wilt find both food and drink. On leaving here, keep straight over yonder hill, then spur with all speed always towards the east. Before three suns have set, thou wilt rest on the Oasis of Meskam, where are encamped the Spahis who are in search of us. Thou wilt be safe with them, although thou wilt not inform them of our whereabouts?"

"No, I promise to preserve thy secret," I said.

Dawn was spreading quickly, and in the grey light I could see more distinctly the part of her countenance left uncovered.

Grasping her slim, white hand, with its fingers laden with roughly-cut gems, I looked earnestly into her magnificent eyes, and again asked, "Is thy decision utterly irrevocable? May I not look for once upon thy face? Think, I have been delivered from a horrible death, yet to recognise my deliverer again will be impossible!"

"You and I are strangers," she replied slowly. "Thou art a European, while I am a homeless wanderer of the desert. If thine eyes do not gaze upon my countenance, I shall have committed one sin the less, and thou wilt never be troubled by any recollections. Memories are apt to be tiresome sometimes, and it is written that the True Believer is—"

"With me thy memory will always remain that of a brave, tender, but mysterious woman, to whom I owe my life."

"That is how I wish thee to think of me. Perhaps I too may remember thee sometimes, though it would be sinful for me to do so. What is thy name?"

"Cecil Holcombe."

She repeated the four syllables with a pretty Arab accent.

"And thine?" I asked, still holding her white hand and gazing into her eyes.

She hesitated. I felt she was trembling. Her breath came quickly.

"Mount, and go," she said. "I—I have risked too much. Besides, thou mayest not discover who I really am. It would be *fatal!*"

"But thy name?" I urged. She seemed bent upon preserving her incognita, and I was growing impatient. That she was lovely I felt sure. No face could be ugly with those magnificent eyes. "Surely thou wilt not withhold from me thy name?"

She was silent. Her slim, bejewelled fingers closed over mine with a slight pressure as she sighed. Then, lifting her eyes, she replied—

"I am called Zoraida."

"The daughter of whom?"

"Daughter of the Sun," she replied, smiling.

"Then thou wilt not tell me the name of thy father?" I said, disappointedly.

She shook her head, replying, "No. To thee I am only Zoraida. My father's name is of no concern."

"And may I not carry with me some little souvenir of this strange meeting?" I asked.

Slowly she drew a quaint, old-fashioned ring from her finger and placed it upon my hand, laughing the while, saying—

"When thou art far beyond the mountains, this will remind thee how near thou hast been to death;" adding anxiously, "Now go, I beg. See! the sun will soon break forth! Do not tarry another instant—for my sake!"

"Zoraida, shall we never meet again?" I asked desperately, for the mystery surrounding her and her strange words caused me to forget the danger of lingering. "Art thou never in Algiers or Oran, or any of the towns by the sea?"

"Sometimes in Algiers. But very, very seldom. Yet even if I were, we could not meet. The Korân forbids."

"When wilt thou visit Algiers again?"

"Perhaps in the month of Rbi-el-tani. Then I go to the koubba of Sidi-Djebbar."

"On what day?" I asked, eagerly.

"Probably on the first Al-go'omah," she replied. "But why dost thou ask? To attempt to meet again would only bring disgrace upon me—perhaps death. Thou knowest full well how strict is our religion, and how terrible is the punishment meted out to those of my sex who hold converse with the Roumis."

"Yes, alas!" I said. "Nevertheless, we shall meet again, I feel certain, because we—"

"I make no promise. But if ever we chance to cross each other's path, thou wilt not compromise me in the eyes of my people?" she urged, with terrible earnestness.

"Never," I replied, fervently. "None shall ever know of our meeting."

"Now mount and go, or we shall be discovered," she begged, in evident alarm. "Remember the directions I have given thee, and know that thou hast my blessing."

With a last look into her big, wonderful eyes, I raised the tiny white hand I had held and kissed it. Then, vaulting into the saddle, I uttered profound thanks for my deliverance, and bade her adieu.

"*Slama!*" she cried, standing erect with both bare arms outstretched towards me. "*Allah Iselemeck. Slama!*"

And digging my heels into the splendid Ku-hai-lan horse she had given me, I shot away like an arrow, and rode for life towards the sand-hills of the Iraouen that looked black and bare against the streak of saffron dawn in the sky beyond.

Chapter Five
Zoraida's Pledge

Over the dunes, regardless of the dust and heat, I rode, well knowing that my life and that of my fair rescuer depended upon my successful escape.

Glancing back now and then, I strained my eyes in the direction of the oasis, half expecting to see a party of Arabs with their long guns held aloft bearing down upon me; but not a living thing was in sight. Again I was alone in that vast, silent wilderness.

About noon, at a spot where a few dry plants and tufts of hulfa grass struggled to maintain a miserable existence, I dismounted in order to rest my tired horse, and eagerly searched the saddle-bag. It had been packed by the mysterious Zoraida herself, and as I drew forth one package after another, I saw how thoughtful she had been. In addition to dates, figs, Moorish biscuits, and a little skin full of water, I drew from the bottom of the bag a bulky Arab purse. Roughly made of crimson leather, ornamented with a crescent and star embroidered in silver thread, it had evidently been well worn. Opening it, I was astonished at finding it full of French napoleons, while in the centre compartment, secured by a tiny flap, was a little scrap of paper. Upon it, traced in pencil in a hurried, uncertain hand, were a number of Arabic characters.

For a long time I puzzled over them. Some of the characters were illegible, and, being run into one another, they appeared to have been written in the dark. At length, however, I succeeded in satisfying myself as to their purport, for they read as follows:—

"Know, O Unbeliever, that thou art welcome to this poor assistance that I can offer thee. Thou, a stranger from far beyond the sea, may some day be able to render assistance to the unhappy woman who severed thy bonds. Thou art named *Amîn* ('the Faithful'). It is by that name that thou wilt be remembered if ever we should chance to meet. Allah, the One Merciful, is gracious, and will guide thee—praised be His name."

This strange note caused me a good deal of thought, as, sitting upon a stone, I ate the dates my mysterious rescuer had provided for my sustenance. Not content with releasing me from certain death, she, a member of a notorious robber band, had given me her purse! Doubtless she was well aware that her people had taken from me everything I possessed, and as reparation had placed some of her own money in the bag. The note, however, was curious, because it made plain the reason why this mysterious Queen of the Desert had taken so much trouble to accomplish my release. She was unhappy, and I could assist her! How? Who was she? what was she? I wondered. Visions of neglect and ill-treatment were immediately conjured up before my eyes; for woman in Algeria is not better off than in other Oriental countries. The victim of a stupid and brutalising social code founded on a religion whose theory is pure, but whose practice is barbarous, she is always contemned or maltreated, a toy to the wealthy, a beast of burden to the poor.

What, I mused, could be the cause of Zoraida's infelicity? Was she, as the daughter of the murderous old Sheikh, leading the usual wretched existence of Arab girls, neglected by her mother and relegated to a corner of the harem in the charge of some ugly old negress? Every Arab woman looks upon a son as a blessing and a daughter as an incubus; therefore it is little wonder that the life of the daughters of wealthy Moors and Arabs is a truly pitiable one. But on due reflection I saw how improbable it was that an outlaw like Hadj Absalam, who, being continually hunted by the French soldiers sent out to capture him, and compelled to be ever on the move in the most inaccessible spots, would cause his family to travel with him. In case of a sudden attack by the Spahis or Turcos, the paraphernalia of a harem would considerably hamper his movements; and that he could be exceedingly active and show serious fight had already been proved times without number.

No. A man of his stamp would never be troubled with his daughter while bent on plunder and murder. There were, therefore, but two other suppositions. Zoraida was either a captive, or Hadj Absalam's wife. This caused me to remember that if a captive she certainly would have endeavoured to fly with me; while the possession of horses and money, her refusal to allow me to gaze upon her face, and her agitation when I pressed her hand to my lips, all pointed to one fact, namely, that my mysterious deliverer, the woman who by her exquisite form and grace had enchanted me, was none other than the wife of the brigand whose many atrocious crimes had from time to time sent a shudder through the readers of European newspapers.

Zoraida the wife of a thief and murderer! No! I could not bring myself to believe it. She was so young, with arms and hands so delicately moulded and eyes so clear and wide open, that it seemed impossible that she was actually wedded to a villain like Hadj Absalam.

Again I read through her note, carefully tracing each of the hastily-scrawled characters. Though ill-formed, it was not owing to lack of education, for the vowels were marked in position correctly in order to make it easier for me to translate. As I held the paper in my hand, it emitted a pleasant sensuous odour. The perfume that clung to it was geranium, the same sweet scent that had pervaded Zoraida when with her keen knife she had bent and freed me from the poison of the asp.

Sitting in the noonday sun, with my burnouse loosened and my arms resting on my knees, that sweet odour brought back vividly the events of the previous night, its horrors, its surprises, its joys. Again I saw Zoraida, gorgeous in her silk and gauze, a vision of loveliness, an ideal of Arab beauty, ready to risk her life to save mine. But it was only for a second; then my memory became hazy again, and it all seemed like some strange, half-remembered dream.

A desert lark rose near me and burst into joyous song. My horse turned its head slowly, and regarded me steadily for a few moments with his large, serious eyes. The utter loneliness in that arid waste, one of the most dreary regions of the Sahara, was terribly depressing.

But on my finger was her ring. The souvenir was by no means a valuable one, yet so dearly did I prize it that I would not have given it in exchange for anything that might be offered. It was of a type common among Arab women; heavy oxydised silver, and around it, in small Arabic characters of gold, ran a text from the Korân, "Allah is gracious and merciful." Taking it off, I examined the inside, and found it quite bright and smooth by constant wear.

Whatever my mysterious enchantress was, or whoever she would prove to be, this was her pledge of trust. And she, whose face I had not looked upon, had named me "the Faithful!"

Yet as I sat thinking, grim, uncanny feelings of doubt and insecurity filled my mind, for I remembered the strange words of Ali Ben Hafiz, and the fateful Omen of the Camel's Hoof.

I had at last become enmeshed as the dead man had prophesied!

Chapter Six
The Man with a Secret

At sundown, three days after my escape from the Ennitra, my eyes distinguished the palms of the Meskam Oasis standing at the foot of a large sand-hill. Zoraida had correctly informed me, for under feathery trees, amid the luxuriant vegetation which one finds here and there in the Sahara, the Spahis and Chasseurs d'Afrique had established an advanced post.

In an hour I had entered the camp, and being taken before the French commandant, related my story. I told him of my journey with Ali Ben Hafiz, of the attack, and of the massacre.

"*Bien*! and you alone escaped!" exclaimed the officer, a thorough boulevardier, who sat before his tent with outstretched legs, lazily puffing a cigarette.

"Yes," I replied.

He was as well groomed, and his moustache was as carefully waxed, as if he were lounging outside the Café de la Paix.

"You were exceedingly fortunate," he exclaimed, rolling his cigarette carelessly. "Those who fall into Absalam's clutches seldom escape. *Diable*! he's the most fierce cut-throat in all Algeria. How did you manage it?"

I hesitated. Had I not promised Zoraida to preserve the secret of their whereabouts for her sake? If her people were to escape, I should be compelled to make misleading statements. At last I replied—

"They left me bound to a tree during the night, and I succeeded in loosening the cords. Finding a horse ready saddled, I jumped upon it and rode away." After I had uttered the words, I saw how lame was my story.

"But how did you know we were here?" asked the commandant, blowing a cloud of smoke from his lips, regarding me rather critically, and then offering me a *chebli* from his case.

"I had no idea," I replied. "Seeing the palms from yonder ridge, I came here to rest. Had I not discovered the oasis, I should most likely have perished."

"You certainly would not have lived many days," he said. "The nearest well is two hundred miles in any direction, therefore, if you had missed this, the vultures would soon have made a meal off you. But," he continued, "describe to me where we are likely to find Hadj Absalam. We have been in search of him these three months, but, strangely enough, his spies appear to watch all our movements, with the result that he evades us in a manner simply marvellous."

I was silent for a moment, thinking.

"I have travelled for three days due north," I said, apparently reflecting. "If you send your men due south three days' journey, they will come upon a small oasis. This must be passed, and still south again, a three hours' ride, there is a larger oasis on the further side of a high ridge. It is there that Hadj Absalam is taking his ease."

"Good!" exclaimed the officer, calling over a Chasseur who was sauntering past with his hands in his pockets and ordering him to send immediately a *sous-officier*, whom he named.

"It's a fine night," he said. "We will start when the moon rises, and, *mon Dieu*! it will not be our fault if we do not exterminate the band, and bring the black-faced old scoundrel back with us. The caravans will never be safe until his head is in the *lunette*."

"But he may have moved by this time," I suggested.

"Then we will follow and overtake him," he replied, brushing some dust from his braided sleeve. "He shall not escape us this time. When I was quartered in Biskra, I knew old Hafiz well. Though prejudiced against France, he was always good to our men, poor old fellow."

"Yes," I said. "Though a strict Moslem, he was most amiable and generous."

At that moment a lieutenant of Chasseurs strode up and saluted.

"Victor," the commandant exclaimed, addressing him, "we leave at once, with the whole of your *enfants d'enfer*, in search of Absalam, who is three days' journey south. This time we will pursue him till we run him to earth. The Spahis will remain;" and, turning to me, he added: "M'sieur Holcombe, you are welcome to stay here also, if it pleases you."

Thanking him, I assured him how deeply I appreciated his hospitality, and then, having been handed over to the care of a *sous-officier*, I was shown to the tent which the commandant ordered should be placed at my disposal, while the Spahis—or *homards*, as they are termed in the argot of the 19th

Army Corps, because of their red burnouses—were busy assisting their comrades to prepare for departure.

Our evening meal of thin onion soup, black bread, and rough, bitter coffee having been disposed of, the Chasseurs, numbering about two hundred, paraded with their horses, and were briefly but keenly inspected by the officer in command, whose name I learned was Captain Paul Deschanel. The inspection over, the commandant addressed his men, and the order was given to mount. Then, amid the shouts of *"Vive les Chasseurs! À bas les Ennitra! Vive la France!"* from the assembled Spahis, the smart troop of cavalry, with the captain at their head, galloped away into the moonlit desert, and were soon lost in the gloom.

As I sat watching the receding horsemen, and inwardly chuckling that by sending them three days' journey into the country of the Inemba-kel-Emoghri, Absalam and his people would be six days' journey distant in an opposite direction, I was startled by a hand being laid upon my shoulder. Turning quickly, I found it was a Spahi.

"M'sieur is English, if I mistake not?" he inquired, with a pleasant smile upon his swarthy but refined face.

"True," I replied. "And, judging from your accent, you are not an Arab, but a Parisian."

"Yes," he said, speaking in fairly good English. "I have been in England once. If you care to spend an hour in my tent, I can offer you absinthe and a cigarette. That is about the extent of the hospitalities of the oasis."

Thanking him for his invitation, I accompanied him, and a few moments later we were sitting in the bright moonlight on a mat spread outside his small tent.

"So you have been in England?" I said presently, when he had told me his name was Octave Uzanne.

"Yes," he replied, with a slight sigh, allowing the water to trickle slowly into his absinthe, and drawing his scarlet burnouse closer about him. It was strange to hear English in this region of silence and desolation.

"Is not the recollection of your visit pleasant?" I asked.

"Ah! forgive me, m'sieur," he exclaimed quickly; "I can never hear your tongue, or think of London, without becoming *triste*. I associate with your great gloomy city the saddest days of my life. Had I not gone to London, I should never have been here, leading the wild semi-barbarous life in an Arab regiment of the Army of Africa. We of the Spahis have a saying, *'N'éveillez pas le chat qui dort'* —but sometimes—"

34 | Zoraida

"It is a good adage, but we cannot always let our sorrows lie," I interrupted sympathetically. He had spoken with the accent of a gentleman, and with the white light of the moon streaming upon his face, I saw that he was about thirty years of age, with a countenance clean-cut and noble, refined and somewhat effeminate. His dark eyes were deep-set and serious, yet in his face there was an expression of genuine *bonhomie*. The average Spahi is feared by Moor and Jew, by Biskri and Koulougli, as the fiercest and most daring of soldiers. In drink he is a brute, in love he is passionate, in the saddle he is one of the finest riders in the world; in the town he is docile and obedient, fond of lounging in the cafés, idling over his eternal cigarette; yet away in the desert, all his old instincts return; he is an Arab again, and knows no measure either in attachment or in hatred. A blow from his scabbard is the only payment when scouring the country for food, a thrust of his sabre the only apology to those he insults, while in the field, seated on his fleet horse, he rides like the wind, and has the strength and courage of a lion.

This quiet, intellectual, bearded young Frenchman sitting cross-legged on the mat beside me, was, I felt sure, a man with a past. One of his comrades came up and asked him a question in Arabic, to which he replied, speaking the language of his regiment like a true-born Bedouin. As we sipped our absinthe in silence for some minutes, watching the camp settling down for the night, it struck me as curious that, instead of being in the Chasseurs d'Afrique, he should be masquerading in burnouse in an exclusively native regiment.

We began talking of England, but he was not communicative regarding himself, and in reply to my question said—

"I desire to live here in the desert and to forget. Each time we return to Algiers, the glare and glitter of the European quarter unlocks the closed page of my history. It was because this wild roving beyond the pale of civilisation was suited to my mood that I became a *homard*."

"Has your experience of life been so very bitter, then?" I asked, looking into the handsome face, upon which there was a shadow of pain, and which was set off by the spotless white haick surrounding it.

"Bitter?—Ah!" he exclaimed, with a deep sigh. "You see me now, dragging out a wretched existence in this wilderness, exiled from my home, with name, creed, nationality—everything changed."

"In order to conceal your identity?" I hazarded.

"Yes, my past is erased. Dead to those who knew me, I am now merely known as Octave Uzanne. I have tasted of life's pleasures, but just as I was about to drink of the cup of happiness, it was dashed from me. It is ended. All I have now to look for is—is a narrow bed in yonder sand."

"My dear fellow," I exclaimed, "don't speak so despondently! We all have our little debauches of melancholy. Cannot you confide in me? Perhaps I might presume to give advice."

Silently and thoughtfully he rolled a cigarette between the fingers of his bronzed hand, completing its manufacture carefully.

"*My* story?" he said dreamily. "Bah! Why should I trouble you—a stranger—with the wretched tragedy of my life?"

"Because I also have a skeleton in my cupboard, and I can sincerely sympathise with you," I answered, tossing away my cigarette end and lighting a fresh one.

Murmuring some words that I did not catch, he sipped his absinthe slowly, and, passing his sinewy, sun-tanned hand wearily across his forehead, sat immovable and silent, with his eyes fixed upon the dense growth of myrtle bushes and prickly aloes before him.

Lighted candles stuck upon piles of rifles flickered here and there among the tents, the feathery leaves of the palms above waved in the night breeze like funeral plumes, the dry hulfa grass rustled and surged like a summer sea; while ever and anon there came bursts of hearty laughter from the Arab soldiers, or snatches of a *chanson eccentrique* with rollicking chorus that had been picked up a thousand miles away in the French cafés of Algiers.

Chapter Seven
A Forgotten Tragedy

Octave Uzanne roused himself.

"My career has not been brilliant," he said slowly, and with bitterness. "It is only remarkable by reason of its direful tragedy. All of us keep a debtor and creditor account with Fortune, and, *ma foi*! my balance has always been on the wrong side. Seven years ago I left the university at Bordeaux with honours. My father was a Senator, and my elder brother was already an *attaché* at our Embassy in London. In order to study English, with the object of entering the diplomatic service, I went over to reside with him, and it was he who, one night, when leaving a theatre, introduced me to the goddess at whose shrine I bowed—and worshipped. We became companions, afterwards lovers. Did she love me? Yes. Though she was a butterfly of Society, though it is through her that I am compelled to lead this life of desert-wandering, I will never believe ill of her. Never! Violet Hanbury—why should I conceal her name—had a—"

"Violet Hanbury?" I cried, starting and looking to his face. "Do you mean the Honourable Violet Hanbury, daughter of Lord Isleworth?"

"The same," he replied quickly. "What!—are you acquainted with her?"

"Well, scarcely," I answered. "I—I merely know her by repute. I have seen her photograph in London shop-windows among the types of English beauty."

I did not tell him all I knew. Vi Hanbury, the beauty of a season, had been mixed up in some unenviable affair. The matter, I remembered, had been enshrouded in a good deal of mystery at the time, but gossips' tongues had not been idle.

"Ah!" he continued, enthusiastically; "I have no need then to describe her, for you know how handsome she is. Well—we loved one another; but it was the old story. Her parents forbade her to hold communication with me for two reasons—firstly, because I was not wealthy, and secondly, because they were determined that she should marry Henri de Largentière, a sallow, wizened man old enough to be her father, but who had been Minister of Education in the Brisson Cabinet."

"Yes," I said; "the engagement was discussed a good deal in the clubs after its announcement in the *Morning Post*."

"Engagement? *Sacré!*" he exclaimed, with anger. "She was snatched from me and given to that old imbecile. I was compelled to fly from her and leave her, a pure and honest woman, at their mercy, because—because—"

He paused for a moment. His voice had faltered and the words seemed to choke him. Flinging away his cigarette viciously, he took a gulp from the tin cup beside him, then, continuing, said—

"Because Violet's cousin, Jack Fothergill, who was one of her most ardent admirers and had declared his love, was discovered one night dead in his chambers in St. James's Street—he had been murdered!"

"Murdered?" I ejaculated. "I don't remember hearing of it. I must have been abroad at the time."

"Yes," he said, speaking rapidly. "Jack Fothergill was brutally done to death with a knife that penetrated to the heart. But that was not all: the stiletto left sticking in the wound was discovered to be mine, a gold pencil-case belonging to me was found upon the floor, and the valet gave information to the police that at ten o'clock that night he had opened the door to allow me to depart!"

In the moonlight his eyes had a fierce glitter in them and his bare brown arms were thrust through the folds of his burnouse as he gesticulated to emphasise his words. There was a silence over the camp, but the gay café-chantant song of Mdlle. Duclerc, with which one of the Spahis was entertaining his comrades, sounded shrill and tuneful in the clear bright air—

> "Je jou' très bien d' la mandoline,
> Ça fait moins d' train que le tambourin;
> Puisque quand on a la jambe fine,
> Ça permet d' la faire voir un brin."

"Strangely enough," my companion continued, after a pause; "I remained that night with a friend, and judge my horror and amazement when next morning I read in the newspapers of the tragedy, and learned that I was suspected of the crime! It was true that I had called upon the murdered man just before ten o'clock, that the pencil-case had been in my pocket, but of the murder I was entirely innocent. Yet how could I prove an alibi, especially when the doctor had given an opinion that death had occurred at ten o'clock—the hour I left! The police were searching for me, but through that long and terrible day I remained in hiding. Once or twice I was tempted to give myself up and bravely face the awful charge; but there was one thing which prevented this. All interest in life had been crushed from my heart by an announcement of two lines in the same issue of the paper, stating that a marriage had been arranged and would shortly take place between Violet and De Largentière. My hopes were shattered, for my love had been cast aside. She had actually accepted the man she had professed to hate!"

"But did you not clear yourself?" I asked. "Surely you could easily have done so?"

"How could I? Were not the suspicions rendered more justifiable by reason of my visit just prior to the crime. Again, I had not returned to my chambers that night, so day after day I remained in hiding. Though innocent, I was not wholly prepared to meet the charge, for I saw clearly that Jack and I had fallen victims of a foul plot. The crime that cost my friend his life was attributed to jealousy on my part, and with an incentive thus invented, I clearly saw that the circumstantial evidence was strong enough to convict me. I sought my brother's assistance, and, half mad with terror and despair, I escaped from England. To return to France would be to run into the arms of the police, so I resolved to come here and in the wild life of the desert to bury the past."

"But by whom was your friend Fothergill stabbed?" I asked.

"Let me tell you," he replied. "Since that day, when like a criminal I fled from the trial I was afraid to face, I have learned only one fact, though not until a year ago did it come to my knowledge. It appears that on the evening of the murder, Fothergill wrote telling me that during a visit to Paris he had discovered certain details connected with the relations between Mariette Lestrade, a pretty singer whose *chansons de poirrot* were well known at the Moulin Rouge and Ambassadeurs and the ex-Minister of Education. He had that day called at Long's Hotel, in Bond Street, where the General was staying, and in the course of a stormy interview threatened that if he still continued his suit, he would expose his secret attachment to this star of the café-concert, and take his cousin to her, so that she might investigate for herself. Lord Isleworth's daughter would have a handsome dowry which was much needed to renovate the departed splendour of the ex-Minister's estate in the Charente, therefore he was obstinate, laughed, snapped his fingers, and defied Jack. This interview took place at four o'clock in the afternoon, and Jack wrote to me from the Naval and Military Club, telling me everything, and stating that De Largentière had threatened his life. This letter was delivered at my chambers the same night, but I was not there, nor did I return, therefore my brother took charge of it and after nearly two years it reached me out here, unopened."

"In face of such evidence as that," I said, "the identity of the actual murderer is not very far to seek."

"No," he said, in a low, harsh tone.

"Why do you not take that letter, face the charge against you, and bring the criminal to his punishment?"

"Why?" he echoed, starting to his feet and looking me full in the face. "Why do I not denounce him, and return to civilisation? Because," he said slowly, in a voice trembling with emotion, "because Violet—the woman I love—is Madame de Largentière. I think only of her. I adore her still. She shall never know of her husband's terrible secret. Her innocent children shall never be branded as the spawn of a murderer!"

As he spoke, there was a bright flash in the dark clump of aloes immediately opposite us, and at the same instant the report of a rifle fired at close quarters caused me to start violently.

Octave Uzanne threw up his arms with a loud piercing cry, and, reeling, fell heavily backward, struck down by a coward's bullet!

Chapter Eight
The Fight in the Meskam

Our eyes were in a moment blinded by a flash, as fifty rifles opened fire upon us from every cover the thick bushes afforded.

For a few seconds, as the sounds of the first volley died away, there was a dead silence. So sudden had been the attack, that my comrades the Spahis stood dumbfounded, but ere the rifles of our unknown enemies were reloaded, fierce shrill yells rent the air, the arms that had been piled were snatched up, horses were untethered, and almost simultaneously with a second volley from the ambush, the *homards*, displaying cool courage, poured into the thick growth of myrtles, hulfa, acacias, and dwarf palms, a terribly withering fire.

The whole scene was enacted ere I could draw breath. The moon had disappeared, and in the darkness rifles seemed to pour forth flame on every hand. Evidently our enemies had been watching their opportunity, and while the camp was busy preparing for the departure of the Chasseurs, they had killed the three men on sentry duty on the other side of the sand-hill, and then crept into ambush, and lay there until the signal was given to open fire.

As the desperate combat commenced, and the fusillade burst forth with deafening report, I felt for my revolver, but my heart sank within me as I remembered that the Ennitra had relieved me of it, and I found myself standing alone and unarmed. A few feet away Uzanne's rifle was lying, together with his bag of cartridges. I dashed towards them and bent to pick them up, but ere I could do so, a big fierce-looking Arab sprang from the myrtles towards me, yelling and whirling his knife above his head.

It was the work of an instant.

I remember feeling his sinewy grasp upon my shoulder, I saw his flashing blade above me, and heard him cry in Arabic—

"Let the dogs perish! Kill them! Kill them all!"

The heavy knife whistled in the air as uplifted it poised aloft for a moment.

Suddenly a shot sounded behind me. My assailant clapped his left hand to his breast and staggered back a few steps, then clutched violently at the air and fell. Glancing quickly in the direction whence the shot had come, I saw my friend Uzanne had with difficulty raised himself on one arm, and, drawing his revolver, had with unerring aim shot the Arab through the heart.

Octave Uzanne had saved my life.

"*Sapristi!*" he shouted, with a laugh, as I dashed towards him. "That was a close shave! *Je lui ai collé un atout sur le nez!*"

"Are you seriously hurt?" I gasped; noticing as the rifles flashed that blood was streaming from his shoulder.

"No," he replied quickly. "I think not. Don't trouble after me now, for I'm no good. I'll patch myself up. Take my rifle and help the others."

Snatching up the weapon, I loaded it, and, flinging myself on the ground behind the root of a fallen palm, I opened fire upon the thick bushes before me. In this way the minutes, full of anxiety, passed in ignorance of our foes. The deafening explosions were incessant, yells and cries of enemy and friend now and then sounded above the firing, and the air grew so thick with smoke, that I could scarcely distinguish the bushes where the Arabs lay in ambush.

As the terrible moments went by, I knew we were fighting for our lives. Altogether our force in camp only amounted to sixty, while we were, as yet, unaware of the character or number of our assailants. That they had dared to attack a military post showed they were present in overwhelming numbers, and, further, that they had waited until the Chasseurs had got away before swooping down to annihilate us.

Lying along the ground near my red-burnoused comrades, I fired as regularly as I was able, until suddenly a bugle sounded. It was the order to mount!

My comrades dashed towards their tethered horses, a number of which had been shot down, and I followed. In the excitement I jumped upon the saddle of the first animal I could reach, and as I did so, the bugle again sounded.

"*I'htaris! sidi!* Keep beside me," shouted a lithe, muscular Spahi, vaulting upon a horse a few yards away. "We'll soon clear out these vermin."

Then, as my companion yelled an imprecation in Arabic and held his rifle high above his head, we all, with one accord, spurred on our horses, and, swift as the wind, tore across the open space between the line of tents and low bushes, dashing into the cavernous darkness of the ambush ere our enemy could be aware of our intention. The result was frightful. Carried on by the wild rush, I found myself in the midst of a sanguinary *mêlée*, where one had to fight one's adversaries literally hand to hand. My companions, whirling their keen blades, and shouting prayers to Allah the while, fell upon their assailants with piercing yells and cut them down in a manner that was truly awful, but it was not until this moment that I discovered that the officer in command of the Spahis had cleverly divided his small force into two detachments, one of which was repulsing the enemy from the front, while the other had made a circuitous charge, and was now outflanking our opponents and slaughtering them in the rear.

Thus the outlaws were quickly hemmed in, and although we were unable to follow them far, owing to the dense undergrowth, yet we silenced their fire.

Then it was that we made a discovery. The Spahi beside whom I had ridden—a splendid fellow, who sat as firmly in his saddle as if he were part of it, and who, while galloping, could fire his rifle with deadly effect— shouted as he drew rein for a moment—

"*Diable*! They are the children of Eblis—the Ennitra!" Hadj Absalam's band had followed me!

The cry was taken up. The news spread rapidly from mouth to mouth, and the knowledge that they were being attacked by the daring marauders for whom they had been searching so long and so fruitlessly, caused every *homard* to redouble his energy, and strike a blow towards their extermination. The audacity of the outlaws roused the ire of these fierce native troopers, for the fact that several Spahis had been shot dead in the first moments of the attack, caused an unanimous resolve to follow up the thieves and give them no quarter.

But scarcely had this decision been arrived at, when the attack was renewed even more vigorously. Concealed amidst the dense tropical foliage, they opened fire with their rifles from a quarter whence we least expected it, and in this direction we rode, only to be received by a fusillade more galling than any that had been previously poured upon us.

Their success, however, was not of long duration. A bugle brought our horses in line, and then, with a terrific rush that none could withstand, we dashed upon them, felling them to earth with shot or sabre thrust.

Suddenly a sharp sting in the left side caused me a twinge, and I felt the warm blood trickling. I hesitated a moment, knowing that I was wounded. With an imprecation the Spahi officer shouted to his men to sweep the marauders away, and in the sudden rush and intense excitement that followed I forgot my mishap. Just, however, as I became separated from my companions-in-arms, my wound gave me a second twinge of pain, and there shot up from the tall grass at my side a brawny Arab, whose white burnouse showed distinctly in the semi-darkness, and whose eyes flashed with the fire of hatred. Seizing my horse's head, he swung round his *jambiyah*, but by good fortune I pulled the trigger of my rifle just in time. The bullet entered his throat, and he tumbled back into the rank grass with a curse upon his lips.

The fight was long and desperate; not merely a skirmish, but a thoroughly well-planned attack by Hadj Absalam's men to annihilate the Spahis for the purpose of securing arms, ammunition, and horses. Whether Absalam himself was present directing the operations we could not learn, although two prisoners we captured both denied that he was with them.

Presently the moon shone out again brightly, showing up both friend and enemy, but the silence of night was still broken by rapid shots, mingled with the loud, exultant shout of the victor and the hoarse, despairing cry of the dying. In that brief hour the scenes of bloodshed were terrible. Little did either the Ennitra or the Spahis value life, and as they struggled desperately for the mastery, they fought with that fierce courage characteristic of the barbarian of the desert.

Amid the wild massacre, when at last my comrades catching their enemies unprepared and making a sudden onslaught cut through them with fire and sword, the thought suddenly occurred to me that this fierce nomadic tribe who had dared to attack us had been spoken of by Zoraida as "her people." Now at last they were being outflanked, unable to reach their horses which had been captured by our detachment operating in their rear, and we were sweeping them down—slaughtering them without mercy!

Sickened by the bloody fight in which I had involuntarily borne a part, and feeling rather faint owing to my wound,—which happily, however, proved a very slight one,—I left my comrades to complete their work of annihilating the murderous band, which they did by following them as they fell back through the tangled vegetation and away across the oasis into the desert beyond, where, with the exception of eighteen who were taken prisoners, the whole of those who had attacked us so desperately were killed or wounded.

Where was Zoraida? As hot and faint I rode back to the spot where my whilom companion Uzanne was lying, I wondered whether the woman, whose half-veiled face seemed ever before my eyes with tantalising distinctness, had accompanied the unfortunate men of her barbaric tribe, or was she waiting with the notorious old cut-throat at a safe distance from the oasis, expecting each moment to learn of a brilliant success, and impatient to assist in the high revelry and divide the plunder?

None of those of her people who had gone forth to attack us would, however, return.

Seventy of them were stretched dead under the bright stars of the Eastern sky, and nearly a hundred were lying with great ugly stains of blood upon their burnouses, racked by the agony of their wounds, and well knowing that ere the morrow's sun would set they would succumb to heat and thirst; that in a few short hours the vultures would lay bare their bones and leave them whitening on the glaring sand.

Chapter Nine
Uzanne, the Outcast

The wild turbulence of that terrible night was succeeded by a peaceful, brilliant dawn.

Already my comrades were preparing to move south, for immediately upon the conclusion of the fight, messengers had been hastily despatched to overtake the commandant, and the detachment would also move on after the Chasseurs at sunset, as the unburied bodies of the marauders would prevent them remaining longer on the Meskam.

My wound—a deep laceration of the flesh where an Arab's bullet had grazed me—proving more painful than at first, I had decided to accompany the messenger who, with an escort, would leave the camp at sundown to travel due north by way of Zaouïa Timassanin and over the barren Areg, bearing the intelligence of the annihilation of the marauders to the headquarters of the Spahis at Tuggurt. For some time I was undecided whether to remain with the military post, or return to civilisation. It was six months since I had left Oran, and for the greater part of that time I had been travelling. I was by no means tired of life in the desert, but the recollection that the mysterious Zoraida intended to perform a pilgrimage to the popular shrine on the outskirts of Algiers, and that if I went south to Zamlen as I had intended, I should certainly lose all chance of seeing her again, caused my decision to recross the Atlas and return.

Late that afternoon, while the glaring sun blazed down upon the motionless bodies of the marauders over which the great dark vultures now hovered, I sat in Uzanne's tent. Stretched upon the ground, my friend, half-dressed, lay with his head upon his saddle. The wound in his shoulder had been roughly bandaged, pending an examination by the surgeon who had gone south with the Chasseurs, and although his bronzed face was a trifle paler, he nevertheless wore an air of utter carelessness.

It was our last chat together, and I had been thanking him for the lucky shot that had knocked over the Arab who had pinned me down.

"*Zut!*" he replied, laughing. "*Eh bien,* old fellow! It was the only man among old Absalam's gang that I could pot. If they had given me a chance, I would have bagged one or two more, but, *diable!* they didn't."

"No," I replied. "They apparently fired point blank at you."

"I don't know why they were so particularly malicious towards me. But there, I suppose it's only my usual bad luck," and he smiled grimly. "One thing is certain, however, we shall not be troubled by old Absalam again for some time."

"Do you think we have entirely broken up his band?"

"No. His people are born marauders, and will continue to plunder and murder until he is captured or shot. He will break out in a fresh place before long. Strange that we can never catch him! He really seems to lead a charmed existence."

"Yes," I said. "He's a clever old villain." Then I commenced to talk to him of his return to France.

"I shall never go back," he snapped, frowning. "Have I not already told you that I have no further interest in life among the people I once knew? When now and then we are quartered in Algiers, its civilisation palls upon me and carries me back to days I am trying to forget. I'm a social outsider; a fugitive from justice. If I cleared myself, it would be at the cost of *her* happiness—why should I go back?"

"But you don't intend to spend the remainder of your days here, in the desert, do you?" I asked.

"Why not? We Spahis have a saying, '*Attaslim éhire, rafîk*'!" ("Resignation is the best companion.") Then, grasping my hand and looking seriously into my eyes, he added, "There is but one thing that troubles me. Violet!—Violet herself believes that I am her cousin's murderer!"

I was silent. How strange it was that I should meet here, so far removed from civilisation as we in Europe know it, a man who held a secret which, if made known, would cause one of the greatest scandals that has ever shocked Society! How bitter were his thoughts; how utterly wrecked was his life! in order that a leader of smart Paris—a woman over whose beauty London had raved—should live in blissful happiness with her husband, this man was leading an aimless, hopeless life, condemned by his friends as a coward and a criminal.

He noticed my look of sympathy, and pressed my hand a trifle harder.

"I do not usually wear my heart on my sleeve," he said, at last. "Indeed, I have told my secret to no one beside yourself; therefore consider what

I have said is in confidence. You are returning to the world I have so ignominiously left, and in all probability we shall not meet again. If we do, and you require a friend, remember you will find him in the Spahi, Octave Uzanne."

"A thousand thanks," I said. "You, who have saved me from an Arab's sword, may always rely upon my devoted friendship. Expressions of vague regret are useless. A stout heart, a clear conscience, and a fixed determination may accomplish many difficulties—they may even effect one's social resurrection—one's—"

"With me, never," he interrupted, despondently. "But see! your horse is ready," he added, glancing at the tent door, before which a soldier stood, holding the fine Ku-hai-lan that Zoraida had given me. "You will have a long ride to-night, and the dispatches cannot wait. You must go."

"Then adieu," I said, rising and shaking his sun-tanned hand heartily. "I hope you'll soon be right again. Till we meet, *au revoir*."

He smiled rather sorrowfully, and his dark eyes wore a wistful look. But it was only momentary. "*Bon voyage*," he said, gaily. "Accept the good wishes of an outcast."

The dispatch-bearer was outside, speaking impatiently and shouting to remind me that we had a long and fatiguing journey before us; therefore a few moments later I was in the saddle, and the messenger, six Spahis, and myself were soon galloping away past the ghastly corpses of Hadj Absalam's followers and out into the trackless appallingly-silent wilderness.

Chapter Ten
Humours from the Desert

Twelve weary days after leaving the Meskam, journeying due north over the hot loose sands of the Great Erg, the hill crowned by the imposing white cupolas and towers of the desert town of Tuggurt came into view.

The scene was charming. It was an hour before sundown, and as we ascended the long caravan route from Ngoussa, a foot deep in dust, the place presented a purely Oriental aspect. Against a background of cool-looking palms, the white flat-roofed houses, the grim walls of the Kasbah, and the domes of the many mosques stood out in bold relief. Riding on, we entered a beautiful grove of tall date palms, the trees which the Arabs say stand with their feet in the water and their heads in the fire of heaven. Under their welcome shade a rivulet flowed with rippling music over the pebbles, and fruit trees and corn were growing luxuriantly, for the oasis is most fertile, although, strangely enough, the abundance of water throughout the Oued Gheir causes a malignant fever which proves fatal to Europeans. The beautiful palm-groves and wealth of vegetation was unutterably refreshing after the heat and glare of the waterless regions of the south; and as we approached the gate, a strange motley crowd of gaily-dressed Arabs of the Beni Mansour, Jews, Biskris, and Negroes came forth to meet us and inquire what news we brought.

Our statement that Hadj Absalam's men had been repulsed and defeated caused the wildest rejoicings, and we made a triumphant entry into the place, followed by a gesticulating throng who apparently regarded us as heroes.

Tuggurt is a curious old town. European civilisation has not yet reached it, for, with the exception of one or two French officers, there are no Christian residents. Built almost entirely of bricks baked in the sun, its low houses join one another, and present an unbroken line save for the two town gates. Secure from attack, its moat is now filled up, and in front of the stone-built Kasbah stands the principal of the twenty mosques, with its high dome and tall slender minarets. Around its ancient market-place, where for hundreds of years slaves were bought and sold, are cool arcades with crumbling horse-shoe arches, while beside it there rises the dilapidated dome of a disused house of prayer, bearing some curious plaster arabesques. Within the *enceinte* of the Kasbah—the scene of a horrible massacre during the revolt of the Cherif Bou Choucha in 1871—stands the barracks, the commandant's house, and the hospital, and it was within those walls, in an inner court beside a plashing fountain, that in the twilight I sat explaining to Captain Carmier, the commandant, how the attack was frustrated.

A French dinner was an appreciable change after the eternal kousskouss, dates, and kola nuts that form one's sustenance on the plains, and as the Captain, a lieutenant, and myself sat over our cognac and cigarettes, I told them of my adventures with Ali Ben Hafiz, and the surprise by the Spahis in the far-off Meskam.

The cool peacefulness of that ancient Kasbah garden, where the veiled houris of Bou Choucha once lounged and plucked the roses, was delightful, and, sitting with the foliage rustling above, there was an air of repose such as I had not experienced for months.

"So the *homards* have gone south to overtake the Chasseurs," Captain Carmier said, as he struck a match on his heel and lit his cigarette after I had told him how valiantly my companions had fought. "How aggravating it is that Hadj Absalam always escapes us!"

"Extraordinary!" remarked the lieutenant, a thorough Parisian, who had just been grumbling at his lot, he having been sent to the desert for three years, instead of to Tonquin, where he might earn distinction and the yellow and green ribbon, as he had expected. "Nothing would please me better than to command an expedition in search of him."

"Search? What's the use?" asked the commandant. "The rapidity with which the old scoundrel travels is simply miraculous. To-day he's here, to-morrow he disappears, and on the third day he is reported completely out of our reach. As on previous occasions, he has, I suppose, retreated beyond Mount El Aghil, and there, idling in his harem, is snapping his fingers and defying us. It is always the same—always."

"Are his headquarters on Mount Aghil, then?" I asked, for amid all the conflicting reports I had never been able to learn the outlaw's actual place of abode.

"It is said that his stronghold is perched on an almost inaccessible rock not far from Tiouordeouïn, and that his household consists of nearly a thousand persons."

"Of whom about half are inmates of his harem," added the lieutenant, smiling. "According to report current among the neighbouring tribe, the Tédjéhé N'ou Sidi, the ladies of his household include a number of Europeans who have from time to time fallen into his merciless clutches. The favourites are surrounded by every luxury, the proceeds of his raids, while those who fall into disfavour, or whose personal charms deteriorate by age, are disposed of in the very simple method of being thrown over the cliff and dashed to pieces upon the rocks beneath."

"Horrible!" I exclaimed. "But why does not the Government send a sufficient force to follow him into his fastness and capture him?"

"For several reasons," answered the commandant. "Firstly, because that portion of the Ahaggar where he has his abode has never been explored; secondly, because, by reason of the zealously-guarded mountain pass by which it is approached, access is impossible except by a strong column, who would meet with a most desperate resistance, and would have to take it by storm. The third, and perhaps most important, reason is, because the region of the Ennitra is declared by all the neighbouring nomad tribes to be a sacred place, where several miracle-working marabouts are buried, and any attempt at desecration by Europeans would certainly cause a holy war all through the Sahara. Therefore the War Department, although the General has urged them times without number to send a column in pursuit of Hadj Absalam, prefer to wait and capture him when in the act of plunder."

"That will never be, it seems," I remarked.

"No. *Il sait le fin des fins*," laughed Carmier. "It is said that he attributes his extraordinary success in evading us to a woman who is gifted with second sight."

"A woman?" I exclaimed, surprised. "She's believed to be a witch, I suppose?"

"Yes, and a young and very pretty one, too. They say her beauty is marvellous, and her power supernatural. While I was in command of the advanced post at Tihodayen, near the salt mines of Sebkha d'Amadghor, three Spahis ventured into the Ikerremoïn Oasis in search of forage, and they declare that they came across her. She was surrounded by a number of slaves, and was lying unveiled under a canopy of white and gold. According to their account, she possesses the *beauté du diable*, her women make obeisance to her, and the men who approach fall upon their knees before her, kiss the ground, and ask her blessing. It is said, too, that Mulai Hassan, Sultan of Morocco, saw her on one occasion when he crossed the frontier, and offered Hadj Absalam an enormous sum for her, but the superstitious Ennitra threatened a revolt if she were sold. Whether that's true I don't know," he added, shrugging his shoulders and sipping his cognac. "She is evidently Queen of the Desert, and I merely tell you what's rumoured."

"But is she Moorish, Arab, or a Negress?" I asked. "What is her name?"

"She is from the mountains, they say, and the Ennitra know her as Daughter of the Sun."

"Daughter of the Sun?" I cried, starting. I remembered that Zoraida had, in reply to my questions, told me that that was her name. Could this strange woman of incomparable beauty, who was believed by her people to be possessed of supernatural power, be none other than my mysterious Zoraida, the woman whose veiled face was in my waking hours and in my dreams constantly before my eyes?

"Is her name familiar?" asked the Captain, noticing my ill-concealed surprise.

"No—not at all!" I stammered. "Surely that designation is common enough among the Arabs! It seems an extraordinary fact, nevertheless, that a young and beautiful woman should direct the movements of a band of outlaws."

"True," replied Carmier, thoughtfully twisting his waxed moustache. "And there is, moreover, considerable mystery with regard to her which nobody has up to the present been able to solve. One thing, however, appears certain, that this veiled prophetess is an inmate of Hadj Absalam's harem."

His words stung me. Could it be possible that this woman who held the murderous nomads under her sway was the same to whom I owed my life? Nay, was it not most probable that she, the graceful incarnation of Eastern beauty whom I adored, was one of the four wives allowed to Hadj Absalam by the Prophet? The mystery was bewildering. The very thought drove me to despair, for I confess I loved her to the verge of madness.

My companion smoked on in lazy contemplative silence. Above, the stars were bright in a steely sky; the ancient court, with its horse-shoe arches, wide arcades, and trailing vines, looked ghostly in the dim light. The quiet was only broken by the running water of the fountain as it fell with pleasant music into its time-worn blue-tiled basin, and the measured tramp of the sentry in the outer court beyond. Upward the cigarette smoke dissolved into the cool night air, carrying with it bitter thoughts of the past, and strange, dreamy visions of an unknown future.

Chapter Eleven
The City of the Sun

I was awaiting Zoraida, my enchantress.

After a few days in Tuggurt, and a lengthened stay in the date-groves of Biskra with my genial friend the General of Division, I found myself once again in old El Djezaïr, that quaint Franco-Arab city known to Europeans as Algiers. Here Western civilisation and Oriental fanaticism mingle, but never blend. It is a city of glare and darkness, of mosques and marabouts, of Parisian politeness and Berber barbarity, of wide, modern-built boulevards and narrow, crooked streets, as yet untouched by the hand of the colonising vandal.

Till a comparatively recent date it was a nest of fierce pirates who were a terror to Europe, and even now one cannot look upon the gigantic mole and other works prior to the French occupation without remembering that they were constructed by Christian slaves, who were beaten, tortured, and made to toil under the blazing sun until their gyves wore into their flesh, and death relieved them of their miseries. The great white Kasbah on the hill-top, once the gorgeous Palace of the Deys, now echoes to the tramp of Zouaves and artillery. If those gigantic walls could speak, what tales of outrage, torture, and butchery they, alas! could tell! In the great harem, where hundreds of English and French women captured by the Corsairs have pined and died, smart officers on colonial service now lounge, smoke, and discuss the topics of their beloved Paris as revealed by the *Petit Journal* and the *Figaro*; while down in the Rue de la Lyre British tourists in suits of astounding check stare in abject astonishment at Fathma or Khadidja, who, veiled and shrouded in her white haick, has descended the ladder-like streets of the native quarter to make purchases in the Rue de Constantine or the Marché de la Lyre.

This City of the Sun is one of violent contrasts. Seen from the sea, it fully bears out its Arab comparison of being a "diamond set in emeralds," for in terraces of intensely white, flat-roofed houses, each with little square windows like pips upon a dice, it rises high upon the bright green Sahel hills. In the centre the Arab town with its cupolas and minarets is crowned by the great fortress, while right and left are the pleasant suburbs of St.

Eugène and Mustapha, their white houses and handsome villas gleaming forth from dark luxuriant foliage.

In the French quarter, the Boulevard de la République, running along nearly the whole front of the town facing the sea, the wide Place du Gouvernement, with its oasis of palms, and the Rue d'Isly, with its avenue of trees, are all hot and full of busy, bustling French; but turn away up any of the side streets from the Rue de la Lyre, cross the Quartier Juif, and in a few moments one is in a bewildering labyrinth of steep, shady, and tortuous streets, so narrow in places that two asses cannot pass with their panniers.

Herein lies the charm of Algiers. Those narrow passages, where the Arabs sit on rush mats outside the *kahoua*, drinking tiny cups of coffee, smoking cigarettes, and killing time by playing *damma*, are the same at this moment as they were in the days of Yousuf Zeri; and although the religious prejudices of the Arab, the Moor, the Jew, and the Biskri have perhaps become somewhat modified by contact with the civilising Roumis, yet their mode of life is still the same, and at heart they hate the Christians as fiercely as ever. Indolent and content, they love to lean upon the long parapet of the Boulevard de la République, gazing with deep-set, thoughtful eyes away over the bright blue sea, to lounge in groups at street corners gossiping, to sit at the garish French cafés driving bargains with European merchants, or hand-in-hand to stroll leisurely across to the mosque to their daily prayers. Side by side with dainty ladies in Paris-made gowns and the high-heeled boots of fashion, Arab women, with foreheads heavily laden with tinkling sequins, their dark, flashing eyes peeping over their veils, and all looking exactly the same in their spotlessly white but hideous out-door dress, shuffle along with waddling gait, and turn to glance surreptitiously at the stranger after he or she has passed.

This wonderful old city of sunlight and shadow, of dazzling brightness and sombre gloom, of strange incongruities of dress, of language, and of religion, was by no means fresh to me. On taking up my quarters at the Hôtel de la Régence, in the Place du Gouvernement, I was welcomed as an old friend, for on several previous occasions, while idling in El Djezaïr, I had made it my headquarters in preference to the suburban hotels on the hill at Mustapha. Before the house a cluster of fine date palms throw a welcome shade, and beyond lies the bay, with the great, misty mountains of Kabylia in the distance. Forming one side of the Place stands the Djamäa el-Djedid, with its plain windowless walls, dazzlingly white dome, and square minaret, whereon at sunset the *mueddin* appears and calls the Faithful to prayer. Here, again, extremes meet. The monotonous voice of the priest mingles with the jingle and chatter of the French café opposite, and Europeans, sipping their bock or mazagran, watch the devout Moslems trooping into the courtyard to wash before entering the house of Allah.

Here, in this the most charmingly cosmopolitan city in the world, where subjects for the artist are presented in perfect panorama at every turn, I wandered and idled at cafés, killing time impatiently, and eagerly awaiting the day on which my mysterious desert acquaintance would go upon her pilgrimage. At last that long-wished-for Friday dawned, and leaving the city early by the gate Bab-el-Oued, I strolled through the charming Jardin Marengo, under the intensely white walls of the handsome mosque built over the shrine of Sidi Abd-er-Rahman, and then out on the road which wound up through the dark, wild ravine of the Bou-Zarea.

In the fresh, cool morning air the walk up that well-shaded road to the Frais-Vallon was delightful, even though the aloes and prickly pears were white with dust and the sun had scorched the foliage of the almond and orange trees. At the top of the glen, where the road narrowed into a footpath, I found a little Arab café, and upon a stone bench before it I seated myself to watch for the woman who held me under her spell.

This smiling, fertile country beside the sea, where grapes, olives, and sweet flowers grew in such wild abundance, was charming after the great wastes of arid sand; and while the birds sang gladly above in the cloudless vault of blue, I sat alone, smoking and sipping a tiny cup of coffee, watching the veiled women in their white baggy trousers and haicks, in pairs and singly, slowly toiling past up the steep road on their way to adore the koubba of Sidi-Djebbar.

That Zoraida should repair to this shrine was puzzling. It added considerably to the mystery which enveloped her. Sidi-Djebbar is the patron saint of divorced Arab women, and, according to a local tradition, whenever a divorced lady makes three pilgrimages to his tomb and drinks of the waters of Aioun Srakna, she will marry again before the next fast of Ramadân. Was Zoraida the divorced wife of some man who had bought her from her parents and had soon grown tired of her? Was she an outcast from the harem?

Thoughts such as these filled my mind as I watched the veiled houris pass in silent, pious procession. To distinguish one from another was impossible. The only way in which I could tell a lady from a woman of the people was by her feet and by the texture of her haick. The feet of the lower classes were bare and thrust into heavy, roughly-made slippers, while on the neat ankles of wealthier women gold bangles jingled, their feet were encased in stockings of silk, they wore tiny Paris-made patent-leather shoes, and as they brushed past, they left upon the air a scent of attar of rose. The women of Al-Islâm are seldom allowed to visit the mosques, so on Friday, their day of prayer, they go on foot to venerate the koubbas of their saints instead.

A weary journey extending over a month, had brought me at last to this spot, yet how among all these shrouded figures could I distinguish the woman I adored? Suddenly it occurred to me that, although I had taken up a position of vantage, Zoraida would not approach me, an Infidel, at any spot where she might be observed; therefore I rose and strolled leisurely on up the steep shaded track that led in serpentine wanderings among the fig trees, oranges, and vines.

Half convinced that her promise would never be kept, and that she was still in the far Sahara, I walked on very slowly for some distance. Suddenly, at a bend in the hill-path, where the wide branches of the cork oaks, the ilex, and the chêne-zeen met overhead, and the giant aloes grew abundantly, a voice amongst the leafy scrub startled me, and a short, stout figure appeared from among the foliage. Glancing round to reassure herself she was unobserved, she ran towards me. Only her eyes were visible, but they disappointed me, for I could see that they were not those of the woman for whom I was searching. She was old; her forehead was brown, wizened, and tattooed.

"Art thou the Angleezi whom Allah delivered into the hands of our master Hadj Absalam? Art thou named the Amîn?" she asked, almost breathlessly, in Arabic.

"Yes," I replied. "Who art thou?"

"Know, O Roumi, that I have been sent by my mistress, Zoraida Fathma," she said, drawing her haick closer with her brown, bony hand. "My lady of exalted dignity said unto me, 'Go, seek the foreigner Cecil Holcombe, *wákol loh inni moshtâk ilich.*'" ("Tell him that I am desiring to see him.")

"To see her? I expected she would be here!" I said.

"Alas! no. The koubba of Sidi-Djebbar cannot be graced by my lady's presence this moon."

"Is she here, in El Djezaïr?" I asked quickly.

"Yes. Although thou hast not known it, her lustrous eyes, the Lights of the Harem, hath already gazed upon thee since thy sojourn here. She desireth to have speech with thee."

"When?"

"Two hours after the sun hath set."

"And where may I see her?" I asked, impatiently.

"Knowest thou, O Roumi, that in the Jardin Marengo there is a path under the wall of the holy Zaouia of Sidi Abd-er-Rahman. If thou wilt meet me there under the great cedar tree when the moon hath risen, I will conduct thee to her presence. My lady hath named thee Amîn, and must see thee."

"I will await thee," I replied. "Go, tell thy mistress that the hours have passed at snail's pace since we met, that the Amîn weareth her ring, and that he hath not forgotten."

"Behold! Some one cometh!" she exclaimed in alarm, as a tall Arab appeared at the bend of the path sauntering slowly in our direction. "I must not be seen speaking with thee, an Infidel, within the sacred precincts of the koubba. Till to-night, *sidi, slama*."

And, turning quickly, the messenger from my mysterious enchantress strode onward towards the tomb of the patron saint of divorce.

Chapter Twelve
An Oath to Messoudia

With eager anticipation of once again meeting Zoraida, I left the Place Bab-el-Oued, and, ascending the steep incline, entered the Jardin Marengo.

The sun had disappeared into the broad Mediterranean, flooding the sea with its lurid blaze of gold; the light had faded, the *muddenin* had, from the minarets of the mosques, called the Faithful to their evening devotions, and the dusky, mystic gloom had now deepened into night. From the garden, situated a hundred feet or more above the sea, on the edge of the city but within the fortifications, a beautiful picture was presented. Above, the square castellated minaret of the mosque of Sidi Abd-er-Rahman stood out distinctly against the calm night sky; below, in the hollow, the houses of the lower town clustered with a dream-like picturesqueness in every line and angle. Beyond, lay the harbour with its breakwater and tall white lighthouse; in the gently undulating water were long perpendicular twinklings of light, and against the darkness, which was not wholly dark, the bold lines and tapering masts of half a dozen vessels were sharply silhouetted. The distant strains of one of the tenderest airs from "Carmen," played by the fine Zouave band, floated upward out of the shadow; and as I stood under the giant cedar which the old Arab woman had indicated, it was hard to say whether one's looking or one's listening brought a finer sense of restfulness and remoteness. It was probably the alliance of the two that gave to those moments their special fascination.

The ancient mosque, under the walls of which I waited, was silent. Among the dark foliage lights glimmered, and overhead in the spacious quiet were a few stars. At last the air from "Carmen" died in its final poignant chords, the succeeding silence remained far a long time unbroken, and the moon shone forth from behind the light scud. Its white brilliance was shedding a silvery light over the trees and gravelled walks, when suddenly I saw, moving slowly in the shadow of the ilex trees, a shrouded figure approaching noiselessly, like some ghostly visitant from the graveyard of the mosque.

A few moments later the old Arab woman with whom I had made the appointment, emerged into the moonlight and halted before me.

"Thou, the Amîn, the stranger from over seas, hast kept thy promise," she said, slowly. "Know, O Roumi, that my lady awaiteth thee."

"Whither wilt thou conduct me?" I asked. "Is the journey long?"

"No," she answered. "First, before I, Messoudia, conduct thee to her, thou must swear by thine own Deity never to reveal to any one, Mussulman or Christian, her whereabouts, or, even though strange things may occur,—more remarkable than thou hast ever dreamed,—thou wilt never seek to discover their cause, neither wilt thou approach her in the future unless she commandeth thee."

The weird old woman's words mystified me. In the moonlight her white-robed figure looked ghostly and mysterious, and her small dark eyes peered earnestly at me over her veil.

"Why should I give such an undertaking?" I asked.

"Because—because it is my lady's desire. It is her words I deliver unto thee; if thou dost not obey, thou canst never enter her presence."

I hesitated. Perhaps, after all, it would be best not to go, for if I were discovered, Zoraida's life as well as mine would most probably pay the penalty. Besides, she might be already married! Some questions I had asked of her servant, when we met at the Frais-Vallon earlier in the day, were directed towards clearing up that point, but I had only received vague, evasive answers.

Noticing my indecision, the old woman continued—"Thy thoughts, O Roumi, are that thy presence in my lady's apartment would be an insult to our creed. O' há kki k lak annoh lise fi hâtha al-amr éhátar." ("I assure thee there is no danger in that matter.")

"And if I undertake to respect her wishes although my curiosity be aroused, what then?" I asked, still undecided.

"My lady will admit thee to her presence, and have speech with thee alone. Remember, O Infidel, she risked her life to save thee, and thou, in return, may now redeem thy promise to her."

"Then I will accompany thee," I said at last, determined to see my fair Enchantress of the Desert again. "And if her commands are imperative, I give my word of honour as an Englishman that I will never make inquiry regarding things I may witness, unless she giveth me sanction."

"May all the blessings of Allah be extended unto thee!" she replied, with evident satisfaction at my resolve, for seldom will a True Believer express such a wish to an Infidel. "I, a Moslem, cannot walk with thee, but follow me, and I will lead thee unto her."

Then, drawing her haick closer, she moved onward in the deep shadow of the orange and ilex trees, while I, with mixed feelings of pleasure and distrust, strode on after her.

I had exchanged my haick and burnouse for European dress, now that I was back in Algiers. The spirit of adventure was strong within me, yet I felt curiously apprehensive of some untoward event. I was about to enter the abode of some fanatical Moslem, to converse with a woman of Al-Islâm, to tread upon ground that must always be highly dangerous to a Christian. Yet the world was before me, and there is always pleasure and excitement in plunging single-handed into its chilling depths.

Ascending the short flight of steps at the side of the mosque we emerged from the Jardin Marengo, and, turning into the broad but unfrequented Boulevard Valée, the highest point of the ancient town, we walked for some distance until nearly opposite the great grey walls of the prison, when suddenly my guide crossed the road and dived into the Arab quarter, a puzzling labyrinth of narrow crooked streets and gloomy little passages, of maze-like windings and dark *impasses*. As we passed down the steep, ill-lit streets, white-burnoused men were squatting in groups on the mats outside their cafés, drinking coffee, playing *damma*, and smoking "the pipe of permanence;" or inside the *kahoua* they lounged upon the benches, discussing the topics of the day. In the deep dens that serve as shops, shoemakers were still plying their trade, makers of horn rings were still at their primitive lathes, and embroiderers were still busily sewing in the yellow lamplight.

The streets were crowded, for it was pleasant in the evening hour, and amid the chatter of Arabic we sped on, wending our way in and out the tortuous turnings until I had no idea in what portion of the Arab quarter we were. The streets bore names in French on little plates, it is true, but after we had crossed the Rue de la Kasbah, the principal native business street, I discovered nothing that gave me a clue to the direction in which I was going. A dozen turns to right and left, now ascending through some dark tunnel-like passage, now descending where the ancient thoroughfare was wide enough to admit three asses abreast, we at last came to where two narrow streets met. Straight before us was an arched door in a great, gloomy, whitewashed house, windowless except for a few little square holes high up, protected by lattices of thick iron bars. The house was very old, built in the time of the Deys, and as my guide rapped upon the door, I noticed that the step was worn deeply by the feet of generations, and above the arch the hand of Fathma in brass was nailed to avert the evil eye.

It was a strange inartistic-looking exterior, but, ere I had time to gaze around, the heavy iron-studded door swung open, and, entering, we passed through a narrow vestibule, or *skiffa*, into a spacious *oust*, or open court, where a vine trailed above and a fountain fell gently into its marble basin. Then, for the first time since we left the Jardin Marengo, my guide spoke. In a low half-whisper, she said—

"Thy voice must not be heard. This meeting is strictly secret, therefore follow me in silence and noiselessly."

"*Ma ansash*," I replied.

"And thy promise?" she whispered.

"My oath bindeth me to obey her."

"Then thou art truly the Amîn. Peace be unto thee, and upon thy descendants and companions," she said. "Hush! make no noise. Let us seek her."

Crossing the dark courtyard, she unlocked a small door, and I followed her in. The mingled perfume of musk, geranium, and attar of rose was almost overpowering, and my feet fell with noiseless tread upon a thick, soft carpet. A great hanging lamp of filigree brass shed a welcome ray, and as we ascended the broad stair, I thought I heard whisperings and the rustle of silken garments. Upstairs, a big, handsomely-dressed negro stood apparently awaiting us, for, with a sharp, inquiring glance and the exchange of some whispered words in Kabyle dialect, which I could not distinctly catch, he conducted me along a well-carpeted passage to the end, where closed plush curtains barred our passage.

As I advanced, he suddenly drew them aside, and in a low deep voice announced me in Arabic, inviting me to enter.

Stepping forward, I gazed around in curiosity and amazement.

I was in the harem!

Chapter Thirteen
Night in the Harem

"Ah, Ce-cil! At last!—at last! *Marhaba*."

There was a movement on the other side of the dimly-lit, luxurious chamber, and from her silken divan Zoraida half rose to greet me. Reclining with languorous grace upon a pile of silken cushions, her hand outstretched in glad welcome, the jewels she wore flashed and gleamed under the antique Moorish hanging lamp with an effect that was bewildering. But alas! from her eyes to her chin a flimsy veil still concealed her features.

Taking her small white hand, I stood by the divan and looked down at her steadily in silence, then raised her fingers slowly and reverently to my lips.

The curtains had fallen; we were alone.

Presently, when we had gazed into each other's eyes with tender, passionate earnestness, I addressed her in Arab simile as light of my life from the envy of whose beauty the sun was confused, and told her how slowly time had dragged along since I had escaped from the poison of the asp; how glad I was to bow once again before the Daughter of the Sun.

She listened to my affectionate words without replying. One of her little pale green slippers had fallen off, leaving a tiny bare foot lying white upon the dark silk.

Her dress was gorgeous, fully in keeping with her costly surroundings. She was a veiled enchantress in gold-spangled embroidery, filmy gauzes, and silver brocade. Her dark crimson velvet *rlila*, or jacket, cut very low at the throat, exposing her white, bare breast, was heavily embroidered with gold, the little *chachia* stuck jauntily on the side of her head was of the same hue, thickly ornamented with seed pearls, while her wide, baggy *serroual*, reaching only mid-leg, were of palest *eau de nil* silk, fine as gauze, and brocaded with tiny coloured flowers. Her vest, that showed below the *rlila*, was of silver brocade, and her sash, of many-coloured stripes, was looped in front, the fringes hanging gracefully. Across her forehead a string of gold sequins was stretched, with a centre-piece consisting of a great cluster of lustrous diamonds, while three particularly fine gems, set in pendants, hung upon her white brow. Around her slim, delicate throat were two splendid diamond necklaces, a dozen rows of seed pearls, and a necklet composed of large, golden Turkish coins. Suspended by four heavy gold chains about her neck was her golden perfume-bottle, encrusted with roughly-cut diamonds and sapphires; on her arms she wore *mesais* of gold and silver studded with gems, her fingers glittered with diamonds, and on her neat, bare ankles golden *redeefs* jingled.

Indeed, she was the fairest and most dazzling woman my eyes had ever gazed upon.

The air of the harem was heavy with sweet perfumes, mingling with the sensuous odour of burning pastilles. In the apartment everything betokened wealth and taste. The silken divans, with their downy, brightly-coloured cushions, the priceless inlaid tables, the genuinely antique cabinets with doors of mother-of-pearl, the Eastern rugs of beautifully-blended shades, the rich embroideries, and the profusion of flowers, all combined to render it the acme of comfort and luxury, and graced by such a bewitching vision of Eastern beauty, the scene seemed more like a glimpse of fairyland than a reality.

"Thou hast not forgotten me, then?" she said, raising herself slowly, and placing under her handsome head a cushion of pale primrose silk.

"No," I replied. "How can I ever forget thee?"

Her white breast rose and fell in a deep-drawn sigh.

"Already Allah, the Most Merciful, hath directed thy footsteps and vouchsafed me the felicity of conversing with thee. Thou hast kept thy promise unto me, O Cecil, for when the *homards* would follow us, thou didst not betray our whereabouts. Therefore I trust thee."

"I assure thee that any confidence thou placest in me shall never be abused," I replied. "Yet," I added, "thou dost not place in me that perfect trust that I have."

"Why?" she asked, in quick surprise.

"Still hidden from my gaze is that countenance I am longing to look upon."

"Wouldst thou have me cast aside my religion? I am a woman; remember what is written," she exclaimed, half reproachfully.

"The adoration of the Christian is none the less passionate than the love of the True Believer," I said. "A woman is not defiled by the gaze of the man she loveth. But," I added thoughtfully, "perhaps, after all, thou hast no thought of me, and my fond belief that in thy breast burneth the fire of love is only a vain delusion."

"Thou—thou thinkest I can care nothing for thee—a Roumi? Why?" she cried, starting up.

"Because of thy refusal to unveil."

She hesitated; her brows were momentarily contracted. Her hand trembled.

"Then, though I cast aside the creed of my forefathers and the commands of the Prophet, I give thee definite answer. See!" With a sudden movement she withdrew a golden pin, and, tearing away her white silken veil, her countenance was revealed.

I stood amazed, fascinated, half fearing that the wondrous vision of beauty was only a chimera of my distorted imagination that would quickly fade.

Yet it was a reality. The face turned upward to mine with a merry, mischievous smile was that of Zoraida, the woman who had now so plainly demonstrated her love.

"Well," she asked, with a merry, rippling laugh, "art thou satisfied? Do I please thee?"

"Thou art, indeed, the fairest daughter of Al-Islâm," I said, slowly entwining my arm about her neck and bending to kiss her. She was fair as the sun at dawn, with hair black as the midnight shades, with Paradise in her eye, her bosom an enchantment, and a form waving like the tamarisk when the soft wind blows from the hills of Afiou.

Her lips met mine in a long, hot, passionate caress; but at last she pushed me from her with firmness, saying—

"No, I must not—I must not love thee! Allah, Lord of the Three Worlds, Pardoner of Transgressions, knoweth that thou art always in my thoughts— yet we can never be more than friends."

"Why?" I asked, in dismay. "May we not marry some day?"

"Thou art a Roumi, while I—I am a dweller in the mansion of grief."

"But all things are possible," I said. "If thou art afraid of thy people, trust in me. Meet me clandestinely, attired in European garments, and we will leave by the steamer for Marseilles, where we can marry."

I uttered these passionate words scarce knowing what thoughts I expressed. As soon as they had left my mouth I was filled with regret.

"No. Ask me not," she replied, firmly. "Already, by bringing thee hither, by unveiling before thee, and by suffering thee to kiss me, I have invoked the Wrath. The curse is already upon me, and—and, alas! I shall pay the penalty soon enough," she added, with a touch of gloomy sadness.

"What dost thou mean?" I asked, gazing into her beautiful, entrancing face.

"It meaneth that I, Zoraida Fathma, am consumed by that sorrow and despair that is precursory of death; that Eblis hath set his fatal seal upon me—that I am doomed!"

Her lustrous eyes, with their arched and darkened brows, looked into mine with an expression of intensity and desperation, and she glanced furtively, as if in fear, into the distant corner of the room, where the light from the great lamp of beaten brass did not penetrate.

"Thine enigmas are puzzling," I said. "What evil canst thou fear?"

A shudder ran through her slim frame. Then she clutched my hand and tightly held it.

"I cannot—I—It is forbidden that I should love thee, O Cecil," she said, sighing and setting her teeth firmly.

"Why?"

"Because a greater and more insurmountable obstacle than our difference of race and creed preventeth it."

"But tell me what it is?" I demanded.

"*Isbir showhyyah,*" ("Have patience a little"), she replied. "Though I may love thee, my Amîn, thou canst never be my husband. I am as much a captive as any of my slaves, and, alas! far, far more unhappy than they."

Why did she have slaves? I wondered. Slavery in Algeria had, I knew, been abolished since the overthrow of the Dey, although in the far south, beyond the Areg, the tribes still held many in bondage.

"Unhappy?" I cried. "What is the cause of thy misery? Art thou thyself a slave, or—or art thou wedded?"

She started, staring at me with a strange expression.

"I—I love thee!" she stammered. "Is not that sufficient? If I wish at present to conceal certain facts, why dost thou desire me to tell lies to *thee*? To my woman Messoudia thou didst take oath to seek no further information beyond what I give thee."

"True, O Zoraida," I said. "Forgive me. Yet the mystery that surroundeth thyself is so puzzling."

"I know," she said, with a tantalising laugh. "But when a woman loves, it is imprudent of her to compromise herself;" and she beat an impatient tattoo with her fingers, with their henna-stained nails, upon a *derbouka* lying within her reach.

I did not reply. I was engrossed in thought. All that she had said made it plainer to me that she was the wife of Hadj Absalam.

She watched me in silence. Then, with a sudden impetuousness, she sprang from her divan, and, standing up, flung her arms about my neck, kissing me passionately. The silk of her *serroual* rustled, her bangles jingled, and in her quick movement she lost her remaining slipper, and stood barefooted, a veritable Queen of the Harem, a houri of Paradise.

"Hark!" she whispered, starting in alarm as we stood locked in each other's arms, while I rained kisses upon her fair face. "Hark!" she cried. "Listen! What was that?"

I held my breath, but could detect nothing.

"My foolish fancy, I suppose," she added, a few moments later, after she had strained her ears to again catch the sounds that had alarmed her. "Think! If we were betrayed! It would mean torture and death!" she said hoarsely, and, disengaging herself from my arms, she walked quickly over to the opposite wall, and, drawing aside a heavy curtain, reassured herself that a door it concealed was securely bolted.

Returning, she flung herself upon her divan among her cushions and motioned me to a seat beside her. Then, taking from the little mother-of-pearl stool a box of embossed gold filled with cigarettes, she offered me one, and, lighting one herself, reclined with her head thrown back gazing up to me.

"We are more than friends, Ce-cil," she said presently, thoughtfully watching the smoke that curled upward from her rosy lips. "I only wish it were possible that I could leave this land and go to thine. Ah! If thou couldst but know how dull and colourless is my life, how rapidly my doom approaches—how horrible it all is!"

"What is this strange destiny that the Fates have in store for thee?" I asked, mystified.

"Have I not already told thee that thy curiosity cannot be satisfied?"

"Yes. But I love thee," I protested. "Surely I may know the character of any danger that threateneth?"

She shook her head, and, taking my hand, noticed upon my finger a plain gold signet ring that had belonged to my father. Slowly she drew it off and placed it upon her middle finger, saying, "I take this in remembrance of to-night."

"But is there nothing I can do to avert this mysterious evil which thou apprehendest?" I asked.

She did not reply. With her face turned towards the painted ceiling, her dark, serious eyes gazed away into space. Her bare breast, with its profusion of pearls and diamonds, heaved and fell as she breathed, and the sweet odour of rose and geranium that pervaded her filled my nostrils with intoxicating fragrance.

"Why canst thou not escape from here?" I continued. "If danger threateneth, fly from it. I will assist thee. And is not Allah merciful? He giveth life and death."

"*Hákk*," she replied. "Yet to leave this place unobserved would be impossible. I have been able by a ruse to gain thine admittance here, but any attempt to leave would only result in my death."

"Are not thy servants amenable to bribery?" I suggested.

"Alas! as they are my slaves, so are they my gaolers. They are charged with my safe custody, and if I eluded their vigilance, they would pay the penalty of their negligence with their lives. Ah! thou knowest not the more terrible of the tortures practised by my people. Thou knowest not the Ennitra. Soon I shall return again to the Ahaggar, and then the Great Desert and the Atlas will separate us. For me escape is impossible. Thou wilt go to thine own land ere many moons, and—and forget me!"

"Never!" I exclaimed, vehemently.

"Thou wilt marry one of thine own women who have no prejudices, and who may go unveiled, like those who come to Mustapha at Ramadân."

"No, Zoraida," I said; "I love only thee."

She gazed long and earnestly into my eyes, at the same time toying with my ring.

"And thou art ready to serve me implicitly?" she inquired eagerly.

"I am. Command me."

"Then know, O Cecil, my life is at stake," she said, in a low, hoarse whisper, drawing herself up with one arm still entwined tenderly about my neck.

"Why art thou threatened?" I asked, in surprise.

"Because I—because I am guilty of a crime; I possess the secret of a hidden marvel. Having dared to penetrate the hideous mysteries of Eblis, one of them, undreamed of and astounding, hath been revealed unto me. Its knowledge placeth in my hands a secret power that I might use with fearful effect, but the awful curse hath now fallen upon me, and I am doomed. Only thy willing assistance can save me. Yet"—and she paused. "Yet I feel doubtful whether thou, a Roumi, wouldst dare to undertake the mission that is necessary for my safety; whether thou couldst place sufficient confidence in me to carry out instructions which to thee may seem so extraordinary."

"I have perfect trust in thee," I said. "I am ready from this moment to serve thee blindly, implicitly, if I can save thee and further the prospect of our marriage."

"Marriage? No! no! Do not speak of it now," she exclaimed hastily. "Hast thou never heard of the truth uttered by our Harikar al-Hakim, who said, 'Marriage is a joy for a month and a sorrow for a life, and the paying of settlements, and the breaking of the back under a load of misery, and the listening to a woman's tongue.' To thee I can promise nothing, for my life may end at any moment."

"But thy death can be averted. How?"

"By rendering me assistance thou canst save me from the awful physical and mental torture—from the horrors of the grave. Wilt thou consent to become my secret agent?"

"Yes. I am ready to perform any task thou mayest require of me."

"Then remember the oath of secrecy thou didst take before Messoudia brought thee hither; for, first of all, thou, trusting to thine own Deity, must enter with me into the presence of the Great Unknown."

And as she touched a little silver gong, the great negro in handsome blue livery, who had announced me, entered the harem and prostrated himself before his mistress until his forehead touched the carpet; while two houris, in clinging robes of white silk, entered bearing a great gold bowl of sweet perfume in which Zoraida, with an imperious gesture, washed her hands, and bade me follow her example.

"Thou wilt not be timid," she asked, "even though we go voluntarily together to the very threshold of the grave; even though we may peradventure taste of the horrors of death?"

"No," I replied, endeavouring to remain calm.

My nerves were strung to their highest pitch, and my heart beat quickly. I stood breathless, watching one of the houris, who lit a small gold lamp that burned with a thin blue flame. What, I wondered, was the character of the strange scene I was about to witness? Zoraida, my enchanting Pearl of the Harem, and I were going together voluntarily into the presence of the Great Unknown!

Chapter Fourteen
Seeking the Unknown

Having placed the quaintly-shaped lamp on the pearl and silver stool in the centre of the harem, the negro went out, returning immediately with a small bronze urn marvellously chased, which on bended knee he carefully handed to his mistress. At a word from Zoraida, her women and the tall Soudanese prostrated themselves facing the table, pressing their foreheads to the carpet. Then, turning to me, she said in deep earnestness—

"Knowest thou that the deeds we are about to commit are a terrible sacrilege? Though thou wilt witness strange things, yet peradventure they may cost us our lives—nay, our very souls."

"Why?" I asked, somewhat alarmed at her sudden seriousness. "Is it imperative that we should risk everything?"

"Every sin beareth its fruit," she replied, as, slowly rising from her divan and holding above her head the urn the negro had brought, she added, "Hath not the Prophet told us that when the earth shall be shaken by a violent shock, and the mountains shall be dashed to pieces and shall become as dust scattered abroad, we shall be separated into three distinct classes? Those who have preceded others in the Faith shall precede them to Paradise. The Companions of the Right Hand shall go and dwell in the Gardens of Delight, among lote trees free from thorns and trees of mauz always fruitful; but the Companions of the Left Hand—how miserable shall they be! They who, like ourselves at this moment, invoke the secret power of Eblis the Terrible, will dwell amidst the burning winds under the shade of the great black smoke. They are the damned, for they, in their error, have gone astray in the Valley of Perdition. Then know, O Roumi! that thou hast chosen to accompany me unto the dreaded Shrine of Darkness, to seek of the beneficent Granter of Requests what is hidden, to face the terrors of the tomb, so that thou mayest hold over thy fellows a power terrific, fatal, awful!"

Her eyes were dilated, filled with a strange, unnatural light, and I stood aghast at her solemn speech.

"Art thou not one of the chosen?" I asked. "Art thou not—"

"Hold thy peace!" she commanded. Then, holding forth the bronze urn, she exclaimed, "See! in this vessel are the ashes of the great Masinissa, the Numidian king, whose body was entombed at Medrassen two thousand years ago. By their light we will search for the Great Unknown."

With a sudden movement she took from the urn a small handful of white dust, and, holding it high over the lamp, sprinkled it slowly into its faint blue flame. In a moment the place was illuminated by a white glare so brilliant that I was compelled to shade my blinking eyes with my hands, while at the same time the apartment was filled with a dense smoke of a light green hue, but so pungent as to plunge me into the agonies of asphyxiation.

Thrice she threw into the flame the ashes of the King; thrice she uttered strange words in a drawling monotone, that were repeated by the three servants who lay prostrate and appalled. Then, dipping her finger in the dust, she drew it across my forehead from left to right, and afterwards made the same sign across her own bejewelled brow and across her bare breast.

"Rise," she said, turning to her servants. "Bring hither the elixir. Then leave us."

All three scrambled to their feet in haste to do the bidding of their imperious mistress, and, after the lapse of a few moments, the two houris in white reappeared, one bearing a tiny bowl containing a colourless liquid, while the other brought between her fingers a long thin poignard, the hilt of which was studded with rubies and turquoises. When they had placed them beside the lamp, and the heavy curtains had fallen behind the two girls, Zoraida turned her great dark eyes upon me, exclaiming—

"Thou wilt ere long learn a wonderful secret which hath been revealed to none on earth except myself. Already hast thou taken an oath never to disclose what thou mayest see between these walls. Know, O Cecil! that by thy passionate love for me thou wilt bind thyself to one who can produce strange effects from simple causes, and who can show thee wonders undreamed of. Yonder knife and potion will bind thy soul unto mine; thou wilt become one of the Companions of the Left Hand, whose habitation is the shadowless Land of Torment, where the burning wind scorches and water scalds like boiling pitch."

"Is there then no hope for those who love thee?" I asked, so mystified and my senses so dulled by the curious odour of the smoke, that I scarce knew what words escaped me.

"None," she replied, sighing. "Neither rest, mercy, nor the Garden of Delights can fall to the lot of he who loveth me."

"Why?"

"Because, by regaining the wondrous secret lost to the world for so many ages, the mark is set indelibly upon thee. Knowest thou not what is written in Al Korân? The Prophet hath declared that when the heavens shall be rent in sunder and shall become red as a rose and shall melt like ointment, then neither man nor genius shall be asked concerning his sin. The wicked will be known by their marks, and they shall be taken by the forelocks and the feet and cast into the place of grievous torments."

"Yes," I said. "But why is the search after this hidden force an act of such heinous wickedness?"

"Because the secret is only to be obtained at the Shrine of Darkness. Dost thou, after the warnings I have given thee, still consent to accompany me among the Companions of the Left Hand—to gain the knowledge that is forbidden?"

I gazed upon her marvellous beauty. Her magnificent eyes, bright as those of the gazelle, were turned to mine with a look of earnest appeal as the little hand I held trembled with suppressed excitement. The mystic rite she had practised had intoxicated me with a burning desire to learn more of these strange revelations that she promised, and, dazzled by her loveliness, I was utterly reckless of the future.

"I do not fear," I replied. "I place implicit confidence in thee, and am prepared to serve thee, and to seek the wisdom so long withheld."

"*Ibtidâ-an*," she exclaimed. "Thou, the Amîn, must be inoculated with the elixir;" and, taking up the gleaming poignard, she felt its point. "It is a deadly decoction. One drop is sufficient to cause death, yet, strangely enough, three drops have only the effect of stimulating the brain and preparing the vision for the strange things of which thou must remain a silent witness."

Taking my hand in hers, she pushed back the sleeve of my coat, exposing my arm. Then, grasping a small rod of glass that lay beside the bowl, she dipped it in the liquid and allowed a single drop to fall upon my flesh. It burned and ate into my arm like an acid, causing me to draw back quickly in pain, but ere I realised her intention, she had raised the dagger and made a punctured wound, thus allowing the poison to enter my veins and mingle with my blood.

"Quick! The second drop!" she cried, dipping the rod into the bowl again.

"It feels like molten metal," I gasped, drawing my arm away. "It—"

"Do not hesitate," she exclaimed concernedly. "If thou dost not receive the three drops into thy veins, the poison will prove fatal. Come, let me conclude the formality;" and, grasping me firmly, she placed another spot of the acid upon my arm and punctured the flesh with her knife, repeating the operation a third time, until I had been fully inoculated with the mysterious virus.

Then, stretching forth her own well-moulded white arm, whereon I noticed several small red spots,—which she explained were the marks of previous inoculations,—she stuck the point of the dagger three times into her own delicate flesh, until the blood flowed and the fluid she had placed upon the spots was wholly absorbed.

Casting the dagger from her with an expression of repugnance, she passed her hand quickly across her brow, saying—

"Henceforward, O Cecil, an affinity existeth between us. Though deserts, mountains, and rolling seas may separate us, our souls will hold converse. We shall no longer be strangers."

The poison was taking effect upon me. Its action was slow, but a strange, sickening giddiness crept over my brain, a feeling that the objects around me were gradually fading. Even Zoraida's voice sounded hollow and distant in the dreamy half-consciousness that the secret decoction of my enchantress produced.

Was she, so young, so eminently handsome, so bewitching, the ingenious sorceress who, according to the rumour current among the Spahis, directed the movements of Hadj Absalam and his daring band of outlaws? Could it be possible that beneath those fair features was a heart so brutal and depraved as to plot murder, robbery, and horrible atrocities? As she stood before me in her dainty silks and flashing gems, she had no appearance of a wild freebooter and desert-wanderer, but rather that of an Oriental child of Fortune into whose languorous life the demon ennui had entered.

Had she not, however, called herself the Daughter of the Sun? Was not that the name by which the *homards* knew the guiding star of the murderous Ennitra?

"Hearken, O Cecil!" she said, placing her hand suddenly to her breast as if a pain shot through her heart. "The inoculation is accomplished, and life is now fast ebbing—we are dying—"

"Poisoned!" I gasped, alarmed. "Thou dost not mean that the three punctures will prove fatal?"

"Thou, the Amîn, hast placed thy faith in me. Of a verity will I reveal unto thee that which is known to me alone. Only by thus inviting death can we seek converse with the Great Unseen who ruleth the Kingdom of Shades. Our mental power, our sensibility, our very souls must be severed from our bodies and concentrated into separate existence, ere we may seek the knowledge that giveth us power. Even now at this moment our souls are parting from our bodies, the dim spark of life flickers, and we stand together on the threshold of the grave!"

I was touched and awed by the extraordinary change that came over her while she had been speaking. Something in her tone appealed to my sympathy, while at the same time her words made my heart sink. A woman lying in her coffin, ready to be buried alive, might have had such a strain in her voice. Her face was white, with that ghastliness which comes in extreme moments to a brunette, and her eyes, starting from their sockets, burned with a dusky, deep-set brilliance. When her voice, that sounded in my ears like a far-off wail, had ceased, she stood motionless, and her countenance assumed an inscrutable mask of quiet, almost serene resignation, behind which something suggested immeasurable depths of poignant suffering. Pale, haggard, and deathlike, she gazed at me with dry, half-parted lips. Then I saw in her wild eyes the fearful but unmistakable light of madness!

I was appalled at the slow, mysterious transformation of the woman I loved.

Chapter Fifteen
At the Shrine of Darkness

Under the singular magnetism of her lustrous eyes, I stood dazed, speechless, fascinated. My head throbbed with the burning of fever, my throat contracted, my limbs trembled as if palsied, and my heart was filled with an all-consuming terror.

Truly I was on the brink of the grave; I was peering into the yawning chasm of the Unknown. Suddenly an awful thought occurred to me. Was Zoraida, my idol, insane?

Bewildered and blinded in the rose-mist of happiness, the deepest significance of her strange actions had been entirely lost to me. Love had predominated everything, for the gracefulness of my Pearl of the Harem had so far surpassed expectation, so dwarfed all former visions of feminine attractiveness, that I had been struck to the heart by her first glance after the veil had fallen from her countenance. Therefore, was it not possible that, in failing to regard her extraordinary acts as those of a person whose mind was unbalanced, I had foolishly allowed myself to fall a victim to her homicidal tendencies? Though I strove to remain calm, I involuntarily shuddered. I tried to speak, but my tongue clave to the roof of my mouth and refused to articulate.

"*Al-ân.* We are ready," she exclaimed at last, still keeping her bright eyes fixed upon me. "With our souls distinct from our bodies, we may now seek the knowledge withheld from mankind. Thou hast, I know, believed me to be a common charlatan, a sorceress who imposeth upon those who put their faith in occult arts. Now, however, that we love each other; now that our souls are wedded in the Unseen, I will invoke the revelation of the extraordinary secret, which, if it pleaseth the Great Unknown, thou shalt hold as my pledge. Prepare thine eyes for the witnessing of strange marvels, and follow me."

Walking towards me, she raised her face to mine, kissing me fondly, then, slowly drawing back, she passed her hand quickly over her aching forehead, and, bidding me accompany her, tottered forward to the hidden door which previously in the evening she had ascertained was secure.

"*Addonya dâr gorour*," ("The world is a house of deceit"), she said, drawing a small key from her bosom. "In the grave there is none. Hovering as we now are, between life and death, with the conquest of the soul over the impulses of the body, we may catch a glimpse of the Unknown. Therefore, let us go down and search for light at the Shrine of Darkness. *Náhhi hâtha*."

The ancient key grated in the lock, and the ponderous door swung slowly open, revealing a narrow stone passage, the darkness of which was cavernous and impenetrable. Taking up the lamp into which she had sprinkled the ashes of Masinissa, she passed through the door, bidding me close it and follow her. Her face was pale and determined, and her wealth of dark hair, that had become unbound, fell to her waist in luxuriant profusion. I crossed the threshold into the close, damp passage, and pulling the door behind me it clanged loudly, the lock securing itself with an ominous snap.

I knew I was a prisoner in this, the innermost and secret chamber of the harem, and held my breath in expectation and alarm. Her sequins tinkled as she walked firmly and upright with the little lamp held high above, as down the long stone corridor that was evidently cut in the thickness of the wall I stumbled on after her, with reeling head and unsteady gait. A strange, sickly odour of cinnamon and musk filled my nostrils, the air was hot and offensive, and upon the rough-hewn walls lodged the dust of ages. A door at the end of the passage groaned as she pushed it open, and the dim light revealed a passage still narrower, running at right angles to that which we had traversed. Down this we walked in silence, until our progress was barred by a thick curtain of dark plush.

Halting, she turned towards me. In her countenance a change had been effected that startled me. The poison with which she had inoculated herself had wrought a terrible transformation. Round her fine, clear, luminous eyes were large dark rings that gave her bloodless face an expression of haggard hideousness, the bloom of youth had faded from her cheeks, now sunken, and her mouth was hard and drawn, showing the agony she was suffering.

"Thou art ill," I exclaimed in alarm. "Let me assist thee."

"No," she replied huskily. "It is the crucial test. Preserve thine own courage, and now, ere we enter the Shrine of Darkness that is the portal of the Kingdom of Shades, let me urge thee, O Cecil! to maintain a level head and clear judgment. Examine what thou seest by the light of reason. Thou hast bound thyself irrevocably to me by the burning of the ashes and the puncture of the poignard, and together we are seeking that knowledge that will give us power over our fellow-creatures. Ours is a solemn investigation, to be undertaken in no spirit of idle curiosity or frivolity, for of a verity we are both fast sinking to the grave, and it is only in our dying moments that the Great Secret of the Unseen World that is forbidden to the living may be revealed unto us."

"I fear not while thou art my companion," I replied, determined not to betray nervousness, although the sickening and excruciating pains in my head caused everything to appear dim and hazy as a dream.

"And to the world thy lips will remain for ever sealed? *Awa lam?*" she asked in earnestness.

"I have pledged myself to preserve silence," I replied.

"Then enter to the Shrine, and perfect peace be upon thee," she said, summoning all her courage and drawing aside the curtain.

Upon the threshold of a grim, dark chamber I stood dumbfounded and amazed at the strange sight that presented itself to my gaze. The apartment was not very large, but the roof was vaulted, the arches were curiously wrought, and by the ruddy light diffused by a single hanging lamp, I saw it was a weird and altogether extraordinary place. Upon the floor was a black carpet, soft as velvet, around the walls were several rich divans, and behind a fine latticework of marble at the farther end of the luxurious dungeon— for such it seemed to be—was a circular altar of agate, jasper, and gold, over which a burning censer of gold was swung by an unseen hand. Behind the altar a large luminous star shone above with a dull red glow, and upon the altar itself stood a small brazier which, burning brightly, rendered the atmosphere close and oppressive.

Such was the extraordinary scene that met my dazzled eyes as I moved forward into the secret chamber.

Zoraida, rushing wildly on before me and uttering a loud cry, fell upon her knees before the altar, bowing until her lips touched the carpet, at the same time murmuring some strange incantation that I could not understand. So rapidly did she repeat the words, and so quickly she swayed her body backwards and forwards, that she was at last seized with hysteria. Suddenly regaining her feet, she raised her hands above her head, uttering a curious supplication in some language with which I was unacquainted.

At that moment I made an alarming discovery. There was a slight movement on the carpet, and, bending to examine it, I was horrified to find that upon the floor were venomous snakes! On the divans asps were lying, with their flat heads erect within their coils, together with vipers and scorpions. On every side tiny brilliant eyes seemed watching us, and now and then a slight hiss was heard from the remoter corners of the place. But Zoraida heeded them not. At the door she had kicked off her embroidered slippers, and now walked barefooted among the reptiles.

When she had concluded her strange prayer, she crossed the chamber hastily, and, tossing the velvet cushions and striped silk covering from one of the divans, there was disclosed an ancient tomb of carved sardonyx that was crumbling by age.

Grasping my hand, she then led me to the altar, whispering to me to prostrate myself before it. Hand in hand we passed the marble screen and threw ourselves down, kissing the ground; then, as we rose, she drew from her breast a small stiletto and pricked her wrist three times with its keen point. Holding it over the burning brazier, she allowed the blood to drip slowly into the fire, each drop hissing loudly as it touched the live coals.

Once she groaned, and a shudder went over her like the passing of the wind of sundown over still water. Then, in a firm voice, she exclaimed—

"Blessed be they who overcome human folly, vanity, and error. Blessed be they to whom the wondrous manifestations of the Terrible Unknown are accorded, for they shall be concealed under the dome of magnificence, and veiled by the curtain of purity. We, Companions of the Left Hand, on whom, alas! no peace resteth, present ourselves in quest of the knowledge of the Crescent of Glorious Wonders, so that our lives may be united and our happiness assured. Fervently pray we that an assurance of favour may be granted unto us, and that the Great Secret, dead to the world through so many ages, may be revealed."

Scarcely had she uttered these words, when from the still swinging censer there rose a single puff of thick smoke. Zoraida was watching for it, and as the smoke dissolved, she remarked to me in low, impressive tones—

"Behold! our petition hath been stamped by the seal of response! It is well. Our quest will not be in vain." Then, after a pause, she added, "Thou, O Roumi! hast believed I am a sorceress and a charlatan. Come hither."

She walked to the sarcophagus, and, grasping the stone that formed the lid, pushed it off with almost superhuman effort, so that it fell heavily down behind. Then, taking up the lamp she had brought, she held it over the stone coffin and bade me gaze into it. With eager eyes I obeyed her, but started back in horror.

It contained a corpse!

An old man of pale complexion, with long white beard, and dressed in the habiliments of the grave, lay stretched with upturned face, motionless in death.

"This man, a holy marabout, died, and entered the Garden of Delights three years ago, yet, behold! his body hath not decayed. His misery hath been changed to peace and his grief to tranquillity," she observed. "That he is actually dead prove for thyself. Touch him."

I bent, placing my hand upon his white cheek. Its contact thrilled me. It seemed icy as marble! The sightless eyes seemed to gaze into mine with a grim, stony stare, and I drew away my hand as if I had been stung.

"*Howa-thâ!*" she cried. "I will prove further that there is no life;" and, raising the knife in her hand, she plunged it into the breast of the corpse.

"Art thou satisfied that he is really dead?" asked Zoraida grimly.

"Yes," I answered, shuddering, for my whole surroundings in that subterranean Chamber of the Serpents were so uncanny, that I began to long for light and fresh air. Was she performing all these strange rites merely for the purpose of impressing and mystifying me; or was she an enthusiastic devotee of some secret sect of Al-Islâm? To poison one's self before invoking the aid of the occult seemed an extraordinary proceeding, and the whole of the rites were so curious, that, fascinated as I was by the mysticism of the East, I regarded them with the most intense interest.

"At the Shrine of Darkness death loseth its sting," she said. "To communicate with Eblis, the Terrible, it is necessary that one who is already a dweller in the Garden of Delights shall return to life and assist us. Here, in this charnel-house, the abode of death and of the serpents, strange knowledge may be imparted; but ere we proceed further, the sacrifice must be made."

Snatching up a viper that lay coiled upon one of the divans, she grasped it dexterously near the head, and, walking to the altar, held it for a few moments above the burning brazier, repeating some weird word's, then, as the reptile squirmed under the pain, she dropped it upon the burning coals.

Flinging herself upon her knees, with her hands outstretched above her head, she again invoked the aid of the mysterious Power. Pushing back her hair, that had fallen over her shoulders, she again rose, and, coming towards me, exclaimed—

"Watch, and I will reveal unto thee the terrible power of Eblis that hath been imparted unto me. *Cathâ!*"

She looked more haggard than before. The strain upon her nerves was evidently awful. Taking my hand, she led me back to the sarcophagus, repeating some words in such a low tone as to be inaudible. Suddenly she dashed forward, and with her right hand made mysterious passes over the face of the corpse.

"Sidi Mammar ben-Mokhala, chosen of the Merciful. Peace! Again I call upon thee, holy man of the Faith, tenant of the tomb of dignity and light of the eyes of the discerning, to assist this Roumi to the sight of the Crescent of Wonders, for none save myself knoweth aught of the way thither. Blessing upon thee, and great peace on those who went before thee!"

She paused. There was a wild look in her eyes, and her bare bosom heaved and fell quickly.

"Arise!" she cried in a loud voice. "I, Zoraida Fathma, Daughter of the Sun, command thy soul and body to reunite for brief space, so that thou mayest minister at this our sacred Shrine."

A sound came from the ancient stone tomb like a long, deep-drawn sigh. There was a slight movement, and then, as I gazed in speechless expectancy, the corpse of the aged marabout slowly rose from its resting-place, white, rigid, and ghastly. The amazing resurrection appalled me. I stood with bated breath, my eyes were riveted upon the weird figure, and I was rooted to the spot. The hair upon my head was lifted as corn is lifted when the wind ceases suddenly, and the sweat rolled from my brow. Truly, this mysterious woman to whom I had voluntarily and blindly bound myself was gifted with some weird power that was utterly amazing and incomprehensible.

Chapter Sixteen
The Crescent of Glorious Wonders

Slowly the dead marabout stepped from his tomb and stood erect before me.

He glided mechanically, rigidly; his limbs did not bend, neither did his eyes move. In his grave-clothes he looked hideous, for so thin was his face that the bones could be seen beneath the brown withered skin, and his fleshless fingers with long nails had the appearance of talons.

"Thou hast never before witnessed the return of the dead to the world!" Zoraida exclaimed, noticing how scared I was.

"Is he really dead?" I asked, feeling somewhat sceptical, and beginning to think I was being imposed upon by some ingenious trickery.

"Dead? I call thee to witness!" she cried, and again drawing her long, keen dagger, she plunged it for the second time into his side.

There was no doubt that it had penetrated.

"Enough!" I gasped. "It is sickening."

"Thou art at last convinced. Good!" she said, withdrawing the knife. Then, turning to the man she had recalled from the grave, she addressed him—

"Greeting to thee who followeth the guidance. Thou who hast enjoyed the pleasures of the Garden of Delights among the Companions of the Right Hand, and hast tasted the sweet waters of Salsabil, knowest the Secret of the Crescent. I, who fear the Omnipotent Avenger, command thee to intercede, that I may gain knowledge whereby to triumph over the Satans of Eblis—on whom may the Merciful not have mercy—and henceforward find perfect peace."

Zoraida looked frightened herself, trembling like a slender cord suspended in a well, yet standing erect and queenly, with her jewels flashing and gleaming with dazzling brilliancy. To her words, however, the marabout made no reply. He remained motionless as a statue, gazing straight at me with his black glassy eyes.

Picking up an asp, a symbol of the Aïssâwà, that was darting over the carpet, Zoraida placed it in his icy hand. His bony fingers gripped the reptile as in a vice as slowly he moved across the strange apartment, and, without uttering a sound, sacrificed it on the blazing brazier.

Motioning me to kneel, and sinking upon her knees at my side, the woman I adored twisted a serpent around her head, and flung herself forward with her lips pressed to the sable carpet. Venomous reptiles were around us, but none ventured to attack. Indeed, she had kicked a viper aside with her bare foot as unconcernedly as if it had been an almond husk.

Strange passes were being made by the dead saint, standing at the altar with his back to us, and as he performed the mystic rite in silence I noticed that the smoke from the censer became thicker, and the fire in the brazier glowed until the iron seemed at white heat. Bowing slowly three times, the marabout stretched forth his hands above his head, and, turning, faced us.

Zoraida's strained voice broke the silence.

"Blessed be he to whom the lifetime of the ruby is as the lifetime of the rose. O thou of exalted dignity, behold me, the least and least worthy of all them that praise the One worthy of praise. May I never endure prosperity as a gift from the accursed, for I seek the Secret of the Crescent, and ask of the One of unbounded favour and infinite bounty that which thou alone canst reveal."

Again the marabout faced the altar, again he made passes over the fierce fire. The censer, still kept swinging by some unseen power, emitted a column of thick smoke, the odour of which, at first sulphurous, then sensuous and overpowering, caused me to feel intolerably drowsy. Then suddenly, with a noise as loud as the firing of a pistol, a great rent appeared in the stone front of the altar, as the slab of jasper broke in twain and a portion fell to the ground.

"Lo! it is at last revealed!" cried Zoraida, turning to me excitedly. "Life remaineth unto us! The poison will take no further effect, since we shall possess the Great Secret."

Bowing to earth, the marabout approached close to the altar, and, dropping upon one knee, placed his hand in the aperture that had been so suddenly created. From the hole he drew forth a semicircular box of time-stained leather, about twelve inches across, and, opening it carefully, took therefrom a piece of rusted iron, shaped in the form of a crescent, about two inches wide in the centre and tapering to horns at each end. Its form was almost like a sickle, covered with strange hieroglyphics deeply graven, and it was about a quarter of an inch in thickness in every part, with a notch in the centre, as if another portion that had once been welded to it had been broken away.

Zoraida, still kneeling, eagerly watched the ghastly figure, who, bowing once again, held the strange object over the flame until it became heated.

"Beseech of the Power, O Sidi Mammar ben-Mokhala, if the secret may be wholly revealed unto the Roumi," she said in a loud, clear voice.

Again the corpse that had been awakened from its sardonyx casket bowed and raised its hands aloft in obedience to her request, as we all three watched the censer. The thin column went slowly up, but the puff of thick smoke—that seemed to be regarded as a sign of the affirmative—was not emitted. Yet again the marabout bowed in silent intercession, but, though we waited for some minutes, no reply was vouchsafed.

"Thou art not a True Believer, O Cecil," Zoraida said, in bitter disappointment. "The Great Secret, although revealed unto me, is withheld from thy knowledge. Alas that it should be so! Truly I bear the yoke of misfortune and taste the venom of grief."

"Of what use is the Crescent?" I said, regarding with curiosity the rusted relic in the bony hand of the aged marabout.

"It is the will of the Unseen that thou mayest not know its Secret," she replied. "Therefore I can reveal nothing."

"But surely thou mayest tell me what it is for?"

"Not at present. Have patience until thou hast passed beyond the portals of this, the Kingdom of Shades."

The silent priest, having heated the iron sufficiently, placed it upon a great gold tray, which Zoraida procured from a corner of the chamber and held for him; then she went out, bearing it with her, and announcing her intention of returning again immediately. Before the broken altar the man from the tomb stood immovable as a statue, his hands uplifted; and there was no sound save the hissing of a snake, hiding in a corner where the light did not penetrate.

Five minutes elapsed; they seemed an hour. When Zoraida re-entered, she bore the mysterious Crescent in her hand, and, strangely enough, her face had assumed much of its usual beauty. In her eyes a look of happiness and contentment had succeeded that expression of mad despair that had for the last half-hour spoiled her countenance, and she appeared to have derived every satisfaction from the strange rites she had practised.

"At last," she cried, "the Great Secret is again mine! A year ago I discovered its existence, but the mere suggestion of its use seemed so utterly absurd, that I hesitated to seek death by the deadly potion until absolutely compelled."

"Wert thou compelled to-night?" I ventured to inquire.

"Yes. Thou knowest I love thee. It was for thy sake that I sought the Great Secret. Thou wert not afraid, and gave me courage to knock at the gate of the dreaded Kingdom of Shades—to face the King of Terrors."

"And yonder marabout? What of him?"

"He will return to the green banks of the river Al Cawthar, whence I called him to do my bidding and act as intermediary. See! I will send him back unto his sepulchre."

Advancing to where the ghastly figure was standing with transfixed gaze without moving a muscle, she placed her hand firmly upon his shoulder.

"Know, O Sidi Mammar ben-Mokhala! thy work hath ended. Thou mayest return to the Shadow of the Lote Tree, and to the houris awaiting thee in the Garden beside the ever-flowing stream. May the blessing of Allah—Gracious Bestower of abundant benefits—ever rest upon thee and thy sons' sons, and may the Destroyer of Mankind—on whom may the Merciful not have mercy—have no power over them. To thy grave I command thee to return, to rest until I again seek thine aid to triumph over Eblis."

She grasped his cold thin hand, and he allowed himself to be led to the sarcophagus as meekly as a lamb. Into his stone coffin he stepped, and then sank back and disappeared. A few moments later, Zoraida beckoned me, and, standing beside the great sardonyx tomb, I peered in. The marabout lay stretched out as before, with wide-open, sightless eyes, and when I touched his cheek, it was hard and icy cold.

"There is no life. See!" she said, and, taking the knife, she once again plunged it into the corpse, afterwards withdrawing it and replacing it in the velvet sheath hanging at her girdle.

The old man had again returned to the Great Unknown, leaving Zoraida in possession of the curiously-wrought piece of metal, the fantastic inscription upon which puzzled me greatly.

Chapter Seventeen
Strange Confidences

Gradually the golden censer ceased swinging; the fire in the brazier slowly died out, and the only light in the mysterious chamber was shed by the blue flame of the lamp that had guided our footsteps thither.

"Come, let us return," she said, with a shudder. She took up the lamp and gazed into the cavernous darkness where the light did not penetrate. Suddenly, just as she was about to turn towards the door, she noticed my face, and became alarmed.

"Ah!" she cried, horrified. "I had forgotten thee. See; thine eyes are already glazing. Thou art dying!"

"Dying?" I gasped, holding my breath.

"Yes. Thou hast not learned the Secret of the Crescent, therefore thou art not rendered invulnerable against the hand of the King of Terrors. The poison hath done its work, and thy spark of life will die out like yonder brazier."

"Why? Dost thou mean that thou hast actually murdered me?"

"I am no murderess," she answered, reproachfully. "Thou hast submitted to the fatal inoculation, yet to every poison there is an antidote." Then, drawing from her breast a little jewelled scent-bottle, about the size and shape of a pigeon's egg, that was suspended by a chain around her neck, she removed the cap and shook into the hollow of her hand a small quantity of a dark brown powder.

"See! place this upon thy tongue and swallow it. Life and health will return to thee, and no ill effects wilt thou feel to-morrow of thy near approach to the Realm of Silence."

She emptied it into my hand, and I swallowed it. The drug was bitter as gall and burned my mouth with fiery pungency, but ere I could make another observation, she had snatched up the lamp and was disappearing through the arched doorway. Following, we retraced our steps along the gloomy corridors, until at last she pushed open a door, and we found ourselves back again in the fragrant, luxurious harem.

Placing the lamp upon one of the little tables of ebony and pearl, she sank upon her divan exhausted, but still grasping the Crescent. Her long hair strayed over her shoulders and breast, and as she lay back in utter abandon she panted as if the strain of the past hour had been too great. Taking one of the great silken cushions I placed it tenderly under her wearied head, then sank upon my knee at her side.

"Tell me, Zoraida," I said. "Tell me more of the strange scenes which I have just witnessed. What giveth thee the wondrous power to recall the dead from the grave, and invoke the assistance of the Great Unknown?"

Turning her brilliant eyes to mine, she hesitated.

"True, O Cecil," she exclaimed, after a short, silent interval, "I have power that is not vouchsafed to some; but what thou hast seen to-night is not so wonderful as the secret contained within this piece of Damascus steel;" and she raised the Crescent for me to gaze upon.

"What secret can a piece of metal possibly contain?" I inquired, almost inclined to laugh at her earnest assertion.

"Thou thinkest that I fool thee," she answered in a tone of reproach. "I tell thee, nevertheless, that knowledge of certain things giveth me power over both friend and enemy, power that I use at will for good or for evil. They who are cursed from my lips find no solace in this life, and descend to Eblis, where hot winds blow and there is no water; but those who have my blessing prosper, grow wealthy, and find peace."

"Have I thy blessing?"

"Thou hast," she murmured calmly, raising her lips to mine in a long, fierce caress. "My wishes are that thou mayest find happiness and riches, and that thou mayest receive the mercy of the Merciful is my heartfelt desire."

"My only happiness is at thy side," I said, with fervent promptitude.

"Ah! it is, alas! but brief," she replied, sighing. "There are circumstances which prevent our marriage—even though we love each other so well."

"Circumstances? What are they? Tell me. Thou always speakest in enigmas."

"The first and most serious is the uncertainty of my life. Even to-night I may die;" and she raised her finely-moulded hand and thoughtfully examined my ancient signet ring upon her finger.

"Absurd!" I said. "What ground hast thou for such gloomy apprehensions? Art thou not safe here, surrounded by every luxury, with slaves to do thy bidding, and guarded from every evil?"

"Not from *every* evil," she replied slowly. "When thou art absent, unhappiness consumeth me, and sadness, like a corrosive acid, eateth away all life and gaiety from mine heart."

"But I may see thee more often, surely? How long wilt thou remain here?"

"I cannot tell," she answered, speaking like one in a dream. "To-morrow thou mayest only find my corpse."

"Bah! Why entertain Despair when Joy desireth to dwell within thine heart? We love each other, and may meet often, even though these mysterious circumstances of which thou speakest may, for a time, prevent our marriage."

With a look of bitter sorrow she shook her head, replying, "No. We must not meet, or our friendship may prove fatal. When I invited thee hither, it was to impart to thee the secret of the Crescent of Glorious Wonders that would give thee power to work for our mutual benefit. But, alas! thou, an infidel, mayest not learn the extraordinary truth; the Unseen hath decreed that thou shalt remain in the outer darkness called Ignorance."

"But how can I act in order to break down this strange barrier that precludeth our happiness? Hast thou—hast thou already a *husband*?"

She started. Her lips quivered, and the colour left her cheeks.

"If I had a husband, I should not ask thee hither, neither would I dare to enter the Kingdom of Shades with thee, a lover. To endeavour to learn my secret at present will be futile. Suffice it for thee to know that there is more mystery to penetrate than thou hast ever dreamed of, and that only by seeking knowledge from afar canst thou hope ever to bring us nearer to each other—to—"

A sigh finished the sentence.

"I am prepared to do anything, to go anywhere, to render thee service," I replied, pressing her jewelled fingers to my lips.

"Then hearken," she said, raising herself upon her arm and looking earnestly at me. "The secret of this, the Crescent of Glorious Wonders, is forbidden thee; yet if thou darest to travel to a distant country far away over the waterless regions beyond the Touareg; if thou wilt penetrate the lands of hostile tribes in the disguise of a True Believer, thou canst learn that which will give thee wealth and power, and will at last bring us together."

"To marry?"

"Yes. To marry."

"Tell me all I must do," I exclaimed excitedly. "Can I learn that which thou callest the Great Secret?"

"Alas! it is impossible," she replied. "If thou wilt undertake this perilous journey, thou shalt carry with thee the Crescent of Glorious Wonders as my pledge that I do not deceive thee, and as a talisman which, if thou canst learn its secret, will make thee wealthy beyond the dreams of avarice."

"But what of thyself—what of happiness with thee?"

"Until thou hast accomplished thy mission, I shall remain with my clansmen awaiting thee. Remember, whatever gossip thou mayest hear, or whatever may be revealed to thee about myself, seek no explanation. Set out upon thy journey as soon as possible, and travel on the wings of haste, for the way is long and the approach difficult. My movements concern thee not until thy return, for although to-night thou art here in the harem, do not forget the awful fate that awaiteth women of Al-Islâm who hold converse with Infidels. Therefore, before I give thee instructions, swear by thine own Deity, thine Allah, to heed nothing that thou mayest see or hear concerning me, but perform thy journey speedily, and learn the Great Secret ere thou seekest any explanation."

"I swear I will obey thee unswervingly. I will act upon thy commands as blindly and devotedly as I have to-night."

"Then know, O Cecil," she said, regaining her feet slowly and standing erect before me, "there is but one spot on earth where the Great Secret may be imparted unto thee, now that it hath been withheld even at the portal of the Land of Shades. Before thou mayest again enter my presence, thou must have gained the power and the riches that it can bestow. Whilst thou art in the distant Desert I shall not forget thee; it is even possible that secret communications may pass between us, for do not forget that in future a fatal affinity existeth between our souls, and that, irrespective of distance, we may have a dream-like consciousness of each other's well-being." Her dark eyes fixed upon me seemed to hold me with a strange magnetism. Truly I was under her spell. Even in the brief space that had elapsed, she had now entirely reassumed her marvellous beauty. Stretching forth her hand she poured water from an ewer of chased silver into two drinking-cups. Over them both she passed her fingers swiftly, and then sipped one of them. The sweet odours that hung about the harem had caused a dryness in my throat, and, raising the other cup to my lips, I took several gulps, while she regarded me keenly.

"Shall I always know thy whereabouts?" I asked eagerly.

"No. There will be a certain affinity between our thoughts, but I shall remain hidden from thee until thou hast returned."

For a few moments we were silent. She was no longer haggard and cold as she had been while the poison coursed through her veins, but the rose-garden of her beauty had forthwith recovered its freshness; in the delicate, rounded limbs and bust there glowed the natural warmth and yielding softness of flesh and blood. Her great lustrous eyes, standing well apart under her darkened brows, the broad white forehead, the perfect nose, the small, well-formed mouth, the pearly teeth, the rounded chin, each added grace to grace. Her beauty was perfect.

"Wilt thou remain here, or go back to the Desert with thy tribe?" I asked, gazing at her enraptured.

"To—to the Desert—peradventure," she replied hesitatingly. "If the *homards* are thrown off our scent."

"What! are thy people about to resume their murderous marauding expeditions?" I asked in surprise.

"I—I know not, Cecil," she replied, laying her hand upon my arm. "I would prevent their terrible crimes if I could, but, alas! it is impossible. Thou knowest not in what constant peril I exist, or—or how unhappy is my life. A single imprudent word may seal my fate. I may be tied in a sack even to-night, and cast into the sea!"

"How can I help thee? How can I save thee?" I asked, with eagerness.

"Only by undertaking the journey of which I have already spoken," she answered slowly. "If thy mission is accomplished successfully, then thou wilt rescue me from a cruel fate—a fate far worse than death."

Chapter Eighteen
A Hidden Tragedy

So earnestly she spoke that I felt convinced there was in her life some hideous mystery, and that those who held power over her she regarded with abject terror. Besides, her frequent allusions to the uncertainty of her life made it plain that she was apprehensive of a swift and terrible doom.

Though some of her words and actions were, strange and incomprehensible, and the effects I had witnessed at the weird Shrine of Darkness had, I reflected, been probably produced by some kind of mechanical ingenuity, yet there was something even more remarkable about this Pearl of the Harem than her entrancing beauty. Her actions led me to the conclusion that she was actually the woman reputed by the Ennitra to be possessed of superhuman power, and every moment I now spent in her company deepened my curiosity concerning her.

The mystery by which she was enveloped was puzzling. I felt myself bewildered.

That she was well versed in Oriental mystic, rites was certain, but whether she had actually produced the results I had witnessed without some ingenious trickery I was half inclined to doubt.

Nevertheless, I loved her blindly. Her beauty fascinated me, and her words in soft, musical Arabic that fell upon my ears entranced me.

"Then thou wilt go?" she said fondly, entwining her arm around my neck. "Thou, the Amîn, to whom may the Bestower of Good Gifts be merciful, art willing to face all the terrors of the long journey for my sake?"

"Yes, Zoraida," I replied, looking straight into her dark orbs. "Already thou hast saved my life. If it lieth within my power I will save thine."

"Then we must lose no time," she exclaimed suddenly. Leaving me, she crossed the harem, and took a sheet of paper and an ink-horn from a little cabinet inlaid with silver and mother-of-pearl, returning to where I was standing. Sinking upon her soft divan, she spread out the paper upon a little coffee-stool, and wrote in Arabic character the following:—

"O revered servant of Allah, learned and mighty, thou whose face is as a lamp unto those who walk in the darkness and in error stray from the path, unto thee I send salutation. The One Worthy of Praise made earth for a carpet, and it is written upon the tablet that Allah, Giver of Good Gifts, is the living One. May he who despiseth the revelation enter into the Companionship of the Left Hand, and dwell for ever in Al Sâhira. To seek an elucidation of the Great Mystery, the Roumi, into whose hands have I given the Crescent of Glorious Wonders, journeyeth afar unto thee. Know, O Friend, deadly peril surroundeth me. Of a verity the day hath come when the Great Secret may be revealed, for by its knowledge my life may be spared. Wherefore I beseech thee to grant him audience, and direct his footsteps into the valley of felicity, for assuredly mine enemies may be dumbfounded if thou wiliest.

"In fear have we flown into the refuge of patience, praying to the Answerer of our Supplications to grant us endurance. When our prayer for the Great Elucidation hath been responded to, the skirts of thine innocence shall be purified from the mire of suspicion, and—if it pleaseth Allah—by the blessing of thy devotions will our petition be heard, and from us will our affliction be removed. May the Beneficent Granter of Requests be gracious unto the Roumi and give him prosperity. Upon thee likewise be perfect peace. Sister."

As she carefully penned the intricate lines, I noticed for the first time that across the back of her right hand—the hand that bore my ring—was a small red scar about an inch in length, and I silently wondered how it had been caused.

"There," she exclaimed at last, as she appended with a flourish the characters "Okht" which apparently she used as her signature, "together with the Crescent of Glorious Wonders convey this my message to Hadj Mohammed ben Ishak, the chief *imam* of the mosque at Agadez. He will understand my desire. Tell him that thou hast accompanied me unto the Shrine of Darkness, where I recovered the key to the hidden mystery, but that knowledge was, alas! not imparted to thee. He will then instruct thee how to act."

"To Agadez?" I echoed, dismayed, remembering that it lay far south beyond the Great Sahara, with nearly two thousand miles of trackless and almost waterless wilderness between it and civilisation.

"Yes; I told thee that the only spot where knowledge can be given thee, and by which thou canst effect my rescue, was far distant. Dost thou fear to travel thither?"

I hesitated in uncertainty. Well I knew how tedious and perilous would be the long journey, for the hostility of the tribes through whose country I should have to pass constituted a terror even as great as the enormous difficulties and frightful hardships that I must encounter for many weeks, perhaps months, in the Great Sahara itself. But the earnest look of pleading in her splendid eyes decided me.

"I will go, Zoraida. If it is thy will, I shall start to-morrow," I said.

"Thou wilt traverse the Great Desert for my sake—for my sake?" she exclaimed, kissing my hand as I took the missive she had folded. "When I named thee the Amîn I was not mistaken. Hadj Mohammed will be expecting thee."

"Why?"

"Because he will receive early knowledge that the Crescent of Glorious Wonders is in thy custody. Remember, if lost, it could never be replaced, having been revealed and given unto us by the Power that is all-powerful. Thou wilt undertake this mission in order to save my life, to save me from the horrible fate that threateneth to overwhelm me. When the Secret hath been imparted, and thou hast used it according to instructions that will be given by the aged chaplain of the daily prayers, then wilt thou return to me—and to peace."

"But how shall I find thee? Many moons may perchance rise and fade ere I return to Algiers."

"Assuredly I shall know thy whereabouts," she replied briefly. "Travel swiftly. The horse I gave thee on the night I severed thy bonds will carry thee back from Biskra to El Biodh. Then with camels travel over the vast northern Touareg and the mountains of Adrar, guarding well thy life through Djanet until thou comest to Mount Equelles. From there thou wilt be compelled to guide thyself by the sun over the Desert to the palms of Issalà, where thou wilt find also dates, forage, and water. Another long and weary course of travel will bring thee at last to Assiou, thence journeying due south past Azarara and along the great rocky valleys of Aïr, where dwell thine enemies, thou wilt at length enter the gate of Agadez, the City of the Sorcerers, wherein the strange mystery lieth hidden."

The exact position of Agadez was, I reflected, somewhat uncertain. Generally believed to be about eighteen hundred miles from Algiers as the swallow flies, it was placed by most maps at the extreme south of the Azarara country, to the west of Lake Tsâd; but among European geographers there was a certain amount of doubt as to its exact position and best approach, for maps of that remote district differ considerably. However, I had decided to set out to seek this aged *imam* for Zoraida's sake, and meant to do my utmost to accomplish my mission.

Leaning before me in silence against a marble column, with her hands clasped behind her head, her jewels scintillating in the softly-tempered light, her sequins tinkling musically, her rich silks rustling, her scented bosom rising and falling as she breathed, she looked a veritable sultana, a woman for whom any man might have sacrificed his very soul.

"Remember always, O Cecil, that my thoughts follow thee," she said softly. "Remember, when thou facest the terrors which are inevitable, that there is one woman who is trusting to thee alone to save her. Perhaps ere long I shall return to our palace in the impenetrable mountains beyond Tiouordeouïn; nevertheless my thoughts will be constantly of thee, for now I am convinced of thy love and fearlessness. May Allah, the One Merciful, guard thee, and may all thine enemies perish!"

Placing my arm slowly around her slim waist, encircled by a golden girdle, I drew her towards me, and she kissed me with hot feverish lips.

"I cannot bear the thought, Zoraida, that thou mayest wander again with thy relatives and clansmen over the burning Desert, and witness those awful scenes of plunder and massacre. Ah! if I could but think that thou wouldst be safe here during my absence."

She sighed, toying with the jewelled scent-bottle suspended upon her breast, the little trinket that contained the antidote.

"Already have I told thee my life is very uncertain," she exclaimed gloomily. "Even to-night I might fall a victim. The tyranny of unpropitious times hath thrown the stone of separation upon us. I might—"

"No, no," I interrupted. "Thou art safe here, surely. Be patient, and keep a stout heart until I return. Thou knowest I love thee dearly, and will strive unceasingly to accomplish my mission quickly and successfully."

"Yes. I shall be thinking always of thee—always," she said softly.

"And when I return I shall have learned the mysterious Secret which is so absolutely necessary for our mutual welfare."

"Ah, Cecil, my Amîn! I love thee! I love thee! As sure as the sun will illumine to-morrow's dawn, so surely will I—"

Her passionate words were suddenly interrupted by the entrance of the big negro who had guarded the door of the harem. He rushed in with a look of abject terror upon his dark, brutal countenance, whispering some hasty words into his mistress's ear that caused her to become agitated and deathly pale.

"Quick! Hasten, or I am lost!" she cried, turning to me.

"What danger threateneth?" I inquired in surprise.

"Leave me! Leave me! Thou must not be discovered!" she exclaimed breathlessly. "Take this, the Crescent, and turn thy face towards the Desert to-morrow. Remember the instructions I have given thee; and, above all, promise to seek no explanation of what thou mayest hear or see regarding me until thou hast returned from Agadez."

"I promise," I replied, as for a second I held her in my arms and our lips met in passionate farewell.

"Quick! The Roumi! In Allah's name, save him!" she cried, turning to the gorgeously-attired Soudanese who stood near, like a gigantic statue.

"Follow," he commanded; and, crossing the room, drew aside some silken hangings, disclosing another small door, of the existence of which I had been unaware.

I turned. Zoraida had flung herself with languorous abandon upon her divan, with her hand pressed to her bejewelled forehead. Her wistful eyes followed me, and as I waved her a last farewell, she said—

"Go, my Amîn! May Allah give thee perfect peace!" Through the open door we passed, and the negro, closing it, bolted it from the outside, leaving us in total darkness.

"Keep silence. Grasp my arm, and I will lead thee," said the man, but ere he had uttered the words, there came from the harem a loud, piercing shriek—the cry of a woman!

It was Zoraida's voice!

"Hark!" I gasped, with bated breath. "Listen! That voice was *hers*! Let us return."

"No," he replied gruffly. "That is impossible."

"But the cry was one of terrible agony!"

"Slaves of the harem never interfere without orders. Death is the penalty of the Infidel found within the precincts sacred to the women," he answered coldly.

I turned to unbolt the door, but his sinewy hand grasped me by the neck, and without any further explanation I was half dragged through several dark, close-smelling passages, and down a flight of broken stone steps, until we came to a heavy door.

"At least thou canst tell me who is the owner of this place," I said, slipping a couple of gold coins into his ready palm.

"I cannot. My mistress hath commanded my silence," he answered, pocketing the bribe, nevertheless.

"May I learn nothing, then?" I asked.

"No. Our Queen of the Desert hath taken every precaution that thou shalt obtain no knowledge of certain facts. For her own sake secrecy is imperative, therefore, if thou holdest her in respect, seek not to loosen my tongue with thy gold."

Then he pushed me gently but firmly outside, and with a parting word closed the iron-studded door again. The key grated in the lock as it was secured, and, gazing round, I found myself in the narrow crooked street.

For a few moments I hesitated. The moon shone brightly, and all was quiet, for it was long past midnight.

After a final look at the gloomy, mysterious house, I plunged into the labyrinth of Arab thoroughfares, and, half dazed by the strange, dreamy experience, I walked on, descending the steep, intricate streets, trusting to chance to bring me into the Place du Gouvernement, in the European quarter, wherein was situated my hotel.

At last, after wandering nearly an hour, I found myself in the Rue de la Lyre, the street of the Algerine merchants, and soon afterwards, having awakened the sleepy Arab porter at the Régence, climbed to my room. Opening the jalousies, I sat for a long time gazing out upon the moonlit Mediterranean. The soft warm wind sighed in the waving palms outside, and shouting came up now and then from the quay, for the mail steamer from Europe had just hove in sight. Deeply I pondered over the strange events of the night, wondering whether I was acting wisely in undertaking the long journey to Agadez. So strange were many of Zoraida's words, that more than once was I tempted to regard her as suffering from mental aberration, yet nevertheless I could not disguise the fact that there was a terrible earnestness in all her words and actions, an earnestness which fully bore out her declaration that her life was at stake.

On the table lay the Crescent of Glorious Wonders, the leathern case of which was evidently centuries old, for it was worm-eaten, tattered, and crumbling. What, I wondered, could be its power? How could it assist me to wealth? How was it possible that a mere piece of steel, with its strange geometrical inscription—that is here reproduced—could bring Zoraida and me happiness and peace?

The idea seemed absurd, nevertheless the mystery was inscrutable. It added fascination to her exquisite charms, and I knew that I loved Zoraida—I knew she held me by her spell for life or death.

Once a gloomy thought arose. I remembered the ominous words of old Ali Ben Hafiz; I recollected the strange Omen of the Camel's Hoof! But I smiled, regarding the superstition, as I had always done, as one of the many unfounded beliefs of the Bedouins, and just as the first streak of dawn showed above the distant peaks of Kabylia, I turned in, resolved to get at least one night's rest in a European bed before setting out upon my long journey from which I might perhaps never return.

For me, alas! it was a night fraught with horrors. What I had seen in that strange house in the Kasbah quarter came back vividly to me, confused and distorted in my dreams. In my horrible nightmare I thought I saw Zoraida, the beautiful woman who loved me, struck down by an assassin's knife. I heard her scream, the same shrill cry of agony I had heard after I left the harem.

This aroused me. The sun was shining brilliantly in its clear vault of blue; there was movement in the great square, and the *garçons de café* were dusting their tables. The scent of the flowers from the stalls below wafted in through my open window. I could sleep no longer, so, dressing again, I swallowed my coffee, and went out, wandering along the sea-shore, breakfasting *al fresco* at the Moorish restaurant outside the Jardin d'Essai, and spending the morning strolling alone, puzzled and thoughtful. Returning to the Régence at midday, the Arab porter handed me a small wooden box about a foot in length, six inches deep, and sealed securely with black wax.

"This came for m'sieur an hour ago," he said.

"For me?" I exclaimed, surprised, glancing at the address, which was in a man's handwriting. "Who left it?"

"A Biskri servant, m'sieur. He said it was most urgent, and I was to deliver it immediately you returned."

Who, I wondered, had sent it?

Mounting the two flights of stone stairs hastily, I at length gained my room. Eagerly I cut the string, broke the great seals, and lifted the lid.

"God!" I cried, starting back in horror when my gaze fell upon the object it contained.

Appalled and breathless I stood, unable to move.

Some moments elapsed before I summoned sufficient courage to again rivet my eyes upon it. The sight was sickening.

The box was lined with black silk, and in it there reposed a woman's hand that had been hacked from the wrist! It was white and bloodless. Rings still remained upon the slim waxen fingers, the nails of which were stained brown with henna. I recognised them! One was the signet ring that had belonged to my father. On the back of the dead hand was a scar. I examined it closely. Yes! it was the same that I noticed while the woman I adored was penning the letter to the *imam* I now carried in my pocket!

Trembling, I touched the lifeless fingers. They were cold as marble.

The hideous, blood-smeared Thing that had been sent me was *the dead severed hand of Zoraida*!

Chapter Nineteen
Dead Fingers

On the black silk the shrivelling, bloodless fingers lay half curved like talons. At first I could not bring myself to gaze upon the mutilated hand I had so recently grasped; but at length, fascinated by the gruesome mystery, I inspected it minutely. On the stiffened fingers diamonds glistened in the bar of sunlight that strayed into the room, and my own ring remained there, a silent witness of some terrible tragedy.

Had Zoraida been murdered? Was she, after all, the wife of a jealous, fanatical Moslem, who had discovered our friendship, and who had wreaked an awful vengeance upon her? As I stood with the horrible contents of the box before my eyes, strange thoughts took possession of me. With startling vividness I pictured the woman I loved, and to whom I owed my life, lying stark and dead, with one hand hacked away and a great ugly wound in her white breast where the assassin's cruel knife had entered. I seemed to see every detail of a hideous crime; on my ears there fell the soft lapping of the sea, and the splash as the body, divested of its silks and jewels, was hurled into the water as unceremoniously as offal by two brutal, stalwart negroes. Had not Zoraida been apprehensive of danger? Had she not told me frankly that her life was uncertain? Yet I had never dreamed of murder!

Alas! death comes swiftly sometimes to inmates of the harem. To-day Zuleika or Zohra, Kheira or Khadidja, may be the favourite, exercising power over her lord, and holding sway through him over the world outside her luxurious prison, but to-morrow she may be a corpse floating out with the tide into the lonely sea.

The sight of the dead hand was sickening. I could not bear it. Replacing the lid upon the box, I stood for a few moments in hesitation, then resolved to rid myself of the ghastly object that had been sent me by an unknown enemy. With the box under my arm, I went out into the glaring sunlight. Half-way across the broad Place, it occurred to me to find the mysterious house to which old Messoudia had conducted me, and with the severed member in my possession to seek an explanation. Did not our mutual pledges give me a right to demand knowledge of Zoraida's welfare? If she had actually fallen a victim to the caprices of a monster, was it not my duty to investigate the affair, and bring to justice the perpetrator of the crime? With such thoughts I crossed the Jews' quarter, and, ascending the long narrow Arab street, the Rue de la Kasbah, leading through the heart of the native quarter, was soon climbing with impatient steps the maze-like labyrinth of shady passages, with their low dark archways and great, gloomy, prison-like houses, among which I hoped to recognise the arched door again. I spent a weary, anxious afternoon. The air was sultry, the Arabs lay stretched on the benches in the *kahouas*, or, squatting lazily on the mats outside, were oblivious to their surroundings. Everything was sleepful. Shoemakers and embroiderers who had ceased work were dozing in their little dens, and as I trudged wearily onward, I passed only a solitary ass with heavily-laden panniers plodding on, followed leisurely by his master, who wore a jasmine flower behind his ear. The stillness was only broken by the far-off voices of some Arab urchins at their play, or ever and anon the thumping of the *derbouka* and the twanging of the *guenibri* floating out of the small closely-barred windows of the harems fell upon my ears as I passed. Surely mine was an unique experience, wandering at will, and bearing with me the dead hand of the woman I loved!

The bright blue sea was like glass, the sky cloudless, and the whole world seemed at peace; yet I was the least peaceful. Carrying the casket containing the horrible souvenir, I stumbled onward, toiling aimlessly and in vain up through the gloomy, crooked passages. Feelings I had never before experienced assailed me with a force that first perplexed and then astounded me. I was afraid; and what rather heightened than diminished the unwonted sensation, was the fact that I was not afraid of anything tangible either in the present or the future, but of something mysterious and peculiar. Every sound jarred upon my nerves, causing the faintest murmur to seem like the utterance of a great dread, as awful as it was inexplicable.

Time after time, finding myself at the boundary of the Kasbah, I again turned and plunged into the narrow, crooked thoroughfares, hoping by wandering in this manner to discover the house to which I had been conducted. Alas! it was a forlorn hope. Messoudia had taken precautions in order that I should not be able to retrace my steps; besides, there were hundreds of houses with similar entrances, and though I strove to decide which was the mysterious residence I sought, I could detect absolutely nothing by which to identify it.

Terror shackled my steps. During those hot, anxious hours I several times traversed the streets from the winding Rue Rovigo to the Boulevard Valée on the opposite side of the town, exploring each of the narrow, ancient lanes lying between the Rue Bab Azzoun and the grim old citadel. Every effort to discover the house where I had spent such eventful hours failed, and at last entering a *kahoua*, and having given the lounging Arabs "peace," I sank upon a bench, and, placing the box beside me, called for coffee.

While the old Arab was brewing it on his tiled stove, a man in a ragged and rather soiled burnouse entered, and, after grunting a greeting, squatted near me, idly smoking his long haschish pipe. He was of rather forbidding countenance, with a thin black beard, and eyes that seemed to flame like torches.

Noticing that I had uttered a salutation in Arabic, one of the customers, a very old man, who was half reclining on a bench opposite me, gravely observed—

"It is not often that the Roumi speaketh our tongue."

"No," I replied, smiling. "But I have lived for many moons among thy clansmen, and have wandered far and wide in this thy Land of the Sun."

My remark interested them, and was received with muttered satisfaction. As I wore European dress, I knew they viewed me with considerable suspicion.

"Hast thou travelled in the Great Desert?" the old man asked.

"Yes," I answered. "With the caravans I have been over the Areg and the Sahara, and," laughing, I added, "I have managed to escape from the clutches of Hadj Absalam—"

"Cursed be his name! May Allah never show him mercy!" interrupted the dark-faced man, who was smoking quietly beside me. I turned, surprised at such a vehement denunciation.

"I heard a rumour at Constantine the other day," remarked my interrogator, "that his men have recently raided the caravan of Ali Ben Hafiz, and massacred the whole party."

"That is quite correct," I replied. "I was with them, and because of my Faith my life was spared so that I might be tortured. But I escaped, and returned hence."

"Praise be unto the Prophet who hast preserved thee!" he said devoutly. "Indeed, Absalam's people are a terror to all. Our brother Ali Ben Hafiz— may Allah show him mercy—was very well known here."

"Yes. Very well known," echoed half a dozen guttural voices.

"He often played *damma* here," continued the old Arab, "and no man was more respected in the Kasbah than he." Then, raising himself and pointing to the end of the low-roofed café, where on the walls hung grotesquely-executed texts from the Korân and gaudily-coloured pictures of the city of Mecca, he added, "See there! once while he was smoking in this *kahoua*, a Roumi who chanced to come in drew that portrait. Dost thou recognise him?"

Interested, I rose and walked to where the little pencil sketch was hanging. Notwithstanding the dim light, I could see that the features of my dead friend were lifelike, and I deciphered in the corner the signature of one of our greatest living English artists.

"It is excellent. The expression on the features is exact," I agreed, and, taking the coffee from the hand of the *kahouaji*, I sipped it, and gave him the ten centimes demanded.

Returning to my bench, I suddenly noticed that while my back had been turned to inspect the portrait, the dark-faced man who had entered after me had risen and quietly departed.

Next second I made a discovery.

"My box!" I gasped. "See! it has gone! *It has been stolen!*"

The Arabs, startled from their lethargy, exchanged black looks of disapproval, some of them muttering that True Believers would never pollute themselves by handling the treasure of Infidels.

"My box has been taken by that man who has just left!" I cried, rushing headlong out into the street, and glancing quickly up and down. But he had vanished like a shadow! No human being was in sight. Frantically I rushed about, peering eagerly into dark corners and gloomy archways in the vicinity, but the man, who had apparently been watching for an opportunity to obtain possession of the box, had disappeared in that bewildering maze of streets and left no trace behind!

At last re-entering the *kahoua*, the customers of which had now risen and were holding a very animated discussion over the dexterously accomplished robbery, I demanded if anyone present knew the man. Everyone, however, disclaimed acquaintance with him.

"He is an utter stranger," said the old man who had been conversing with me. "To judge from his face, he cometh from the Areg."

"Evidently he hath no friendship for Hadj Absalam," observed one of the Arabs grimly, as in the midst of an exciting argument he stopped to light a cigarette, carefully extinguishing the match with his fingers.

"But my loss is irreparable. That box contained" —I hesitated. Then I added, "It contained great treasure."

"May Allah consign the thief to Hâwiyat for ever!" exclaimed one of the men calmly.

"May the Prophet send thee consolation!" added another. "Against Fate thou canst not arm thyself," observed a third. "May the entrails of the thief be burned!"

To such remarks I returned thanks, and, heedless of the questions they asked concerning the value of the contents of the stolen box, I stood deep in thought. Though the circumstances were somewhat suspicious that my attention should have been diverted in the manner it had, still there was no mistake that the portrait was actually that of my murdered friend; and, further, the thief had not, as far as I had noticed, spoken to any of those around him. Expert pilferers as the Arabs mostly are, I could not in this instance bring myself to believe that I had been the victim of a plot. Again, it was not a pleasant reflection that the thief might have stolen it thinking it contained valuables, and then, finding the hideous object inside, would in such a case most likely give information which would lead to my arrest for murder! My guilt would be assumed, and to prove my innocence I should experience considerable difficulty.

On the other hand, however, the circumstances pointed strongly to the theory that the ragged ruffian had dogged my footsteps in order to obtain possession of the casket. But for what reason? The box had been wrapped in brown paper, there being nothing whatever in its exterior to excite undue curiosity. Was it possible that the thief might have been aware of its contents? Was the possession of this startling evidence of a gruesome tragedy of imperative necessity? If so, why?

None of these questions could I answer. I felt that the robbery was not an ordinary one. It was an enigma that I could not solve. The hand, with its rings, had been stolen from me by one who was evidently an expert thief, and, recognising that any attempt to recover it was useless, I thanked the Arabs in the *kahoua* for their condolences, and left, turning my steps slowly towards the European quarter.

I recollected that I had promised Zoraida to set out that night on my journey into the distant Desert. Again and again her earnest words in her own musical tongue rang in my ears: "Thou wilt go for my sake," she had said. "Remember the instructions I have given thee; and, above all, promise to seek no explanation of what thou mayest hear or see regarding me until thou hast returned from Agadez. Thou wilt undertake this mission in order to save my life, to rescue me from a horrible fate that threateneth to overwhelm me!"

Had she already succumbed to the fate she dreaded?

Utterly powerless to obtain any information that might lead to the elucidation of the extraordinary mystery, I at length, after calmly reviewing the situation over a cigarette under the palms in the Place Bresson, resolved to keep my promise to her, and before midnight I left the City of the Corsairs on the first stage of my long, tedious journey southward towards the sun.

The temptation to return to England and leave the mystery unsolved had indeed been great, yet I could not forget that I had pledged my word to a woman I loved better than life. She had declared that I alone could save her, and trusted me. These thoughts caused my decision to attempt the perilous journey. Is it not, indeed, true that sometimes beauty draws us with a single hair towards our doom?

Why, I wondered, had she been so intensely anxious that I should refrain from seeking any explanation of these strange, ever-deepening and perplexing mysteries? Her words and actions were those of a woman apprehensive of some terrible tragedy that she was powerless to avert; and even though I started that night from Algiers fully determined to learn the secret of the Crescent of Glorious Wonders I carried, and its bearing upon her welfare, yet that shrill, despairing cry I had heard after leaving her presence still sounded distinctly in my ears, the dolorous, agonised wail of the hapless victim of a hidden crime.

Chapter Twenty
After the Fâtiha

Again I found myself alone in the vast, sun-baked wilderness, where all is silent, and the pulse of life stands still.

Twenty-eight hours over one of the most execrable railways in the world had taken me back to Biskra, where I remained a day, writing letters home to England, and otherwise making preparations for a lengthened absence from civilisation. Then, mounted on Zoraida's fleet horse, I set forth for Tuggurt.

Though the sun's rays were scarcely as powerful as when I had travelled over the same ground three months before, yet the inconveniences and perils of the Desert were legion. In order that the Arabs I met should not deem me worth robbing, I cultivated a ragged appearance; my gandoura was of the coarsest quality worn by the Kabyles, my haick was soiled and torn, and my burnouse old and darned. I had purchased the clothing second-hand in the market-place at Biskra, and now wore a most woe-begone aspect, my only possession of value perceptible being a new magazine-rifle of British pattern. Yet stored away in my saddle-bags I had food, a fair sum of money, a more presentable burnouse, and, what was more precious than all, there reposed in its rotting, worm-eaten leather case that mysterious object, the Crescent of Glorious Wonders. Zoraida's letter to the *imam*, however, I carried in my wallet in the pocket on the breast of my gandoura.

Terribly wearying and monotonous that journey proved. Only those who have experienced the appalling silence and gigantic immensity of the Great Sahara can have any idea of the utter loneliness experienced by a man journeying without companions. In that dreary waste one is completely isolated from the world amid the most desolate and inhospitable surroundings, with the whitening bones of man and beast lying here and there, ever reminding him with gruesome vividness of the uncertainty of his own existence. Knowing, however, that I should be unlikely to fall in with a caravan travelling south until I reached El Biodh, I pushed onward, and after five days reached Tuggurt, where I was the welcome guest of Captain

Carmier, the only European there, his Parisian lieutenant having gone into the Sidi Rachid Oasis in charge of some native recruits.

As the captain and I sat together smoking and sipping our absinthe under the cool arcade with its horse-shoe arches that runs across the now deserted harem-garden of the Kasbah, I retailed to him the latest news I had picked up in Algiers.

"We know nothing here in this uncivilised oven," the officer said, laughing, and at the same time flicking some dust from off his braided coat-sleeve. "The Paris papers are always a fortnight to three weeks old, and, there being no postal service, I have to send to Biskra for them."

"But you have very comfortable quarters here," I said.

"Comfortable! Oh yes," he replied; "but the life is abominably monotonous. I would rather be in command of an advanced post down in the south. There one leads a wild, free life and has plenty of enjoyment. Take Deschanel's squadron of Spahis as an instance. You have already had some experience with them, so I need not describe the rollicking life they lead, scouring the plains in search of that daring old pirate, Hadj Absalam."

"Have you heard anything of the old chieftain lately?" I asked eagerly.

"No. Since the sharp brush with Deschanel's detachment he seems to have mysteriously disappeared. After the defeat of his band we did our best to capture him, feeling that with his power broken he would fall an easy prey. I at once organised detachments of Spahis, Chasseurs, and Turcos, who for nearly a month patrolled the Desert, made inquiries of all the neighbouring tribes, and did their utmost to discover the direction in which the fugitive had gone. But, as usual, all was in vain."

"Then he has again escaped you?"

Carmier nodded, blowing a cloud of smoke upward from his lips. "He seems to move from one place to another imperceptibly, for when he flies he leaves not a clue by which he can be traced. Only last week the Sheikh of the Ourlana, who had just returned from Algiers, told me positively that he saw him, dressed as a Jew merchant, enjoying himself at one of the cafés on the Boulevard de la République. That, of course, is *un conte en l'air*. The old rascal may be daring, but he would never risk arrest by going to Algiers."

I remained silent. Was it not most likely that while Zoraida sojourned beside the sea, the Pirate of the Desert would be there also? I did not, however, tell him of my enchantress, but agreed with him that such an assertion was incredible. When presently my friend had invited me to remain with him a couple of days, and I had accepted, he suddenly asked me—

"Where are you going when you leave here?"

"To Agadez."

"To Agadez?" he echoed in concern. "You are not going alone? It is not safe. Surely the mere love of adventure has not induced you to set out on such a perilous ride?"

"I am fulfilling an urgent mission," I answered vaguely.

"*Bien*! and one fraught with more dangers than you imagine. What possible object can you have in risking your life in journeying to the City of the Sorcerers, which, if all reports are true, is extremely unsafe for Christians on account of the fanatical character of the inhabitants?"

"The object of my journey is a secret," I said. "I have promised to attempt it, and must accomplish it at all hazards."

"And the person you have promised is a woman—eh?" he hazarded, laughing.

"Who told you?" I asked, starting in surprise.

"Oh, I merely guessed," he answered. "But, speaking candidly, I would urge you most strongly to abandon the idea."

"I cannot," I said. "All my happiness—my whole future depends upon whether I accomplish the journey successfully. Besides, I have not hesitated before to cross the Desert, why should I now?"

"Because many of the regions through which you must pass to get to Assiou to join the route to Agadez are peopled by tribes intensely hostile. Their prejudice against Europeans is even greater than in Morocco, therefore it will require considerable courage to face such insurmountable barriers."

"It is not a question of courage," I said; "it's a matter of duty."

Scarcely had these words fallen from my lips when the quick clatter of horse's hoofs sounded in the outer courtyard, and a few minutes later a Spahi orderly came towards us, saluting his officer, saying—

"An Arab has arrived in haste from Es-Safla bearing important news."

"Bring him in," Cannier replied.

In a few moments a tall, thin, aquiline-featured Bedouin, dirty, stained by long travel, and wearing a very ragged burnouse, stalked in, and, wishing us peace, handed the captain a letter, which he tore open and immediately read.

"*Dieu*!" he gasped, starting up. "A reverse! The Ennitra, with the Arabs of the Ouled Ba' Hammou, have risen, and, attacking the Spahis and

Chasseurs near Aïn Souf, massacred the whole of them! As far as is known, not a single man has survived, Paul Deschanel himself succumbing to his wounds a few hours after writing this report, which has been forwarded to me by the Sheikh of the Kel-Ahamellen, our friends. The slaughter must have been awful, for, according to the Sheikh's letter, the enemy treated the wounded and prisoners with the most fiendish barbarity."

"Horrible!" I said. "Poor Deschanel! He was an excellent friend to me."

"He was good to everybody; one of the best soldiers serving under the Tricolour, poor fellow." Then, turning to the Arab, who was unconcernedly rolling a cigarette, he thanked him for delivering his Sheikh's message, and told the orderly to look after him. Again and again Carmier eagerly perused the report, penned in a shaky, uncertain hand by the dead officer, and, much affected, he read me extracts from the black record of treachery and brutal butchery, a record which spoke in the highest terms of the fearlessness of his men and the cool bravery they displayed, even though in face of the overwhelming hordes death was a foregone conclusion from the outset of the fight. The massacre had taken place at the well of Dhaya, where the Spahis had halted on their way to In Salah, and as they had been surrounded at night and cut up, it was evident that my friend Octave Uzanne, the man who had so nobly sacrificed everything in order that the woman he loved should live happily with her husband, had, alas! fallen.

Indeed, I was filled with a grief no less poignant than that experienced by Carmier, when I remembered that those valiant comrades with whom I had fought side by side when we defeated Hadj Absalam's piratical cut-throats in the Meskam had now been treacherously attacked and ruthlessly butchered. The captain, however, gave himself little time for reflection over the sad incident. Calling for writing materials, he sat down and penned an explanatory note to the General of Division, who happened to be at Biskra making his inspection. He recommended that a punitive expedition should be immediately dispatched into the hostile district, and stated, that if the War Department in Paris sanctioned it, he himself could furnish half the men.

In an hour, a smart Spahi, with his rifle slung at his back over his scarlet burnouse, mounted his horse under the great arched gate of the Kasbah, and into his hands the captain gave the dispatch, ordering him to ride with all speed to Biskra, where, by travelling incessantly and changing his horse at five Arab villages he named, he could arrive within three days.

The man, placing the letter in his capacious breast pocket, saluted, and, setting spurs in his horse, sped rapidly away; after which Carmier, pleading that he had some further dispatches to attend to, left me to wander at will through the great courts of the ancient fortress. Presently I came across the Arab who had brought the sad news from his Sheikh, and who, after his meal was now squatting under a shady arcade lazily smoking. Leaning against one of the twisted columns, I questioned him further upon the reverse, but he apparently knew very few of the actual facts. He told me that he intended to return to In Salah on the following day, and it at once occurred to me that we might be travelling companions as far as El Biodh. Knowing that this man, whose name I learnt was Gajére, was trustworthy, otherwise he would not have been sent by the friendly Sheikh, I suggested that we should perform the journey together, an arrangement which met with his heartiest approval.

When the *mueddin* called from the tall minaret of the great white mosque at sundown, I watched the man of the Kel-Ahamellen wash his feet and hands in the courtyard and enter to recite his Fâtiha, and to ask Allah to give us peace upon our journey over the great barren plain where death is ever-present.

Strangely enough, however, I chanced to be lounging with the captain near the gate of the Kasbah, when, an hour later, the devout Moslems came trooping out, and as I looked across to the narrow doorway, I saw Gajére emerge, accompanied by an unkempt-looking Arab whose face struck me as strangely familiar. The pair stood for a few moments hand in hand, engaged in excited conversation, until suddenly they detected my presence. Then, exchanging quick, significant looks and uttering *slaamas*, Gajére and his friend parted, the latter striding quickly away in an opposite direction, and, turning a corner, was soon lost to view. Notwithstanding the dim twilight, however, I had made an astounding discovery, for I recognised the man who had fled so quickly as the Arab who had sat next to me in the little *kahoua* in Algiers—the man who had stolen the cut-off hand!

Had he followed me? If so, with what purpose? I felt convinced that his presence and his friendship with the man from the Desert boded evil, and throughout that night grimly-apprehensive thoughts caused me the most intense anxiety.

By no mere coincidence was it that we should thus meet. The unkempt, fierce-looking ruffian had some sinister design in dogging my footsteps, and the nature of this object I was determined at all costs to ascertain. Therefore, I did not hesitate to adhere to previous arrangements, and, regardless of the consequences, I set out with Gajére.

Chapter Twenty One
A Startling Revelation

Day after day for a whole fortnight Gajére and I rode onward together, passing through Temacin, El Hadjira, and the arid Chambâas region. Now and then we halted at Arab villages in the oases, but the greater part of our time was spent in the dry, waterless wilderness. He was an intelligent fellow, full of anecdote and *bonhomie*, a splendid horseman, and in every sense a typical Bedouin. Yet, somehow, I could not get rid of a strange feeling of insecurity such as I had scarcely ever before experienced.

These vague apprehensions of impending evil were increased by an incident which occurred one night while we were sleeping under the little lean-to awning which served as a tent. We had halted at a small fertile oasis after we had been on our journey eight days, and under the cool waving palms had stretched ourselves for the night. I suppose I must have been asleep nearly two hours, my head pillowed upon the saddle-bag containing the Crescent of Glorious Wonders, when suddenly I was awakened by my companion stirring. In a moment I became filled with suspicion, and with bated breath lay—determined not to betray my watchfulness. Gajére at first sat up listening intently; then, as he bent over and found my eyes closed and my breathing heavy and regular, became apparently reassured. The little awning did not admit of one standing upright, but my treacherous fellow-traveller, moving slowly and noiselessly in order not to disturb me, bent once again to make certain that I had no knowledge of things about me.

Those were anxious, exciting moments. With closed eyes I lay prostrate and helpless, well knowing the futility of a struggle with that sinewy son of the Desert, in whose grasp I should quickly be as helpless as a child. I was unable to draw my revolver without attracting his attention, and knew myself to be in a position of extreme peril. Unaware of his designs, I breathed heavily, and waited. Seconds seemed hours, for the terrible thought occurred to me that he was in league with the sinister-looking thief, and his object was murder. I felt assured that I was to fall the victim of a foul conspiracy.

At last he rose, and, with his eyes still fixed upon me, drew from his sash his long curved knife with its carved handle. I shuddered. The edge of the murderous weapon was keen as a razor. Muttering some guttural malediction in Arabic, the exact purport of which I could not catch, he placed the knife between his teeth and suddenly turned and crept silently out upon his hands and knees, halting in front of the tent, as if listening. Was he waiting the advent of his fellow-conspirator before assassinating me? I strained my ears to catch every sound. Among the dense tropical foliage there were many strange noises; the distant cry of a jackal broke upon my ear, but I could detect no sound of human voices. Again a noise sounded quite close to me, and, stretching forth my hand, I grasped my revolver. The noise was receding, and by slightly turning I could see in the dim half-light the indistinct figure of Gajére creeping slowly away in the shadow as stealthily as a beast of prey.

What could be his object? I wondered. That he meant murder was apparent by the readiness in which he held his knife, and as I was the only person besides himself in that lonely region, I confess I viewed the situation with mingled alarm and dread.

Fully a quarter of an hour elapsed. The suspense was awful, for Gajére had now crept away, and was lost in the wild undergrowth of hulfa and aloes. Perhaps he had gone to give the signal to the scoundrel who had followed me from Algiers! Feeling that my revolver was fully loaded, I grasped it firmly, and lay on the alert in readiness to spring up and defend myself.

The loneliness was appalling. Dismal howls came from the small pond where wild animals were drinking, but in the gloom I could detect no moving object, and began at last to think that my companion had deserted me. At length, however, he returned as quietly as he had departed. I expected to see a second dark form, but breathed more freely when I reassured myself that he was still alone. His knife had been replaced in its sheath, and after halting a few seconds, and holding his quick ear towards the wind so as to catch every sound, he entered, and, throwing himself down again beside me, was quickly asleep.

I scarcely closed my eyes during the remainder of that night, fearing treachery, yet nothing further transpired to confirm my suspicions of his intention to assassinate me, and his mysterious actions puzzled me considerably.

One evening at sundown, when we had halted two days distant from El Biodh, and we were eating our kousskouss together, I succeeded in inducing him to become more communicative about himself.

"I was born and bred in the Desert," he said, in answer to my inquiries. "The sand of the Areg was my cradle, and I have been a wanderer through the Sahara ever since."

"Have you no fixed abode?" I asked.

"None; only my tent. We of the Kel-Ahamellen are no town-dwellers; the Desert is our home, and in the oases we seek our rest. Sometimes our caravans travel to El Golea or Touat, and at rare intervals even into Morocco, but our men are always glad to leave the towns and return to us. I, too, shall not be sorry to return to my wife and children, who are encamped with our tribe at the well of Tadjemoult. Next moon—if Allah willeth it—we shall set out on our yearly pilgrimage to Mount Hikena, under the shadow of which is the holy tomb of Azaká n Akkar—to whom may the Merciful give peace."

"I recollect," I said at length, determined if possible to learn something of the man who had robbed me,—"I recollect that on the night before we turned our faces from Tuggurt, whilst leaving the mosque, thou wert in close conversation with a man. Who was he?"

"A stranger," he replied abruptly, glancing quickly at me with suspicion.

"Not a stranger to me," I said meaningly. "I recognised his face."

"Thou knowest him?" he exclaimed, surprised. "Then thou art forewarned to take precaution for thine own safety."

"Why?" I asked in alarm. "Surely thou hast not hidden from me thy knowledge of some impending evil?"

"Thou art a Roumi, while I am a servant of the Prophet," he answered. "Infidels are our enemies, and it is forbidden that we should warn our foe of our plans for attack."

"Is there danger, then? Doth this man bear me malice for nought?"

"Know, O Roumi," he said solemnly, "thou art indeed in grave peril. I should not tell thee, only the man who addressed me in the courtyard of the House of Allah made an infamous proposition to me, and afterwards I discovered that he was called Labakan, of the tribe of the Ennitra, and one of the most renowned cut-throats of Hadj Absalam, the Terror of the Desert."

"The Ennitra?" I cried. "And he is following me?"

The Arab slowly nodded, rolling his cigarette thoughtfully. "What villainous proposal did he make to thee?" I demanded quickly.

"He offered me a bag of gold to assist in thy murder," my companion replied hesitatingly.

"And thou hast refused—eh?"

"Though we of the Kel-Ahamellen may thieve and plunder, we do not stain our hands with blood," he said proudly. "The men under the green banner of Hadj Absalam have times without number attacked, murdered, and robbed us, carrying off our women to their harems, and selling our children into slavery beyond Lake Tsâd. This man called Labakan, son of Omar, who invited me to help him in his foul plot against thee, is the same who has acted as leader on many of those murderous expeditions."

"But why should he be so desirous of killing me?" I asked. "He explained that thou hadst on one occasion escaped from them after being taken prisoner, and that, hidden in thy saddle-bag thou hast a treasure of enormous value."

"Treasure? I have no treasure," I said. "A man doth not carry his wealth with him when passing through the land of his enemies."

"Labakan said the treasure was neither gold, silver, nor precious stones, but that thou hadst in thy possession something which belonged to their tribe, and which they had solemnly sworn to regain, even though the attempt might cost the lives of those who followed thee. In further speech he told me that Hadj Absalam—the despot who ruleth his people with a rod of iron, and whom may the Merciful doom to all the horrors of Hâwiyat— had ordered him to follow thee to the ends of the earth to regain the lost treasure. If he succeeds, he is to obtain as a reward the most beautiful houri of the Desert Pirate's harem, but if he doth not accomplish his mission successfully within twelve moons, his head will fall under the sword of the executioner."

"Did he tell thee of what this valuable treasure consists?"

"No. He only said that if lost to his people it could never be replaced."

"And dost thou really think that this villain actually meaneth to obtain by foul means the contents of my saddle-bags?" I asked, feeling somewhat uncomfortable at this startling revelation.

"Alas! I do. Of this, the most unscrupulous caitiff of the Ennitra, thou must beware. Take heed of thine own safety when we part. Never relax thy vigilance while in the land of Al-Islâm, and may the Merciful One guard thee in thy perilous journey to Agadez."

"Is this man Labakan alone, or is there a conspiracy to murder me?" I asked.

"I am afraid, from what he hath told me, there is a widespread plot to compass thy death," he said. "Apparently thou hast incensed them exceedingly by learning some strange secret which they desired should never be divulged. As death closes the mouth, Hadj Absalam hath ordered that thou shalt be slain. Under such circumstances I hardly think it wise that thou shouldst venture alone through the Valley of Aïr."

"It is imperative," I answered; "I must not halt until I enter the gates of Agadez. To me also the result of my mission is a matter of life—or death."

"May thy treasure be preserved unto thee, and may Allah—the One Merciful to whom be boundless praise—give thee strength to overcome all thine enemies. May they be vanquished and be swept from the earth to the burning land of Al Sâhira like grains of sand before the sirocco," said he earnestly, hitching up his burnouse.

"I tender thee thanks for thy warning, Gajére," I said. "For thy action thou wilt indeed receive the reward of the One Worthy of Praise, and drink of the waters of Al Cawthar, which are sweeter than honey, whiter than milk, and cooler than the snow."

"And thou wilt, I hope, believe some day that Allah is the One Lord of the Three Worlds, and that Mohammed is his Prophet," he murmured devoutly, looking at me with his deep-set eyes.

But I did not answer. I had no intention of entering upon a controversy on religious subjects, but sat pondering deeply over the plot against me, which evidently had for its object the recovery of the Crescent of Glorious Wonders. His suspicions of approaching attack had caused him to arise in the night, and, armed with his keen blade, reconnoitre for the crafty assassin. He was, after all, my friend and protector. How, I wondered, could Hadj Absalam know that the mysterious object was in my possession? Surely Zoraida had not told him? Yet might he not in his rage, after learning of the catastrophe his tribe had sustained by the loss of the Wonderful Crescent, have taken up a scimitar and struck off her hand?

The thought was horrible.

However fearless I might have been of the terrors of the Desert, I could not close my eyes to the fact that this murderous ruffian Labakan was going about offering as payment for my murder a bag of gold, and I knew that ere long an attempt upon my life would most surely be made. Mine was decidedly a most unenviable position, and when at El Biodh two days later, I bade farewell to my faithful friend Gajére, the earnest blessings he invoked upon me aroused within me an additionally apprehensive feeling of insecurity.

This journey I had undertaken because of the passionate love I entertained for Zoraida, but I could not forget the grave prophecy of old Ali Ben Hafiz, when the Omen of the Camel's Hoof had been revealed. Had he not told me that it was always fatal to love, and in the majority of instances fatal to the lover?

Yet thoughts of Zoraida trusting in me gave me renewed courage, and I resolved to push onward to the south with a stout heart, and endeavour to gain the mysterious knowledge that was necessary to bring to us both the peace, happiness, and riches of this world.

Chapter Twenty Two
Mákita's Enemies

Though I sought the advice of the cadi of the strange old Arab town of El Biodh, and also explained my desire to several of the Sheikhs whom I met, I could hear of no one going in my direction. To set out into the naked Desert alone would, I knew, be a most foolish proceeding, therefore I could do nothing but wait until, through the good offices of a man to whom Gajére introduced me before his departure, I obtained permission to accompany a caravan of the tribe Kel-Imanan, whose chief town is Djanet, about two hundred miles on my route, and one morning, after I had remained as the guest of the friendly Arab for a week, I once more found myself on the back of a camel, and from my elevated seat cast a last glance over the pleasant picture presented by the oasis.

(The word "Kel" denotes the habitual residents of a Saharan district.)

Our caravan, headed by the Sheikh Mákita, numbered about ninety souls, and included men, women, and children, who with fifty camels had been to In Salah with salt and dates, and were now returning with cotton and silk goods, which would eventually find their way into the country in the far south beyond Lake Tsâd. Mákita and I were soon very good friends, but from the moment we started I observed that he ruled his people in a most despotic manner. They were Children of the Sun, with whom theft is no crime, and revenge is virtue.

The first hours of our journey were pleasant enough, for we passed through a beautiful palm-grove bordered by scattered gardens, where the people were busy in the cool of the morning irrigating the corn and vegetables. They came out to see us depart, but without expressing any feeling, hostile or otherwise. After a mile and a half the plantation ceased, and presently we entered a luxurious valley between three and four miles broad, rich in herbage and full of ethel trees, which crowned the tops of small mounds. Several other valleys, rich in sebót and adorned with talha trees, brought us to the well of Gara Beïda, where we encamped for the night at the foot of some cliffs of considerable height, which were to be ascended on the following day.

Commencing our task at dawn, we found the precipitous path wound through loose blocks, and the ascent proved most difficult. The loads had in many instances to be taken off the camels, and we all had to climb on foot up the steep, narrow way over the rugged red sandstone. The ascent took over two hours, and at last we found ourselves on a great rocky level destitute of herbage, stretching away as far as the eye could reach. This region was the wildest, most barren, and most difficult to traverse that I had ever experienced, and it was then that I realised the wisdom of old Mákita, who had prevailed upon me to leave Zoraida's horse behind and mount a camel.

Very slow and tedious our journey proved for four days, the rough nature of the ground making it exceedingly difficult for the camels, until on the fifth day we began to descend by a narrow rocky ravine into a deeper region, amid scenery that was grander than I expected to find in that arid country. Here I saw plants and flowers, the most noticeable among the latter being one that grew about twenty feet high, bearing a white and violet flower which my Arab companions called "tursha." There were also the jadariyeh, the shiá, and the damankádda and dum palms, all of which, however, are familiar to the traveller in the Great Sahara. There was a small torrent too, the bed of which was overgrown by wild melons, and beside the rippling water we halted for the night, prior to moving out into the wilderness again.

Few, however, moved far from the camp that evening, for my dark-faced companions spoke with timorous exclamations of the numbers of lions which infested the valleys. While the camels browsed greedily upon the fresh allwot, the monotony of the evening was relieved by performances by Mákita's musicians and the dancing of several Soudanese slave girls.

On the following day we entered a much wilder country, and for a week we plodded on over the hot dry sand, during which time we only came across one well. The sun was blazing, its fiery rays beating down upon us more fiercely as we travelled further south. The choking clouds of sand raised by the camels, the inability to wash, and the continual consuming thirst, were some of the many discomforts we had to bear. Within sight of a great barren peak called Mount Telout, rising dark and rugged some three thousand feet above the level of the trackless, sandy waste, we passed, and entered the inhospitable country of the Izhaban. Not until a few days later, when we had halted at a well called Djerdeb for our noonday rest, did Mákita coolly inform me that the country through which we were passing was the territory of a slave-raiding tribe, the Kel-Fadê, who had on several occasions besieged their town Djanet, and had even gone so far as to threaten Rhât, the principal town of the Northern Touareg.

"But dost thou apprehend attack?" I asked concernedly, as we squatted together under the shadow of a tree, a little apart from the others.

"It is as Allah willeth it," he replied gravely, stroking his grey beard and taking a deliberate pull at his long pipe. "One of the camel-drivers, however, hath declared that he detected a horseman of the Kel-Fadê in hiding in the valley through which we passed two days ago. It is possible that he is a scout; if so, we may find ourselves compelled to fight."

"Was it absolutely necessary to pass through this region? Could we not have avoided it?"

"No. On the plain called Admar neither man nor beast can exist, for there are no wells, and the region remaineth unexplored. In a week we shall enter the gates of Djanet. Till then, we must be vigilant and watch warily, lest we are surprised. If we were, it would peradventure mean death or slavery for all of us."

This was not reassuring. Previous experience had taught me how deadly were the feuds between the various desert tribes possessed of souls of fire, and how fierce and sanguinary were the struggles when collisions occurred. I had not forgotten the swift, awful fate of the caravan of Ali Ben Hafiz, nor the bloody combat with the fierce freebooters of Hadj Absalam; and when I reflected that the packs of our camels contained very valuable merchandise, and that nearly a quarter of the number comprising our party were women and children, I confess I had some misgivings.

As the succeeding days passed in perfect security, and as the Sheikh, to judge by his jubilant manner, considered that the danger of attack was over, the apprehensions passed entirely from my mind. Though the heat was intense and the journey monotonous, our long string of camels plodded onward at the same slow, measured pace day after day, regardless of the fiery sun. At night in the moonlight, when the wind blew in short refreshing gusts, the camel-drivers would sit and play *damma*, the women would chatter and scold their children, and the musicians would twang weird Arab airs upon their queer-shaped instruments or thump on their *derboukas*, while ebon-faced damsels danced on the mat spread for them. Indeed, under night's blue arch life in a desert encampment has an indescribable charm that is irresistible to those of roving disposition, to whom the hum of cities is a torture and who have thrown off the conventional gyves of civilisation to wander south beyond the Atlas.

In the dull crimson light of the dying day, that made the foliage of the palms and talha trees look black as funeral plumes above us, we halted at the well of Zarzäoua in a small oasis in the centre of a wild rocky district known to the Arabs as the Adrar. It was, the Sheikh informed me, only three days distant from Djanet, and the approaching termination of the journey, which had extended over four months, put everyone in a good humour. On the morrow we should cross the boundary, and my companions would enter their own country; then the remainder of the journey to their town would be devoid of danger.

At the hour of prayer each of our men prostrated himself towards Mecca, and old Mákita, a very devout and bigoted Moslem with Time's deep furrows on his brows, cried aloud the following words, which were repeated by his people, who at the end of every sentence kissed the ground.

"O Allah! bless and preserve and increase and perpetuate and benefit and be propitious to our Lord Mohammed and to his family and to his Companions, and be Thou their preserver. O Allah! these Thy people are delivered. One and all, may Thy Blessing rest upon us. O Allah! pardon our sins and veil our faults, and place not over us one who feareth not Thee, and who pitieth not us, and pardon us and the True Believers, men and women, the quick of them and the dead, for verily Thou, O Allah, art the hearer, the near to us, and the answerer of our supplications."

Then, after reciting the testification, and drawing their palms down their faces, they went through a two-bow prayer, and the devotions, throughout exceedingly impressive, ended.

Immediately there was bustle and activity. Camels were lightened of their packs and allowed to browse at will upon the long oat grass, a tent was quickly pitched for the Sheikh, a fire was kindled, the kousskouss was cooked, and as the dim twilight darkened into night and the moon's rays shone like silver through the feathery palms, sounds of singing and revelry awakened the echoes of the fertile grove. Mákita and I had given ourselves up to cigarettes and calm repose as we squatted on a mat and lazily watched the terpsichorean efforts of a thick-lipped young negress, whose movements were exceedingly graceful as compared with those who had on previous evenings essayed the same performance for our entertainment. The cool breeze fanning my sun-seared cheeks gave me a feeling of perfect peace and ease after the heat and burden of the long weary day, and lolling upon the cushions spread for me, the monotonous chant of the people assembled and the measured thumping of tom-toms almost lulled me to sleep.

Suddenly the sound of a shot startled us.

The music ceased, and the men, with ears alert, exchanged quick glances. Loud fiendish yells rent the air, and in a moment, almost before anyone could seize a gun, a hundred dark-visaged horsemen, with their white burnouses flowing behind, swept down upon us, firing their long rifles indiscriminately and shouting the most horrible maledictions.

Within a few seconds a fierce fight had commenced. The shrieking women and children flew into the thick dark undergrowth, while the men, seizing their arms and obtaining cover where they could, kept up a sharp fusillade, which had its effect in temporarily checking our assailants. Fortunately my magazine-rifle was at hand, and it proved a most deadly weapon. Our men were mostly splendid shots, but the enemy, who proved to be the Kel-Fadê, had the advantage of vastly superior numbers.

The fight was desperate. Dismounting, and leaving a dozen of their number lying dead, our enemy withdrew among the palms, whence they poured upon us a galling fire. Mákita and I, lying on the ground beside each other, discharged our rifles steadily whenever a white-robed figure showed itself among the trees. Without betraying any fear, the old Arab reloaded time after time and shot as coolly as if gazelle-hunting, an example that was followed by his men, some of whom, however, were falling under the quick volleys from the enemy.

For fully a quarter of an hour the fight continued, when suddenly loud triumphant yells burst forth as a second party of horsemen rode down upon us. Then we knew defeat was inevitable. Against nearly two hundred Arabs armed to the teeth we could make no further stand, yet, as the reinforcements dashed among us, our men sprang up, and a second later a dozen horses were riderless. Again and again rifles rang out and men fell to earth mortally wounded, but the steady fire from the palms opposite was playing fearful havoc among us, and my companions were each moment falling back lifeless. Yet not a man was dismayed; each, struggling desperately for his life, bore his part in the hasty defence. Considering the suddenness and vigour of the attack, it was indeed surprising that we could offer such a stubborn resistance, for up to the present the losses of our assailants were much heavier than ours; nevertheless, by degrees, the firing of the Kel-Fadê grew more rapid, and was, alas! more effectual.

Once the hostile Arabs made a rush in our direction, but we were prepared. Having my magazine fully loaded at that moment, my rifle proved an effective addition to those of my companions, but again and again the effort of the enemy was repeated, and though some men fell every time, they at last succeeded in rushing right in upon us.

Standing in deadly peril, each moment was one of the most intense excitement, when in the dark shadow rifles flashed, and hoarse, fierce yells sounded above the firing as the tall Arabs dashed forward to secure us as prisoners. The struggle was desperate, literally hand to hand, when suddenly I heard a loud wail, and the Sheikh dropped his rifle, stumbled forward, and fell heavily to the ground. Then, for the first time, I remembered that the Crescent of Glorious Wonders—my treasure which if lost could never be replaced—was in my camel's pack, lying with the others about two hundred yards from where I stood! Turning, I saw in dismay that a number of the Kel-Fadê had already cut open the packages of merchandise and were examining their booty. Covering one of the men with my rifle, I picked him off, but as he fell, I saw that at a little distance from the others a tall thin Arab had opened my pack and was rifling it.

Meanwhile by the death of Mákita my companions had become demoralised. They saw that to attempt to drive off their assailants was an utterly forlorn hope, for though they never relaxed their fire for a moment, yet half of their number were lying dead or wounded, and most of the women and children were in the hands of their deadly enemy. A fight between these Sons of the Desert is always a stubbornly-contested butchery, and this was no exception. My friends made a gallant stand against an enemy treble their strength, but at last the brave fellows felt themselves overpowered, and suddenly acknowledged their enemy's superiority, although they fought on hand-to-hand to the very last. In the awful *mêlée* I found myself close to where the camels' packs were piled.

The tall thin-faced Arab who had been turning over my saddle-bag drew forth the old leather case, tore it open, and took out the Crescent. Holding it in his hands, he regarded it with evident curiosity, but in an instant I sprang upon him. The knowledge of its value as the means of securing to Zoraida and myself peace and happiness gave me courage and a strength almost demoniacal. Indeed, I was surprised at my own actions, for, falling upon him, I snatched the mysterious object from his grasp, and ere he could raise his flashing blade, I had drawn the knife from my sash and buried it in his breast.

The moment was one of desperation. I had struck the blow unerringly, and with a loud cry he fell backward a corpse.

Ere I could recover from the shock my deed caused me, I felt myself seized by three stalwart Arabs, whose fierce, determined faces told me I need expect no mercy, and though I struggled violently, cords were quickly slipped upon my wrists, and in a moment I found myself helpless as a babe.

Though I clung to the Crescent of Glorious Wonders with all the strength I possessed, it was wrenched from my grasp from behind, and that so quickly in the confusion and horrible bloodshed that I failed to discover into whose possession it had passed!

My heart sank within me and I became filled with dark, gloomy forebodings. The treasure that had been confided to my safe custody by

Zoraida I had lost, and with it had vanished in an instant all hope of winning her! Had not she plainly told me that the successful accomplishment of my mission would save her life?—yet I had now lost the strangely-shaped steel, the mystic properties of which were known to only two persons in the world!

Was this dire catastrophe prophetic of the end?

In those few seconds the hope that for so many weeks had buoyed me and incited me to push determinedly onward to my goal; the anticipations that some day I should return to civilisation and claim as my wife the most lovely woman I had ever gazed upon, were shattered by this double disaster that had so suddenly befallen me.

While the Crescent remained in my possession, and I was free to journey southward, there was still, I felt, a possibility of some day reaching Agadez. With my treasure filched from me the object of my journey had, however, gone. Though I had travelled so many weary miles towards the City of the Sorcerers, my efforts on Zoraida's behalf were thus rendered entirely futile, and reflection only filled me with such black dismay and despair, that, had not my knife been wrested from me, I verily believe I should have dealt myself a fatal blow.

My zealously-guarded treasure had in a second passed from my keeping into unknown hands that would most probably toss it away as worthless, yet how could I recover it now that I had been captured by these fierce, brutal slave-raiders, who were reputed to be among the most merciless of the wild freebooters of the Desert?

The disaster overwhelmed me. Bound hand and foot, I stood powerless in the hands of my enemies. The morrow's sun to me might never rise!

Chapter Twenty Three
The Treasure of Askiá

Brief were the moments allowed me for lamentation over my irreparable loss. Amid the wild scenes of carnage the thief had disappeared, and though I just caught a glimpse of his profile, his features had been partially hidden by the haick surrounding his face, and in the dark shadow it was impossible to distinguish his countenance sufficiently to again recognise him. Had my treasure consisted of gold or gems there would have been some ground for hoping for its eventual recovery, but a mere piece of rusted metal, apparently valueless, would doubtless be quickly cast aside. Even now— even while I stood helpless in the hands of my captors—it might have been already tossed away into the rank vegetation of the oasis; it might be lying hidden and unheeded within a few yards of me! Yet so tightly was I bound hand and foot, that the cords cut into my flesh each time I attempted to move. While three tall fierce men of the Fadê, armed to the teeth and as sinister-looking a trio as ever it had been my lot to meet, mounted guard over me, others were with scant mercy securing those of my companions who had survived the sudden ferocious attack, while the remainder of the band gleefully investigated the contents of our camels' packs, replacing them upon the animals ready for transportation to their own region.

Those of the captured caravan who struggled to get free were shown no quarter. One of my whilom friends, a fine, stalwart fellow, held fast by several of the hostile band quite close to me, fought desperately to rescue a woman of his tribe who was being brutally cuffed by two hulking fellows. For a few seconds he struck right and left, felling one of the men who held him, but ere he could rush forward to protect the defenceless female, a quick knife-thrust caused him to stagger and fall.

"Cowards!" he gasped in his death-agony. "May Allah curse thee and thy sons' sons! Thou canst not fight fairly! Thou canst only strike by stealth, and make war on women. May thy bodies moulder and drop limb from limb; may the flames of the Land of Torments devour thee; may thine accursed dust be scattered afar by the sirocco, and may thy souls descend into Hâwiyat."

"Silence! Wouldst thou, son of a dog! speak thus insolently unto thy masters?" cried the dark-faced brute who had dealt the cowardly blow. "Go thou to join the Companions of the Left Hand, and may torments ever rack thee in the fire unquenchable! Take that—and that!" and, bending, he raised his hand swiftly, burying his long dagger twice in the prostrate man's breast.

One agonised groan and the unfortunate Arab rolled over a corpse. The murderer's companions laughed heartily.

Scenes of relentless butchery such as these were occurring on every hand. Our fierce captors were merciless; their hatred deadly. A word was quickly followed by a cruel, unerring blow that either maimed or proved fatal. A wounded slave is only an encumbrance, therefore, in almost every instance, when an enemy's knife struck, it entered a vital part. The horrors of that night were sickening, the bloodshed truly awful. Men, women, even children were slaughtered out of the mere fiendish delight felt by the victors in causing agony to their vanquished foe, and passive and appalled I stood in the grip of my enemies, wondering vaguely how soon I too should share the same fate as those whose horrible death I was being compelled to witness.

The sun had already risen an hour when my captors lifted me upon a horse, securing my feet so that I could not dismount, and soon afterwards we moved away, an armed man riding on either side of each prisoner. From the first it occurred to me that only by affecting the religion of Islâm could I escape death, therefore from that moment I spoke only Arabic, declaring myself a native of Mequinez and a True Believer. My accent in speaking Arabic and the whiteness of my skin my captors attributed to my Moorish parentage, and, judging from the manner in which the sinister-faced Sheikh of the slave-raiders inspected me, I was considered a valuable prize.

Leaving the palms, we struck due south through a great clump of batum trees into the barren, inhospitable region of the Admar, the desert that has never been explored by Europeans, and which is still a blank upon the maps. On setting out we travelled quickly, perhaps owing to the great dreariness of the country and the impulse of the camel-drivers and their beasts to get to their homes. Gradually, however, the day grew very hot and uncomfortable, a stifling west wind scattering the sand of the dunes into our faces and totally obscuring the way. Keeping along the valley, wild and desolate, sometimes nearly a mile wide, we had on our left a broad mount, rising first with gradual ascent, but in its upper part forming a steep and lofty wall which the two men guarding me called El Khaddamiyeh. Passing along a small defile and crossing another valley, which my captors called the Tanarh, we once more gained the great open desert of ever-shifting sand.

"Once I crossed this plain alone in face of the sirocco," observed one of the men guarding me to his companion. "I would not attempt it again for all the Treasure of Askiá."

The Arab addressed grunted, but made no reply, and there was a long silence.

"What is the treasure of which thou hast spoken?" I asked, interested, after a pause. "I come from the north, and have never heard of it."

The dark-faced warrior of the Fadê, giving me a quick glance, asked—

"Art thou ignorant of our great forefather Askiá?"

"None knoweth his fame in Morocco," I replied. "Was he a man of power?"

"While he lived he was the Most Mighty of the Sahara. If thou hast never heard of the Great Sultan who was so wealthy that he preferred to wear a crown of iron to a diadem of gold, I will render thee explanation:— Hadj Mohammed Askiá, the most powerful of the Sónghay conquerors, lived in the year of the Hedjira 311, or a thousand years ago, and was a just but warlike ruler. His wrath was feared from Gógo even unto Mourzouk, and those who disobeyed him were put to the sword relentlessly. Having by constant battle extended his kingdom so as to include the regions now known as Kátsena and Kanó, he two years later led an expedition against the Sultan of Agadez. After a siege lasting nearly six moons, the Sultan of the Ahír was killed, and the City of the Sorcerers fell and was looted, together with the dead Sultan's palace and the houses of many rich merchants who dwelt near. Soon afterwards, however, the vengeance of Allah, the Omniscient, descended upon the conquerors, for the city was smitten by a terrible plague of bloodsuckers the length of the little finger-joint, and Askiá's people, panic-stricken, deserted their ruler and fled. Askiá, gathering together the whole of the plunder he had secured, amounting to an enormous quantity, packed it upon a number of camels, and with four faithful followers set out at night secretly for his own stronghold far away at Gógo."

"A caravan worth plundering," I observed, smiling.

"Yes," he replied, with a broad grin. "But, strangely enough, no reliable facts ever came to light regarding the Great Sultan's subsequent movements. With his camels, his followers, and his gold and gems, he set out into the desert and disappeared. Alas! woe succeedeth woe, as wave a wave. Some declare that he went to Egypt and again became a ruler among men, but we of the Fadê believe that the Great Treasure was buried. The story-tellers relate that Askiá, having travelled for one whole moon from Agadez, found himself still in the desert, with both food and water exhausted. He and his companions were lying on the sand dying, when there appeared in the heavens a mirage of green fields, in which a Christian in a white robe was standing. The visitant addressed the great chieftain, telling him that the only manner in which to save his life and those of his followers, was to abandon his treasure, upon which there lay a curse, and travel straight in the direction of the rising sun. Askiá promised, but instead of abandoning his wealth he buried it, and then started off, as directed, in search of the oasis. Still within sight of the spot where the treasure had been hidden the travellers were so jaded that they were compelled to halt for the night, and during the darkness, it occurred to the Sultan that his four men, knowing the spot, would in all probability return before him, seize the gold, and carry it off. Therefore, in order to preserve the secret, he rose, and with his scimitar slew those who had been true to him. Then a curse again fell swiftly upon the Mighty Potentate, for ere dawn appeared he too had succumbed, and the knowledge of the place where the treasure lieth buried thus became lost for ever."

"And has no one been able to discover its position?"

"No," he replied. "The gold and gems of fabulous worth remain still hidden."

As prisoner in the hands of the Kel-Fadê I was guarded carefully, together with my companions in adversity, during the four weeks we were journeying in the wild sandy regions of the Great Sahara. Our taskmasters took a brutal delight in keeping us without water as long as possible, and the awful agonies of thirst I endured in those blazing days while crossing the Admar will ever be vivid in my memory. Cuffed, beaten, and half-starved, we were dragged onward over the hot dusty plains towards the town of Assiou, situate on the direct caravan route from Mourzouk to Agadez. It was a source of some satisfaction to know that my captors were taking me towards my goal, yet my perilous position seemed utterly hopeless, for I had lost the Crescent of Glorious Wonders, and been robbed of everything I possessed, with the exception of Zoraida's letter to the *imam*, which, for safety, I had concealed in the rope of camel's hair I wore twisted around my head.

Before we had been a week on our journey, two of Mákita's men, exhausted by the barbarous treatment they had received at the hands of their conquerors, sank, and were left behind upon the sand to die. Treated like cattle, and compelled to bear the blows of our inhuman masters, we received only dates with a little kousskouss, just sufficient to keep us alive, and any who grumbled were secured by a rope to one of the camels and made to trudge over the stony wilderness until he or she sank from sheer exhaustion. On three occasions was this terrible punishment administered, and each time the unfortunate prisoner, when overcome by heat and fatigue, was left a prey to the huge grey vultures who, expecting carrion, followed us with ominous persistency.

A fortnight after our annihilation, we passed through the great valley of the Anahet, a sorry band of smileless captives, each apprehensive of his doom, and after halting for two days under the palms of Azatteli, where there was a rich supply of herbage, principally of the kind called *bu rékkebah*, and of *el hád*, the camels' dainty, we resumed our journey into a waterless region resembling a sea of bare rocks with patches of sand, until we reached the Marárraba, a great heap of stones which marks the boundary line between the countries of Rhât and Aïr, close to which we halted, apparently in order to await another caravan. This spot is held in religious awe by the Kel-Fadê, who each placed a stone upon the gigantic heap of granite blocks.

For several days we remained there. One afternoon the male prisoners were assisting the women, who had been set by their captors to grind the corn. Our taskmasters guarded their tents, keeping them hard at work with lash or bastinado, and while the encampment was hushed in its siesta, I was roughly awakened from a doze by the villainous old Sheikh of the Kel-Fadê, who, finding me stretched upon the sand, in the shadow of one of the tents, after some fatiguing work I had just completed, administered a vigorous kick, the effects of which I felt for some days.

"Rise! son of a dog! Hasten, or thy movements shall be quickened in a manner thou wilt not like."

As I scrambled to my feet, rubbing my eyes, he commanded me to follow him to his tent, and after he had settled himself upon his divan, together with two of his chief men, he subjected me to a severe cross-examination as to my past, and my capabilities.

When I had related to him a long imaginary account of my career in Morocco, and entertained him with an exciting story, he suddenly asked —

"What trade hast thou followed?"

"I was a *hodja* (letter-writer) in Mequinez, and afterwards in Algiers," I replied.

"Then thou shalt write me a letter," he said, and, ordering an ink-horn and writing materials to be brought, he dictated a message regarding some merchandise. When I had finished, he inspected it, while I stood by in trepidation, fearing lest he should detect the many mistakes I had made in tracing the Arabic characters. Evidently, however, he could not read, though he made a pretence of doing so, for he expressed complete satisfaction by a sharp grunt, and a deep pull at his pipe.

"Art thou a musician?" he inquired presently.

"I can play the *kanoon* and the *guenibri*" I answered, and in a few moments one of the strange-looking two-stringed Arab instruments, fashioned from the shell of a tortoise, covered with skin, was handed to me. As it happened, I had long ago learned to manipulate the strings of the *guenibri*, and at once gave the old Sheikh an illustration of my talent for native music.

"Good," he said at last. "Thou art a musician. I must consider what I shall do with thee. Leave now and return to thy slumbers, for thou wilt not always be enabled to take thine ease in the shadow."

The men squatting on either side of their chieftain grinned at their lord's witticism, and as I turned wearily away, I wondered what fortune the next turn of the kaleidoscope of life would bring to me.

Yet I cared little. I had, alas! lost my mystic talisman, and with it had disappeared all hope of securing the hand of my peerless Queen of the Desert.

Chapter Twenty Four
Slave of the Sultan

To describe our dreary journey through the barren unknown desert at greater detail would serve no purpose. The way lay mainly over a gigantic plain interspersed by small sand-hills and naked ledges of rock, speckled with ethel bushes half overwhelmed by sand. For days there seemed not a breath of air, and the desolate monotony was terribly exhausting. Now and then we came upon wells with herbage and a few sebót and talha trees, but the long stretches of sand within sight of Mount Azben were frightfully fatiguing for man and beast, the ground at all times being either gravelly, rocky, or strewn with loose pebbles.

Arriving at length at Assiou, a small town in an oasis on that great arid plateau called the Tahassaza, the centre of an important caravan trade, my male companions and myself were very soon led into the market-place, a square open space, and under the arches of the low whitewashed colonnade we were allowed to lounge and wait. At last we knew the worst. We were to be sold into slavery!

The place was agog with caravans arriving and departing, and on all hands men and women, mostly negroes and negresses from the Soudan, were being sold after long and loud haggling. Many, too, were the silent bargains effected by pairs of traders standing quiet and immovable in the middle of the noisy, bustling, pushing crowd, each with a hand under his neighbour's burnouse, and grasping his arm as if engaged in feeling the other's pulse. They were making use of the conventional signs, consisting of certain pressures of the finger and knuckle joints, each having a recognised value and significance, and by employing them they were effecting business without attracting the notice of the gaping onlookers, who would listen and offer their advice.

Among the human wares for disposal were many young Arabs of the Kel-Tin-Alkoun, the Iguedhadh, and other tribes who were weaker than their neighbours, together with some comely women, the latter creating the keenest competition among the dealers. Those who were fat enough to fulfil the Arab standard of beauty were being sold for large sums, while the more slim were disposed of to the highest bidder.

Buyers and sellers were squatting together in little groups, sipping coffee, eating melons, and smoking cigarettes while they gossiped, and as money passed from hand to hand, husbands were torn for ever from their wives, and children gazed for the last time upon their parents. This market of human flesh, which the strenuous efforts of the French and British Governments have failed to suppress, was indeed revolting, yet the scenes were not so heartrending as might have been imagined, for the majority of the women, when they were unveiled for inspection, evinced pleasure at the prospect of a new lord, while the men, finding themselves in the hands of their enemies, squatted in melancholy silence, utterly regardless of their fate.

For me escape was hopeless. Fully a dozen well-to-do Arabs had viewed me, each being urged by the Sheikh of the Kel-Fadê, who acted as showman and extolled my virtues, to purchase me. He described me as a Moorish letter-writer, musician, and man of wisdom, but the price he required appeared quite prohibitive, until a splendidly-dressed Arab, evidently of the wealthier class, made a close examination of me. In compliance with his request, I played a tune on the *guenibri*, and after nearly half an hour's bargaining, I at last saw the Sheikh accept a bag of gold; and then the man in a *helái* burnouse and ornamented Ghadámsi shoes coolly informed me that I must in future consider myself the property of His Majesty the Sultan of Agadez.

For the moment my delight was unbounded. I was going, after all, to Agadez! But courage failed me when I recollected that I was a slave, and that the Crescent of Glorious Wonders had been filched from me and was utterly lost.

Three weeks after I had been purchased by the agent of the potentate, I found myself a prisoner in the great irregularly-built Fáda, or palace, of His Majesty Hámed e' Rufáy, the mighty Sultan of the Ahír. I was one of the slaves of Amagay, His Majesty's chief eunuch, my duties being to burnish the arms of the ever-vigilant guardians of the Sultan's harem, and, when required, to discourse music for the delectation of the Grand Vizier Mukhtar, President of the Divan, and his suite. The great palace, situated on the outskirts of the town though within the walls, covered an enormous area, and was a kingdom within itself. Like a fortress enclosed by grim massive walls were beautiful gardens, spacious courtyards with fountains and cool arcades, and in these sumptuous buildings there dwelt the officers of state; while, in the inner court, to which none had access save the eunuchs and the Sultan himself, was situated the royal harem. Outside the one entrance to this, the most private portion of the luxurious Fáda, was a smaller court devoted to the eunuchs and their slaves, while the single passage communicating was closed by three iron doors, at which gigantic negroes fully armed stood on guard night and day. To obtain admission to the Court of the Eunuchs no fewer than five gates had to be passed, each with three doors, whereat stood janissaries—whose lawless and powerful prototypes beside the Bosphorus are historical—barring with gleaming scimitars the passage of the would-be adventurer. Each court, with its massive, frowning walls, was a colony in itself, preserving its own individuality, its inhabitants never mixing or passing into the forbidden domains of its neighbours. Thus the great gilded palace was a prison to its inmates, except the royal princes and the officials of His Majesty; and the janissaries had no dealings with the eunuchs, nor did the officials of the Sultan's Great Court of Audience fraternise with those of His Majesty's private apartments.

This luxurious city within a city, housing nearly seventeen hundred persons, was magnificent in its proportions, for as one entered court after court towards the quarters of the women, the appointments grew richer and more costly, until, in the Hall of the Eunuchs, the ceilings were of sky-blue with stars of gold, the floors of polished marble, the walls adorned by delicate frescoes and arabesques, and the slender columns of rare marble supporting the horse-shoe arches were carved with exquisite taste and glistened with gold. Indeed, the great palace was a maze of buildings, courts, gardens, and spacious halls, in which, however, the autocratic ruler was rarely seen. He mostly spent his time in his own apartments adjoining the Hall of the Eunuchs, and was only seen to his scheming and intriguing *entourage* when seated on the Great White Divan. Before him every member of the household quaked with fear, for he was a man whose displeasure meant death, whose smile bestowed wealth and luxury, whose harsh word brought upon the hapless victim of his displeasure the bastinado and disgrace, or whose commendation made him chief among men. He was ruled by harem influence; indeed, the doves of the gilded prison held in their hands men's lives and fortunes. A whispered word in the ear of their lord would cause a courtier's head to fall under the executioner's sword, or a soft caress secure his appointment to high official position, with fat emoluments. Through every court, from the fierce guardians of the outer gate to the innermost quadrangle where beautiful houris lolled among their silken cushions around a fountain of fragrant perfume, dark plots were constantly being hatched and carried out. Men and women almost daily fell victims of the jealousy, hatred, or avarice of their fellows, and life was indeed insecure in a *ménage* where the unheeded handmaiden of to-day might be the all-powerful Sultana of to-morrow; where the Grand Vizier might be decapitated by the negro executioner within an hour, and the meanest slave of the Fáda appointed vizier of the Ahír in his stead; or where the Pearl of the Harem who had displeased her cruel, fickle master by some petty shortcoming, might have a silken cord slipped over her white neck by the brutal Chief of the Eunuchs, die of strangulation, and her body be given to the vultures without knowledge of her fault.

A remnant of the autocratic sway of Turkey which still holds Tripoli under its rule, the Sultan was himself "the State." His so-called ministers were simply the favourites of the hour. Justice was bought and sold. Every office was directly or indirectly purchased, small remuneration or none at all being paid, the holders recouping themselves by plunder and oppression, tempered by the fact that at any moment they might be forced to disgorge by the Sultan, left to rot in loathsome dungeons, or be beaten or tortured to death.

Amid these strange surroundings I lived and toiled. By day, in the little niche in the massive wall of the Court of the Eunuchs that was assigned to me, I burnished the scimitars, scabbards, knives, and steel girdles of the custodians of the harem. At night, when the stars shone above the open court, and the breeze stirred the leaves of the trailing vines, I would take my *guenibri* and, in obedience to the order of my taskmasters, pass into the hall of the Grand Vizier, and while that high official lounged upon his divan surrounded by his officers, I, with three other musicians, would squat at the corners of the mat spread before him, and play accompaniments to the dancing of his female slaves. To the monotonous thumping of the tom-tom, the mournful note of the *guenibri*, and the clashing of cymbals, the women barefooted performed slow Eastern dances, scarcely moving their feet, yet gracefully swaying their bodies, and whirling scimitars above their heads in a manner that was marvellous, or with wild abandon they would trip a kind of Spanish dance with the tambourine.

Week after week, surrounded by the dazzling splendour of the gorgeous palace, I led a weary life of abject slavery. Ill-treated and cuffed by the stern black taskmaster whose duty it was to see that I performed the work allotted to me, I felt many times inclined to regard escape as utterly hopeless. While on my way to the palace, I caught sight of the Mesállaje, the principal mosque with its great square minaret, and though I had still retained Zoraida's letter to Hadj Mohammed ben Ishak, the chief *imam*, I had no means of presenting it. Nevertheless, buoyed constantly by expectation, I worked on, seeking as far as possible to obtain the good graces of my fierce

Soudanese slave-master, and never ceasing in my endeavours to devise some scheme by which I might obtain freedom.

One evening, when I had been toiling throughout the day burnishing some accoutrements that were rusty until my arms pained me, my taskmaster brought information that His Excellency the Grand Vizier would require no music that night; therefore, remaining in my little den near the gate of the harem that served as workshop and living-room, I took my ease. I must have slept, for I was awakened by the stern voice of one of the eunuchs saying—

"Quick! take this, clean it and return it to me. I will wait."

He handed me a long, keen scimitar, the blade of which was wet with blood!

It was night. All was quiet. The courts, so full of colour and animation during the day, were hushed in silence, for the huge palace seemed asleep. Above, bright points of light shone, but there was no moon, and the Court of the Eunuchs was in darkness, save where over the gate of the harem a great swinging lamp of brass shed a yellow uncertain light upon the tall statuesque guards. Without questioning the man, I quickly washed his sword, cleaned it with cloths, and re-polished it with my stone. Then, with muttered thanks, he replaced it in its scabbard, and, stalking towards the harem, passed through the heavy iron doors and disappeared.

A bloody drama had been enacted! Another secret tragedy had occurred within those grim, massive walls that concealed the gorgeous Courts of Love!

Even as I gazed wonderingly at the great arched doorway through which so many hundreds of women had passed never to return alive, its iron portals again opened, and there appeared four black eunuchs, gaily attired in bright blue and gold, bearing upon a board some long object covered with a black cloth, from beneath which bright silks and filmy gauzes showed. Silently they marched onward close to where I stood, and as they passed, I saw a woman's bare white arm hanging underneath the sable pall. It swung limp and helpless as the men strode through the court with their burden, and when they had gone, there remained on the still night air a subtle breath of attar of rose.

The pretty head of one of the Pearls of the Harem had been struck off by order of Hámed e' Rufäy—the iron will of the great Sultan, Ruler of the Ahír and Defender of the Faith, had been obeyed!

Chapter Twenty Five
The Eunuch's Scimitar

What dire events had led to the summary execution of the beauty who had just been carried out a corpse? Probably she had held brief sway over His Majesty, ruling the land from her soft silken divan, until one of her jealous sisters had, by intrigue, succeeded in displacing her in her fickle lord's affections, and immediately the new favourite's influence was sufficiently strong, she had used it to cause the death of her discarded but troublesome rival.

Sitting in my little den, with the shutter half closed, I was trying to picture to myself the scenes of brilliant festivity, of fierce hatred, and merciless revenge that were ever occurring within those zealously-guarded Courts of Love, when suddenly I heard Arabic spoken softly quite close to the entrance to my workshop. Without stirring, I listened with bated breath.

"But apparently thou dost not fully realise that, now the Sultana Krenfla is dead, our power hath vanished," exclaimed a voice, the tones of which I instantly recognised as those of the Grand Vizier.

"*Nakrifoh colloh,*" replied his companion. "Thou art indeed right. Well do I remember that when we were but janissaries at yon gate, we conveyed messages for the pretty Krenfla to her lover, and sometimes would allow her to secretly meet him. But he was killed in the war against Awelimimiden, and then his mistress, having mourned for him many days, devoted herself wholly to our lord the Sultan, and became Sultana. In recognition of our services as Cupid's messengers, she caused our advancement, you to be Grand Vizier of the Ahír, and I to be Chief of the Eunuchs. But, alas! her sway hath ended, and consequently our careers are abruptly cut short. To-morrow we too may lose our heads—who knoweth?"

"True, O Amagay! unless Allah showeth us mercy, the death of Krenfla sealeth our doom. If it pleaseth our lord the Sultan to fall under the bewitching caresses of Khadidja, our degradation and dismissal will be inevitable; while if Zobeide should secure the favour of Hámed, her power will be immediately directed towards our decapitation. Long hast thou held in the harem the lives of the houris in thine hands, and in consequence thou art held in awe and hatred; while, to tell the truth, I, as Grand Vizier, have ruled with the sword and bastinado, and the people would rejoice could they see my head mounted on a spear in the Azarmádarangh (place of execution). But," His Excellency added with a pause, "art thou convinced we shall not be overheard?"

"Quite," replied my master reassuringly, peering in at my half-open shutter, but failing to detect me in the deep shadow. "Fear not eavesdroppers here. In thine own pavilion the very walls have ears; here, in the Court of the Eunuchs, it is different."

"Then it is thine opinion that we must act quickly if we would save our heads?"

"*Ma akindana al-ân wákt lilliakb*" ("We have no time to play at present"), acquiesced the Chief of the Eunuchs.

"*Taakâla challina náhn al-ithnine natáhaddath showy-yah,*" the Grand Vizier said. Then, dropping his voice until I could scarcely catch his words, he continued, "Viewed from all sides, our position is one of extreme peril, therefore we must set ourselves to avert the disaster which threateneth. The choice of the Sultan remaineth between Khadidja and Zobeide, and even to-night one or other may secure His Majesty's favour. In any case, our necks at this moment lie under the scimitar of the executioner, therefore must we act swiftly, firmly, and in a manner that showeth not mercy."

"But how? I can see no way of saving ourselves except by flight."

"Thy suggestion is impracticable. Such a course would condemn thee," interrupted the Grand Vizier. "Unless we could first secure the contents of the treasury, flight would avail us nought, and even then we should be overtaken ere we could get away to the Tsâd. No; long have I foreseen the downfall of Krenfla, and have evolved a scheme by which men shall still abundantly utter the memory of our great goodness and sing of our greatness."

"Thou hast? How?"

"Listen. My words are for thine ears alone," whispered the Grand Vizier. "My opinion is that Hámed, our Sultan, hath ruled the Ahír for sufficient time. Dost thou agree?"

"Yes," replied the Chief of the Eunuchs eagerly. "Art—art thou thinking of his deposition?"

"Hath it never occurred to thee that his son, 'Abd-el-Kerim, who is already in his twentieth year, is now fitted to rule?" he asked slowly.

"Once or twice I have reflected that the youth hath been always under our tuition and influence, and that, trusting us as implicitly as he doth, we should be absolute masters were he to reign in his father's stead."

"Truly, O Amagay, thou hast wisdom. If we placed 'Abd-el-Kerim upon the White Divan, I should most certainly remain Grand Vizier, while thou mightest even secure a post more lucrative than Chief of the Eunuchs. Instead of death, such an event meaneth for us increased wealth and the retention of our power."

"But how dost thou propose to effect this sweeping change?" asked Amagay, interested.

"Render me thine assistance, and the means are simple. Our Sultan Hámed hath already ruled too long," exclaimed Mukhtar, adding, in a low, intense voice, after a pause, the ominous words, "He must die—to-morrow!"

"Dost thou then intend to assassinate him?" gasped the Chief Eunuch, amazed at the bold daring of the high official's suggestion.

"Certainly. If he were thrown into prison, those who now bask in his favours would raise a serious agitation for his release; whereas, once dead, his memory will immediately be forgotten, and we shall hold the fortunes of the Fáda entirely in our own hands. Think, O Amagay, will it not be better to act fearlessly, and by one sharp, decisive blow attain increased riches and honour, than to remain inactive and fall hapless victims to the hatred of those black-eyed doves in yonder cage who would deliver us unto the sword. We must decide upon our policy now—to-night."

"Hast thou the co-operation of any others in this thy daring scheme?" asked his companion.

"Yes, the Chamberlain, and the Aga of the Janissaries have both promised to bear their part; but thine own trusty, unerring scimitar must deliver the death blow."

"No! no!" he cried in a low voice. "By the Prophet! I cannot strike. My nerve would fail!"

"Bah! Didst thou not strike off the heads of rebellious houris by the score; didst thou not for two years act as executioner in the Place of Azarmádarangh, where heads fell under thy keen *doka* every day? Surely thou, of all men, hast courage with thy sword and confidence in thine arm? A single blow, and the deed is done!"

"But suppose I fail?"

"Even then, our fate will be not one whit the worse than it is at this moment," answered Mukhtar.

There was a short pause. Then Amagay, who had apparently become convinced by the strength of his fellow-conspirator's argument, answered—

"I agree with thee, O Mukhtar. Thy mouth uttereth wisdom. Only the mighty Hámed's death can save us; so, if Allah willeth, my keen steel shall strike the tyrant to the dust."

"Then we shall count upon thee," exclaimed the Grand Vizier, apparently well pleased. "Hearken, and I will show thee how the removal of His Majesty can be best accomplished. He hath sent information to the Keeper of the Treasure that to-morrow, after the midday meal, it will please him to repair unto the Treasury, in order to choose jewels to present to his new favourite. The jewels of great price are to be laid out for his inspection. On his way from the court to the Treasure House he will be compelled to pass across the Great Hall of Audience and through the long, dark passage that divideth that chamber from the Court of the Treasury. In that passage are niches where one mayest remain concealed, and it is there that thy steel must strike."

"But may not others accompany him?"

"Leave that unto me. After he hath eaten, I shall detain him in conversation about certain pressing matters of state, so that his guards will pass before him, and he will walk alone past the spot where thou art secreted with thy companions, the Chamberlain and the Aga of the Janissaries. Then wilt thou rush out, and in a second the Sultan Hámed will be no more."

"Will not the guards rush back and kill us?" the Chief Eunuch asked doubtfully.

"No. The conspiracy hath already been well planned in every detail. When the tyrant falleth, the heads of Khadidja and Zobeide will be struck off by thy guardians of the harem, and thus will the three persons whose power threateneth us have disappeared, and so secretly that not twenty of those within the Fáda will be aware of the tragedy."

"Thou art indeed, O Mukhtar, a man of much foresight and one fitted to rule," exclaimed Amagay, in admiration of the old villain's cunning. "True, the Sultan Hámed is as a shadow betwixt us and the shining of the sun, and he must be removed. In thee, upon whom the One Merciful hath bestowed bounteous wisdom, I place my trust, and will assist thee in placing upon the Great Divan 'Abd-el-Kerim, the Son of the Doomed. Thy servant's scimitar shall strike this daring blow for liberty. Peace."

"Hush! Listen!" whispered the Grand Vizier in a tone of alarm. "One of thy men approacheth from the harem. Let us part to allay suspicion. I will await thee in my pavilion two hours after the sun hath arisen. Until then, *slama!*"

A slight jingling of keys and softly-receding footsteps; then all was quiet again.

Alone I sat for a long time reflecting upon the secret of the great plot of which I had accidentally obtained knowledge. At noon the Sultan Hámed, dreaded throughout Fezzan, Tripoli, and the Sahara as the most powerful and tyrannical of rulers, would be struck down, and his son proclaimed monarch, while the assassination would, no doubt, bring death to many of the inmates of the harem. The palace was asleep, its lotus-eating inmates little dreaming of the great *coup d'état* that had been so cunningly planned, or of the startling sensation in store for them. The black guardians of the harem stood silent and statuesque on either side of its carved portals, and the dead silence of the Court of the Eunuchs remained unbroken.

Enslaved as I was, my thoughts were always of liberty whereby I might deliver Zoraida's message to the *imam*, and I now saw in this knowledge of the attempt on the Sultan's life a means to regain my freedom. Though excited over the discovery, I resolved to remain calm and act judiciously, for I foresaw that any desire I might express to seek audience of His Majesty would arouse suspicion among the conspirators. Through that night I pondered deeply over the strange events of the past few months, endeavouring time after time to convince myself that Zoraida no longer lived. Yet my mind refused to accept any indistinct theory of which I had not absolute proof. She had entrusted to me a mission in which, alas! I had by sheer ill-luck failed, nevertheless I recollected her earnest words when she had given the Crescent of Glorious Wonders into my keeping, and it was more than possible, I argued, that the *imam* was daily expecting my arrival and wondering what mishap had befallen me.

From him alone I could obtain the Great Secret, yet what would that knowledge avail, now that I had lost the mysterious half-circle of steel? Where was Zoraida? If alive, she would, I reflected, probably be journeying with her people in the Great Desert, the all-powerful prophetess of the most desperate band of fleet horsemen that ever rode over the Sahara. She, the dazzling, mysterious Daughter of the Sun, held in awe by the Ennitra, was possibly directing their marauding expeditions, sharing the plunder with her own delicate fingers, and causing death and desolation among neighbouring caravans; yet, when I recollected how at heart she hated that life of rapine and murder, how she shrank from the position in which, by some unaccountable combination of circumstances, she was forcibly held, my blood rose within me. Had she not acknowledged that she loved me? Were we not actually betrothed? Truly, the Omen of the Camel's Hoof which I had ridiculed had been a presage of impending evil that was gradually being fulfilled. Mystified by the strange, weird rites that Zoraida had practised, fascinated by her marvellous beauty, filled with admiration at the cool courage she had displayed when saving my life, I had travelled steadily onward, meeting misfortune with a smile and disregarding danger and fatigue, until my capture. Then I knew that to declare myself a Christian would mean certain death, so I had been compelled, much against my will, to conceal my nationality and act as a devout follower of the Prophet until an opportunity for escape should present itself. That opportunity, I felt, was now at hand, and though the flush of dawn appeared, sleep came not to my eyes, for I sat devising various schemes, one of which, however wild and hazardous, it was imperative should be carried out successfully before noon.

As the sun rose, and the great courts of the Fáda grew animated, I resumed my work, burnishing swords, spears, and shields until they shone like mirrors, yet keeping an ever-vigilant eye upon the gate of the harem, in case His Majesty should emerge. Unfortunately, the Sultan seldom cared to pass outside his private apartments. Only once had I seen him, and then only at a distance. To all save his high officers and body-servants he was absolutely unapproachable. When he made a tour of the palace,—which I learned was of very rare occurrence,—he was surrounded by men-at-arms with drawn swords, and none dared address him for fear of incurring his displeasure, which meant unceremonious decapitation.

As the hours sped on, and the shade in the sunlit court grew smaller, I began to consider all hope of averting the triple tragedy futile. Once or twice, Amagay, a giant in stature, had passed and repassed with heavy, thoughtful brow and arms folded under his burnouse, as if preoccupied with the details of the widespread conspiracy, and my astonishment was sudden when presently he entered my den, and, drawing his splendid scimitar, the hilt of which was encrusted with jewels, said—"This weapon hath no edge upon it. Sharpen it quickly. Whet it upon thy stone."

With hands trembling with excitement, I took the great sword, such as could only be wielded by one of enormous strength, and proceeded to sharpen it as he commanded.

"Take thy time. Make the blade so keen that it will cut a single hair."

"Thy will be done, O lord Amagay," I answered, not daring to look up lest my agitation should betray me, while the Chief of the Eunuchs lit a cigarette, and, lolling against the door, watched me until I had sharpened to a keen edge the scimitar that was to strike dead the Sultan Hámed. Then, replacing the weapon in its scabbard, he settled the hang of his burnouse and strode away.

By the shadows I became aware that the noon was nigh. I had sharpened the assassin's weapon, yet I dared speak to no one of the foul plot about to be carried out. For aught I knew, many of those around me were implicated, and my confession that I had acted as eavesdropper would certainly bring wrath upon me. If I could only see the Sultan, one word could save him. But how?

Suddenly I conceived a most desperate plan. It seemed utter madness to attempt it, yet, knowing that my liberty, my whole future, depended upon frustrating the terrible *coup d'état*, I was determined to risk everything. There was little time to lose, so I set about my preparations immediately. In my little den I had a canister half full of gunpowder and about a dozen cartridges. Boring a hole through the lid of the tin box, I placed the cartridges within, and, taking an old piece of flexible hoop iron, I bound it tightly round the sides and ends of the canister, taking care, however, to leave open the hole in the lid. Thus the bomb was quickly constructed, and, placing it under the bench at which I worked, I sprinkled a train of powder from it, and when all was ready, I lit a rudely-constructed slow match.

Hurriedly ascertaining that the match was fairly alight, I left the place, and, with my copper pitcher, lounged leisurely across to the well close to the gate of the harem, as if to obtain water. Scarcely had I gained the impassable portals when there was a bright flash, followed by a terrific explosion that shook the palace to its very foundations, wrecked my workshop, and tore up the masonry like pasteboard.

In an instant the most intense excitement and confusion prevailed. The two guards at the door of the harem, almost taken off their feet by the concussion, left their posts panic-stricken, and, with others who emerged from the seraglio, rushed over to the scene to ascertain the cause, while, in a few seconds, the court was filled by officials, eunuchs, soldiers, and slaves.

The moment for which I had been waiting had arrived. The outer gate of the harem was ajar, and while everybody was hurrying in alarm to the spot where the explosion had occurred, I managed to slip inside unobserved. Dashing along into the unknown region of the Fáda, scarcely daring to breathe and unaware of what armed resistance I might encounter, I sped like lightning across a wide, tiled hall, where, to my delight, I saw the second iron door was also half open. Passing this, I crossed yet another similar hall, rather smaller than the first, and leaped towards the third and last door. It was closed.

Grasping the great iron ring that served as handle, I tried to turn it, but though I exerted all my strength until the veins stood knotted on my forehead and the perspiration dropped from me, it would not yield. Fate was against me—I was doomed to failure. The door was locked!

Chapter Twenty Six
In the Courts of Love

Again and again I tried the handle, failing utterly to move it. Another moment's delay might cost me my life!

Shaking the great door in frantic desperation, and turning to see whether I had been detected, I suddenly noticed that on each side of this gate hung heavy curtains of bright yellow silken brocade. One appeared to have been disarranged, for it did not hang in such graceful folds as the other, and this attracted my attention. After a careful examination, I discovered a small square handle in the centre of the gate, painted black, so as to appear as one of the big nails with which the door was studded. In a moment the truth flashed upon me. Eagerly I tried the handle, and found I could turn it with ease, and that a small and cunningly-concealed door, just large enough to admit one person, was the means by which the private apartments of His Majesty could be entered.

Stepping through without hesitation and closing the door silently after me, I found myself in a great wide court, with fine arched arcades on either side. In the centre a splendid fountain of perfume was playing, the sparkling, scented water falling into a huge basin of crystal. The spectacle was gorgeous and dazzling. The brilliant colours, the green palms, the rich brocades, the woven carpets, the glittering gold with which the arcades were decorated, and the glimpse of cool and beautiful gardens in the vista away through several open courts, seemed a veritable fairyland.

From the great gilt perfuming-pans, columns of thin blue smoke diffused sensuous odours. Bright-eyed women with faces of flawless beauty were half-sitting, half reclining on their luxurious divans, lazily smoking cigarettes, or allowing themselves to be slowly fanned by their slaves. Resplendent in bright-hued silks, heavy gold ornaments and flashing gems, some were seated in little groups gossiping, others had stretched themselves on silken couches in languid indolence, while one or two, leaning against the columns of marvellously-carved marble, with their delicate hands clasped behind their heads, were indulging in day-dreams—dreams perhaps of joyous hours bygone before they were torn away from the ones they loved to adorn the Sultan's harem. With brows covered by strings of pearls and sequins, white arms with massive bracelets, bare bosoms half hidden by necklaces and scintillating gems, bare feet encased in tiny slippers embroidered with gold and jewels, and neat ankles heavy with golden bangles, the beautiful prisoners of Hámed the Mighty were idling away the day with careless, dreamy indifference amid the sweetly-scented atmosphere of love.

Entranced by the wondrous scene of beauty, I stood for a few seconds while my eyes travelled quickly around in search of His Majesty. He was, however, not present; therefore, summoning courage and dashing forward, I sped on through the three great Courts of the Sultanas towards the distant garden, beyond which I had heard lay His Majesty's private pavilion. Without daring to notice the profound sensation my sudden appearance was causing throughout the harem, I ran quickly through court after court, until, just as I had gained the great arch which led into the garden, my passage was barred by a big black eunuch who had recognised me as a slave.

To close with him would have been folly, for his muscles were like iron; therefore, redoubling my speed, I bent down quickly just as he was about to grasp me, and thus dodged under his hands. Pursued, I rushed across the beautiful garden, red with roses and green with many leaves, along the edge of a clear lake, through an open gate, and into a richly-furnished magnificent pavilion, the pavement of which was of polished sardonyx and agate.

In the centre was a great baldachin of amaranth silk enriched with long fringes of silver, stretched on twelve pillars of twisted gold, and underneath there sat upon the Great White Divan, Hámed, son of Mohammed el Bákèri, the all-powerful Sultan of the Ahír. Upon his head was a turban of pale green silk, in front of which was a splendid diamond aigrette, while the robes he wore were of rich white silk brocade. Behind His Majesty stood two negro slaves cooling him with large fans of peacocks' feathers. Around him were his gorgeously-attired body-servants, to whom he was giving some instructions, being just about to rise from his midday meal. As I burst upon them, with the gigantic eunuch in pursuit, the guards were in a moment on the alert, and those who were prostrate before their sovereign sprang to their feet and drew their swords.

"Seize him!" cried the eunuch excitedly. "He is a slave who hath escaped!"

"My gracious lord the Sultan!" I gasped breathlessly, prostrating myself before the royal divan as the slaves pounced upon me. "Hear me, I beseech thee! Let not thy servants remove me before I have spoken."

"The slave hath merely some paltry grievance," exclaimed the eunuch, with ceremonious obeisance.

"It is no grievance," I cried wildly. "I come to give thee warning, O Sultan, Mighty of the Earth, that ere the shadows lengthen thou wilt die!"

"Silence, slave! Heed what thou sayest!" the Sultan thundered, pale with anger as he rose stately and superb from his divan. He was tall and of majestic presence, though his dark, sinister features bore distinct impress of the vile and brutal passions which actuated him. "Silence!" he cried again, and his servants fell before him with genuflections inspired by awe. "Slave! thou, who hast passed the portals of the private courts of thy Sovereign to prophesy his discomforture, hast dared to address thy Ruler without leave! Knowest thou not that none are allowed in this our pavilion unless commanded, under pain of instant death?"

"I come to forewarn thee, O August Ruler, of impending evil—"

"Stop thy chatter, dog!" he shouted, his face livid with sudden passion. The storm burst, and the dark cloud, swollen with his accumulated exasperation, exploded in a tremolo full of threats. When the Sultan Hámed broke out, he was terrible. "I heed not the croakings of a common slave who—"

"But men, jealous of thy position, have plotted to compass thy death ere to-day's sun hath set!"

"Liar! Thou art indeed demented," he cried, in full combustion. Then, in the frightful rumbling of his phrases, in the incessant crackling of his words, he roared bitter corrosive invectives that caused his robust frame to vibrate as they issued forth. Suddenly, turning to his trembling body-servants, he added, "Seize him! Let his prophetic tongue be torn out as a punishment for daring to predict evil in our presence!"

"Hear me, I pray thee, Just and Mighty one, slow to anger and of great mercy! It is to save thy Majesty's life that—"

"The Sultan of the Ahír desireth not the aid of a slave!" he answered proudly. "I would send thee to execution at Azarmádarangh at once, only I think thy mind is deranged, and if so, thy boldness is not of thine own fault. But the chatter of the idiot annoyeth the sane, therefore thy tongue shall be removed, so that, though mad, thou wilt in future be dumb." Turning quickly to my captors, he added, "Let him be cast into prison and rendered speechless. Away with him!"

For this rebuff I was totally unprepared, and my courage sank.

"Wilt thou show no mercy towards thine humble slave, who hath risked his life to prostrate himself before thee and give thee warning?" I ventured to cry earnestly, in final appeal.

"Take him from my sight," commanded the Sultan, waving his hand angrily. "See that his glib tongue wags not after sundown."

"Merciful Allah!" I implored, struggling violently with those who held me. "Behold, I am thy slave, O lord the Sultan! Hear me, I beseech of thee!"

But His Majesty, uttering a string of voluble curses upon my family through generations, turned his back towards me with a gesture of impatience, and I was unceremoniously hurried from his terrible presence.

The Sultan had, however, stepped from his divan, therefore, at the entrance to the pavilion I was held back by the four stalwart guards in order to let him pass through to the spacious Hall of Audience. Surrounded by his body-servants, he strode along with regal gait and keen, observant eye; then, after he had gone, I was dragged onward at a distance behind not so great as to prevent me watching his progress.

Gaining the Hall of Audience, one of the most gorgeous apartments of the Fáda, Mukhtar, the Grand Vizier, suddenly appeared, and, bowing low, craved a hasty and private word with his royal master. The plot was being carried out before my eyes! The Sultan, halting at the entrance to the long arched arcade that gave access to the Court of the Treasury, waved his hand, motioning those surrounding him to pass onward.

The armed janissaries standing erect and mute as statues along the walls of the audience-chamber exchanged expectant glances full of meaning, and I knew that they were anxiously awaiting the commission of the dastardly crime. I would, even at that moment, have shouted a last warning, but, alas! the men in whose hands I stood powerless had gagged me in compliance with the desire of their irate master.

Until the servants and guards had passed through the long dimly-lit arcade and crossed the paved court beyond, Mukhtar held his royal master in earnest conversation, then, prostrating himself humbly, he rose and took his leave, while His Majesty, hitching his robes of spotless silk about him, moved onward briskly and alone down the silent arcade.

Upon Mukhtar's lips a momentary smile of satisfaction played as he stalked away. It told me that the doom of the Sultan Hámed was at hand! Walking still in the grip of the guards, I watched the upright and truly regal figure of His Majesty receding until he had passed half-way along the great arched corridor. Then suddenly a second figure was sharply silhouetted against the brilliant sunlight at the end of the vista. A strong arm was raised, a gleaming scimitar whirled aloft, and a loud cry of surprise and dismay echoed until it reached the spot where we stood.

Next second the headless body of Hámed, Sultan of the Ahír, lay at the Chief Eunuch's feet, and upon the polished marble pavement a dark, ugly pool was rapidly forming.

My four captors, paralysed and amazed, released me and dashed along towards the prostrate body of their master, but in an instant the scimitars of the guards of the Hall of Audience were hovering over their heads, and after a desperate but brief struggle they were secured and gagged.

So swiftly indeed had the secret assassination been accomplished, that, ere I could realise that the plot had been carried out, the body had been thrust into a sack and removed, slaves who had actually held water in readiness had washed the stains from the marble, and almost before one could regain breath, every trace of the terrible crime had been erased.

Chapter Twenty Seven
The False Cadi

The gulf of accident lies between what is and what might have been. Strangely enough, the very tragedy which I had endeavoured to avert saved me from the torture and imprisonment to which the brutal autocrat had condemned me, for when my guards were hurried away to the prison cells, and I explained to my master, the murderer Amagay, the fate to which the dead Sultan had condemned me without telling him the cause, he bade me return immediately to the Court of the Eunuchs, sending two of the guardians of the harem to escort me thither.

Thus once again I became a slave and prisoner. Escape seemed hopeless, and the delivery of Zoraida's letter impossible. Though so near the one person who held the Secret of the Crescent, I was yet held in bondage, unable to seek him, unable to fulfil my promise. The beautiful face of Zoraida with its dark, wistful eyes was ever before me, and my thoughts were constantly of the mysterious one of enchanting loveliness who had placed her faith in me. Time does not change a heart, and love memories are not written in sand—they last while life lasts.

The explosion in my workshop had, I ascertained, been attributed to accident, therefore, as soon as I returned, I found another corner, and, removing those of my polishing stones and cloths that had escaped injury, I resumed my work, resolved to hope on and wait. So swiftly and silently had the *coup d'état* been carried out, that only the conspirators themselves knew of it, those of the dead monarch's bodyguard who had witnessed the brutal assassination being all safely in prison pending the Grand Vizier's decision as to their fate. True, the sudden disappearance of the Sultan caused some anxiety in the harem and among the Fadáwa-n-serki, or royal courtiers, but this was at once allayed by a report that was spread that His Majesty had unexpectedly set out upon a journey.

It was only at night, when Khadidja and Zobeide, the Sultan's two favourites, were, without warning, decapitated by the eunuchs in the centre of one of the Courts of Love, that the doves of the gilded cage vaguely guessed the truth. Trembling, they huddled together upon their mats, none knowing who might fall the next victim of the wrath of their absent unknown lord.

That night, and through many nights following, dark terrible dramas were enacted in that dazzling female hive. The plots, jealousies, and intrigues of the past were bearing fruit, and when darkness fell, eunuchs would bring me their scimitars wet with blood to be cleaned and burnished, while others carried out the bodies of the fair ones in silent gloomy procession. More than once I saw upon a passing bier a form that moved and struggled desperately, though no cry came from beneath the black pall. They were those unfortunate ones doomed to torture, who at daybreak would be conveyed by the guards far into the desert, secured, and there left to die of heat and thirst, affording a feast for the flies and the great grey vultures.

The history of the Sultans of Agadez is a bloody story—one long chapter of murder, fierce combats, and poisonings, that, had the secrets ever leaked out, would form a startling volume. How many dark plots had been hatched within those painted walls! What passionate love, what unbridled hate! A despot is always all-powerful; but the Sultan Hámed was a despot of despots. A favourite one day; the next a carcase eaten by dogs at the city gate. A wife one day, robed in brocade and dazzling with diamonds; the next a slave washing the feet of her who only a day ago waited upon her, and was cuffed and beaten at her command. Truly indeed the Grand Vizier Mukhtar and his accomplice, the Chief of the Eunuchs, were now revenging themselves upon those who had sought to compass their downfall, and the scenes of fiendish cruelty and bloodshed witnessed nightly within those gorgeous Courts of the Sultanas must have been awful. Until the new monarch could be publicly proclaimed, they ruled the Fáda, and were removing with horrible brutality those of its inmates whose existence might in the future prove detrimental to their interests.

At last, on the morn of the Nahr-el-Djemäa following Hámed's assassination, his son 'Abd-el-Kerim was publicly proclaimed Sultan of the Ahír. Through the city of Agadez the news spread rapidly, announcements were made in the camel market and in the market of slaves, the cadis gave forth the astounding intelligence from their divans, invoking at the same time the blessing of Allah, while from the great gates of the Fáda horsemen spurred away fleet as the storm-breeze, through the oasis and across the lonely Desert for many days, bearing the news to the furthermost limits of His Majesty's domains.

So carefully had the secret of the tragedy been preserved, that until that day the people knew not that their ruler had died, and with the intelligence there came the news that his son was already reigning in his stead. None mourned, but in the palace and throughout the land there was general feasting and rejoicing. Even the slaves were allowed a day of idleness, and I, among them, lolled upon the bench in my den, and enjoyed a calm siesta, notwithstanding the life and movement in the wide sunlit court outside. Glad of the brief relaxation from wearying toil, I dozed through the hot, brilliant afternoon, and only awakened to a consciousness of things about me by words being whispered into my ear.

"Awake, O Roumi," exclaimed a negro, hunchbacked and of dwarfed stature, whom I beheld standing before me. "Take care lest thou attractest the attention of thine enemies."

I started up, alarmed that the deformed stranger should have discovered my creed. A Christian would, I knew, quickly meet his death at the hands of that fierce fanatical people.

"How—how darest thou declare that I am no believer in the Prophet?" I demanded, with feigned anger.

"Hush! Fear not. Thou art the one who hast journeyed from afar over the Great Desert, and art detained as slave of the Sultan. For thee I bear a secret message."

"A message. Who hath sent it?" I gasped.

"I know not," he answered. "See! it is here;" and, slipping his hand into mine cautiously, he left in my palm a small pomegranate. "Remember that thine enemies regard thee with suspicion, therefore make no sign, and do not open it until I have passed through the outer courts. At last I have, by good fortune, been enabled to reach thee unnoticed amid the crowds now congregated everywhere. May the Giver of Mercy—whose name be ever praised—preserve thee, strengthen thine arm, and guide thy footsteps into the paths of freedom."

And without another word my mysterious visitor slipped away, and in a moment I lost sight of him amid the gaily-attired throng who, promenading in the spacious court, across which the shadows were already lengthening, smoked and discussed excitedly the all-absorbing topic of the unexpected accession of young 'Abd-el-Kerim as their lord and master.

Eagerly I cut open the pomegranate when I thought myself unobserved, and discovered in a small cavity from which the fruit had been removed a scrap of parchment cunningly concealed. On opening it, the following words, penned in ill-formed Arabic characters, met my eyes—

"Know, O Roumi, faithful lover of Zoraida, beauteous Daughter of the Sun, a friend sendeth thee greeting. Remain watchful, for when the moon hath shed her light two hours, thou, Slave of the Eunuchs, mayest be rescued. A friend that thou canst trust with thy life will utter the word '*dáchchân.*' (Smoke of a pipe.) Then obey, follow without seeking explanation, and thou mayest pass unchallenged the vigilantly-guarded portals of the Fáda, even unto the outer gate where freedom lieth. Upon thee be perfect peace."

The paper almost fell from my hands. At last secret steps were being taken to secure my release! But by whom? The mention of Zoraida's name told me that by some unknown means the *imam* had discovered me, and was exerting every effort to secure my rescue from the palace-fortress, a task which, I well knew, was no easy matter. Gazing upon the message, I remained spellbound. Anticipations of freedom gave me a certain amount of happiness, yet the bitter recollection that the strange object which Zoraida had entrusted to my care was lost irretrievably, filled me with gloomiest forebodings. Over nearly two thousand miles of rugged mountain and sun-baked wilderness I had travelled, on an errand the aim of which had suddenly vanished, and the vague uncertainty whether Zoraida really still lived caused me to view the result of this attempt to leave the Fáda with a cool indifference begotten of despair.

Weeks of hard, monotonous toil had caused me to look upon my future with hopelessness, and regard life within the Court of the Eunuchs as preferable to an aimless freedom without the woman I loved. If she were dead,—if, as I half feared, the mysterious disaster which she dreaded had actually fallen upon her,—then life's empty pleasures had no further attraction for me. By day and by night, dreaming or waking, the horrible vision of the white cut-off hand, with its thin, shrivelled fingers and its scintillating gems, haunted me continuously, strengthening my misgivings as to her safety, and horrifying me by its ghastly vividness.

Why had it been stolen from me? Why, indeed, had it ever been sent to me, and by whom? All were points as deeply strange and mysterious as the hidden properties of the lost Crescent, the marvels of the secret chamber in the weird old house in Algiers, or the identity of Zoraida herself.

The shadows in the spacious court crept slowly onward, the warm tints of sunset flooded the great open space aglow with colour and alive with promenaders, and as I resumed my work, brightening scimitars and daggers until they shone like mirrors, the brilliant rays deepened into a fiery crimson, then faded in a mystic twilight.

Toiling on in order to pass the intervening hours more rapidly, I watched and waited until the moon shone forth, and then, anxious and impatient, I held my ears open in readiness for the secret word. By the flickering light of an oil lamp I was engaged cleaning the jewelled handle of a dagger, when, on turning suddenly, I was startled to observe a tall, dignified-looking man of middle age in the silken courtiers' robes of the Fadáwa-n-serki.

"*Dáchchân!*" he whispered, adding quickly, "Extinguish thy lamp. We must not be observed."

Involuntarily I bent to blow out the flame, but, suddenly remembering that no true son of Islâm would commit such an unholy act, I put out the light with my fingers. As I did so, he quickly slipped off his robe, revealing the fact that he wore two similar garments, one over the other, and a second later he produced a yellow turban, similar to the one he himself was wearing.

"Trust in me, O my friend," he whispered. "Assume this disguise, and follow me."

I dressed quickly, and, arranging the turban upon my head, we were about to leave when, pointing to the long dagger upon the bench, he said in an ominous undertone, "Take that with thee. Peradventure thou mayest want it."

Snatching it up, I placed it in my sash, and quickly we went forth together.

"Remember thou art no longer a slave," he whispered.

"Have no fear, but bear boldly thy part as one of the Fadáwa-n-serki."

Without any attempt at concealment, we walked onward together in the brilliant moonlight to the gate leading to the Court of the Janissaries, whereat stood two great negroes, their naked swords gleaming in the white moonbeams. Holding my breath, I scarce dared to gaze upon them, but, after an inquiring glance at us, they pushed open the heavy gate, ceremoniously allowing us to pass into the first vestibule. Again we passed the second gate unchallenged, and then the third, finding ourselves in the great court of the guardians of the Fáda. Some of the brightly-attired soldiers of the Sultan were squatting under the spacious arches, smoking *keef*, amusing themselves with *damma*, or taking coffee, while others strolled about in pairs gossiping. The presence of the Fadáwa-n-serki was nothing unusual, therefore we attracted no notice as in silence we crossed the court to the great dark portals, beyond which, again unchallenged, we passed, gaining a smaller court, where a fountain plashed with cool refreshing sound into a basin of carved porphyry. Through this region of the Fáda we went without inquiry being addressed to us, and, judging from the obsequious manner of the guards, I felt convinced that my unknown friend was some high official whom janissaries dared not question.

Another court was passed, and as I was wondering who my rescuer might be, we came to the great outer gate, which, next to the gate of the harem, was the most carefully guarded entrance in the whole of the Fáda. As we approached, the chief of the guards, a Soudanese of great height and muscular development, loudly demanded our business.

My heart gave a leap, and again I held my breath. The result of this interview would, I knew, decide my fate. If it were discovered that I, a slave purchased by Hámed's gold, was endeavouring to escape, a sudden and violent death was the punishment I must expect.

"Art thine eyes so dimmed as not to recognise 'Abd e Rahman, cadi of Egemmén, and Hadj Beshir, sheikh of the Kel-Ikóhanén? Open thy gate quickly and let us pass. We have no time to bandy words, for we are on an urgent mission for our new lord the Sultan 'Abd-el-Kerim."

The black giant, either recognising my companion, or becoming impressed by the importance of our rapid departure, bowed ceremoniously, and shouted to his men to unbar the door in the great dark arch. In the deep shadow six janissaries were drawn up on either side, armed with long curved swords, and as we stood in the full, bright moonlight, they could easily see our faces distinctly, though they themselves remained hidden. Chains clanked, and slowly the heavy door that never opened after sunset grated upon its hinges; then, having given peace to the chief of the guard, we were about to pass out into the city, when suddenly one of the soldiers cried—

"Hold! That man is a false cadi! He is the fierce pirate of the Desert known as Hámma, and is a terror to our people along the shores of the Tsâd! The other I recognise as a slave of the eunuchs!"

The words caused the greatest sensation among his companions. For a moment they remained dumbfounded at our audacity.

"Seize them!" cried the chief gate-keeper, rushing forward excitedly. Next second a dozen scimitars were playing around us, but ere we could be secured my mysterious companion had drawn his formidable knife from its sheath, and with a dexterous blow had sent the first man who laid a hand upon him reeling back, stabbed through the heart.

In an instant I drew the dagger I had brought with me, and as I did so, closed with a big negro who endeavoured to hold me. I fought for life, and the struggle was short and desperate. Having gained the outer gate, I was determined to escape, and I defended myself with greater strength than I had imagined I possessed. As the negro wrestled with me, clasping me in his iron embrace in an endeavour to throw me to the ground, we swayed backwards and forwards, both exerting every muscle to gain the mastery. Suddenly I felt my strength failing, for the pain caused by his grasp was excruciating, but with a quick movement I managed to wrench my right arm free, and with my dagger struck him a blow in the throat which caused him to release his hold. Then, staggering, he fell back mortally wounded.

With a spring like that of a leopard, another negro pounced upon me, while a second seized me by the shoulder. It was a critical moment. Capture I knew meant death, and as I turned in struggling with my latest assailants, I saw my companion struck a coward blow by a scimitar from behind. He fell like a log, and, judging from the terrible wound inflicted on his skull, death must have been instantaneous.

His fate filled me with a strength that was almost demoniacal, for while the others assembled round the prostrate bodies of the false cadi and the man he had killed, I fought desperately, determined to struggle on till the last. My knife, wet with the blood of the first janissary who had attacked me, was still in my hand, and, feeling myself being overpowered by the fierce black-faced brutes, I dealt one a blow in the side which caused him to spring away, and as he did so, I again brought the keen blade full across the other's face, inflicting a frightful gash. Shrieking with rage and pain, he released me, clapping both hands to his ebon countenance.

A moment later I dashed headlong into the darkness, followed at full speed by half a dozen enraged and howling janissaries who, waving their scimitars, cried: "Kill the slave! Let him not escape! Kill him! Kill him!"

Chapter Twenty Eight
On the Pinnacle of Al Arâf

It was a mad dash for liberty. Ignorant of where my footsteps would lead me, I sped swiftly onward across a great open space, which I afterwards learnt was called the Katshíu, past the Mesállaje, or Great Mosque, with its high square minaret, and running beside the walls of several spacious whitewashed buildings, evidently the residences of wealthier merchants, I turned the first corner I came to, and, passing a stagnant pool, found myself in a maze of squalid, narrow, ill-built streets, which, though bearing marks of former grandeur, were unpaved and filthy. The houses, mostly of one storey, were mean, flat-roofed, and half in decay, and as I wound my way through the unlighted, crooked thoroughfares, I could still hear the hurrying footsteps and shrill cries of the palace guards, who, eager for revenge, were determined that I should not escape them.

Panting, well knowing that a halt meant death by torture, I ran forward until I found myself in the Erárar-n-Zákan, or Camel Market, a small square with the usual arched arcade running along one side. Then, the angry shouts of the janissaries sounding on my ears, I resolved upon a desperate expedient, namely, to dash along a street which led back in the direction I had come, and so return towards the Mosque. Even in my desperation I was determined to seek the holy man and deliver Zoraida's letter which for so many months had reposed in the little leathern charm-case suspended round my neck; but as I rushed headlong across a deserted market-place and emerged into an open space, I noticed a youthful Arab horseman mounted and leading a horse saddled but riderless.

My footsteps attracted him, and, having gazed at me for a moment intently, and apparently taking in the situation, he spurred across to cut off my retreat. As he rode down upon me, his flowing white robe looking ghostly in the darkness, my heart sank, for I was thoroughly exhausted and no longer hoped for freedom.

Judge my amazement, however, when, pulling up suddenly close to me, he exclaimed—

"Peace! Mount yonder steed quickly, and let us away! *Dáchchân!*"

The word gave me courage. It had been uttered by the mysterious man who at the cost of his own life had accomplished my deliverance! The fierce, brutal guards, accompanied by a number of Arabs who considered it sport to hunt a slave, were still in full cry after me. Already they had gained the Katánga, therefore, without losing a moment, I rushed towards the horse, swung myself into the saddle, and sped away like the wind, my rescuer leading.

Shots sounded in rapid succession, but we remained unharmed, and with loud, angry curses sounding in the distance, we rode speedily forward, to where there was a breach in the city walls, and then away through the fertile oasis. As in silence we pressed onward at a wild, mad gallop, I was filled with admiration at the magnificent manner in which my companion sat his horse. He seemed merely a youth, for he was not tall, and his haick, well drawn over his face, half concealed his features, yet he rode at a pace that was killing, regardless of obstacles or the uneven nature of the ground.

"For me this day hath indeed been one full of events," I managed to gasp at length, when, in ascending the rising ground, our horses slackened.

"And for me also," he replied, without glancing towards me. "How sad it is that the daring Hámma, hero of a hundred fights, should have fallen in his valiant attempt to rescue thee!"

"Yes," I answered. "He fought bravely, indeed. But how didst thou know of his death?"

"I was awaiting thee outside the mosque opposite the Fáda gate, with a horse for Hámma and thyself," he answered. "I saw him fall, and then I witnessed thy flight. I could not reach thee in time, but by the shouts of the janissaries I knew the direction thou hadst taken, and posted myself in readiness. Praise be unto Allah that thou hast escaped those fiendish brutes!"

"But it is all a mystery," I said. "Tell me who plotted my deliverance; why should it be attempted by an outlaw?"

"I know nothing," he replied, "save that it was imperative that thy life should be saved."

"Why?"

"Because thou art the Amîn, and the Well-Beloved."

"What dost thou know of me?" I asked, in surprise. "Nothing, beyond the fact that thou, who hast undertaken a secret mission, fell into the hands of the slave-raiders and became a prisoner in the inner court of the Fáda."

"Then thou art aware of my mission?"

"I am aware that thou art a Roumi from across the sea."

"Knowest thou Hadj Mohammed ben Ishak, the *imam* of the Mesállaje?" I asked.

"Yes, I knew him. He was a man pious and full of learning."

"What! hath the Avenger claimed him?"

"No. He hath gone on a journey."

"On a journey?" I cried in dismay. "When will he return?"

"I know not."

We had reached the brow of the hill, and our horses started off again at the same terrific pace as before. Noticing our saddle-bags were packed as if for travel, I inquired where we were going, but the only answer vouchsafed was—

"Trust thyself unto me."

For another hour we rode onward through a great grove of date palms, until at last we plunged into a dense tropical forest, along what appeared to be a secret, unfrequented path. Presently, however, my guide suggested that we should rest until sunrise, and, dismounting, we unsaddled our horses, and, throwing ourselves down with our heads upon our saddle-bags, slept soundly.

It was bright daylight when, on opening my eyes, I made an amazing discovery. The sex of my companion had changed! My guide to whom I owed my freedom was not a youth, as I had believed, but a young and pretty Arab woman, whose bright-hued silk garments had been concealed by a man's burnouse, while on her head she had worn the fez and haick instead of the dainty embroidered cap and sequins which she had now resumed.

"Thou art astonished at my transformation," she laughed roguishly, standing before me with her pretty face unveiled. "Man's attire doth not suit me in the light of day."

"Why hast thou practised such deception upon me?" I asked, amazed.

"Because it was necessary. It was arranged that I should merely hold the horses in readiness, but when thou alone escaped, it became imperative that I should act as thy servant and guide."

"I owe thee a great debt indeed," I said. "Tell me thy name."

"My name and tribe are of no consequence," she answered. "An explanation will be given thee some day; at present I am bound to secrecy."

"Even though thou art of the sect of the Aïssáwà and of the tribe of the Ennitra—eh?" I asked.

"How didst thou know?" she asked, startled. But I refused to satisfy her curiosity, although, truth to tell, I had noticed neatly tattooed upon her forehead a serpent, the symbol of the more fanatical of the followers of Sidi ben Aïssa, and upon her wrist was a curiously-wrought Kabyle bracelet of white metal, similar in form to one Zoraida had worn. The presence of this woman so far south puzzled me greatly, and I sat silent and thoughtful while she produced from her saddle-bag some dates, with a little skinful of water in which úzak seeds had been dipped, and which I found a cooling and refreshing drink.

When we had eaten, she twisted her haick around her head, leaving just a slit for her eyes, then she sprang lightly into her saddle and we moved on again. Our way lay through a great thicket, where the mimosas and abísga attained such an exuberance as I had never before seen in the Sahara, and being closely interwoven by "gráffeni," or climbing plants, were almost impenetrable.

As we rode along the secret path, I endeavoured to persuade her to tell me of Zoraida, but her lips were closely sealed. She admitted that she had heard of the Daughter of the Sun, but with artful ingenuousness declared that she had never seen her.

"I have heard that she died in Algiers somewhat mysteriously," I said, watching her dark eyes narrowly.

"Yes," she exclaimed, quite calmly. "I have heard a similar report, and it is a curious circumstance that none have seen her since she went to El Djezaïr."

"She could foretell coming events and divine the thoughts of those with whom she came into contact," I observed.

"True, O Roumi. Whenever she accompanied our people into battle, they returned with much spoil and many slaves. Her love was a fierce, unbridled passion, and her hatred bitter and lifelong."

"And the Sheikh, Hadj Absalam, what of him?"

"I know not. I am merely thy servant and thy guide. Ask me not things of which I have no knowledge;" and with this rebuff she commenced chattering and laughing gaily, leading the way through the dense forest in the depths of which it would have been easy enough to lose one's self and perish. That she had before traversed the secret route was apparent, and her anxiety to push onward showed her impatience to bring our journey to a conclusion. Any little gallantry I offered when she found herself in difficulty owing to her dress catching in the twigs was accepted with dignity and murmured thanks, but regarding our ultimate destination she refused to utter a single word, beyond stating that for three days longer we should be travelling companions, and vaguely hinting that the journey might prove beneficial to my interests.

Riding at slow pace behind her through the tangled tropical vegetation, where flowers grew in wild, luxuriant profusion, and monkeys, alarmed at our appearance, swang from tree to tree, I reflected how utterly fruitless my journey over the Great Desert had proved. The mysterious conspiracy of silence regarding Zoraida into which everyone seemed to have entered appeared directed against myself, for with the exception of what she had told me with her own lips, I knew absolutely nothing of her. The mystic rites practised in the secret chamber, the discovery of the Crescent of Glorious Wonders, and the unknown object of my mission to Agadez, were all enigmas so puzzling as to drive me to the verge of madness. Although a strenuous, desperate effort had been made to release me from the Sultan's palace, nevertheless every precaution had apparently been taken in order that I should obtain no knowledge of Zoraida's past, of her present whereabouts, or even whether she still lived.

For a brief rest we halted about noon, ate our scanty meal which my pretty guide prepared, and then, declaring that she was not fatigued, we moved on again, still through the great forest unknown to geographers that seemed appallingly weird and impenetrable. I had no idea that the Oasis of the Ahír comprised such an extensive tract of wooded land. From the sun it appeared as though we were travelling in a north-westerly direction. The path wound and turned in a manner that would have been puzzling and amazing to the stranger, and at times it was lost sight of altogether, as if to prevent those who discovered it accidentally from following it up.

The afternoon passed, and the mellowing rays of sunlight glinting through the trees tinted the long tresses of my fair companion, who, having now removed her haick, laughed and talked gaily, telling me of her exciting adventures as the child of a thieving band. Though she would not utter Zoraida's name, she told me many curious things. She had, it appeared, been in the camp of the Ennitra when, after the successful attack on the caravan of Ali Ben Hafiz, I had been brought in and sentenced to be tortured with the asp, and she told me how, after I had escaped, Hadj Absalam had sworn vengeance and sent a force after me. This force it was who subsequently attacked the Spahis and was slaughtered by them.

"And why art thou here, so far from thy mountain home?" I asked presently, determined if possible to elucidate some of the tantalising mystery which seemed ever increasing.

"I travelled alone to Agadez to arrange with Hámma to effect thy liberty," she answered. "Allah, the One Gracious and Merciful, hath preserved thee, while he who dared to enter the Fáda fell under the janissaries' swords."

"Allah grant his soul peace!" I said, adding fervently, "I am truly thankful to thee. Thou art indeed brave to risk so much, to accomplish this lonely journey, and to trust thyself upon this lonely path."

"A woman of the Ennitra knoweth not fear," she answered proudly. Then, with a calm, serious look, she added, "I am the servant of one who could not travel here in person. Allah directeth whom He pleaseth and casteth the unbeliever into the torments of hell. To-day thou standest upon the pinnacle of Al Arâf, the partition which divideth everlasting joy from eternal sorrow. Already the test hath been applied to thee, and it hath been proved that thou art the Amîn—the Well-Beloved."

"Thou knowest the ordeal through which I am passing with feet treading the unknown paths of ignorance where the light of truth shineth not. Canst thou not give me one word of hope as to the successful accomplishment of the mission that hath been entrusted to me?" I asked, rather surprised at her enigmatical speech.

"I give thee no empty word of confidence. Thine own courage and stout heart in this strange land wherein thou art wandering will, in itself, prove a test the severity of which will not be forgotten. Peace be upon us, and upon all righteous servants of Allah!"

With this last sentiment I expressed devout concurrence, and under the foliage reddened by the crimson afterglow we wended our way onward until we came to a small rivulet, where we halted, watered our horses, and prepared our food. Then, when it had grown dark, my fair guide, wrapping herself in the burnouse she had worn when I first met her, lay down to rest, arranging herself in a manner which showed her to be a true Bedouin to whom sleeping under the starlit canopy of heaven was no fresh experience.

Next day and the day following went by in a similar manner, with the exception that, having passed through the forest, we found ourselves on the edge of the oasis, and with our horses well pleased at the freedom, we galloped out straight as an arrow into the wild, inhospitable wilderness, which stretched away as far as the eye could discern, a great arid, barren plain. She sat her horse splendidly, as side by side we rode onward hour after hour, stopping now and then to drink from our water-skins, yet not once did she complain of the terrible burning heat or fatigue. On the contrary, there was always in her dark sparkling eyes a roguishness that is the peculiar charm of all Oriental women, and she entertained me with many stories of the valour and chivalry of her tribesmen. That night we encamped in the desert, and at dawn on the third day moved onward again towards our unknown goal.

An hour before sundown she suddenly drew rein, and, shading her eyes with her little sun-tanned hand, cried—

"Behold! They are within sight!"

Straining my aching eyes in the direction indicated, I saw in the far distance a small speck against the horizon, which proved, on our approach, to be a clump of palms, and almost as soon as I had been able to make them out, I noticed that we had been observed, and that a Bedouin horseman in white burnouse was spurring out towards us.

In half an hour we met. As he came nearer, there appeared something about him that seemed to me familiar, and when at last he galloped up, amid the jingling of his horse's trappings, holding his rifle high above his head, I recognised his dark evil face.

It was the rascally caitiff Labakan, who had followed me so suspiciously from Algiers, and against whom the dispatch-bearer Gajére had forewarned me! The man who gave me greeting was the sinister, villainous-looking outlaw who had stolen the cut-off hand!

Chapter Twenty Nine
Labakan

Misgivings were aroused within me by the discovery, but, concealing them, I gave him "peace," as in flowery language and with many references to Allah's might, he bade me welcome to their shade. Scarcely deigning to notice the brave girl who had secured my liberty and acted as my guide, he wheeled round and rode beside me, expressing hope that I had in no way suffered from my detention within the Fáda of Agadez, and uttering profuse greetings with every breath.

To these I remained somewhat indifferent. I was wondering what fate was about to overtake me, and whether, after all, I had not been ingeniously betrayed into the hands of my enemies. This dark-visaged brigand who had followed me nearly two thousand miles had evidently done so with evil purpose. His words of well-feigned welcome and apparent delight at my arrival at that lonely spot were the reverse of reassuring, and, for aught I knew, I was about to fall into some cunningly-devised trap. The reason of this strange vengeance which he apparently desired to wreak upon me remained a hidden and mystifying enigma. To my knowledge, I had never harmed him, and, indeed, previous to our meeting in the *kahoua* in Algiers, I had never before set eyes upon him. Yet, with the fire of a terrible hatred burning within his heart, he had tracked me with the pertinacity of a bloodhound over the Great Sahara, through the many vicissitudes that had befallen me, and at last, by his clever machinations, I was now actually being led irresistibly to my fate!

At first the thought flashed across my mind that the woman whom the outlaw addressed as Yamina had brought me there, well knowing the reason this villain desired my release. Why had she observed that I was standing insecurely upon Al Aráf, between paradise and torment? Did not that imply that there was a vile plot against my life? Heedless of the outlaw's well-turned Arabic sentences, I pondered, half inclined to condemn her. Yet no, I could not. She had, I felt sure, rescued me without dreaming that I should fall a victim under the knife of a secret assassin, and as she rode along in silence, unveiled, and looking a trifle pale and jaded, I was compelled to admit that to secure my release she had placed her own life in serious jeopardy.

At length we galloped into the small palm-grove that surrounded a well where camels and horses were resting, and a sharp turn brought us upon a small encampment. I half expected to fall into an ambush, and my hand instinctively sought the hilt of the dagger that had done me such good service at the Fáda gate, but when the shouts of the assembled men, all of them fierce-looking, well armed, and carrying daggers and powder-horns, gave me hearty welcome, I became reassured, dismounting, and following my enemy to the principal tent, before which a morose old Arab sat smoking his long pipe. He was very old, with a dark face thin and wizened, yet age had not dimmed the pair of keen, searching eyes he fixed upon me.

"Behold! the stranger!" exclaimed Labakan, as we advanced.

"Roumi from afar, thou art welcome to our encampment," the old man exclaimed solemnly, removing his pipe and waving his brown, bony hand.

"Blessings on thy beard!" I answered, when I had given him peace. "As a stranger in this thy land, I appreciate thine hospitality, even though I know not the name of my host."

"Thou art weary, thou hast journeyed long through the forest and over the plain, and thou requirest rest," he went on, motioning me to the mat spread beside him, and ordering a slave to bring me food and water. I was in the camp of my enemies, which accounted for his disinclination to tell me who he was. Besides, I heard conversations being carried on in *tamahaq*, the dialect of the Touaregs, in order, apparently, that I might not understand. Whatever the object for which I had been conducted to that lonely spot, the chief of the encampment treated me as his honoured guest, and gave me to eat the best fare his people could provide. Such conduct was exceedingly puzzling, and, after I had eaten the kousskouss and chick peas, and accepted the pipe he offered, I suddenly asked—

"What have I done that I should merit this thy friendship?"

"Are we not commanded to succour our friend's friend?" he answered. "Thou owest me no debt of gratitude, for it was Labakan yonder who arranged thine escape from the Fáda;" and, raising his hand, he indicated the outlaw of the Ennitra who had stolen the severed hand, and who was now smoking a cigarette, and lounging lazily with another man as repulsive-looking as himself at a little distance from us.

I was silent. Was it not at least remarkable that the man who had offered Gajére gold to assist in my murder, should now exert himself so strenuously on my behalf? Expectation fettered me.

"Fidelity towards a friend, magnanimity towards an enemy, are the pride of my people," the old man continued. Then, turning towards me, he added, "Thy brow beareth traces of a poignant grief. Perhaps we may be able to calm thy sorrow, for we would most willingly help a brother, though he be of different creed."

His words struck me as ominous. Was he joking grimly, meaning that my sorrow would be "calmed" in death?

Nevertheless I replied to his confidential address: "I feel much relieved by thy words, O friend, for in thine eyes there lurketh no treachery. True, I have passed through many terrible days since last I trod mine own far-distant land; yet I have no sorrow, only the regret of what might have been which is common alike to True Believer and to Roumi."

"Why dost thou journey in this the land of thine enemies?" asked the strange old man, calmly puffing at his pipe.

"I have a secret object," I replied, still keeping my eyes upon the hulking lounger who remained in conversation with one of the armed band, now and then casting furtive glances towards me. "I am seeking a phantom fortune."

"Ah! thou art young. Thou hast the careless indifference that youth giveth, and art no doubt prepared to meet Eblis himself if he promiseth an adventure. Yet, alas! the mark upon thy brow telleth me that the canker-worm of love eateth away thine heart. Fair tresses oft ensnare a man, and cause him to seek Sindbad's diamond valley, of which the story-teller singeth."

Evidently he was aware of my mission to that distant region!

"When one is wounded by the keen shafts of a woman's eyes, there is no peace," I said, impressed by my venerable companion's seriousness. "True love createth a mad fascination, a partial insanity that refuseth to be calmed."

"And so it is in thy case, I wager," he observed. "From thy mouth fall pearls of wisdom. Yet to-day, how little of genuine love is there among thy people, the Roumis! Have I not witnessed it among the Franks of El Djezaïr! Fascination is a gift of Allah; it hath no limits of age or condition. It is as indescribable as the steam that propelleth thy caravans of iron, or the invisible power that carrieth thy commands along wires of great length; therefore, it is not possible to simulate it. Yet what a tendency there existeth among thy people from over seas to coquette with love! We True Believers when in El Djezaïr, gaze upon the white uncovered faces of thy women in the streets, in the gardens, in the cafés, everywhere, and watch them in amazement. In the people of Al-Islâm, as in the Infidels, the heart is the same; but it seemeth to us that thy women, foolish and vain, know not true affection, and live only to attract men by feigning an imitation of love that is ridiculous. It astoundeth us."

"Thou speakest of what we term flirts," I said, surprised that he should have observed so keenly the manners of European society as portrayed at Algiers. "It is true that fashion hath taken a wrong turn. Tragic, romantic, frivolous, and heroic love-affairs will succeed each other, for the heart of a woman beateth alike under the gauzes of Al-Islâm and the tightly-laced corsets of Christianity, and the pulses of the Bedouins of the Desert and the idler of the Franks are alike moved by a pretty face; but, as thou rightly sayest, the fashion of flirtation only leadeth to factious disturbances, misery, and ruin."

"Thy criticism is just, O Roumi! Truth never loseth its rights, though falsehood may have a long day. Thy women, who affect love in order to be considered fascinating, are the falsehoods of thy society, veritable houris from Hâwiyat. A woman who loveth deeply, passionately, really, though wrongly, may have our pity, compassion, sympathy, but she who simulateth a passion for vanity's sake hath neither. We of Al-Islâm feel a pity for the heart that breaketh beneath a smile; we honour a hidden sorrow; but for the trifling, idle, gay, and foolish married woman of thy people, who with uncovered face seeketh to fascinate the men who move about her, we entertain no such feelings. She feigneth love for them, entranceth them, and then—may Allah confound her!—she mocketh them. Such is one of the developments of thy so-called Christian civilisation!"

He spoke the truth; I was compelled to admit it. Was there any wonder that a devout Moslem, witnessing the ways of European society, where the women bare their chests at night for the public gaze, and laboriously try to appear to have done something wrong, in order that scandal may be whispered about them,—"being talked about" being the high road to fashionable eminence,—should express amazement at the commanding egotism of those of our fair sex who consider it "smart" and a necessary adjunct of fashion to be seen flirting. How utterly contemptible must our whole social system appear in the eyes of these wise, thoughtful Sons of the Desert, who, far from bustling cities and the ways of men, dream away their silent, breathless days!

The old man, although a pleasant companion, would answer no question I addressed to him, and though I felt safe under his protection, yet the presence of the man Labakan caused me considerable uneasiness. When the last rays of sunset had faded, and some negro girls danced before our tent, the evil-visaged scoundrel sat beside me smoking haschish. In a semicircle the people squatted, listening with rapture to the humdrum voices of the singers and story-tellers, mingling with the thumping of *derboukas*, and the shrill notes of the flute-like *djouak*. From time to time a prolonged "Ah!" plaintively modulated, was uttered in applause of the song, dance, or story; and as I spoke now and then with him, I watched his face narrowly, detecting in his eyes a crafty look of unmistakable hatred. When he laughed, his white teeth shone spectral in the twilight, and when he addressed me, his thin, sinister face was so nigh to mine that I could mark each line that Time had turned upon his sallow cheeks, and watch the slow, cruel smile that wrinkled about his moving lips.

When at length the camp grew quiet, and I cast myself down to rest, all slumber was prevented by reason of the terrible sandstorm that sprang up, roaring over the oasis and screaming most melancholy in the palms. In claps of the veriest passion, the sand-laden, suffocating wind swept through the clumps of trees, and the night was in the possession of a thousand evil powers that seemed to mock at me. In that hour but one hope held me; but one fear. Death seemed to shriek about the tent, and wander whining through the storm-torn trees; on my heart Fear laid his chilly fingers, tightening his hold, and straining as though drawing me nearer to the end. But determined to remain calm and defiant, in order to learn the Great Secret, I was prepared to encounter all risks, even in that wild, unknown country, in the camp of the outlaws. In the midst of the howling sirocco, two furtive figures, almost obscured by the whirling sand, passed my tent silently. The misty silhouettes were those of Yamina and Labakan! Swollen to a monstrous horror, Fear, a hideous, torturing spectre, loomed beside me, and all past delight, all future evil, laughed me to derision in his presence. Through the night the tempest raged with fury unabated, and as I lay with my hand grasping my only weapon, my knife, I knew not from one moment to another whether a coward's dagger would strike me a swift death blow. Thus, vigilant and feverishly anxious, I waited until the sandstorm passed and the dawn was no longer obscured, then rose, half surprised that I still lived to witness the glorious sunrise.

Judge my amazement, however, when, on gazing round, I found that the tents had disappeared, and I was alone!

In the hours of darkness during the storm, the camp had been struck, the camels packed, and even while I lay with eyes and ears open, the Bedouin band had silently departed, leaving me to my fate in an unknown region! Even the spots on the sand where the fires had burned had been carefully dug over, and every trace of the recent encampment had been carefully obliterated. Tied by its nose-cord to a palm was a *méheri* camel, kneeling upon the sand with bent head, disconsolate and neglected, and as I gazed around among the tall trunks, seeking to discover whether any of the band remained behind, I suddenly caught a glimpse of a fluttering burnouse.

"*Sabâh elker!*" ("Good morning!") I shouted in greeting, but next moment I was startled to recognise in the approaching figure the lean, sinewy form of Labakan.

"*Slamalik!*" ("Good day to you!") he cried, hastening towards me with a broad, fiendish smile upon his coarse, brutal features. "Thou art forgotten."

"Thy people could scarcely have overlooked me when they left my tent untouched," I said, angered that this man should still be haunting me like an evil shadow. "Besides, they departed by stealth, so as not to attract my attention. For what reason have they plunged again into the desert?"

"For reasons known only to ourselves," the crafty brigand replied, displaying his teeth in the hideous grin that seemed natural to him. "A secret message received after *el maghrib* made it necessary to move."

"Didst thou fear attack?"

"We fear nothing, save the wrath of Allah," was his prompt reply, as without further words he proceeded to pull down my tent and pack it quickly upon the back of the kneeling camel.

"We of the Roumis endeavour to be loyal to those who eat salt with us," I said, presently. "Thy people, however, desert the stranger to whom they give succour."

Shrugging his shoulders, he drew his haick closer about his narrow chest, replying, "If thou hadst full knowledge of our affairs, thou wouldst be aware that circumstances had combined to render it imperative that my people should leave this spot, and proceed by a certain route, of which thou must remain in ignorance. In order, however, that thou shouldst not be left to starve in this vast region of the Great Death, I am here to guide thee onward to a spot where we may in two days rejoin our friends."

Of all men he was the last I should have chosen as travelling companion, for treachery lurked in his curling lip, and in his black eye there beamed the villainous cunning of one whose callous hands were stained by many crimes. To refuse meant to remain there without food, and quickly perish, therefore I was compelled, when he had carefully removed all traces of the tent, to mount the camel, and submit to his obnoxious companionship. He had his own camel tethered near, and as he straddled across the saddle the animal rose, and together we started out upon our journey.

Chapter Thirty
The Hall of the Great Death

Labakan's appearance was just as unkempt, his burnouse just as ragged, as on the day he snatched from me the box containing the horrible souvenir. As we rode side by side into the shadowless plain, he addressed many ingenious questions to me about my past. His thinly-veiled curiosity, however, I steadfastly refused to satisfy. That he knew more of me than I had imagined was quite apparent, otherwise he would not have taken such infinite pains to secure my escape from the palace of the Sultan. Puzzled over his strange conduct, I journeyed with him throughout the greater part of the day. Conversing pleasantly, and making many observations that contained a certain amount of dry humour, he never for a moment acted in a manner to cause me further misgivings. With the craftiness characteristic of his piratical tribe, he was endeavouring to disarm any suspicions I might perchance entertain, if—as to him seemed impossible—I recognised him as the man who followed me into the little *kahoua* in the far-distant city.

After nearly five hours on the level, sandy plain, under the torrid rays of a leaden sun, we passed along a valley, desolate and barren, until we had on our left a broad mount, rising first with gradual ascent, but in its upper part forming a steep and lofty wall. Then, having passed a small defile and crossed another valley, we gained the open, stony *hamada* (plateau) again, and travelled on until, in the far distance, I detected a great, gaunt ruin. Plodding onward wearily through the furnace-heat of sunshine, we reached it about two hours later, and halted under its crumbling walls.

Like a solitary beacon of civilisation, the ruined arches of a great stronghold rose over the sea-like level of desolation which spread out to an immense distance south and west. The rugged, uneven valley below, with its green strip of herbage, continued far into the stony level, and beyond, northwards, the desolate waste stretched towards a great dark mountain.

Astonished, I stood gazing at the spacious dimensions of this time-worn relic of the power of the ancients. It seemed half a castle, half a temple, built of hewn stone, without cement, and ornamented with Corinthian columns. Apparently the place had suffered considerably by the depredations of the

Arabs, who, during succeeding centuries, had carried away most of the sculptures; nevertheless, there was much about this relic of a bygone age to excite curiosity, and to cause one to recollect the fact that years before our era the Romans had penetrated as far as that place. That their dominion was not of a mere transitory nature the ruin seemed clearly to show, for it had nearly two thousand years ago been a great castle, and, no doubt, a centre of a departed and forgotten civilisation. Yet to-day this region is unknown to European geographers, and upon both English and French maps of the Great Sahara it is left a wide blank marked "Desert."

Of Labakan I learnt that it was known to his people as the Hall of the Great Death. According to the Arab legend he related, a Christian ruler called the White Sultan, who lived there ages ago, once made war upon the Sultan of the Tsâd, defeating him, and capturing his daughter, a girl of wondrous beauty. Intoxicated by success, and heavily laden with booty, the White Sultan returned to his own stronghold, followed, however, by the defeated monarch, who travelled alone and in disguise. Attired as a magician, he obtained audience of his enemy, then suddenly threw off his disguise and demanded the return of his daughter. But the White Sultan jeered at him, refused to part with the pearl of his harem, and ordered the sorrowing father to leave his presence, or be consigned to a dungeon. He withdrew, but as he went he cast his ring of graven jacinths upon the ground, and prophesied that ere two moons had run their course, a disaster, terrible and crushing, would fall upon his Infidel foe. Then, retiring to a cavern, he lived as a hermit, and through the months of Choubât and Adâr, for fifty-nine nights and fifty-nine days, he invoked continuously the wrath of the Wrathful upon his enemy. On the sixtieth day his prophecy was fulfilled, for a terrible fire from heaven smote the palace of the White Ruler, and the poisonous fumes from the burning pile spread death and desolation throughout the land. Through the whole of the White Sultan's broad domains the death-dealing vapours wafted, and the people, the wise men, ministers, and the Sultan himself, all fell victims to the awful visitation. The only person spared an agonising death was the daughter of the Sultan of the Tsâd, who, after the fire was subdued, found the treasure stolen from her father untouched, and carried it back with her to the shores of the Great Lake. Thus was she avenged.

"Since that day," added the pirate of the desert, "the Hall of the Great Death, with its courtyards and gardens, has been tenantless, the wealthy city that once surrounded it has been swallowed up by the shifting sand, and so completely did Allah sweep away the dogs of Infidels, that even their name is now unknown."

Much interested in this magnificent monument of the Roman occupation, I left Labakan squatting and smoking in its shadow to wander through the ruins. Upon the centre stone of the arched gateway that gave entrance to the great hall I deciphered the inscription "PBO. AFR. ILL.," (Provincia Africae illustris.) encircled by a coronal, while below was a trace of a chariot and a person in curious attire following it on foot. Besides a representation of an eagle and a few Berber names roughly graven, I could, however, find no other inscription on the portals, so proceeded to examine the grey walls of the inner courts.

While thus engaged, a stealthy movement behind me caused me to start suddenly, and as I did so, I beheld my enemy!

Silently, with his long, bright knife ready in his hand, he had crept up, and at the very instant I turned he sprang upon me. Ere I could unsheath my poignard, he held my throat in iron grip, and his eyes, flashing like those of some wild animal, were fixed with murderous hatred upon mine.

"Thou art at last in the Hall of the Great Death, which is the Grave of the Infidels, and thou shalt die!" he cried, holding his knife uplifted ready to strike.

I was held to the spot, stricken by a sudden dread.

"So this is how thou treatest the stranger who falleth into thy merciless clutches!" I gasped, scarcely able to articulate, but struggling desperately.

"Thou, dog of hell, art no stranger!" he said, with a string of blasphemies. "Thou hast escaped from our camp and brought upon us disaster, defeat, and dishonour. Thou hast obtained actual possession of the Crescent of Glorious Wonders, and even at this moment there is concealed upon thy person a secret message to the Hadj Mohammed ben Ishak, of Agadez. Confess where thou hast hidden the Crescent, or thou shalt assuredly die!" His knife was poised aloft; his hand trembled, impatient to strike me down. Yet I was powerless in his grasp!

"I cannot tell thee!" I answered.

"Thou liest!" he cried. "Dost thou deny also that thou hast any secret message addressed to the *imam*, upon thee?"

"I deny nothing," I gasped. "It was thee, paltry pilferer, who stole the box from me in the *kahoua* in Algiers; thee who offered Gajére a bag of gold to assist in my murder! I know thee, Labakan! Rest assured, that if thou killest me, my assassination will speedily be avenged."

His fierce, brutal countenance, hideously distorted by uncontrollable anger, broadened into a fiendish grin as, with a loud, defiant laugh, he cried—

"Hadj Absalam is Sultan of the Desert, and Labakan his Grand Vizier. We care naught for Infidels who seek to avenge thee, nor for the *homards* who bear arms against us. Speak! Dost thou still refuse to disclose the hiding-place of the Crescent of Glorious Wonders, or to deliver unto me thy secret message?"

"I do," I gasped.

"Too long then have I tarried and wasted words upon thee, courier of evil!" he shrieked, shaking me in his rage and tightening his painful grip upon my throat. At that moment, however, I succeeded in wrenching free my right hand from the outlaw's grasp, and, desperately clutching the hilt of my thin, curved blade, unsheathed it. It was a struggle for life. Again he grasped my wrist and held it immovable.

"Cur of a Christian! thou who hast sought to bring ill-luck, disaster, and destruction upon us, shalt no longer pollute True Believers with thy baneful presence!" he roared furiously, adding, "Die! rot in the grave of the Infidels that is called the Hall of the Great Death! Curse thee! May Eblis condemn thee and all thine accursed race to the horrible tortures that are eternal, and may Allah burn thy vitals!"

"Thou hast brought me here to murder me!" I cried. "Yet I am willing to explain to thee the whereabouts of the Crescent, if thou wilt tell me of the fate of Zoraida, Daughter of the Sun."

"The Lalla Zoraida?" he cried, in surprise. "Then it *is* true thou knowest her! We have not been mistaken! Thy dog's eyes have rested upon her unveiled face; her beauty hath been defiled by thy curious gaze, and she hath spoken with thee, telling thee of wonders the secret of which she was charged to preserve under penalty of death!"

"She hath told me nothing," I answered, still helpless in his murderous grasp. "For many moons have I journeyed over oasis and desert, *hamada* and dune, in search of the truth, but nothing, alas! hath been revealed."

"She entrusted to thy keeping the Crescent of Glorious Wonders; she unveiled before thee, an Infidel; therefore the punishment to which she was condemned is just."

"What was her punishment?" I gasped breathlessly. "At least tell me whether she still lives."

"The hand that wrought treacherous deeds was sent thee, so that thou mightest gaze upon the result of thy gallant adventure," he answered sternly.

"Yes, yes, I know. Its sight was horrible!" I said, shuddering, his words bringing back to my memory the cold, dead, bejewelled lingers in all their sickening hideousness.

"Disgraced in the eyes of the people of Al-Islâm, untrue to her creed, faithless to her people, she hath already received the just reward of spies and those who play us false. The vengeance of the Ennitra shall also fall upon thee!"

"Was she murdered?" I demanded. "Tell me."

"She, the One of Beauty, who was possessed of powers strange and inexplicable, exhibited to thee wonders that none have seen, marvels that she alone was able to work," he continued, murder lurking in every line of his dark, forbidding countenance. "The Great Secret that hath for generations been so zealously-guarded by our people she gave into thine unscrupulous hands. To thee, a dog of a Christian—upon whom may the wrath of Allah descend—she transferred her power, thus allowing her people to be ignominiously defeated and slaughtered by the *homards*. Of the disasters that have fallen upon us, of the misfortune that ever dogs the footprints of those of our men who set out upon expeditions, of all the discomforture that hath been experienced by us; nay, of the terrible doom that hath overtaken the perfidious Daughter of the Sun who entranced thee, thou art the author."

"Merciful Allah!" I cried loudly. "I have been unconscious of having brought catastrophe upon thee. True, I am not of thy creed, but—"

"Silence, thou bringer of evil! Let not the name of the One of Might pass thy polluted lips," he cried, glaring into my face with fierce, passionate anger. "To thee we owe the loss of the Marvellous Crescent. With it our good fortune hath departed. Crushed by defeat, the downfall of Hadj Absalam seemeth imminent, owing to the false, fickle sorceress Zoraida—may Allah burn the hell-vixen!—having fallen under thine amorous glances. Upon thee her power hath fallen, and as thou refusest to give back to us that which is our own, thou shalt not live to witness the rising of to-morrow's sun."

"Doth thy Korân teach thee to murder those who are innocent?" I shouted in a tone of reproach, struggling strenuously, but in vain, to free my hand.

"The Book of the Everlasting Will saith that those who fight against the True Believers and study to act corruptly shall be slain, or shall have their hands and feet cut off, and that the Infidel shall have none to help him."

"Loosen thine hold!" I cried again, vainly exerting every muscle. "Felon and outlaw! thou hast seized me by coward stealth, fearing to fight in open combat. If thine hand strikest me, my blood will swiftly be avenged!"

"Spawn of a worm! I have brought thee hither to kill thee!" he hissed between his firmly-set teeth. "Christian dog! Son of a dungheap! Thou, whose ill-favoured white features so fascinated the One of Beauty as to cause her to forsake her people and leave them powerless in the hands of their hated enemies—thou hast uttered thy last word! To-morrow thou wilt be carrion for the vultures!"

"Curse thee, cut-throat!" I shrieked, turning my dagger upon him, but only succeeding in inflicting a gash upon his brown wrist. "Thou, brigand of bloody deeds, hast followed me here into the distant desert to assassinate me secretly, to satisfy thy craving for the shedding of blood, but I prophesy that thou wilt—"

In the terrible death-embrace the words froze on my parched lips. His brown, sinewy arm fell swiftly between my aching eyes and the golden blaze of sunlight. A sharp twinge in the breast told me the horrible truth, and the hideous, dirty, repulsive face glaring into mine seemed slowly to fade into the dark red mist by which everything was suddenly overspread.

I felt myself falling, and clutched frantically for support, but with a nauseating giddiness reeled backwards upon the sand.

A rough hand searched the inner pocket of my gandoura, and tore from my breast my little leathern charm-case, without which no Arab travels. Upon my ears, harsh and discordant, a short, exultant laugh sounded hollow and distant.

Next second a grim shadow fell, enveloping me in a darkness that blotted out all consciousness.

Chapter Thirty One
Kaylúlah

Insanity had seized me. Dimly conscious of the horrible truth, I longed for release by death from the awful torture racking me.

The pain was excruciating. In my agony every nerve seemed lacerated, every muscle paralysed, every joint dislocated. My brain was on fire. My lips dry and cracking, my throat parched and contracted, my eyes burning in their sockets, my tongue so swollen that my mouth seemed too small to contain it, and my fevered forehead throbbing, as strange scenes, grim and terrifying, flitted before me. Pursued by hideously-distorted phantoms of the past, I seemed to have been plunged into a veritable Hâwiyat. Forms and faces, incidents and scenes that were familiar rose shadowy and unreal before my pain-racked eyes, only to dissolve in rapid succession. My closest friends mocked and jeered at my discomforture, and those I had known in my brighter youthful days renewed their acquaintance in a manner grotesquely chaotic. In this awful nightmare of delirium scenes were conjured up before me vividly tragical, sometimes actually revolting. Bereft of reason, I was enduring an agony every horror of which still remains graven on the tablets of my memory.

Over me blank despair had cast her sable pall, and, reviewing my career, I saw my fond hopes, once so buoyant, crushed and shattered, and the future only a grey, impenetrable mist. My skull seemed filled with molten metal that boiled and bubbled, causing me the most frightful nauseating torment which nothing could relieve, yet with appalling vividness sights, strange and startling, passed in panorama before my unbalanced vision. By turns I witnessed incidents picturesque, grotesque, and ghastly, and struggled to articulate the aimless, incoherent chatter of an idiot.

Once I had a vision of the green fields, the ploughed land, the tall poplars and stately elms that surrounded my far-off English home. The old Norman tower of the church, grey and lichen-covered, under the shadow of which rested my ancestors, the old-fashioned windmill that formed so prominent a feature in the landscape, the long, straggling village street, with its ivy-covered parsonage and its homely cottages with tiny dormer windows peeping forth from under the thatch, were all before my eyes, and, notwithstanding the acute pain that racked me, I became entranced by the rural peace of the typical English scene to which I had, as if by magic, been transported. Years had passed since I had last trodden that quaint old street; indeed, amid the Bohemian gaieties of the Quartier Latin, the ease and idleness of life beyond the Pyrenees, and the perpetual excitement consequent on "roughing it" among the Arabs and Moors, its remembrance had become almost obliterated. Yet in a few brief seconds I lived again my childhood days, days when that ancient village constituted my world; a world in which Society was represented by a jovial but occasionally-resident city merchant, an energetic parson, a merry and popular doctor, and a tall, stately, white-haired gentleman who lived in a house which somebody had nicknamed "Spy-corner," and who, on account of his commanding presence, was known to his intimates as "The Sultan."

I fancied myself moving again among friends I had known from my birth, amid surroundings that were peaceful, refreshing, and altogether charming. But the chimera faded all too quickly. Green fields were succeeded by desolate stretches of shifting sand, where there was not a blade of grass, not a tree, not a living thing, and where I stood alone and unsheltered from the fierce, merciless rays of the African sun. Fine sand whirled up by the hot, stifling wind filled my eyes, mouth, and nostrils, and I was faint with hunger and consumed by an unquenchable thirst. Abnormal incidents, full of horror, crowded themselves upon my disordered intellect. I thought myself again in the hands of the brutal Pirates of the Desert, condemned by Hadj Absalam to all the frightful tortures his ingenious mind could devise. Black writhing asps played before my face, scorpions were about me, and vultures, hovering above, flapped their great wings impatient to devour the carrion. I cried out, I shouted, I raved, in the hope that someone would release me from the ever-increasing horrors, but I was alone in that great barren wilderness, with life fast ebbing. The agonies were awful! My brain was aflame, my head throbbed, feeling as if every moment it must burst, and upon me hung a terrible weight that crushed my senses, rendering me powerless.

Visions, confused and unintelligible, passed in rapid succession before my aching eyes, and I became awestricken by their revolting hideousness. The dark, villainous face of Labakan grinned at me exultingly, and the scarred, sinister visage of Hadj Absalam, the mighty Ruler of the Desert, regarded my agonies with a fierce, horrible expression, in which the spirit of murder was vividly delineated. Suddenly despair gave place to joy. Demented and rambling, I imagined that my hand was grasping the Crescent of Glorious Wonders, the lost talisman that would restore me to happiness with the woman I loved. But, alas! it was only for a brief second, for next moment in a sudden pang of excruciating pain a darkness fell, and everything, even my physical torment, suddenly faded.

I think I must have slept.

Of time I had no idea, my mind having lost its balance. My lapse into unconsciousness may have lasted for minutes or for days, for aught I knew. At last, however, I found myself again wrestling with the terrible calenture of the brain. My temples throbbed painfully, my throat was so contracted that I scarce could swallow, and across my breast acute pains shot like knife-stabs.

Dazed and half conscious, I lay in a kind of stupor. In the red mist before my heavy, fevered eyes a woman's countenance gradually assumed shape. The pale, beautiful face of Zoraida, every feature of which was distinct and vivid, gazed upon me with dark, wide-open, serious eyes. Across her white brow hung the golden sequins and roughly-cut gems, and upon her bare breast jewels seemed to flash with brilliant fires that blinded me. Nearer she bent towards me, and her bare arm slid around my neck in affectionate embrace.

Almost beside myself with joy, I tried to speak, to greet her, to tell her of the treachery of the outlaw who had struck me down; but my lips refused to utter sound. Again I exerted every effort to articulate one word—her name—but could not. A spell of dumbness seemed to have fallen upon me! Her lips moved; she spoke, but her words were unintelligible. Again I tried to speak, yet, alas! only a dull rattle proceeded from my parched throat. Upon her face, flawless in its beauty, there was an expression of unutterable sorrow, a woeful look of blank despair, as slowly and solemnly she shook her head. Her arm rose, and its sight shocked me. The hand had been lopped off at the wrist! Then, with her beautiful eyes still fixed upon mine, she bent still closer, until I felt her lips press softly upon my cheek.

Her passionate kiss electrified me. From my brain the weight seemed suddenly lifted, as the phantom of the woman I loved faded slowly from my entranced gaze. So distinctly had I seen her that I could have sworn she was by my side. Her warm caress that I had been unable to return, was still fresh upon my cheek, the tinkle of her sequins sounded in my ears. The sweet breath of attar of rose and geranium filled my nostrils, and the fair face, full of a poignant, ever-present sorrow, lived in my memory.

Thus, slowly and painfully, I struggled back to consciousness.

It was sunset when the villain Labakan struck me down, but, judging from the brilliance of the bar of sunlight that fell across me when at last

I opened my eyes, it was about noon. At least twenty hours must have elapsed since I had fallen under the assassin's knife; perhaps, indeed, two whole days had run their course!

As I stretched my cramped, aching limbs, a sudden spasm shot through my breast, causing me to place my hand involuntarily there, and I was amazed to discover that my gandoura had been torn open and my wound hastily but skilfully bandaged with strips torn from a clean white burnouse. Who could have thus rendered me aid? Labakan certainly had not, therefore it was equally apparent that some other person had discovered and befriended me. Again I glanced at the bandages in which I was swathed, and found they were fastened by large jewelled pins that were essentially articles of feminine adornment. It seemed cool and dimly-lit where I was lying, and presently, when full consciousness returned, I made out that I was in a subterranean chamber built of stone and lighted from the top by a crevice through which the ray of sunlight strayed. Let into the dark walls were iron rings. They showed that the place was a dungeon!

With some of my clothing removed and my body covered by a coarse rug, I was lying upon a broad stone bench, and when presently I felt sufficiently strong to investigate, I was astonished to discover that my couch had been rendered comfortable by a pile of silken and woollen garments—evidently the contents of a woman's wardrobe—which had been placed on the stone before I had been laid thereon. Upon the floor beside me lay a small skin of water, some dates, Moorish biscuits, and sweetmeats. Whoever had brought me there had done all in their power to secure my bodily comfort, and it seemed evident that I owed it all to a woman. Apparently she had emptied the contents of her camel's bags in order to make me a bed, for my head was pillowed on one of the soft silken cushions of a *jakfi*, and the blanket that covered me bore a crude representation of Fathma's hand in order to avert the evil eye.

(Jakfi: A kind of cage mounted on a camel in which the wealthier Arabs carry their wives across the desert. Sometimes called a *shugduf*.)

Who, I wondered, had snatched me from the grave and placed me in that silent underground tomb?

The painful throbbing in my head that had caused my temporary madness was now gradually abating, and after considerable difficulty I succeeded in raising myself upon my elbow, gazing anxiously on all sides with calm consciousness. The opposite end of the curious stone chamber was plunged in cavernous darkness, and I strained my eyes to ascertain what mystery might there be hidden. While doing so, my gaze fell upon a piece of paper which lay upon the water-skin close to my hand. Taking it up eagerly, I held it in the golden streak of sunshine, and saw upon it Arabic characters that had been rudely traced, apparently with a piece of charred wood. After considerable difficulty, on account of the hurried manner in which the words had been scrawled, I deciphered it to be a message which read as follows:—

"Praise be to Allah, opener of locks with His name and withdrawer of veils of hidden things with His beneficence. Upon thee, O stranger from beyond seas, be the best of blessings, and salutation, and perfect peace. O Elucidator of the Great Mystery, know thou that a friend hath given thee succour and will not forsake thee, even though the vials of murderous wrath have been poured out upon thee. If thou readest these words, hope for thou mayest yet confound the plots of thine enemies and discover that which thou seekest. Though strange things may meet thine eyes, fear not, for in the darkness there is yet light. Thy presence will be demanded ere long. Therefore rest and recover, in the knowledge that thou art under the secret protection of an unknown friend. Praise be upon thee, and may Allah's wrath fall heavily upon those who seek thy destruction!"

A sudden faintness again seized me. The paper fell from my nerveless grasp, as with a strange, sinking feeling I lapsed again into unconsciousness. Hours must have passed; how many I know not, but when I again awoke, the grey light of early dawn was struggling through the small crevice. My wound felt easier, and, supporting myself upon one arm, I drank a few drops of water from the skin. Close to my hand I found a tiny paper packet bearing the label of a French pharmacy in Constantine which showed it to contain quinine. The drug would, I thought, prove beneficial to me, so I swallowed some of the powder, and ate two or three dates to remove the bitter taste. As the light increased, and I found myself in full possession of my faculties, I re-read the mysterious message, and commenced a minute examination of my bandages. The latter had been skilfully adjusted, evidently by a woman. With the exception of a dull soreness in my chest, the pain had left me, and my temperature had fallen considerably. The fever had abated, and I felt confident that the drug that had so frequently been of benefit to me in the past would once more prove serviceable. I tried to rise, but could not, therefore I lay throughout that day, vaguely wondering where I was and how I came to be there alone, yet not uncared for. My eyes fixed themselves upon the impenetrable darkness of the opposite end of the mysterious chamber, vainly striving to pierce the gloom. Now and then a lizard or some other reptile would emerge from the crevices and scuttle along over the stones in search of food, otherwise there prevailed the dead silence of the tomb.

I desired to rise, in order to ascertain whether I was actually a prisoner. The entrance to the strange chamber was apparently at the opposite end, hidden in the darkness. As the light grew stronger, I examined the walls, finding they were constructed of huge blocks of stone now black with age. Indeed, my surroundings were decidedly uncanny, and although the place was cool, yet light and air would have been preferable. Satisfying my hunger with some *ajwah* (dates stoned and pressed into a paste) and *kahk*, (a kind of bread), I spent the day in alternate dozing and silent thoughtfulness until the single ray of sunlight disappeared, and night crept slowly on. For hours I slept, and when I awoke refreshed, it was again day. My wound seemed even less painful, and, having eaten and drawn some water from the skin, I succeeded, after some difficulty, in rising. The woman's dresses of silk and gauze that had formed my couch were sadly creased and tumbled, and upon some of them were dark, ugly stains where blood had flowed from my breast.

But it was my intention to explore thoroughly and without delay the sepulchral place into which I had been so mysteriously introduced. I had not the slightest knowledge of where I was; and could only suppose that some persons, having found me, had taken me to that chamber, and, being compelled to continue their way, had left all they could devise for my comfort. Yet, whoever had done this knew me, and was well aware of the object of my journey, facts which were plainly proved by the message traced in charcoal.

Girding my loins with my sash, and sticking into it the jewelled-hilted knife which I found lying near, I started, with unsteady gait caused by weakness, on a tour of investigation. With my feet falling noiselessly upon the dust of years, I strode to the opposite end of the chamber, where the light did not penetrate, and then discovered that it led into a second chamber of about the same size, situated at right angles with the one I had been occupying. At the further end of this bare, gloomy apartment a faint glimmer showed in the arched roof, where the light struggled through between a long but narrow space between the massive masonry. Groping onward, my foot suddenly caught some object, and, stumbling, I fell prone upon my face. As I put out my hand to break the fall, I grasped something, over which a moment later I ran my hands to ascertain its nature. Horrified, I drew back with a cry.

My fingers had touched a heap of bones!

Regaining my feet, I stood for a few moments in hesitation, but ere I stepped over the obstruction to move forward, my eyes had grown accustomed to the gloom, and then, where the shaft of uncertain light struck the wall a grim and startling spectacle met my gaze. Lying in a niche similar to that in which I had spent so many hours of agony and unconsciousness was a complete human skeleton! With the grey light struggling through the roof and falling full upon it, the remains presented an appearance hideous and ghastly. The lower part of the skull had fallen away, an arm had dropped off, and the cavities where eyes once gleamed gave the upturned skull a hideous appearance. A wisp of long dark hair, twisted and matted, was still attached to the skin of the skull, a portion of which seemed mummified, and upon the thin finger-bones that rested upon the stone some rings of gold and tarnished silver still remained. By the length of the hair, the character of the rings, and the fact that on one of the ankles there still remained a bangle, it was apparent that the remains were those of a woman.

Approaching closer, I examined the bones, and found a small collar of iron encircling the neck, to which was attached a chain that was riveted to a ring in the wall a few feet away. The woman, whoever she had been, had died in captivity.

Looking around, I was surprised to notice another object crouched down against the wall, and this proved on investigation to be the skeleton of a second woman, chained like the first, and who had evidently died while seated cross-legged upon the floor. In the soft dust that had been whirled in by the sandstorms, skulls and bones of all kinds were lying about in profusion, showing that in that dungeon captives were either murdered or starved to death, and that the corpses of previous victims were allowed to remain there and rot within sight of those confined there. What horrors must those prisoners have suffered, compelled to spend day and night with a body in the most hideous stages of decay!

I stood gazing at the gruesome remains. For several days had I lived in this charnel-house, in ignorance that the bones of the departed were my companions, but now, on discovering the truth, I desired to leave the tomb-like dungeon without delay.

Near the skeletons were two saddle-bags apparently well filled, but I did not pause to investigate their contents, for I was too anxious to leave the place. True, the written message; said I should gaze upon strange things, but I had been utterly unprepared for the discovery of these hideous relics of the dead. Onward among the bones with which the place seemed thickly strewn I groped, in eager search of some means of exit, until I came to the wall at the further end of the dark chamber; then, failing to discover any door, I started to go slowly around the place, feeling the walls carefully with both hands. Nearly two hours I spent in a search that was tedious, and which in my enfeebled condition caused my wound to pain me considerably.

All, however, was in vain. Noon came and went, and my active fingers travelled rapidly over every portion of the rough, dust-covered walls of the rectangular dungeon, but no trace of a door could I discover, though I made a systematic investigation of every portion of the place. There were no means of escape. It seemed suspiciously as if I had been brought there and walled in to share the fate of the other unfortunate wretches whose whitening bones told so horrible a tale!

Sinking upon the couch that had been arranged for me by unknown hands, I endeavoured to devise some means of extricating myself. If it had been intended that I should die in that gloomy tomb, why had means of sustenance been provided for me; why had my janitors provided me with a bed composed of a woman's wardrobe? The letter told me to rest and to recover in order to pursue my search. Alas! had I not been pursuing a will-o'-the-wisp? Had I not been actually in Agadez, and passed under the shadow of the mosque, yet unable to seek the old *imam* who held the key to the mystery? The Crescent of Glorious Wonders—the strange object that was to bring Zoraida and me prosperity and happiness—was lost, and, weak and ill, I was now a shattered and rudderless derelict drifting on the lonely sea of despair.

Time after time I deciphered the mysterious message I had found by my side when consciousness returned to me, but it brought no satisfaction. Anxious to escape from that grim sepulchre, yet failing to discover any way out, I paced to and fro, wildly agitated. It was indeed strange. I had certainly been brought there, yet there was no door through which I had passed. I examined the whole of the roof minutely as far as I was able, but there was nothing whatever to show that entrance was gained from the top, while every part of the walls was of stone, which led me to the conviction that there was no secret door. Again and again I stumbled onward, with eager hands feeling the ancient, roughly-hewn blocks, but failing to discover anything to raise my hopes. Indeed, as the afternoon wore by and the light slowly faded, I became dejected, feeling that at last I had fallen hopelessly into the hands of enemies who had resolved that, walled up in that sepulchre, I should endure the tortures of hunger and thirst, and afterwards die a horrible and lingering death.

I ate only a few mouthfuls of *kahk* and took only a few drops of water, just sufficient to moisten my parched throat, for I was determined not to give in without a struggle, and therefore intended to make my supplies last as long as possible. After an elaborate calculation, I arrived at the conclusion that with economy I should have sufficient to sustain life for about a week, therefore I partook only of what was absolutely necessary for subsistence.

Through the crack above my couch I could see daylight had faded, and at last, in despair, I cast myself down, wearied and faint, and fell asleep.

My wound became very painful, and I think the delirium must have again crept over me, for during the night strange phantoms seemed to haunt me with horrifying vividness, and my mind became partially unbalanced by the mental torture which fastened itself upon me. Through those long dark hours wild words that had neither context nor meaning fell from my fevered lips, as periods of imaginary joy were succeeded by hideous debauches of despair. Consciousness returned after I had indulged in a *kaylúlah*, (a sleep about 9 a.m. It is believed among the Arabs to cause poverty and wretchedness), and when the narrow bar of sunlight fell across me, I rose and ate the few mouthfuls of food I allowed myself. Then once more there commenced a search for means of egress.

Every crevice and corner I searched diligently, hoping to discover some secret door; but in an hour I paused to rest. Feeling weaker, for the least exertion overcame me, I suddenly remembered the two saddle-bags, and out of sheer curiosity, and perhaps a desire to occupy my time, resolved to see what they contained. Dragging one of them into the light close to my couch, I drew the knife from my sash and ripped it open. It contained a miscellaneous collection of articles almost valueless, yet to me they were of considerable interest, as they were mostly of European manufacture, and at some time or another had evidently belonged to unfortunate travellers. A couple of watches bore the names of London makers, and there were knives from Sheffield, several British-made revolvers, a sovereign purse, and other things which belonged unmistakably to Western civilisation.

After I had turned out the first bag, I dragged in the second and cut it open in a like manner, finding a similar assortment inside. One by one I pulled them out, inspected them, and cast them in a heap upon the floor, when suddenly I grasped some object larger than the rest and drew it forth.

Its appearance amazed me. I could scarcely believe my eyes, half persuaded for the moment that I had again lapsed into delirium, and that it was merely a chimera of my disordered imagination. But no, I was in perfect possession of all my senses. My eager, trembling fingers tore open the worm-eaten leathern case, and a second later there was disclosed to my gaze an object which caused me to utter a loud cry of joy.

I had regained that for which I had long mourned as lost. Reposing in its case, uninjured and apparently untouched, was that half-hoop of cabalistically-engraven iron upon which all my hopes were founded—the Crescent of Glorious Wonders!

Chapter Thirty Two
The Ghuzzat of the Senousya

Grasping the Crescent with both hands, I examined it minutely, convincing myself that it actually was the strange object that Zoraida had given me. I recognised its curious engraving and the undecipherable hieroglyphics that had so puzzled me.

How it came to repose where I had discovered it was a profound mystery. Apparently the thief of the Kel-Fadê, who had snatched it from me, had replaced it in its case and pushed it into his saddle-bag along with the miscellaneous proceeds of other raids, and then, by some means, both the bags had been deposited in that chamber for safe keeping. The entrance to that gruesome sepulchre was, no doubt, a hidden mystery, therefore the thief imagined his treasure safe from prying fingers. But I had regained it, and meant to retain possession of it, and to learn the great insolvable Secret even though my life might be jeopardised. If Zoraida still lived, I might, after all, be enabled to carry out her extraordinary commission, and so earn that peace and happiness that was my promised reward. By this thought hope revived within me, as with redoubled energy I endeavoured to detect some means by which to escape. With the Crescent of Glorious Wonders once again in my possession it was my determination to return to Agadez, even at the risk of arrest, and seek Mohammed ben Ishak, the one person in the whole world who could impart to me the abstruse knowledge upon which depended my future. Yet, with the Crescent within my grasp, and only a few days distant from Agadez, I was, nevertheless, an utterly helpless prisoner, doomed to the companionship of the ghastly dead, until I too should pass the threshold of the Silent Kingdom.

Through the day I searched for means of exit, unceasingly examining the roof of my prison, but finding nothing to lead me to suppose that a door was concealed. How I had been placed there was a mystery. Once, about noon, I was startled by hearing a voice deep and resonant, yet I reassured myself that it was merely fancy, and that I was alone. After long search, I ate and drank, then sat helpless and dejected, examining my regained prize, which, alas! was still useless to me. To return to Agadez with it in my possession seemed a forlorn hope. All my thoughts centred upon the woman whose grace and beauty held me enmeshed. In a frenzy of madness I rose and paced that silent unknown tomb where hideous, crumbling skeletons seemed to mock me, and where the stillness and gloom were so complete and appalling.

Suddenly an object caught my eye that I had not before noticed. Close to the niche in which the bones of one of the victims reposed, an iron ring was fastened in the wall about a foot from the floor. The slanting ray of light from above was falling at that hour quite close to it, revealing that the dust encrusting other parts of the floor had been removed in the vicinity. Upon the white beaten earth there was a large dark stain, about the size of my hand. This aroused my curiosity, for it appeared suspiciously like a stain of blood, and I remembered that my wound was still open when I had been brought there. The thought flashed across my mind that some secret mode of entrance was therein hidden, yet I examined carefully the ring, and found it an ordinary one, evidently used to chain up prisoners, and securely embedded in a huge block of roughly-hewn stone about two feet square.

My hands carefully felt the ring, but it was rough and deeply rusted, showing that it had not been used as a handle. It was curious, though, why the dust should have been removed from the floor at that spot, and why at that place only should there remain a trace of blood. With the hilt of my knife I rapped upon the stone, but there was no sound to give rise to further suspicion, neither was there any opening around the block. It fitted closely like the others, and had probably been built in there for centuries.

Taking the ring in both hands, I tugged at it, at the same time, however, feeling the effort was useless. The idea of moving a gigantic block of stone of that size was preposterous, and when I found I had expended my strength in vain, I laughed aloud as I wiped my brow. Pausing, I again examined its surroundings minutely. Though there was nothing whatever to show the block was movable, I instinctively felt that some secret mode of exit lay concealed there.

Again a voice startled me. Like a muffled wail it sounded, and I was undecided as to whether it might not have been caused by the wind passing over the crevice above that admitted light and air into the charnel-house. Having rested to regain breath, I essayed another attempt. Setting my feet firmly on either side of the block, I threw my whole weight backward, and pulled frantically at the ring of iron. Holding my breath, and setting my teeth firmly, I was exerting every muscle, when suddenly there was a harsh, grating sound.

The great block of stone moved forward nearly six inches!

In my weak state the smallest exertion produced hard breathing, therefore I was compelled to pause for a few moments in intense anxiety. At last I had discovered the secret!

Again I tugged at the great rusty ring, moving it towards me still further. Then, on careful investigation, I discovered that the block of stone was not solid, but formed the front of a great stone drawer, long and narrow like a coffin, and just large enough to admit the body of a man.

By dint of herculean effort I drew the great drawer out nearly four feet, then, taking the Crescent of Glorious Wonders in its worm-eaten case, together with some *ajwah* for sustenance, I entered the coffin-like receptacle. With difficulty I squeezed through the shallow trough, that proved several feet longer than the thickness of the wall, and, to my relief, I found myself, a moment later, in a narrow, subterranean passage, enveloped in an impenetrable darkness. With feet falling silently in the thick white dust, I felt my way along for some distance, taking several abrupt turnings, until strange noises caused me to halt, listening breathlessly.

Human voices were raised in a solemn, mournful chant!

Noiselessly I crept forward in the darkness, coming at length to a blank wall, and then, turning sharply to the right, a thick plush curtain arrested my progress. Drawing it aside slightly, and with infinite care, I gazed in wonderment upon a scene weird and remarkable. It held me spellbound.

The underground apartment was about fifteen feet wide, forty feet long, and nine feet high, with one end slightly raised as a kind of platform. Illumined by a great fire that burned in a sort of brazier in the centre, there were nine flat stones ranged round, and upon these sat aged, white-bearded Arabs. They were councillors of one of the secret societies of Al-Islâm. Around were assembled other younger Sons of the Desert, presenting a strange and weird appearance. Each bore an ostrich feather, stuck in the rope of camel's hair that encircled his head, and carried in his left hand a green-painted *derbouka*.

The councillors, swaying their bodies in unison, were uttering strange, monotonous incantations, when suddenly a very old and feeble man, in scarlet burnouse, descended from the platform where he had been enthroned, bearing in his hand a small black snake that writhed and twisted itself around his bony wrist. Advancing to the brazier, he cast the reptile into the fire, and as it was consumed, the whole of those present set up a long, shrill wail.

"Accursed be the race of dogs!" they cried. "May the entrails of the Infidels who have over-run the glorious land of the True Believer be burned

Zoraida | 183

like yonder serpent, and may the pestilence overtake them. May the vultures lay bare their bones, and may their dust be scattered across the plains, even unto the Great Sea."

The words revealed to me their purpose. During my travels, I had, on many occasions, heard rumours of secret Moslem societies, although their existence had often been denied in the European press, the Paris *Figaro* excepted. Frequently had I longed for an opportunity of investigating these associations, formed for the purpose of concerted and decisive action against the Christians, and now, by a most curious circumstance, I found myself present at one of their secret meetings. The most violent and far-reaching of these organisations was, I had been told, the Ghuzzat, a development of an offshoot of the Senousya, and was composed of the wildest fanatics of the Aïssâwà sect who were followers of the elder Senousi, a Shereef, or descendant of the Prophet. Leaving Mecca some years before, the marabout had wandered through Egypt, Tripoli, and Tunis, finally building a large *zawya* (Hermitage) at El-Beida, near the fountain of Apollo. At that time the Arabs of the province were pagans. He preached against the Christian invaders, healed the sick, performed "miracles," and established for himself a reputation, so that the Bedouins carried his fame across the Desert, through the Oasis of Ojila-Jalo, into Wadai and Mourzouk, Agadez, and Timbuktu, and even into Morocco. The present head of this society for the simultaneous massacre of all Christians throughout the Soudan, was a descendant of Senousi, named El-Mahdi, and its members were the most mad-brained fanatics, who took oaths upon the Korân to exterminate the dogs of Infidels. (El-Mahdi. Meaning "Led by God." There are many families of that name in the Sahara.) Thus it was with combined interest and trepidation that I stood gazing upon a remarkable sight that no European had ever before witnessed. Though the Christian invader had been tolerated along the Barbary littoral, it was apparent that the fierce hatred and treachery of Al-Islâm was only stifled, and the teaching of fanatical societies, such as these, was that all Roumis should, in an unguarded moment, be massacred without mercy. Indeed, the weird chant that fell upon my ears at that moment was to the effect that Allah, Requiter of good and evil, bade them rise and revenge the wrongs that followers of the Great Prophet had suffered at the defiling hands of the accursed.

The blazing brazier was, I noticed, very similar in shape to that in the mysterious chamber in Algiers, to which Zoraida had conducted me. Could it be that she too was a member of this widespread secret league to secure the extermination of the Christians?

The chant concluded, the strange rites of the Ghuzzat (Fighters for the Faith) commenced. After performing a *sujdah*, (a single "prostration," with the forehead touching the ground, performed from a sitting position), the whole of those present recited the Surat-al-Ikhlas, which is also sometimes called the Kul Huw' Allah, or the Declaration of Unity, of which the following is the translation:—

"Say, He is the one God!
The eternal Allah!
He begets not, nor is He begot!
And unto Him the like is not."

The aged man in the scarlet burnouse, who seemed to be the high priest of the order, turned towards the raised platform, and, amid a sudden silence, clapped his hands. When lo! a curtain at the rear was drawn aside, revealing a kind of small circular hut, built of dried palm branches, with an opening at the top. Those assembled cried aloud, as if in fear, but the priest comforted them with an Ayat, or Korânic verse, and almost at the same moment, eleven men, barefooted, with their burnouses cast aside, marched in single file before the hut.

The secret ceremony was a strange admixture of religion and paganism, for, as they descended from the dais and marched round the circle of seated councillors, the chief sprinkled them with blood from the tip of an ostrich feather. Then they were lined up with their backs to the hut, and in the uncertain light shed by the flaming brazier presented a most weird spectacle. Suddenly, at a word from the man in the red robe, the conspirators gathered around, thumped their *derboukas*, and set up a plaintive howl, while the eleven kept perfect cadence with the right foot.

A slight pause ensued, when the eleven turned and moved onward, until the first—a lad not over ten years of age, apparently just initiated into the mysteries of the foul plot against Europeans—reached the mysterious hut. Then, halting for a second, he deliberately plunged his arm down the hole in the top, and, amid low, guttural expressions of approbation that sounded from all sides, dragged forth a huge serpent, about five feet in length, and the size of a man's wrist. Struggling desperately, he attempted to hold it about four inches from the head with his teeth, but at first he could not open his mouth wide enough, and this seemed to cause the onlookers considerable anxiety. The head of the reptile was to the left, and to break the dead weight of the great snake, the lad held its writhing body up with his left hand. The boy was not four feet in height, so the contrast was remarkable. At length, however, he succeeded in fastening his teeth firmly in the serpent's back, and the march and chant were resumed, to the accompaniment of monotonous drumming. The man behind the snake-carrier took his feather from his head and seemed to be chasing the serpent towards the left, so as to keep the reptile's fangs from the lad's face.

The third man picked out a snake from the little hut and carried it as did the boy, while the fourth acted as the second man did; thus it went on till eight of the men were in motion. By the time the fifth couple were ready to take a snake, the first had completed a few circuits of the space. Then he took the reptile from his mouth and gently threw it upon the ground, where it lay motionless in a state of catalepsy, and, marching round while the onlookers prostrated themselves, murmuring strange incantations, he again reached the hut, and took another of the writhing reptiles. This was continued until all the snakes had been used.

Meanwhile, the reptiles that had been thrown at the feet of the silent, statuesque councillors of the order were brushed by feathers by half a dozen men, and then handed one by one to the conspirators grouped around, who gripped them near the head, and, while holding them still and motionless at arm's length, recited a declaration of adherence to the secret league. When all the snakes had gone through the weird ceremonial, and were in the hands of the dark-faced wanderers of the plains, the grave councillors rose, and their places were taken by a similar number of mysterious-looking women, enveloped from head to foot in black haicks, which entirely covered them, except for the two holes through which their bright eyes peered.

As they seated themselves upon the flat stones, the note of the dismal chant was changed to a more shrill one, and the men, led by the venerable chief of the conspirators, formed a circle around them, while each drew from beneath his burnouse a *Hamáil*, or pocket Korân.

"The grave is darkness and good deeds are its lamp," they commenced chanting, moving slowly round the seated women. Then followed a supplication which commenced, "O Prince! O Ruler! O Ancient of Benefits! O Omniscient! O Lord of the Three Worlds! O Thou who givest when asked, and who aidest when Aid is required, receive this our prostration, and preserve us from dangers, and make easy our Affairs, and broaden our Breasts."

From the remainder of their remarkable prayer I gathered that as they, the Ghuzzat of the Senousya, had been able to hold in submission the venomous serpents in their hands, so would they, on the day when the standard of revolt was raised in Algeria, in Tunis, and in Egypt, hold in their clutches the swaggering Roumis who had defiled their land. Then, as they proceeded one after another to kill the reptiles, they declared, with one accord, that with as little compunction as they now treated these snakes, so would they slaughter without mercy the men, women, and children of the Infidels. Their extermination, like vermin, would alone, they declared, "bring coolness to the eyes of True Believers."

Suddenly, almost before I was aware of it, the eyes of the aged chief met mine! I had, in my eager desire to witness the strange scenes, indiscreetly pulled back the curtain too far, revealing the whole of my head!

The high priest, clapping his hands, produced in a moment a dead silence.

"Lo!" he shouted in a loud voice. "My sons and daughters, prying eyes have fallen upon us. We are discovered!"

His words produced an effect that was electrical. Fifty voices, with one accord, demanded further explanation.

"We have, O children, been watched from behind yonder curtain!" he cried. *"Our secret is known!"*

I waited for no more. A dozen fierce fanatics dashed towards the spot where I had been standing, but without thinking of any place of refuge, I plunged down the dark passage. In a second I was pursued. Oaths and vows of vengeance sounded behind me, and with the Crescent of Glorious Wonders grasped tightly in my hand, I sped onward until I ran headlong against a wall. Turning quickly at right angles, I found another long, unlighted subterranean passage. Dashing headlong down it, I turned to right and then to left through its intricate windings, and as the footsteps of my pursuers sounded behind me, I suddenly became aware that I was retracing my steps to my tomb-like dungeon. From those who sought me I could expect no mercy. Death only could expiate my crime. I had discovered the intentions of Al-Islâm, and even though I might declare myself a follower of the Prophet, I had not been initiated into the mysteries of the Ghuzzat, and would therefore be put to death as a spy.

The fierce fanatics, with knives unsheathed, were at my heels, and, redoubling my speed, I tore along, stumbling over the rough floor and grazing both legs and arms in my wild flight. To strike me down the conspirators were straining every muscle, yet I managed to keep on, until, taking two sudden turns immediately after one another, I remembered that I was near the entrance to the secret chamber.

It was my only chance. If they were unaware of the existence of the charnel-house with its crumbling bones, then, perchance, I might escape. In the darkness I could distinguish nothing. What if I had passed the entrance, and came at last to a blank wall! The thought unnerved me. Voices behind me sounded harsh and deep, still I dashed onward until my feet caught in something, and, stumbling, I fell.

I knew the accident must result in my death. In a few moments the keen knives of the conspirators must reach my heart.

My hands came into contact with stone. Frantically I grasped it, realising with gratification that I had fallen over the great coffin-like drawer that gave entrance to my prison. In a second I recovered myself, and, entering the half-open trough, crawled through it, with the Crescent still in my hand.

Finding myself on the opposite side of the wall, I lost no time in grasping the iron ring, and, with the last strenuous effort of which I was capable, succeeded in dragging the drawer towards me. It was done on the impulse of the moment; then I waited, not daring to breathe.

Hurrying footsteps sounded outside, with shouts of "Death to the spy! He holdeth our secrets, and must not evade us! Kill him! His entrails shall be burned with the snakes!"

Nearer they came, as if searching for the secret entrance.

In pulling the drawer inside I had closed it, and, clinging on to the ring, determined that it should not be opened while strength was left to me.

For a second the footsteps, sounding dull and muffled in the dust, seemed to halt outside. Then joy filled my heart a moment later, when they hurried onward, and the angry cries receded in the distance.

Evidently, with the stone trough drawn inside, nothing remained in the subterranean passage to denote the whereabouts of a hidden entrance. Likewise it was apparent that they knew not the existence of the secret sepulchre.

Panting and exhausted, I sank upon the ground. I had again escaped!

Chapter Thirty Three
A Penalty of Beauty

The glimmer of sunset struggling through the chink above faded quickly. Upon my strained ears the sound of hurrying footsteps fell, but again died away. My pursuers were returning after their fruitless errand. Yet would they relinquish the search now they knew a stranger held their secrets?

The conspiracy was against Christians in general and the power of France in Algeria and Tunis in particular, therefore they knew that if the military authorities in Algiers were acquainted with the facts, the great Army of Africa would be held in readiness to crush the revolt in its earliest stages. No doubt the memory of the great insurrection which commenced at Souk Ahras in 1871, and which eventually proved so disastrous to them, had not yet been obliterated, and they still recollected how, although the revolt spread everywhere through Kabylia at the word of the Sheikh el-Haddad, yet their people had struggled in vain against the invaders, and the standard of Al-Islâm was at last torn down by the Infidels, and their mosques were defiled by their conquerors' feet. Since that day, Turcos, Spahis, Zouaves, artillery, and infantry had posts everywhere throughout the French sphere of influence, and conspiracy was punishable by the guillotine. True, the plot I had discovered was being perfected beyond the frontier, yet the conspirators were no doubt members of a tribe under French rule, therefore amenable to the laws of their conquerors. Thoughts such as these caused me to reflect that these men who had schemed revenge were not likely to content themselves with the knowledge that I had escaped. If, as I supposed, I was still in the ruined Hall of the Great Death, it would be impossible for a man to get away unnoticed, the ruins being situated on high ground in the centre of a barren wilderness. But evidently they were unaware of the existence of that secret chamber, and doubtless they considered my sudden disappearance most remarkable.

As, however, the dead silence remained unbroken, I at length resolved to wait patiently till the morrow, and in the pitch darkness groped my way towards my couch. The violent exertion had almost exhausted me, and I sat for some time feeling very faint and ill. My wound pained me considerably, for the bandages had shifted and haemorrhage had again been produced. Presently, however, I felt better, and after a draught of water and a few dates, I stretched myself and fell asleep.

Until the streak of sunlight told me that the noon had passed, I waited patiently, with ears open to catch every sound, and, hearing nothing, I at last resolved to make another dash for liberty. Placing some food and the leathern case containing my prize in my sash, I pushed forth the stone drawer gently and crept through its narrow aperture. Gaining the dark passage, I hesitated for a few seconds, then decided to explore it in the opposite direction, for I had no intention of again approaching the chamber wherein the secret rites had been performed. A few feet from where I had emerged, the passage, like a rabbit's burrow, declined steeply, and grew so narrow and low that I was compelled to stoop. Advance was difficult in the darkness, yet I crept on, hoping to arrive eventually at some exit. To my disappointment, however, the passage penetrated still deeper into the earth, and gradually narrowed until I was compelled to creep along on all fours. The atmosphere was choking, and I began to fear asphyxiation.

Suddenly I emerged into what appeared to be a larger space, and my feet struck stone steps. Finding I could now stand upright again, I ascended, wondering whither they might lead. Not a ray of light showed, and in the darkness I stumbled onward, for the steep stairs were worn and in some places fallen away. As I toiled upward, the air seemed more fresh, and I felt that in the immediate vicinity there must be some outlet from that subterranean labyrinth. Gaining the top, I groped about until I felt a door strengthened by strips of iron. It was small, but very heavy. What, I wondered, did it conceal?

Discovering a handle, I slowly turned it. To my satisfaction, the door yielded noiselessly, and I found myself in a great luxuriously-furnished chamber, the air of which was fragrant with attar of rose and the downy divans were of pale yellow silk.

Scarce daring to enter, I paused. It was, I could see, a woman's apartment.

A man's deep voice was raised in anger, and I saw lying in a lazy attitude on a divan before me, with her hair unbound, a beautiful girl with face unveiled. She was richly dressed in silk of palest heliotrope, with a heavy golden girdle and a tiny sleeveless zouave jacket of rose-pink velvet, heavily trimmed with gold. Her skin was as fair as an Englishwoman's, but her eyebrows were darkened with kohl, and her forehead was almost hidden beneath its sequins. A dainty little fez trimmed with seed pearls was set jauntily upon her handsome head, and as she lay, one bare foot hanging over the edge of the divan in an attitude full of languid grace, she toyed with her rings, and her bejewelled breast heaved and fell in a long, heavy sigh.

Her companion, a well-dressed Arab, tall, long past middle life, with a face in which brutality was strongly marked, was striding up and down the sweet-scented apartment, hurling at her fearful imprecations and insults, and expressing profound disgust that he had ever stooped to caress her.

My feet fell so noiselessly upon the soft carpet that neither had noticed my entrance, therefore I stepped back, re-closing the door, but leaving it ajar, in order that I might witness the domestic disagreement.

"Thine harsh words wound more deeply than thy blows," she observed, with a sigh, as the man paused to gain breath.

"By my beard, wench! thou art verily the off-scum of Eblis, upon whom the mercy of the One Merciful can never rest! Thou hidest in thine heart secrets, and refusest to tell me that which I demand. I will degrade thee, woman, to the meanest slavery; thou shalt wash the feet of those who have been thy slaves. Though thou art a beauteous damsel—a houri fitted for the Sultan of the Ahír—thou—"

"Hast thou lived thy threescore years, and failed to discover that sometimes the face is not an index to the mind?" she interrupted, with a flippant air.

"With thee, accursed betrayer of secrets and worker of iniquity, have I learned that soft caresses may prove as the coils of a venomous serpent, and that a woman's lips may conceal poison!" he cried, halting before her with clenched fist.

Throwing her head back upon her silken cushion, she laughed at his passion.

"Thou thinkest that thou hast cleverly deceived me—eh?" he hissed. "Thy dark eyes sparkle like the stars, because thou, thrice-cursed offspring of Satan, knowest that—that I have been fooled, tricked by thee, who hast received from me every luxury! Had it not been for me, thou wouldst have been at this moment the slave of some common camel-driver, and—"

"Even that would have been preferable to imprisonment within thine harem. Would that thine accursed generosity had been showered upon some other woman than upon me," she cried, rousing herself and looking straight and fearlessly into his angry, bearded visage. "True, in return for thy favours, I have tried to love thee. Thou hast been pleased to exalt me to be chief of thy wives, to bestow upon me jewels of great price, and to place me above those who were envious because their faces pleased thee not. Towards thee I have been faithful, and I have ever kept thy private affairs locked within my bosom."

"And thou hast now exposed the greatest of all our secrets—the intentions of the Senousya!" he said.

"I tell thee thou liest!" she cried in anger, clenching her small white hand; "I have divulged nothing—I swear!"

"Perhaps not personally; nevertheless thou hast been instrumental in allowing the designs of our brotherhood to become known, and punishment will of a verity overtake thee. May the judgment of Allah fall upon thee! upon thy father, and upon thy tribe of murderers and harlots, and may their vitals be devoured by the fire unquenchable! Thou, bringer of evil upon our house, hast done thy best to thwart the *Jihad*, (Holy War) against the dogs of Infidels."

"I cannot understand thy meaning," she said, puzzled. "Thine accusations are as complicated as the lock of the Holy Ka'abah."

"Vile offspring of Shirm!" he cried in a sudden paroxysm of passion, seizing her roughly by the wrist. "To feign ignorance will not avail thee. I have discovered the depths of thy perfidy. Perhaps thou wilt deny that, on thy return hither with thy slaves, thou didst discover amid the ruins of the Hall of the Great Death a man who had been wounded?"

She started, turned pale, and looked at him with an expression that betrayed fear of his terrible wrath.

"Thou, cursed handmaiden of hell, viewing this stranger from beyond the Atlas with compassion because his face found favour in thine eyes, bound up his wound, and, placing him in a *jakfi* upon one of thy camels, secretly bore him hither. Though thou didst not know him, thou gavest him food, and tended him while he lay fever-stricken and unconscious; and when thou arrivedst here, thy women, acting under thine orders, assisted thee to secrete him in some place the existence of which thyself only hast knowledge. Speak!" he added, twisting her white arm until a cry of pain escaped her. "Speak, woman! tell me if I utter the truth."

"Release me, brute!" she cried, springing to her feet, with her beautiful eyes flashing angrily. "Thinkest thou that I will endure thy tortures longer? No! I hate thee! I will depart. Another may rule thine harem, and may she find her position happier than mine hath been!"

"But remember thou art my prisoner. Dost thou admit or deny what I have said?" he demanded, pale with passion.

"If thou accusest me of infidelity, I can deny it upon the Book of the Everlasting Will," she replied, drawing herself up haughtily. "Other allegations I deign not to answer, even though thou art my captor, and I am in thy power."

"Then know, O woman of evil, who hast been defiled by the eyes of a stranger, the man thou hast aided now holdeth the secret of the Ghuzzat, and—"

"He—he hath learned of the plot against our Oppressors?" she gasped. "Tell me, how did it occur?"

"At the council of the Brotherhood he was discovered behind a curtain in the secret Chamber of Assembly, and no doubt can exist but that he watched and obtained knowledge of our rites and intentions. Upon me, therefore, will fall the fierce and fatal wrath of the Brotherhood, for within my walls hath their secret been betrayed!"

"But—how did he gain the Chamber of the Assembly?" she stammered.

"Thou canst best answer that question," the old Arab replied sternly.

"I am in ignorance, truly," she declared, a deadly pallor overspreading her fair countenance. "I have done naught of which I am ashamed."

"But canst thou not, perfidious wench, see that our secret is out?" he continued angrily. "The stranger, though pursued, disappeared mysteriously, and though every search hath been made, he hath not been found. By this time he is most probably on his way into Algeria, where he will spread the warning, and thus the armed hordes of the Roumis will be on the alert, and our aims utterly defeated."

"And thou hast attributed the misfortune of thy fellow-conspirators to me?" she exclaimed, in a tone of reproach.

"I tell thee thou alone art the author of the evil that hath befallen us," he cried, with flashing eyes. "For women of Eblis who betray True Believers, the fire of hell is already prepared. There, the flame and smoke shall surround thee like a pavilion, and if thou beggest relief, thou shalt be relieved with water like molten brass that shall scald thy face. The mischief is worked, the secret is divulged, and already the Brotherhood are leaving, never to return. Thee, devilish daughter of Waila, have we to thank for introducing secretly a spy into our midst!"

"I have acted as I thought fit. Leave my presence!" she commanded, with imperious gesture. "I will no longer suffer the brutal insults of a man I hate. Ere the sun hath set I shall have freed myself of thine hateful bonds and left thine accursed roof."

"Thou shalt never go from here alive!" he hissed in her ear, holding her slim white wrist and dragging her roughly towards him. "Already thou, the cause of our downfall, hast defiled thine hands with the blood of a stranger, and allowed him to obtain knowledge whereby our secret designs will be thwarted. For such offences there is but one penalty. It is death!"

"Thou, who art tired of me, bring these accusations in order to justify my murder!" she gasped in indignation and alarm. "My people have not forgotten, and assuredly will they seek blood revenge."

"Enough!" he growled between his teeth, as in a second he drew a knife from his waist, and, clutching her by the throat, forced her upon her knees. "Thou art the handmaiden of Al-Dajjâl, and the mark of the Câfer is set upon thy brow. Thou shalt die!"

She shrieked as his powerful arm poised in mid air.

"Spare me! Spare me!" she implored piteously. "Be thou merciful!"

But he jeered at her appeal, and, forcing her backward in his iron clutches, gripped the gleaming, murderous weapon.

"Thy people, thou Misriyah! will never know thy fate, for ere sundown thou wilt be as offal, and vultures will strip thy bones," he said, with a fiendish grin. "See! this my knife seeketh thy polluted heart."

Unhesitatingly I dashed forward, springing upon him from behind and wrenching the weapon from his grasp. I was not a moment too soon, for in another instant the keen steel would have been plunged into the heaving white breast of the fair, fragile jewel of the harem.

"Who, pray, art thou, who darest obstruct me?" he demanded angrily, turning upon me in amazement.

"Thy wife hath saved my life, and it is my duty to save hers," I answered boldly.

"See!" she panted, suddenly recognising me. "See! it is the stranger who was wounded!"

"The stranger who hath learned at his peril the secret of the Ghuzzat," he added, with grim sarcasm. "As he is thy protector, he is most probably thy lover also!"

"That I deny," I answered quickly. "I have known nothing of this lady until to-day."

"Liar!" he shrieked in rage. "Thou boldest our secret. Only thy death will expiate thine eavesdropping!" and ere I could realise his intention, he had drawn a second knife from his waist and made a desperate lunge at me. With difficulty I managed to parry the blow, and for a few moments we engaged in deadly combat. His young wife, alarmed, rushed to a door which led into a beautiful courtyard, and shouted for help. Her cries were answered immediately by two black slaves of gigantic stature, who, in obedience to her commands, flung themselves upon their master, twisted the knife from his fingers, and in a trice had bound his hands behind his back with a cord they seemed to have brought for the purpose.

"Slaves! Suffer not thine hands to thus defile me!" he cried, with a look of murder in his flashing eyes, but they gagged him immediately.

His wife, addressing the two negroes, exclaimed—

"It is as I expected. He hath attempted to strike me to earth, and had it not been for this stranger, I should have been murdered. Three days ago I gave thee certain instructions—carry them out."

"We will, O Lady of Great Beauty," they both replied.

"Then remove him."

The two black giants opened the small door by which I had entered, and almost before the old Arab could mumble a protest, they had hurried him out and down into the dark subterranean passage that led away into the unknown maze below.

"That course is my only chance of escape," she said, turning to me in explanation, when the door had closed. "Had I fallen, thou too must have perished, for thy food in the secret chamber could not have lasted long," she panted, holding her hand to her breast as if in pain.

"I have to thank thee for rescuing me from death," I said. "I had no idea who was my deliverer until I overheard thy conversation."

"But thou didst not obey the instructions I left thee in my letter," she said in a tone of reproach. "Searching for a means of exit, it seemeth, brought thee unto the Chamber of Assembly; hence my disgrace and thine own peril."

"But thine husband—whither have they taken him?"

"To the chamber in which thou hast remained hidden these few days. Before he is placed there, he will be rendered unconscious, so that he may not know of the secret entrance. There will he remain while I reach a place of safety."

"Merely detained?" I asked dubiously.

"Yes. Though in his wrath he tried to kill me, I bear him no malice, for when I get back to mine own people, I shall be safe. If he discovers how to get out of his prison, then he will live. If not"—and she shrugged her shoulders.

"Though thou art his wife, thou dost not appear to regret thy departure."

"Why should I, when I have been detained here over a year against my will? If thou only knewest the dreary life a woman leadeth in the hands of a brute she hates and despises—ah!" and she shuddered.

"Then thou wilt now regain freedom?" I said, surprised.

"Yes. For many moons have I waited in patience for this moment, and at last I have accomplished what I sought. Already the preparations are being made. My two trusty slaves will return when their work hath been accomplished, and in an hour camels will be packed in readiness for our journey."

"Our journey? Dost thou intend that I should accompany thee?" I asked.

"Certainly. To disguise thyself as a female slave, veiled and enshrouded by a haick, is thine only chance of escape. *La bodd annak taroóh maaki!*" ("You must go with me") and she sank back again upon her divan, as if the exertion had utterly exhausted her.

"Thou art stronger than when I found thee lying as one dead in the ruins of the great Palace of the White Sultan," she exclaimed, as she lay stretched among her cushions, with her bright, beautiful eyes looking up to mine. "Dost thou feel well enough to withstand the fatigue of travel?"

"Yes, quite," I answered. "But ought we not to prepare for flight immediately?"

"There is no need for haste," she answered. "This is mine own private apartment where none dare enter, so take thine ease, for we must journey far before *el maghrib*."

All trace of her agitation had now disappeared, and as we chatted calmly, I asked, "Why didst thou take compassion upon me—a stranger?"

"I had accompanied two of the wives of the man who hath held me in hateful bondage on a portion of their journey towards Assiou, and in returning we halted to rest under the shadow of the Hall of the Great Death. There I discovered thee, and, in order to give thee succour, was compelled to resort to the expedient of placing thee within the secret chamber. Some time previously I had heard that thou wert journeying south."

"Who told thee? What didst thou know of me?"

"I knew that thou, a Roumi, hadst undertaken to reach Agadez in order to perform a secret mission, and that thou hadst proved loyal and true to the woman who loved thee. For her sake as well as for thine I snatched thee from certain death, and if Allah giveth us His mercy and blessing, we both shall now regain our freedom."

"Art thou aware of the name of the woman to whom I am betrothed?" I inquired, in amazement.

"She is—or was—called Zoraida, and was known to our people as the Daughter of the Sun."

"Thy people? Then thou art of the tribe of the Ennitra?" I exclaimed.

"True," she answered, with a smile. "I am the daughter of those who have so long and eagerly sought thy destruction."

"But what of Zoraida? Tell me; is she still alive?" I asked anxiously.

"Alas! I am uncertain. Here in this my prison only strange and vague rumours have reached me. Once I heard that she had been murdered in Algiers, but soon afterwards that report brought by the caravans was denied, and since then much curious gossip regarding her hath been circulated. The last I heard was, that, disguised as a camel-driver, she had followed thee to Agadez."

"To Agadez?" I cried. "How long ago did that astounding news reach thee?"

"Early last moon. One of my slaves heard it while travelling with some of the women to Assiou. I am inclined to regard it, however, like so many other rumours, as mere idle talk of the bazaars, for only a few days before that, I heard of her holding sway at the palace of our lord Hadj Absalam."

"Canst thou tell me nothing authentic?" I asked, disappointedly.

"Alas! nothing," she answered, with a sigh. "Our Lalla Zoraida is mighty and of wondrous beauty, but the mystery that surroundeth her hath never been penetrated."

Chapter Thirty Four
Under the Green Banner

Through a vast, barren wilderness, peopled only by echoes, we journeyed over drifted sand-heaps, upon which every breath of the hot poison-wind left its trace in solid waves. It was a haggard land of drear silence, of solitude, and of fantastic desolation. In the Desert a vivid sense of danger is never absent; indeed, even more so than upon the sea, for the mere lameness of a camel or the bursting of a water-skin is a disaster that must inevitably prove fatal to the traveller.

Our caravan consisted of ten persons only, six trusted and well-armed male slaves, two females, my pretty companion, and myself. Our departure from the great ancient stronghold in which the handsome girl had been held captive had not been accomplished without much exciting incident; but luckily my disguise as a female slave, in ugly white trousers and a haick that hid my features, proved complete, and, the imperious pearl of the Sheikh's harem having announced her intention of journeying to Assiou to join his two other wives, we were at last allowed to depart without any opposition on the part of her husband's armed retainers. The whole thing had been most carefully arranged, and the details of the escape were cleverly carried out without a hitch.

On setting out, Lalla Halima—for such she told me was her name—and myself, as her attendant, travelled together in one *jakfi* placed upon a swift camel, gaily caparisoned with crimson velvet; but as soon as we had got fairly away, I slipped off my white shroud, and, resuming a fez and burnouse, mounted one of the animals whereon our food was loaded. In camping during those blinding days under a dead, milk-white sky, I spent many pleasant, idle hours with Halima, and when travelling—which we usually did at night—we generally rode side by side. Notwithstanding the terrific heat, life in the Desert seemed to suit her far better than the seclusion of her sweet-perfumed harem, for, true child of the plains as she was, she felt her heart dilate and her pulse beat stronger; declaring to me that she experienced a keen enjoyment in "roughing it" in that trackless wilderness. Indeed, the spirits of all of us became exuberant, the air and exercise seemed to stir us to exertion, and, altogether, we constituted a really pleasant party.

Lolling lazily at her ease among the silken cushions in her *jakfi*, she would chat with charming frankness through the night, as in the moonlight we plodded steadily onward guided by one of the slaves to whom the route was familiar. She told me all about herself, of her childhood, spent in the barren desert of the Ahaggar, of a visit she paid to Algiers one Ramadân, and of the attack by the Kel-Fadê upon the little village of Afara Aouhan, her capture, and her subsequent life in the harem of the Sheikh. From her I gleaned many details regarding her people, of their wanderings, their power in the Desert, and their raids upon neighbouring nomad tribes. Many were the horrible stories she told me of the fierce brutality of Hadj Absalam, who was feared by his people as a wicked, unjust, and tyrannical ruler, and who, despising the French military authorities, delighted in the torture of Christian captives, and endeavoured to entice the Zouaves and Spahis into his mountain fastnesses where he could slaughter them without mercy. The Great Pirate's impregnable palace, the fame of which had long ago spread from Timbuktu to Cairo, she described in detail, and if what she said proved correct, the place must be of magnificent proportions, and a very remarkable structure. The harem, she said, contained over four hundred inmates, the majority of whom had fallen prisoners in various raids, but so fickle was the pirate Sultan of the Sahara, that assassination was horribly frequent, and poison, the silken cord, or the scimitar, removed, almost weekly, those who failed to find favour in the eyes of their cruel captor.

Yet, regarding Zoraida, I could gather scarcely anything beyond the fact that the subjects of Hadj Absalam knew her by repute as the most beautiful of women, and that few, even of the female inmates of the palace, had ever looked upon her unveiled face. One evening, as we rode beside each other in the brilliant afterglow, I admitted how utterly mystified I was regarding the woman I loved; to which Halima replied softly—

"Who she is no one can tell. Her name is synonymous for all that is pure and good, her benevolence among our poorer families is proverbial, and she possesseth a strange power, the secret of which none hath ever been able to discover."

"Thou didst tell me that thy people sought my destruction," I said. "Dost thou know the reason for their secret hatred?"

"I have heard that thou holdest the mysterious power of defeating thine enemies once possessed by the Lalla Zoraida, and that until thy death it cannot return to her," she answered. "But thou dost not seem so terrible as report describeth thee," she added, with a coquettish smile.

I laughed. It was nevertheless strange that my would-be assassin Labakan had made a similar allegation. Remembering that I was accompanying my fair companion upon an adventurous journey to an unknown destination, I said—

"Though we have travelled together these six days, thou hast not yet told me whither our camels' heads are set."

Puffing thoughtfully at the cigarette between her dainty lips, she replied, "Already have I explained that I am returning to my people. The route we are traversing is known only to the trusty slave who guideth us and to mine own people, for there are no wells, and no adventurous traveller hath ever dared to penetrate into this deserted, silent land of the Samun."

"Is it not known to thine enemies, the Kel-Fadê?" I asked, recollecting with bitterness that to the marauders of the tribe that had held her in bondage I also owed my captivity in the Court of the Eunuchs.

"The Kel-Fadê have never penetrated hither," she answered, gazing away to where the purple flush was dying away on the misty horizon. "In three days—if Allah showeth us favour—we shall reach the rocky valley wherein my people are encamped. *Ana fíkalák hatta athab ila honâk.*" ("I am very anxious to get there.")

"But for what reason are thy people so many weeks' journey from their own country?" I asked.

Moving uneasily among her cushions, she contemplated the end of her cigarette. Apparently it was a question which she did not care to answer, for she disregarded it, exclaiming grimly, "I wonder if the occupant of the secret chamber will discover the means of exit?"

"Suppose he faileth? What then?"

"He will share the fate that hath befallen others immured there," she answered, raising her arched brows slightly.

"Immured there by thee?" I hazarded, smiling.

"No," she replied, with a musical laugh. "Thou must not judge me with such harshness, even though my life hath become embittered by captivity in the harem of a monster I hated."

Suddenly I recollected the strange recovery of my mysterious talisman, the Crescent of Glorious Wonders, which was now reposing safely in its case within one of the bags beneath me. Evidently it had been hidden with other booty taken from the caravan with which I had travelled by some one who had regarded it with curiosity.

"Is the existence of that hidden prison known to anyone besides thyself?" I inquired.

"Why askest thou that question? Art thou afraid my lord will escape ere we reach a place of safety?" she exclaimed, with a low, rippling laugh.

"No," I replied. "I have a serious object in seeking information."

"What, wert thou troubled by unwelcome visitors?" she asked, smiling mischievously.

"No; on the contrary, the silence was appalling and the companionship of the dead horrible."

"Ah, forgive me!" she exclaimed apologetically. "It was not my fault that I could not have the place cleared of the bones. There was no time. But in my written message I told thee to fear not."

"But whoever placed me there knew of the secret entrance," I urged.

"True," she answered. "Two of my slaves—he who guideth us towards the encampment of the Ennitra and the man leading yonder camel—carried thee to thine underground tomb, and placed food there for thee."

Her words gave me instant explanation. From the first the countenance of our guide had seemed familiar, and I now remembered where I had seen it. He was one of those who had held me when the Mysterious Crescent had been wrenched so suddenly from my grasp! No doubt it had come into his possession with other loot, which, in order to secure to himself, he had hidden in that place where none could obtain entrance. As he rode on top of his camel quite close to me, I peered into his dark, aquiline face and found its features unmistakable. It was he who had secured me, who had subjected me to slavery, and who had mounted guard over me until I had been purchased by the agent of the Sultan Hámed. Apparently he had not recognised me, and as I again held my treasure safely in my own keeping, I had no desire to claim acquaintance with this slave, who was himself a slave-raider. They were all brave, sturdy fellows, loyal to their mistress, a quality that I admired, for both she and I had interests in common in putting a respectable distance between ourselves and the irate Sheikh of the Kel-Fadê.

"If thy people seek my death, am I not unwise in accompanying thee into their midst?" I queried, after a pause.

"By thine aid I, one of their daughters, have escaped from the bonds of their enemies, therefore fear not, for though the Ennitra rule the Desert harshly with rifle and bastinado, they harm not those who lend them assistance."

I told her of my first experience of Hadj Absalam, and how I had been tortured with the snake, concealing the fact that Zoraida had set me at liberty.

"*Tabakoh câsi.* (His disposition is cruel.) He is hated even by our own people," she exclaimed, when I had concluded. "His brutality is fiendish to us and to strangers alike; but when Infidels are brought into his presence, his rage is absolutely ungovernable. Thy torture was not so horrible as some I myself have witnessed. Once, near Téhe-n-Aïeren, at the foot of Mount El Aghil, a young Zouave soldier strayed into our camp, and, being captured, was brought before him. Because the Infidel's eyes had rested upon one of his women, he ordered them both to be gouged out and sent to the French commandant at Ideles. Then the man's ears followed, then his nose, then his hands, and after keeping him alive in fearful torture for nearly three weeks, the body of the wretched prisoner was covered with date juice and placed upon an ant-hill, where he was literally devoured by the insects."

"Horrible!" I said, shuddering. "Are such tortures common among thy tribe?"

"Alas!" she answered, rearranging her pillow; "cruelties such as these are frequently practised, even upon us. Neither men, women, nor children are safe. Those who give our mighty lord offence always pay the penalty with their lives, but never before they have been tortured."

"Yet thou art anxious to return among them?"

"Yes," she replied, with an earnest look. As she lay curled up in her cage-like litter, she had the air of a little savage with the grace of a child. "I do not wish to be loved as I have been, like a slave," she added in a confidential tone.

"But thou hast ruled the harem of the Sheikh, and hast been chief of his great household," I observed.

"True," she answered. "But there are circumstances in our lives we cannot forget; there are people who dwell always in the house of our memory."

I nodded. The truth was easily guessed.

"Two days before being torn from my people," she continued bitterly, "I met, by mere chance, a man of mine own people whom I have never ceased to remember. It was a chance meeting, and by no fault of mine own was my veil drawn aside. Neither of us spoke, but I knew we loved each other. My father told me he was one of the most daring of the men-at-arms

Hadj Absalam sends against the *homards*, a notorious thief and cut-throat, to secure whose capture the Roumis away at Algiers have offered two bags of gold." She sighed, then added simply, "Though he may be a murderer, I shall love him, even until Allah bringeth me to Certainty." (The hour of death.)

She spoke with the passionate ardour of her race. The love of the Arab woman knows neither the shame nor the duplicity of vice. Proud of her submission as a slave, she can love even a murderer without losing any of her self-respect. In her eyes, her tenderness is legitimate; her glory is to conquer the heart. The man she loves is her master, she abandons herself to him without failing in any duty. A daughter of Al-Islâm, she fulfils her destiny according to the moral traditions and beliefs of her country, and she remains faithful to them by loving the man she chooses; her religion has no other rule, her virtue no other law.

"And you have escaped in order to seek this man?" I observed, smoking calmly.

"Yes. I seek him because I love him. His eyes gave me a sign of affection, the remembrance of which time hath not effaced. I shall find him, even though I am compelled to journey from Ghat to Mequinez, or from the Tsâd to Algiers." The eventuality did not occur to her that, being a warrior of an outlaw band, his bones might long ago have been bleaching in the Desert like those of so many of his fellow marauders. Such a thought, I reflected, would cause her acute anxiety, therefore I did not suggest it. She was hopeful, confident, content; tender and passionate in her love, fierce and relentless in her revenge. Night had fallen, and as under the myriad stars we travelled over rising ground towards the camp of the Desert pirates, she formed a delightful study. Her ingenuous ignorance and intuition of coquetry, the Eastern fascination striving with modest reserve, charmed and amused me, and although the wind commenced to blow up choking clouds of fine sand, compelling her to adjust her veil, yet she would not draw the curtains of her *jakfi*, but continued chatting until we halted an hour after dawn.

The slave guiding us predicted a sandstorm, therefore, before encamping, we turned our faces towards the Holy City, and, as pious travellers, recited the Hizb al-Bahr, the prayer which is supposed to make all safe on either land or sea. Halima with her slaves prostrated themselves upon the sand, and in impressive tones repeated aloud the prayer that commences—

"O Allah, O Exalted, O Almighty, O All-pitiful, O All-powerful, Thou art my God, and sufficeth to me the knowledge of it!" and which has the following strange conclusion:—"Thou didst subject the Moon and Al-

Burak to Mohammed, upon whom be Allah's mercy and His blessing! And subject unto us all the Seas in Earth and Heaven, in Thy visible and in Thine invisible Worlds, the Sea of this Life, and the Sea of Futurity. O Thou who reignest over everything, and unto whom all Things return. *Khyas! Khyas! Khyas!*" (Mystic words that cannot be translated.)

Halima told me afterwards that in this great waterless region of shifting sand, so fraught with perils, a storm was always brewing and the dreaded poison-wind always blowing, therefore men raised their hands to pray as they crossed it.

At sunrise three days later my pretty companion was lying unveiled in her *jakfi*, smoking and chatting to me, her two women riding a little distance behind, when our guide suddenly raised a loud shout of warning which in a moment alarmed the whole caravan. Halima instinctively twisted her veil across her face as she inquired the cause.

The slave drew up his camel near her, replying, while he glanced to make certain that his gun was loaded, "Know, O beauteous Lalla, that we are discovered! Six mysterious, armed horsemen are spurring towards us!" and with his finger he indicated the direction in which his keen, hawk-like eyes had detected them. We all gazed away into the dusky grey where he pointed, and there I saw several mounted Bedouins tearing headlong across the desert in our direction, their long guns held high above their heads, and their white draperies flowing in the wind.

Each of us grasped our rifles, prepared to fight for the protection of our fair charge, while Halima herself, pale and determined, drew a long and serviceable-looking poignard from her girdle and felt its edge. It was evident that the strangers had from afar espied Halima's *jakfi*, and were resolved to possess themselves of its occupant. In this country of lawless slave-raiders those who show fight are treated with scant mercy, therefore we could expect no quarter, and dismounted ready for the combat. On came the horsemen, fleet as the wind, until they got within a short distance of us, when suddenly, without slackening, and still holding their weapons high above them, they poured out a sharp, decisive volley upon us. It was a warning that they intended attack, and that we might surrender if we were so disposed. The bullets sang over our heads unpleasantly, but no one was hit, and without hesitation our seven rifles rang out almost simultaneously. Again and again we fired, but without result, for the six fierce Sons of the Desert galloped onward, shouting a weird war-cry, and dashed in upon us, calling upon us to lay down our arms. One of them, evidently the leader, swinging himself from his grey stallion, seized Halima by the wrist before we could prevent him, but in a second, with a sudden movement, the harem beauty had slashed him with her dagger, inflicting an ugly wound across his hairy arm.

Raising his rifle, he would have shot her dead, had not one of her slaves flung himself between them, crying—

"Pause, O strangers! Tell us of what tribe thou art. If thou leviest tax upon us in this thy country, our Lalla is prepared to accede to thy just demands. If a hand is raised against her, the wrath of the Kel-Fadê will assuredly fall upon thee!"

"Naught care we for the Kel-Fadê, who are accursed by Allah, for they pray not, neither go they upon pilgrimages!" the man answered, with a harsh laugh. "From the waters of the Tsâd, even unto the green slopes of the Atlas, we hold power supreme, and none dare withstand us, for we are feared alike by the Roumis of Algeria and the True Believers of the Desert." Then, brandishing his *jambiyah* (a very keen crooked dagger) above his head, he added, "We are of the Ennitra, and our lord is the mighty Hadj Absalam, Sultan of the Sahara!"

"Then hear me, O brothers!" Halima exclaimed in a loud, firm voice. "I am thy sister!"

"Our sister? But thou art of the Kel-Fadê, our enemies!" the horsemen cried with one accord.

"True. Hear thou mine explanation. Dost thou not remember that the Kel-Fadê—whom may Allah confound!—attacked and burned our village of Afara Aouhan?"

"The sons of dogs killed my father in the massacre," declared one of the men, a brawny giant, who stood leaning on his gun.

"Mine shared the same fate. He was the *oukil*," cried the beautiful girl, whose veil had in the struggle been torn away.

"His name—quick!" exclaimed the leader of the marauders in surprise.

"Hámed ben Abderrahman."

"Then thou art—"

"His daughter Halima."

The black-bearded scoundrel immediately released her, and, bowing, expressed sorrow at having caused her undue alarm, after which, in a few quick sentences, she told him of her captivity and her escape, afterwards presenting me as one by whose aid she was enabled to return to her own people. She did not, however, declare me to be a Christian, therefore they thanked me and gave me peace. They told us that we were distant three hours from the encampment, which they, as scouts, were guarding, but advised us to rest till sundown, as the poison-wind was unusually virulent. Acting upon their suggestion, our tents were pitched, and the six outlaws ate with us, afterwards wrapping themselves in their burnouses and sleeping through the long, blazing day. From them I could gather but little regarding the movements of their people, and though I mentioned that I had heard many reports of the wondrous powers possessed by their Daughter of the Sun, they nevertheless preserved a studied silence. They did not even descant upon her beauty, as I expected they would do. They only grunted approbation. Towards four o'clock, Halima, wrapped in her haick, came from her tent, and very shortly afterwards we were on our way to the camp, guided by the six cut-throats of Hadj Absalam, who rode along with careless ease, carrying their weapons across their saddles, smoking cigarettes, and talking gaily. Strange indeed was this latest freak of Fate. Long had I regarded these people as the most deadly of my enemies, yet I was now entering their camp as their friend!

Our way wound among bare rocks and hills of granite and over broken ground, weird in its desolation, flanked by high blocks and boulders. Several parties of horsemen, evidently scouts, appeared, but, on recognising our escort, allowed us to pass unmolested, until at length, about the hour of *el maghrib*, we came to a vast cleft in the hideous face of earth, and, passing through, found ourselves in a valley in the midst of a great encampment. The ravine seemed covered with tents; indeed, it appeared as if a whole army had encamped there, and I was not surprised when one of the outlaws told me that the fighting force numbered over three thousand.

On descending the rocky defile, I saw in an open space in the centre of the camping-ground three tents close together and more handsome than the rest, while against the clear, rose-tinted evening sky there waved over the centre pavilion the dreaded green silken banner of Hadj Absalam.

"Then thy lord is present with thee?" I exclaimed in surprise, addressing the marauder who rode beside me.

"Yes. When he leadeth us we fear no evil, for he is the Great Sultan of the Sahara, who cannot be overthrown."

Wending our way slowly onward among the tents, our arrival caused a good deal of excitement and speculation among the robbers, who doubtless believed us to be captives. One incident impressed me as especially remarkable. Just as we had entered the camp, three women, enshrouded in silken haicks and wearing their ugly, out-door trousers, were strolling together slowly, as if enjoying the cool zephyr after the breathless day.

No word escaped either of them, but one reeled and clutched her companion's arm, excited and trembling, as if her eyes had met an apparition. I smiled at her intense agitation, wondering whether she had recognised in Halima a hated rival; but until we had turned to wend our way among the tents, she stood motionless, staring at us fixedly through the small aperture of her veil, apparently much to the consternation of her two companions.

The tragic little scene, though unusual, was apparently not noticed by my companions.

Was it Halima's presence that caused the closely-veiled woman such sudden and profound consternation—or was it mine?

Chapter Thirty Five
Betrayed!

That night, as I lay without undressing in the little tent the outlaws of the Desert had assigned to me, I was kept awake for a long time by the sound of voices and the clang of arms. While half the camp slept, the remainder were apparently cleaning their rifles, and sharpening their *jambiyahs*, preparatory, I presumed, to some wild foray. For a long time I lay wondering whether Halima would find her undeclared lover in the camp, or whether he was lying in the sand, sleeping until the blast of Israfil's golden trumpet. Under my pillow reposed the time-worn case containing the Crescent of Glorious Wonders, but my letter of introduction had, alas! been filched from me by Labakan. Was it not possible, I thought, that this evil-faced scoundrel was in the camp. If so, what more probable than that, finding he had not killed me as he intended, he would denounce me to Hadj Absalam as the Roumi who had escaped them after being condemned to death? Such reflections were not calculated to induce sleep; nevertheless, weakened as I was by my wound, the journey had greatly fatigued me, and at last I grew drowsy and unconscious, and became haunted by strange dreams.

I must have been asleep for some hours when a light pressure upon my shoulder awakened me.

"Utter not a word," whispered a soft female voice in my ear. "Danger besetteth thee, but thou, O stranger, art with friends solicitous of thy welfare."

Turning, I glanced upward, and the streak of moonlight that entered revealed a woman enshrouded so completely by her garments that I could not tell whether she were old or young.

"Who art thou?" I whispered, now wide awake and on the alert at her warning of danger. About her there clung an odour of attar of rose.

"I am but a messenger. Rise and follow me in silence," she answered.

"Whither dost thou desire to conduct me?" I inquired, rather dubiously, for I had a vague, apprehensive feeling now that I was among these murderous outlaws.

"To the presence of one who must speak with thee immediately. Ask no further question, for in a few moments thine eyes shall behold, and thine ears shall hear."

Silent and motionless she stood awaiting me, looking like a ghost in the bright moon's rays. Wondering who desired an interview with me at that hour, and half suspecting that Halima had something secret to communicate, I rose, replaced my haick, rearranged the hang of my burnouse, and then announced my readiness to accompany my mysterious visitant.

"There is no Ilah but Allah," the woman whispered piously. "May the Ruler of Death grant unto thee perfect peace!"

"And upon thee peace," I answered, as in obedience to her silent injunction indicated by her raised finger, I followed her stealthily out.

"Let thy lips be sealed," she whispered, conducting me past many tents the occupants of which were soundly sleeping. Silently we sped onward, until we came to the open space, in the centre of which were erected the three pavilions of the pirate chieftain. The entrance to the centre one was guarded by four superbly-dressed negroes with drawn scimitars, who stood motionless as statues. On seeing me, they raised their glittering blades, and made a sudden movement as if to bar my progress, but on a sign from my veiled guide they immediately fell back, allowing us to pass unmolested. Next second, however, a man's voice sounded, and the armed outlaws closed around me. I glanced back, and saw in the white moonbeams the crafty, villainous face of Labakan!

He laughed exultantly, as I saw to my chagrin how cleverly I had been tricked.

Helpless in the hands of these five armed warriors of the plains, I was hurried unceremoniously into the large and luxurious pavilion. On the ground rich rugs were spread, and divans had been improvised out of saddles and boxes. Above, from a lamp of curiously-worked brass, a subdued light fell upon the occupants, three men who, stretched at their ease, were smoking. The central figure, attired in a large white turban and a rich robe of bright amaranth silk, was that of an old man of patriarchal appearance, and as he lifted his head at our entrance, our eyes met.

It was Hadj Absalam!

Betrayed into the hands of my enemy, I stood helpless and dismayed. I had hoped he would not recognise me, and that I should pass as the rescuer of Halima until an opportunity of escape presented itself; but, alas! some one had detected me, and, without doubt, the person responsible for my discovery was the adroit assassin Labakan, the self-styled Grand Vizier of the Sahara, who now stood grinning with pleasure at my discomfiture.

Removing his chibouk, the Pirate of the Desert glared at me fiercely for several moments without uttering a word, slowly raising himself into a sitting posture, an example followed by his two brutal-looking companions. The air was heavy with tobacco smoke that seemed to hang like a pall over the three occupants of the divan.

Labakan, raising his brown, sinewy hand towards me, was the first to break the painful silence.

"Behold! O gracious Master!" he cried. "Report hath not lied. Thine enemy liveth!"

The great Sheikh of the Ennitra rose, his countenance livid with rage.

"Lo! it is verily the accursed son of Eblis, thief of our secrets!" he burst forth in fiery passion. "At length thou art revealed unto us! Thou—who hast brought upon us despair, defeat, and death, who hast defiled the land that we inhabit—art now within our power, and, upon the Book of Everlasting Will, I swear thou shalt not escape. For many moons hast thou evaded us, and though our horsemen have scoured the plains of Ahaggar, the Areg, and the Ahír, even unto the waterless Desert of Tibbou, in search of thee, thou disappearest like the shadow of a cloud. Neither the terrors of the wilderness, nor the knife of our servant Labakan, have daunted thee, but at last thy career hath ended—at last thy doom is nigh!" he cried, thundering forth the final sentence, and shaking his clenched and sinewy fist.

"True, O Ruler of the Desert," I answered, as he paused to take breath, "I have again fallen into thine hands, yet the judgments of the Bedouins are tempered with—"

"Again?" he ejaculated, his black eyes full of angry fire. "All yes! I remember. Thou wert put to the torture which we reserve for dogs of thine accursed race, and thy strength burst the bonds that held thee."

"The influence of this son of an unbeliever, who hath stolen our power, was the cause of our defeat when our brave sons attacked the *homards* on the Oasis of Meskam," added Labakan, apparently determined that the Great Sheikh should forget none of the allegations against me.

"The Ruler of the Desert hath no need of the promptings of a secret assassin," I exclaimed, fiercely turning upon him.

"Silence, dog!" roared the Bedouin chieftain. "Add not to thy crimes by thus rebuking Allah's chosen. By thy clever machinations hast thou learned our secrets and divested us of our power. Thrice have the armed men of thy brethren, the Infidels, attacked and defeated us; thrice have we been compelled to flee from those who have plotted to conquer the True Believers, and all owing to thy crafty theft of the unseen power that once was ours. While thou livest, thou bearest upon thee influence to work our destruction wheresoever we go, but when thou hast been consigned to the darkness of Hâwiyat, then will power and success return unto our people. Ere to-morrow's sun hath set, thou shalt be a corpse, for Allah is swift in punishing."

"He, the One to be praised, is also gracious and merciful," I added. "Dost thou, who hast performed thy *sujdah* within the Harem of Al-Medinah, forget thy Korân?" I asked reproachfully.

"Mention not our Faith with thy polluted lips!" he cried, adding, "'The Infidels are smitten with vileness wheresoever they are found.'"

These words of the Prophet, with which he endeavoured to crush my argument, gave the utmost satisfaction to the men about me, who murmured approbation in an undertone, and nodded their heads expressive of admiration at the wisdom of their sinister-faced, tyrannical chief.

"For many moons have I dwelt within thy land, O mighty Sultan of the Sahara," I said. "Though I have ever acted with honour towards thy people of Al-Islâm, yet I am far spent with travel, and clothed with calamity as with a garment. Why seekest thou my death?"

"Have I not already told thee? Thou hast filched from us the wondrous secret power by which we vanquished our enemies; the unseen force that hath enabled us to rule the Desert. While thou remainest alive, of a surety ruin and extinction threaten us."

"But I am, alas! ignorant of thy strange allegation," I said, earnestly endeavouring to get the angry Arab to speak more calmly. "By what means have I taken from thee this extraordinary influence that once was thine? Tell me, for a slave may not be condemned for an unknown crime."

"Thou knowest well," he answered distinctly, with loud emphasis and glittering eye, placing one hand upon the hilt of his jewelled *jambiyah*, and standing erect with regal air. "It is useless for thee to deny deeds which have worked our defeat, and actions that must ere long be the cause of our downfall."

"I deny nothing, O mighty Sheikh of the Ennitra," I protested. "Years ago, thy valiant race filled me with admiration, and because of that, I learned to speak thy tongue, and read the commands of the Prophet. Times without number have I been the willing servant of thy people of Al-Islâm; nay, even to-day have I brought hither under my protection a fair woman of thy tribe, whom I assisted to escape from a harem in the land of thine enemies."

"A woman?" he exclaimed, with an expression of surprise, and, turning to his attendants, asked, "Who is she?"

"She is named Halima, O Master," answered Labakan. "To me hath she explained that the Infidel intended to convey her to his own land, and only by a ruse did she succeed in getting to our camp. He carried her off from the harem of the Sheikh of the Kel-Fadê, in order to possess her himself."

"Miserable parasites!" ejaculated Hadj Absalam angrily, on hearing the mention of the hostile tribe, "May their vitals be devoured by insects, and may their bodies be given unto the wild beasts! Did the chief of these locusts of the sands hold our kinswoman in bondage?"

"Yes," I answered. "We escaped from the palace of the Sheikh together."

"Behold, O Master!" said the bandit who had attempted to kill me. "He admits that they journeyed in company. He tried by force to cause her to fly with him across the Atlas and beyond the sea, unto the land of the Infidels."

"It's a lie!" I shouted warmly. "Bring her hither, and let her, O Sheikh, relate unto thee her story."

"Already she hath told it," the old chieftain replied. "Already thou art proved to be no respecter of our women, for thine eyes have defiled their unveiled faces, and by thy speeches hast thou caused them to forget the commands of the Prophet, and look upon thee, a white-faced son of offal, with favour."

"My acquaintance with any woman of thy race will not preclude her from drinking of the fountain of Salsabil," (a spring in Paradise), I answered defiantly.

"Thou wilt deny next that thou hast ever spoken with our beauteous Daughter of the Sun!" exclaimed the irate Despot of the Desert, who, as he uttered Zoraida's name, bowed low in reverence, an example imitated by all his followers.

"I deny not my actions, neither shall I attempt to refute the allegations made against me by a murderer," I answered.

My captors laughed jeeringly. I knew by their manner that they were determined that I should die, and I expected no mercy. Yet, despite an inward feeling of despair, I determined to show a bold front. I had been betrayed; but they should not see that I feared them.

"Secretly hast thou entered her private apartment, and remained there alone with her. To thee, son of Malec (the principal angel who has charge of hell), she hath disclosed our secrets—secrets which thou now holdest; hence, thou art the one Infidel in the world who possessest power to work evil upon us."

"Whatever secrets I may have learned I have not used," I protested firmly. "With me a secret remaineth always a secret."

One of the men who had been reclining on a divan smoking, rose, whispering a word into the ear of his angry master. For a moment Hadj Absalam reflected, then asked: "What was the nature of this secret revealed unto thee?"

"To the Lalla Zoraida I promised not to disclose."

"But if, peradventure, I chose to regard thy crimes leniently,—if I even spared thy life,—wouldst thou not explain the nature of the secret wonders thine eyes have beholden?"

"No," I answered firmly. "Not all the Treasure of Askiá, added to my liberty, would unlock my lips."

"The Treasure of Askiá!" gasped the Hadj, glancing quickly round to his attendants with an expression of amazement and alarm that reflected itself upon their countenances. "What knowest thou of it?"

"In the Desert I learned the story of the great king's hidden wealth," I replied innocently.

"Ah!" cried the Sheikh, with sudden ferocity. "I had expected as much. Truly thou art a son of Eblis whose actions are accursed; truly hast thou tasted of the bitter fruit of Al-Zakkum, which hath its roots in hell!"

"Peace be upon thee, O Ruler!" I said. "Thy servant knoweth naught of any such thing as this whereof thou speakest, for never hath he committed any deed to warrant this thy wrath." But he flew into a fit of uncontrollable rage, and hurled upon me every curse that his voluble tongue could utter. To argue was useless. I tried to induce him to explain how I had stolen from his people the secret of their victories, declaring that I held no power which could detract from the success of their raids. But he would vouchsafe no answer to my questions, and only shouted his intention of submitting me to a most horrible series of tortures, before my body should be given to the vultures. The old despot's anger was fearful to behold. He stamped, he raved, he tore into shreds his silken garments, and actually foamed at the mouth.

Zoraida | 213

Voiceless, I stood before him. Amid these fierce marauders, who regarded not the lives of enemies or friends and were awaiting impatiently the order to hurry me off to my death, I was a doomed man. The frowns of Fortune had never been so ominous as at that moment.

Suddenly he paused, panting and breathless, his eyes aflame with hatred, and his face hideously distorted by anger and revenge.

"Speak, dog of a Christian!" he shouted. "Speak! or, by the Prophet and the One, thy profane tongue shall be torn out by the roots. How earnest thou to possess thyself of the Crescent of Glorious Wonders? What hath its possession availed thee? Answer, or—"

There was a sudden movement among the men behind me, who with one accord uttered ejaculations of surprise, as the Sheikh's threat was interrupted by a loud voice crying—

"Silence! Let not another word pass thy lips, on pain of the most damnifying curses that tongue can utter!"

Turning sharply to ascertain who dared thus command the dreaded Sultan of the Sahara to close his lips, I beheld a woman with bare, beautifully-moulded arm outstretched, pointing imperiously towards the proud, regal figure on the divan. The pirate Sheikh trembled before her, staggered as if he had received a blow, then stood silent, not daring to complete the sentence.

Her sudden appearance had caused a pallor to creep over his countenance, as anger gave place to fear.

Advancing, the strange veiled figure stood before the divan just in front of me, with face turned away and arm still uplifted, as in the lamplight her bracelets flashed and gleamed with dazzling brilliancy. She was a veritable Light of the Harem, dressed superbly in gauzy garments of palest mauve, with magnificent jewels in her hair, upon her brow, upon her bare white breast, and upon her delicate ankles. Her heavy golden girdle was richly studded with rubies and sapphires; her long dark tresses, unbound, fell in rich profusion upon her bare shoulders; and about her there clung a sweet, subtle breath of geranium that filled my nostrils. Her attitude was marked with a strange suppleness, astonishingly graceful, and the men who had held me captive before their tyrannical master fell back, as if awestricken by her dazzling presence.

"Hearken!" she exclaimed in clear, musical Arabic, as she unwound the veil from her face. "Knowest thou me?"

"We do! Peace be upon thee, O beauteous Woman of Wisdom, O Lady amongst Women!" they answered with one accord, even to the Sheikh himself, all bowing before her abashed.

"Then behold! I stand at thy divan of judgment to answer for the offences of this Roumi, who hath, by cowardly device, been delivered into thine hands!"

Turning, she suddenly faced me. I was rendered mute by amazement. The woman before whom these outlaws bowed as if in worship was none other than Zoraida!

Upon me there gazed, with unmistakable glances of affection, the calm, beautiful face that had for so long existed only in my dreams, but which was at this moment before me, a living reality!

For an instant my tongue refused to articulate, but, dashing forward and seizing her right hand, I rained kisses upon it, notwithstanding the fierce, guttural exclamations of disapproval uttered on all sides by my enemies. That the lips of an Infidel should thus defile a woman of Al-Islâm, was to them infamous; but in that brief second, the woman I loved whispered in imperfect French—

"Obey. I may save thee!"

The horrible souvenir I had received in Algiers flashed across my mind, and I sought her hand. Almost beside myself with joy, I found it was intact and uninjured! The severed member that had been sent me, and afterwards stolen so mysteriously, was not Zoraida's!

"By what right dost thou, O Daughter of the Sun, interfere between thy Ruler and his foes?" the old Sheikh asked angrily at that moment.

"Against me have thine unfounded allegations been levelled," she answered bitterly, standing by my side, holding my hand in hers. "It is true that this Roumi and I have met, and that he holdeth certain secrets; but I warn thee that if a hair of his head is injured, of a surety will the fearful vengeance of the Unknown fall upon and crush thee and thy people."

"Thou canst not—thou shalt not wrest him from our hands!" cried Hadj Absalam, boiling over with rage. "My will hath already been spoken. He shall die!"

"Then the peril is thine," she said in slow, impressive tones. Her hand quivered, and I could see that she was trembling lest her bold and gallant effort to save my life should prove unavailing.

"Already hath he brought the direst evil upon us," cried the Ruler of the Ennitra. "Besides, for aught we know, he may be the mysterious stranger who, according to report, was present as spy at a meeting of the Ghuzzat, held by the Kel-Fadê, and who escaped so strangely."

"How thinkest thou that a Roumi can understand our symbols of the serpents? Even if he were the mysterious eavesdropper, what could he have gathered with regard to our brotherhood?" she asked, adding, "It seemeth thou art determined to take his life, so thou formulatest unfounded charges against him!"

"Bah! he is thy lover," the sinister-faced old brigand observed, with a sneer. "In thine eyes he is no doubt innocent."

"I acknowledge that upon mine own head should be the punishment for the evils that have befallen our people. Yet, nevertheless, I declare unto thee—"

"If thou lovest a dog of an Infidel," cried Hadj Absalam, interrupting, "thou art no longer worthy our confidence." Then, turning to those about him, he asked, "Do I give utterance to thy thoughts?"

"Yes. Thy words are words of wisdom, O Ruler," they answered with one voice.

Releasing my hand, she raised her alabaster-like arm towards the chief of the outlaws, exclaiming in a loud voice, "If the Ennitra have no longer confidence in me, I will to-night sever the bond that bindeth me to them. Into battle have I led thy people many times, against Infidel and the enemy of our own race alike, and thou hast vanquished thy foes, and compelled them to bite the dust. Against thee have the legions of France been arrayed, yet powerless, and at this moment, thou, Hadj Absalam, art the mighty Sultan of the Sahara, the ruler whose power causeth all men to tremble, from Ghat even unto far Timbuktu. To-day thou hast advanced to this spot hopeful and confident, prepared to wage a war that must be bloody and deadly; but as thou hast lost faith in thy Daughter of the Sun, I shall leave thee to thine own devices. If thou killest the man I love, I shall depart. We twain are in thine hands."

"Canst thou not, O Ruler, kill the false Prophetess too?" suggested a voice from behind. I recognised the tones as those of Labakan!

"If thou takest my life, thou too wilt fall within one moon under the fiery scimitar of Azraïl, even though each man hath the strength of Jalût and the courage of Al-Jassâsa," she exclaimed, with the calm dignity of a queen.

The men jeered at her prophetic utterances, but she looked at them with withering scorn, and heeded them not. For my life she was striving, and cared for naught else. Her beauty intoxicated me, and I stood, even in those critical moments, entranced, as I had before been, by her extraordinary loveliness.

"Al-Sijil hath registered thy deeds," she continued, casting calm, imperious looks at the brigandish band about her. "If thou committest the crime of shedding the blood of those who possess the power by which thou existest as the most powerful people of the Desert, thou wilt assuredly never lave in the stream Zenjebil."

Her words created a visible impression upon them, and seriously they whispered among themselves, until suddenly their Sheikh addressed them, saying—

"Already have I decided that the Infidel shall be put to the torture, that his ears shall be cut off, his eyes put out, and his tongue removed. Are those thy wishes?"

"Thy will be done, O Ruler," they answered; and Labakan added, "Our Woman of Wisdom hath no longer power to lead us unto victory. She is enamoured of this accursed Christian dog who bringest the direst evil upon us."

"Then away with him!" cried Hadj Absalam, waving his arm towards me. "Let his hands be lopped off, and let his end be one of long suffering."

Four men seized me roughly, and were dragging me out, when Zoraida, advancing a few steps, uttered a final earnest appeal. In her beautiful face was a look of intense anxiety, as she stood alone in the centre of the pavilion, pale, erect, queenly.

"Hearken!" she cried wildly. "If this man—who is not our enemy—be put to death, remember that upon thee will fall the curses of one whose incantations can produce good or evil, life or death! Thou sayest that he holdeth the power that I should hold, but I tell thee—"

"Hath he not by thine aid possessed himself of the Crescent of Glorious Wonders?" interrupted the Sheikh.

"The Crescent is no longer possessed by an Infidel," she answered quickly. "During a fight with the Kel-Fadê it was lost, and hath since that time lain undiscovered."

"I found it at—"

"Hush! Remain silent," she whispered, speaking in broken French and glancing at me significantly.

"The Crescent, O Mighty Ruler, hath been seen in his saddle-bag," Labakan urged, muttering a curse under his breath.

"The leathern case may be there," continued Zoraida, with intense earnestness, "but undoubtedly the Crescent of Strange Wonders, the mysterious secret of which is as impenetrable as the wall of Dhu'lkarnein (built to prevent the incursions of Gog and Magog), was lost among the plunder secured by our enemies. It is probably still in the hands of the Kel-Fadê."

"Let the Infidel's saddle-bags be at once searched," ordered the chieftain, and two men hurried forth with that object. I stood anxious to see what turn events would take when the strange object was found secreted in the bag that had served me as pillow, but judge my amazement when, a few minutes later, the men returned with the case, declaring that they had found it empty! Had it again been stolen from me? When they announced the futility of their errand, a smile of satisfaction played about Zoraida's mouth, a fact which puzzled me when I reflected how explicit her instructions had been over its safe custody.

"If it remaineth in the hands of the Kel-Fadê, we must compel them to restore it, or fight as an alternative," said the Sheikh decisively. "We must repossess ourselves of it at all hazards;" adding thoughtfully, "The Great Secret which it conceals must be revealed unto us. Knowledge of its utility in revealing the mystery must be obtained, even at the point of the sword."

On all hands muttered words of approbation greeted this declaration. Then, after a slight pause, he continued—

"If the Roumi possesseth not the Crescent, he cannot hold our vanished power!"

"Why then should he die?" queried the woman whose face had mastery over me.

"Because he is of the accursed race, and hath defiled with his eyes thine own countenance, and those of other of our daughters."

"But thou wilt not darken the world unto me at this moment—when I am leading thee to glorious success and the acquisition of great wealth?" she urged on my behalf.

"And if he liveth—what then?"

"He will accompany us. The country we are entering is already known unto him, thus will he be enabled to choose our route, and lead us to a great and decisive victory," she argued.

The old Sheikh paused, consulting in an undertone with his two advisers who had smoked on in contemplative silence. Anxiously Zoraida and I awaited their verdict, not without feelings of despair, for we both had realised the terrible prejudice against me. At last, however, Hadj Absalam exclaimed—

"The sentence of death by torture having been declared upon the Infidel, it must remain. Nevertheless, it will not be carried out until the result of our expedition hath been seen. If we are victorious, then shall he lead us against the Kel-Fadê, in order to recover the Crescent of Glorious Wonders."

"My Amîn!" whispered Zoraida in French, with tears of joy in her brilliant eyes. "Thou hast a brief respite; use it well. We must now part, but remember that I love thee always—always!"

"But the Crescent?" I gasped. "How shall I act?"

"Remain patient. For the present thou art safe, but be wary of the man who hath already attempted to take thy life. He may strike thee a secret blow at the orders of Hadj Absalam. Go thou back to thy tent and sleep, and when opportunity ariseth, I will communicate with thee, and direct thy footsteps unto the path of freedom."

Then, snatching up her flimsy veil, she deftly twisted it across her face, and walked out with regal gait, proudly acknowledging the obeisance of the dark-faced outlaws, who in apparent fear bowed before her.

A few minutes later, I was back again in the tent from which I had been so mysteriously called, and until the dawn, sat coolly contemplating the remarkable and unexpected turn events had taken.

Chapter Thirty Six
The Bond of Blood

Sleep was impossible. Thoughts of Zoraida absorbed me. Her position was an extraordinary, yet perilous one, and she herself was still enveloped in a mystery that seemed utterly impenetrable. Apparently she was well aware of the secret plans of the Senousya, and by her grace and beauty had charmed these wild, merciless outlaws, ruling even Hadj Absalam himself. Queen of that fierce piratical band, she seemed to have held them so completely under her sway, that the great Sultan of the Sahara himself had been led by her into battle, and had carried out her orders with implicit confidence and passive obedience. The whole situation seemed unintelligible. It appeared impossible that this fair woman, scarcely more than a girl, with such amazingly beautiful features and gracefully-moulded half-bare limbs, who seemed to lead an exotic existence, half consumed by the ennui of the harem, should be responsible for the plunder and carnage, the heartless outrages and brutal massacres, which had during the past few years appalled both Christians and True Believers throughout North Africa. Yet had I not already heard rumours of this from the Spahis? Was it not now proved by her own admissions that she had led the Ennitra against the Zouaves, Turcos, and *homards*?

Why, I wondered, had the dead hand been sent to me; why had some unknown person endeavoured to convince me of her death; why, indeed, had those who knew her all conspired to keep from me the knowledge that she still lived? The facts formed a strange enigma which I hoped would ere long be solved, for this latest disappearance of the Crescent of Glorious Wonders had added considerably to the mystery. Nevertheless she had promised to communicate with me, so I existed from hour to hour in intense expectancy, hoping to receive a summons to enter her bewitching presence.

I had not long to wait, for, on the following evening, while the people had assembled on the opposite side of the camp and were performing their evening prayer, I was strolling slowly past the three silken pavilions of the self-styled Sultan, when suddenly there appeared at the door of one of the two smaller tents, that were zealously and constantly guarded by armed men, a black female slave. For a few seconds she disappeared, then, coming forth again, she beckoned me. As I approached, my passage was immediately barred by a dozen unsheathed swords, but on a word from the negress the men's arms were relegated to their scabbards, and I followed her into the pavilion.

The sweetly-scented interior was replete with every comfort and luxury. From a golden lamp above a soft, subdued light fell upon bright divans, velvet hangings, dark-hued rugs, and little mother-of-pearl tables, whereon there stood fresh fruits in vessels of gold; while stretched upon a lion's skin, with which her low couch was covered, lay Zoraida, a radiant, dazzling vision of beauty.

Throwing down her cigarette as I entered, she raised herself upon her elbow and greeted me with a smile of glad welcome, at the same time ordering her slave to bring me cigarettes, and motioning me to a seat beside her.

In silence our hands clasped until the negress disappeared. She had gone to mount guard at the door, in order to give us warning if enemies approached. The armed guards were, Zoraida explained in a few hasty words, her own trusted servants, and would keep my presence a secret. Thus placing me at my ease, and assuring me that we had naught to fear, she entwined her bare arms around my neck, and, gently pulling my head down to hers, kissed me passionately.

"Through long, weary days, my Amîn, have we been parted. So long! And thou hast always been so faithful, so unswerving in thy devotion unto me!"

"I have merely striven to fulfil my promise," I said, enravished by her beauty, and returning her tender caress. "For many moons have I journeyed in order to accomplish the mission I undertook, yet until yesterday I mourned for thee as dead. Canst thou imagine my joy now that we are once again together?"

"Ah!" she exclaimed, throwing one arm over her head, as her white, scented bosom, half-covered with flashing jewels, slowly rose and fell. "Thou didst think me dead? Perhaps it would have been better for me— better for thee—if I had really died. On the night we parted I was near indeed to death."

"How?" I asked anxiously. "I heard thy screams, but was held powerless to return and render thee help. Tell me what occurred?"

"Strive not to penetrate secrets that are mine alone, Ce-cil," she answered, kindly but firmly. "I can only show thee evidence of the coward's blow;" and raising herself into a sitting posture, she tore asunder the transparent, pearl-embroidered lace which was the only covering of the upper part of her body, revealing to my astonished eyes a great ugly wound only half-healed. She had been struck in the left side, half-way between arm-pit and waist, evidently with a keen, crooked *jambiyah*, which had inflicted a terrible injury. The white, delicate flesh was red and inflamed around a deep wound about three inches in length, from which bandages had apparently only recently been removed.

"Who attempted thy murder?" I asked, enraged that anyone should thus strike down a defenceless woman.

"An enemy," she answered, readjusting her filmy garments, the transparency of which caused her no concern. The gauzes of the harem had always been her attire from childhood, and she knew nothing of rigid Western conventionalities. To the fair daughters of Al-Islâm the follies and foibles of Parisian fashion are a mystery. It is the mission of the inmates of the harem to look beautiful, but they trust to their own personal attractions, not to Worth's creations or Truefitt's coiffures. The corsets, tailor-made gowns, and other arts that transform a hag of sixty into a "smart" Society woman, are unknown in the dreamy Courts of Love, for the velvet zouaves, the gauzy *serroual*, and the garments of brilliant silk brocade are practically the same from Fez to Teheran.

"Name the man who struck thee!" I cried. "He shall answer to me."

"No, no," she replied, turning slowly among her luxurious cushions, causing her golden anklets to jingle. "It is best that, for the present, thou shouldst not know."

"But a dead hand, with thy rings upon its lifeless fingers, was sent to me, and I thought thou hadst—"

"Yes, yes," she answered quickly, interrupting. "But thou mayest not know for what object the severed hand was sent thee. Forget the incident now; some day shalt thou know all."

"When?"

Taking my hand gently in hers, she raised it slowly to her lips, replying, "When we are free to love each other."

"Are we not free now? What obstacle is there?"

"One that seemeth insurmountable," she answered, looking earnestly at me with her fine dark eyes, so full of love and passion. "By a secret bond am I held unto the Ennitra, and thou alone canst sever it and give me freedom."

"How?" I asked eagerly.

"By faithfully carrying out the mission that I entrusted unto thee; by obtaining the secret from Mohammed ben Ishak at Agadez."

"I have done my best," I said. "I have actually been in Agadez, but only as slave in the Fáda of the Sultan."

"Yes," she replied, with a sweet, tender smile, lifting her dark lashes for an instant; "already have I heard of thy perilous adventures, of the gallant attempt thou hast made, risking thy life fearlessly among thine enemies for my sake. True, we love each other devotedly, but, alas! we—we are not yet free;" and her bright eyes became dimmed with tears.

"When shall we have liberty?" I asked, entwining my arm about her neck, so that her sensuously-beautiful head pillowed itself upon my shoulder.

For a few moments she remained silent; then, gazing up into my eyes with an intense, wistful look, she answered—

"When thou hast learned the Secret, and used it upon our mutual behalf; then only can I extricate myself from the Bond of Blood."

"The Bond of Blood! What is that?" I asked eagerly.

"Ah, no!" she responded, with a touch of sorrow in her voice. "I am unable to give thee explanation. When thou hast gained the Secret, then wilt thou learn the truth, and penetrate the veil of Great Mystery. Until that day have patience, and seek not that which must remain hidden."

"But I—I have lost the Crescent," I blurted forth despondently.

"It is in my possession," she replied, with a smile, rising from her divan, kneeling beside me, and placing her arms about my neck. "When last night I recognised thee on thine arrival in our camp, I foresaw thy deadly peril. Labakan, who had been ordered to kill thee, was also aware of thy presence; therefore I had thy travelling companion, Halima, brought before me, and from her ascertained that on thy journey thine eyes had been constantly upon one of thy saddle-bags. I therefore felt confident that the Crescent thou hadst lost had been recovered. Later, I caused search to be made among thy belongings, and it being found there, it was abstracted and brought hither."

"Hadst thou a reason for this?" I asked, puzzled.

"Yes. I knew that if the Crescent of Glorious Wonders were found in the possession of thyself, an Infidel, no argument of mine would save thee from death."

"But thou hast again rescued me, Zoraida," I murmured in ecstasy. "Again my life hath been in thine hands."

"I love thee," she responded, briefly and simply.

"And thou art risking everything for my sake—even thy position as Queen of the Ennitra!"

"Art thou not doing the same for me?" she asked. "As lovers it is our duty to assist each other, and to stand together in the hour of danger."

"How didst thou know I had lost that which thou hadst entrusted to my care?" I asked, much interested in this remarkable phase of the extraordinary affair.

"I ascertained that when thou wert a slave in the Fáda thou hadst not the Crescent. Then I learnt of the circumstances of thy fall into the hands of the Kel-Fadê, and it was at once apparent that it was they who had filched it from thee."

"Thou didst not know how I recovered it?" I asked, transported by her beauty.

"No," she answered. "Tell me; I am interested to learn the truth;" and with charming ingenuousness she imprinted upon my cheek another warm, affectionate kiss.

Briefly, I told her of my journey after my adventurous escape from Agadez, of the dastardly attempt to take my life, my strange rescue, and my wanderings in the gloomy subterranean passages beneath the Sheikh's palace. As I related how I had suddenly entered the hall where the conspirators of the Senousya had assembled to practise their mystic rites, she grew excited and alarmed, eagerly drinking in every word of my description. When I had finished, she placed her hand upon my arm, and said with intense earnestness—

"Tell no one of this, O Ce-cil! Thine eyes have beholden, and thou hast, alas! learned the secrets of the League of Terror. I fear that the punishment of eavesdroppers may be meted out to thee. Know thou that the terrible vengeance of the Senousya is so far-reaching that the man or woman it condemneth can never escape a violent death, even though he or she may flee beyond seas unto the uttermost corners of the earth. Wherever shineth the sun, there also are emissaries of the Senousya. Therefore take every precaution for thy safety; tell no one of the knowledge thou hast thus acquired; and upon the subject of the Holy War remain always silent as the grave. Take warning, and exercise caution—for my sake. The vengeance is always fatal!"

"I will heed thy words," I said. "But I care naught for enemies while I am nigh unto thee;" and as I drew her slowly towards me, her lips met mine in a warm, entrancing caress, enough to make any man's senses whirl.

"I—I wish we could meet daily," she declared wistfully; "but for thee to tread the enchanted ground of my pavilion is impossible. At the peril of our lives, and by the connivance of those placed as janitors over me, am I enabled to-night to speak with thee for one brief hour, to hear thee tell me of thy love." Then, grasping my hand tightly, and gazing with a fervent love-look into my face, she added, "For days, for weeks have I been longing to see thee, hoping against hope. In the dim, silent seclusion of mine own apartment strange rumours and distorted reports have reached me regarding thy fate. Although those I employed lied unto me, I felt confidence in thee. I knew thou wouldst strain every nerve to obtain knowledge of the Great Secret that is essential to our happiness. We meet now only to part again; to part perhaps for a few days, perhaps for many moons. Let me dwell within thy memory, so that thou wilt ever remember that she who loveth thee followeth thee unseen, and that all her trust is in thine own brave heart."

She spoke with the fierce passion of love, and in her fine brilliant eyes tears were welling. I was silent in the devout worship of my entrancing idol—this woman whose face was perfect in its beauty, whose supple figure and exquisite grace charmed me, and whose soft, tuneful Arabic sounded as sweetest music. With her slight form in my embrace, her cheek, fresh as an English girl's, lying upon my breast, her long dark unplaited hair straying over my white burnouse, she filled me with a restful, dreamy languor, a feeling of perfect enchantment and bliss, enhanced by the heavy perfumes and the sensuousness of her luxuriant surroundings.

"While wandering afar, the thought of thine affection hath given me heart; thou art always my Pole Star, my light, my guide," I said, enraptured. "Though I have failed to obtain the knowledge which I sought, it was purely owing to the fickleness of fortune."

"Yes," she answered gravely. "I know thou hast done thy best. Yet there are still means by which thou canst ascertain the truth, and elucidate the Great Mystery."

"How?"

"By becoming one of us; by bearing arms under the green banner of Hadj Absalam, and accompanying us to Agadez."

"Art thou actually on thy way thither?" I asked, amazed. "Surely it is dangerous?"

"Dangerous only for the Sultan of the Ahír," she laughed.

"I cannot understand," I said. "What is the object of thy journey?"

"The same as the object of all our expeditions," she answered, the smile dying from her lips. "The trade of the Ennitra is marked always by rapine and murder, plunder and bloodshed;" and she shuddered.

"Do thy people intend fighting?" I asked.

"Hearken, and I will give thee explanation," she said excitedly. "For many moons hath Hadj Absalam contemplated an attack upon the Sultan of the Ahír, and the looting of the great Fáda wherein thou wert held a slave. At last the expedition hath been arranged, and is now being carried out. Divided into four sections, our people, mustering all their strength for the supreme effort, have stealthily moved hither, and are now encamped at various points on the border of the Sultan's territory, ready to advance upon Agadez like swarms of locusts at the moment the drum of victory is conveyed unto them. Armed to the teeth, and eager for a struggle that must be brief though deadly, they are awaiting the completion of our plans. Two days hence all will be ready, the drum that beateth us to arms will be carried forth, our tents will be packed, and, acting in conjunction with the three other forces of our fighting men, we shall advance, dealing blows swift and terrible among a people who little dream of the approach of an enemy, and are entirely unprepared."

"Hast thou actually a sufficient force to attack the almost impregnable kasbah of Agadez?" I asked incredulously.

"Yes. In two days the green standard will be raised, the drum will be sent round to the three other camps, and with one accord shall we sweep onward to the great stronghold of the Ahír."

"And thou desirest that I should become a Bedouin of the Ennitra—an outlaw of the Sahara?" I said.

"Thou *must!*" she answered, with enthusiasm, her slim lingers closing tightly upon my hand. "Dost thou not see that I have obtained a respite for thee, only on condition that thou throwest in thy lot with us?"

"What is this mysterious influence which Hadj Absalam declareth hath been transferred unto me?" I inquired, eager to ascertain the meaning of the strange words she had so boldly addressed to the robber Sheikh.

But she laughed, and, evading my question, answered with light coquetry—

"The power that draweth us together; the influence that causeth us to love each other."

"But why didst thou urge thy Ruler to compel me to become a freebooter?"

"It was my last extremity," she said. "I pleaded for thee, and—almost failed. To fight beside us is thine only chance of reaching Agadez, and of finding he whom thou seekest."

"To be near unto thee I am prepared to join thy people, even though they are mine enemies," I said, as she looked into my eyes with trusting gaze.

"Although thou wilt be near me, thou must never seek to have speech with me," she exclaimed quickly. "We meet here at imminent risk, but we must not again invite the wrath of those who desire thy death. To thee I must be as a stranger, for remember that thou art a Roumi, and thy very glance defileth mine unveiled face!" and she laughed lightly.

"Ah! the religious prejudices of thy people are indeed curious," I said. "How long must we affect this estrangement?"

"Until Agadez hath fallen, and thine errand be accomplished."

"But if thou hast the Crescent in thy possession, canst thou not snap thy bonds and escape with me?" I suggested. "Surely thy place is not upon the field of battle, amid the carnage that must inevitably ensue from such a combat?"

"Impossible!" she answered, moving uneasily, and wafting to me the sweet perfume that clung to her draperies. She was agitated, for her hand holding mine trembled violently, and her lips were tightly compressed. "The Bond of Blood bindeth me more firmly than fetters of steel, and if I attempted to desert the camp, the death of both of us would be inevitable. No! To Agadez must we advance. From to-day thou art an outlaw of the plains, and I am thy leader! Obey me, but speak not; for upon thy silence and obedience dependeth thy life. Hidden in my possession the Crescent will remain until such time as thou wilt require it; then, once inside the Great Mosque, the secret knowledge will be imparted unto thee, and will peradventure be of profit."

"It grieveth me sorely to think that thou, the woman I adore, art the head of this fierce band of murderous marauders, and wilt lead them to commit merciless massacre and pillage, to—"

"Ah, no!" she cried, raising both her hands as if to arrest my words. "Reproach me not, O Ce-cil! I cannot bear it *from thee*! Thinkest thou that were I not compelled, I would be the cause of this widespread death and desolation; thinkest thou that I would urge onward these wild hordes to deeds horrible and revolting? Thou believest I have a heart of stone, that I have no woman's tenderness, that—that I, a woman of the Desert, am"—

and, unable to complete her sentence, she burst into a passionate torrent of tears.

"No, Zoraida, I blame thee not," I tenderly hastened to reassure her. "I know there are circumstances connected with thine hidden past of which I have no knowledge, therefore I love thee fondly, awaiting the time when thou art enabled to renounce thy people and become my wife."

"What canst thou think of a woman such as I?" she sobbed bitterly. "Even to thee, so faithful as thou hast been, I am compelled to still preserve my secret, appearing in thine eyes as one to whom the clash of arms is sweeter than the music of the *derbouka*, and the wail of the vanquished the pleasantest sound upon mine ear!"

"But thy position is not of thine own choosing," I said, quietly endeavouring to soothe her.

"No!" she cried wildly, starting up. "I hate it all! Though each raid enricheth me with gold and jewels of great price, yet there is a curse upon the treasure, obtained, as it is, by the relentless slaughter of the weak. Ah, Ce-cil! if thou couldst only know how acutely I suffer, how these jewels upon me glitter with the fire of deadly hatred as each one telleth its mute but horrible story, a story of rapine and murder for which I—the woman thou lovest, the woman who would willingly give her life for thee—am responsible! Is not my existence one of hollow shams, of feigned daring and wretched duplicity? I loathe myself; and were it not that I look forward to happiness with thee, I would—I would end it all with this!" and she drew from her breast a small keen dagger, with hilt encrusted with turquoises, that she always kept concealed there.

"Speak not of that," I said firmly. "Place thy knife in its sheath. I love thee, Zoraida, I trust in thee, and none shall ever come between us."

"Dost thou place thy faith in me implicitly, notwithstanding that I appear in thine eyes debased, and am unable to give thee explanation?" she asked, half credulously, through her blinding tears.

The jewels upon her flashed with a brilliancy that was dazzling, and the sweet odours of her apartment seemed intoxicating.

"I do," I answered, fervently kissing her with a mad, fierce passion. "Indeed, had it not been for thine exertions, my bones would long ago have been stripped by the vultures."

"Ah! my Amîn, thou too art performing for me a mission, the result of which will effect stranger things than thou hast ever dreamed," she exclaimed earnestly; adding, "Our story-tellers relate wondrous things, but none have described such marvels as thou shalt behold. I told thee in Algiers that I was in peril of death, and that thou couldst avert the danger that threatened. These words I now repeat, and trust in thee to save me."

"To save thee I will again face our enemies fearlessly, and strive to reach the *imam* who holdeth the Secret, even though I have been told that the Omen of the Camel's Hoof hath been revealed unto me," I said, entranced by her beauty, and smiling in an endeavour to chase away the gloomy shadow that seemed to have settled upon her.

"Yes," she answered, slowly winding both arms about my neck, and looking up to me with big, tear-stained eyes. "The mark, to thee invisible, is upon thy brow, yet hath not that presage of evil already been fulfilled in thy failure to elucidate the Mystery of the Crescent? Is it not possible that henceforward good fortune and success may attend thine efforts?"

"Truly, O my beloved One of Wondrous Beauty!" I said, "thy words renew hope within me, and restore confidence. I will seek the *imam* of the Mesállaje, and at any risk learn the hidden wonders."

In silence she gazed at me with a look of unutterable sadness. The pallor of her countenance enhanced her delicate beauty, and the trembling of her hands showed me how intensely agitated she had become. She loved me with all the fiery passion of her race, yet it seemed as though she kept from me, with tantalising persistency, just those facts I desired explained. She seemed half incredulous, too, that I should be prepared to make another strenuous effort to reach Mohammed ben Ishak merely upon the expression of her desire, for after a short silence, during which her peach-like cheek, fragrant with perfume, lay against mine, she suddenly exclaimed—

"Dost thou, O Ce-cil! believe me blindly, even though I admit to thee that I—I am unworthy thy generous love? To me, alas! debased and degraded as I am, the fruit of the great lote tree is forbidden, and the water of Salsabil may never cool my lips." Then, sinking upon her knees before me, she suddenly burst again into tears, covering her face with her hands.

"Come," I said, "let not thoughts of thy past cause thee unhappiness. There is danger; and we must arm ourselves, and both bear our burdens bravely."

"Ah!" she cried in accents of poignant bitterness, "it is impossible that thou canst ever love me sufficiently to make me thy wife, even when thou, at last, knowest my story. See!" and, throwing out her arms wildly, she stretched forth her open palms towards me. "See! I am held to this horde of cut-throats by gyves invisible yet unbreakable! I kneel before thee, my Amîn! a despicable, vile-hearted woman, whose whole life hath been one of ignominy and deceit, whose very name is a by-word of reproach! Forsaken by Allah, defamed by man, I confess myself unworthy thy thoughts. I cannot—nay, I will not bring upon thee disgrace and shame, for my hands!—they are stained by heinous crimes!" she added hoarsely, bowing low and hiding her face.

Taking her by the wrist, I was about to assist her to rise, when she snatched away her arm as if she had been stung.

"No, no!" she cried in heart-thrilling tones. "Place not thine hand upon me! My touch polluteth thee! It will perhaps be best—best for both of us if we part to-night to never meet again!"

"Tell me," I demanded quickly, "have not thy crimes been committed under compulsion?"

"Yes, they have! I swear—they—have!" she answered brokenly.

"And thou art the wife of Hadj Absalam?" I said fiercely, half convinced that I spoke the truth.

"Ah! no, no!" she protested, with feverish anxiety, raising her pale, haggard face imploringly to mine. "Judge me not too harshly," she cried. "Though the awful stigma of sin lieth upon me, and my life is accursed, yet here at thy feet I tell thee I am neither wife nor slave. I have suffered no man to hold me in fond embrace, nor to kiss my lips, save thee. I take oath upon the Book of Everlasting Will."

"Canst thou not tell me why thou, a pure and innocent woman, art here among these barbaric Sons of the Desert?" I asked, now convinced by her terrible earnestness that my suspicions were groundless.

"I am not innocent, I confess to thee. How can I be, when to my vile cunning is due that inhuman butchery which causeth the Ennitra to be held in terror throughout the Desert? Until thine eyes met mine, I knew neither mercy nor remorse, but now—Faugh! I see my crimes in all their revolting hideousness, and I—I hate—I loathe myself—for I am the Slave of the Destroyer!"

"Let us bury the past," I said, slowly and with sincerity, assisting her to rise, and, holding her again in my arms, I rained passionate kisses upon her sequin-covered brow. "Though much that is incomprehensible remaineth like a curtain obscuring thee, yet I am satisfied that I bestow not my affection in vain—"

"Ah, my Amîn! thou knowest not how dearly I love thee," she interrupted, raising her lips slowly until they met mine.

"I can gauge thy feelings by mine own," I answered. "Thou must leave this life of outlawry; but ere thou canst escape from thy people, I am compelled to gain certain knowledge. This will I strive once again to accomplish; but in the meantime I desire not to gaze down the uninviting vista of thy past, or tear the veil from unpleasant facts that thou wouldst hide from me. I am confident in the knowledge that thou art neither a wife nor an inmate of thy Sheikh's harem, and that, though morally guilty of the massacres that have sent a thrill through two continents, yet thy position hath, in some way unexplained, been thrust upon thee. I consider this in considerable measure palliates thy crimes, and—"

"I vow I have acted always against my will—always! It was horrible!" she interrupted.

"Yes, I know," I said, tenderly stroking her long silky hair. "Thou hast my love, sympathy, and forgiveness. Some day, when we are wedded, peradventure thou wilt tell me how thou earnest to rule this piratical band."

"It was to save mine honour," she declared, with fervour.

"Then I will demand no further explanation," I said. "It sufficeth that we are confident in each other's love."

"Yes, we are, we are!" she cried, with a wild outburst of passionate affection, kissing me again and again. "I have spoken the truth as clearly as circumstances will allow, nevertheless, thou hast faith in me. Thou art still my Amîn, generous and true. For thee will I live in the hope of eventual freedom, and should misfortune overtake us, by thy side will I die!"

"Let us anticipate success," I said.

"Yes," she answered, smiling, as she dashed away her tears.

"If thou gainest the Great Secret, thou wilt obtain strange knowledge, which will prove to thee amazing, and reveal an unheard-of marvel. Therefore strive on. Though thou mayest see me sometimes, seek not to hold converse with me. Remember always while thou art with us that we are watched closely by those only too eager for a pretext for killing thee. Indeed, if thou wort discovered here, thine head would quickly be smitten off and mounted upon thy tent-pole, so likewise any attempt to speak with me would inevitably cause a dozen knives to pierce thine heart. Henceforth we are strangers until I restore to thee the Crescent, and thy mission is safely accomplished."

"I will preserve silence, and seek thee not."

"Make me one other promise," she exclaimed in grave earnestness. "Whatsoever thou mayest witness during our advance upon Agadez, never wilt thou think ill of me. Remember always that I am forced to act as I do in order to preserve mine own honour."

"I promise," I replied, sealing the compact with a lingering, ecstatic kiss.

Next second her slave entered excitedly, with the news that prayers were over, and that the people were flocking back to their tents.

"Thou must, alas! leave me, my Amîn," Zoraida cried, on hearing the negress's unwelcome announcement. "Would that we could spend some hours longer together! but we must not run too great a risk. May Allah, the Merciful Protector of the weak, watch over and guide thee, and may thy footsteps fall in paths of peace. *Slama. Allah iselemeck!*"

Our leave-taking was tender and affectionate, for I saw how fervid and passionate was her love, nevertheless she compelled me, firmly yet kindly, to tear myself from her, and a few minutes later I was seated in dreamy thoughtfulness outside the little tent which my enemies had given me.

A few brief days, I reflected, and my fate would be decided. Would the mystery of the Crescent of Glorious Wonders, with its undreamed-of marvels that she had promised, ever be revealed?

Chapter Thirty Seven
By the Drum of Nâr

The bid for fortune was desperate and perilous.

I had become an outlaw, a member of one of the most daring bands of freebooters that ever robbed a caravan or tortured a wanderer of the plains. To the civilising influence of French authority Hadj Absalam was as defiant and his identity as mysterious as the Mahdi himself; while his followers were for the most part an ill-dressed, well-armed horde, whose torn and dirty burnouses and general negligence of attire showed plainly that they were Desert rovers, whose ramshackle tents were their only homes, and whose existence depended on the result of their depredations.

The knowledge that I was an Infidel, combined with the secret inflammatory utterances of Labakan, created bitter prejudices against me, causing them to jeer and make matters exceedingly unpleasant generally. Among that legion of marauders I had not a single friend, with the exception of Zoraida and Halima, neither of whom were ever visible. Fierce guttural oaths and exclamations of disgust that a dog of a Christian should be permitted to live among them were muttered by dark-skinned, evil-faced ruffians, who squatted idly before their tents cleaning guns, burnishing knives, and filling powder-flasks. Sometimes, after I had passed, they would spit upon the ground to emphasise their contempt, or openly declare that I was a harbinger of evil, a precursor of defeat.

Affecting to take no notice of the variety of insults flung into my face, I suppressed any rebuke that rose to my lips, remembering Zoraida's words, and determined that when the time came, I would show them that a Christian could handle a rifle with as deadly effect as a True Believer.

The long hot day following my interview with the woman I loved I spent in lonely unhappiness, and my sense of insecurity was very considerably increased by receiving a secret visit, at the mild and balmy dawn of the following day, from one of the men who, after assisting Halima and myself to escape from the Sheikh's house, had accompanied us on our journey. On recognising him, I extended to him a warm greeting, much gratified that at last I had found a friend; but I paused when, raising his hand quickly, he exclaimed in a deep whisper—

"Hush! Let not thy voice be heard! I come to thee, unseen by thine enemies, to give warning unto thee!"

"Is there danger?" I gasped.

"Know, O Roumi," he answered, "thine enemy Labakan—on whom may Allah not have mercy!—hath formed a dastardly plot to kill thee! Our Lady of Beauty, Halima, hath heard of it, and sendeth thee word. Be careful of thyself, or of a surety thou wilt yet fall beneath the knife of the assassin."

"Tell the Lalla Halima I send her greeting. Thank her for placing me upon my guard, and from me give unto her perfect peace," I said; adding, "Is it possible that I might see her?"

"Alas! no," the man replied in consternation. "Seek not to converse with the women of the Faith of our Lord Mohammed. The eye of the Infidel defileth them."

"Why?" I asked, laughing at the Moslem prejudice which even his friendship could not stifle.

"It is written," he answered piously.

Without attempting to argue the point, I learnt from him, in reply to my questions, that in travelling to the camp we had journeyed due south, and that the valley where we were in hiding was called Akoukou, distant seven days from Agadez, and almost inaccessible from that city. Other hordes of the Ennitra had migrated in small parties, so as not to attract the attention of those they intended to attack, and were now congregated to the number of about four thousand, one body being at the Efigaguen Oasis to the north-east of the City of the Sorcerers, another at the well of Enouaggued, and a third lying in ambush to the north-west, in a secluded valley in the waterless wilderness known to the Arabs as the Kahir d' Ibn Batouta.

With that cunning of which the Ennitra were past masters, they had gradually moved from their own region across the Great Desert, many of them under the guise of traders, to the points indicated, and now, having collected their forces, had practically surrounded the country of the young Sultan Abd-el-Kerim, and for several days had been awaiting the order from Hadj Absalam to make a concentric movement upon Agadez.

He told me that in our camp we had over three thousand fighting men, but that, even with such forces at their command, we should experience some hard fighting, for the men-at-arms of the Sultan of the Ahír were more than double our number. Then he questioned me as to my future movements, and I told him briefly that I intended to fight side by side with the warriors of Hadj Absalam. To this he answered—

"Verily, O Roumi, thou art a friend of the Faith. May Allah honour thy face and perfect thy light! May the One Giver of Life abandon thee not to the consequences of thy sins without pardoning them, or to thy griefs without consoling them, or to thy fears without removing them!"

"I salute thee with salutation, O friend," I answered. "To our Lalla Halima, and unto thee likewise, I hope to be enabled to show my thankfulness, for I was a stranger, and thou didst give me succour."

"Some day thou wilt turn from thy paths of infidelity," he murmured in an impressive tone, his dark, deep-set eyes riveted upon mine. "If Almighty Allah, the Omniscient, pleaseth, thou wilt at last know the great Truth and drink of the fountain of joy and gladness. Verily, none but He can remit a sin; of a truth He veileth our offences, broadeneth our breasts, and causeth our last words in the supreme hour of life to be the words, 'There is no Ilah but Allah.'"

Assuring him that I was no "abuser of the salt," that I entertained nothing but profound respect for the people of Al-Islâm, and thanking him for conveying Halima's message, we wished each other a cordial farewell, and he crept away from my tent without apparently having attracted any attention.

My wound was still rather painful, yet the fever had entirely left me, and I felt much better, although far from strong. Throughout the greater part of the blazing day I remained alone in my tent, drowsily smoking some cigarettes Zoraida had given me, and making a meal of some dates and lentils brought by a negro who was one of Hadj Absalam's slaves. An hour before *el maghrib*, however, a great consternation seemed to be produced throughout the camp, for armed men hurried past my tent, and the few women who had accompanied them into the land of their enemies waddled along after them, closely veiled. Evidently something unusual was taking place, therefore I donned my burnouse, tarboosh, and haick, and, strolling out, followed the crowd to the open space before the three pavilions of the self-styled Sultan of the Sahara.

Here the marauders had assembled, and were the most brigandish-looking horde of ruffians that my eyes had ever encountered. As I pushed my way in among the throng, the abhorrence in which I was held was plain, for scowling men drew aside their burnouses so that they should not come in contact with me, and women shrank from me and turned away to avoid my glance. Fortunately I was enabled to get to the front of the great ring of spectators that had been formed, and as I did so, the crowd opened to allow the tall, regal figure of Hadj Absalam to advance into the open space, followed by the two cadis who had lounged on his divan when I had been brought before him, as well as his Grand Vizier Labakan, and four other men in silken robes. Wild with excitement, the crowd raised their voices, shouting—

"*Howa-thâ*! O Just and Generous Ruler! *Marhaba*! O Sultan of the Great Desert! Hail! O Conqueror of Roumis, O Exterminator of Infidels! O Fearless Defender of the Faith! Hail! Hail! Hail!"

Halting in the centre upon an improvised dais, the old Sheikh, arrayed in robes of bright green silk embroidered with gold, and wearing in his white head-dress an aigrette of sparkling diamonds, raised his hands, an action which commanded instant silence.

"Know, O my people! thy Sheikh standeth now before thee!" he cried in a loud voice, as with resolute bearing he gazed round upon the circle of bronzed and bearded faces. "He hath decided that the time hath come when it is meet for thee to spur onward unto Agadez; that the hour hath arrived when salutation should be sent unto our brethren, so that they may co-operate with us in the swift and merciless attack. If there be anyone who craveth to offer advice unto us, let him now speak."

The Pirates of the Desert whispered expressions of satisfaction among themselves, but no word was uttered in response to Hadj Absalam's invitation. Several minutes thus elapsed, when suddenly there was a movement in the crowd in the direction of the pavilions, and then the fierce piratical band again shouted themselves hoarse in enthusiastic cheers and utterances of welcome, as a veiled woman, wearing a dainty zouave of amaranth velvet embroidered with emeralds and seed pearls and *serroual* of golden sheen, advanced and took up her stand on the daïs beside the Sheikh, being followed by six men armed to the teeth and mounted on splendid Arab stallions. She was attended by two female slaves, who, between them, carried an ancient conical-shaped drum, the skin of which was almost black with age. Having placed the instrument on the ground, they unveiled her.

The woman who had received the wildly-enthusiastic plaudits of the robbers was Zoraida!

Pale, erect, calm, she gazed slowly around her, apparently in search of someone, and heedless of a second outburst of cordial welcome. Suddenly her eyes met mine. She started visibly, turned a shade paler, I thought, then set her teeth firmly, as if bracing herself up for some supreme effort.

Her handsome face, with the slight touch of sorrow in its expression, looked even more beautiful than in the subdued light of the harem, and as the brilliant sunset tipped her dark unbound hair with gold and fell upon her breast, whereon lay a great single emerald suspended by a chain of pearls, she seemed standing in hesitancy, as if shrinking from some action she was compelled to perform. Once again she lifted her long lashes in my direction, but only for a second, for, drawing a deep breath, her gaze wandered round the sea of dark, anxious countenances, as she raised her white bare arm heavenward.

In a moment there was a dead silence. The men about her, who had given vent to words of admiration on seeing her unveiled, were breathless in expectancy.

"Behold! my people! At my feet lieth the Drum of Nâr!" she cried in clear, resolute tones, though at first there seemed a slight quiver in her voice. "Times without number hast thou and thy forefathers gone down into battle to its sound. Its note is to thee of a verity a note of victory; to thine enemies a knell of speedy death. To its tones hast thou defeated the legions of the Infidels, and to its roll canst thou now, if thou wilt follow me, overthrow the Sultan of Agadez."

"Wheresoever thou goest, there also will we go!" shouted the evil-looking crowd enthusiastically with one accord, flourishing their rifles high above their heads. "Lead us, O our Malieah! (Queen) O Beauteous Daughter of the Sun! O Bringer of Victory! We will follow thee!"

"Give ear unto me!" she cried again, silencing the wild tumult of enthusiasm with uplifted hands. "I would have brief speech with thee before we commence the advance to Abd-el-Kerim's stronghold. Verily I tell thee that—"

"Cease thy chatter, I command!" cried Hadj Absalam, in a sudden ebullition of anger. "Have I not forbidden thee to address unto the people words other than those which have received my sanction?"

Glancing towards him, the colour left her face, and she trembled as if in fear, but the people, noticing the dispute, cried loudly, "Let the Lalla, Queen of the Noor, speak unto us, O our Father! In her wisdom do we place our trust." This popular demonstration in her favour gave her courage, and heedless of the fiercely-uttered imprecations of the pirate chieftain, Zoraida, drawing a long breath, continued—

"For many moons now past there hath been amongst thee, my foster-brethren, signs of discontent," she said.

"Grim whisperings have caught mine ear, and many a sinister rumour regarding myself hath been conveyed unto me. To-day, ere we set out towards the dazzling Palace of Delights, where some of us will peradventure find a grave, I desire to render thee personal explanation."

She paused, glancing at me with unwavering eye. Every voice was hushed, every face expectant.

"It hath been alleged against me that I have betrayed the secret of the Crescent of Glorious Wonders, but before thee all I deny it. Some have said that I have delivered the Crescent itself into the hands of a Roumi. Behold! I have our treasure still in my hands!" And as she drew it from beneath the folds of the bright-coloured silken scarf that girt her waist, and held it aloft, her words were greeted by loud, ringing cheers.

"Those who declare that our power hath been weakened by the supposed loss of the Crescent may here witness it for themselves," she went on. "It hath further been alleged that the presence of an infidel in our camp bodeth ill-fortune; but I, thy soothsayer, tell thee that his companionship will be of the utmost value unto us. Already hath he been held captive in the great Fáda, and, knowing its intricate courts and pavilions, will render valuable aid in serving as guide when, in the supreme moment, we make the final onrush. Think, then, those of you who seek by sinister device to encompass the death of this stranger from beyond seas! Stay thine hands, thou who art seeking to destroy the one man who can show us the means whereby we can reach the Hall of the Great Divan!"

Every eye was turned upon me with mingled scorn and surprise. Zoraida was endeavouring to ensure my safety! A wild excitement seemed to burn in her veins, and after a few seconds' pause she again proceeded—

"This expedition requireth the fall strength of each one of us, therefore let none seek to wreak vengeance upon his neighbour. Heed these the words of thy Daughter of the Sun, whose prophecies have been fulfilled, and whose curse falleth swiftly upon her enemies. The barriers of Agadez, held by the peerless scimitars of Abd-el-Kerim, can only be broken by the gallant, patient 'brothers of Zoraida'—the soldiers of destiny. Accept the Roumi who hath eaten thy salt as thy clansman, for of a verity he is a friend of True Believers, and will fight by thy side under this the glorious banner of the Ennitra, our green standard that striketh terror into all hearts from Khartoum unto Timbuktu! Let not thy belief in our power be shaken, but act with one accord, follow me with faith, and, striking down thine enemies, thou shalt dash onward through the iron-barred gate of the great Fáda, whence thou wilt bring forth many camel-loads of treasure and many scores of slaves. Verily, I tell thee, thou shalt drive thine enemies to their doom, even as cattle are driven unto water."

Hadj Absalam stood scowling, with folded arms. His Argus eyes were everywhere. By the expressions of approbation and loudly-uttered promises to carry out her wishes, it was plain that Zoraida's words had the effect she desired. Over this fierce horde of cut-throats she exercised such regal sway that her every wish was law. So attentive were they to her utterances, that it seemed as if her marvellous beauty entranced them, causing them to fight for her. How strange was her position; how strenuously was she struggling on my behalf! An undying bitterness, a hatred born of fanaticism, the scorn of the Moslem for the accursed Roumi, had been conquered by her words; for ere she had finished speaking, the fierce warriors of the Desert, who a few minutes before had cursed me under their breath, were wildly enthusiastic, and gave me "peace" on every hand.

Again raising the mysterious Crescent above her head, she demanded in a loud voice, "Hast thou still confidence in me?"

The echoes were awakened by shouts in the affirmative, and one man near me cried, "We fear not the stars when the moon is with us."

"And thou entrustest to me the success of this bold dash into the stronghold of our most powerful enemy?" she asked again.

"Thou art our light!" they cried. "Lead us, O Daughter of the Sun! and we will follow thee."

"Is the Roumi yonder thine ally and friend?"

"Yes," they answered. "Already have we given him 'peace.'"

"May the Giver of Good Gifts bestow upon thee blessing!" I cried, in acknowledgment of their declaration of friendship. I was about to address some words to the woman I loved, when suddenly I remembered she had forbidden me to speak, and stood gazing at her in silence. Upon the sinister face of Hadj Absalam there rested a dark look of displeasure. Zoraida was doing her best to save me, but in the crafty eyes of the Sheikh there lurked treachery and deadly hatred.

A pause ensued. Zoraida, standing erect and glancing around her, smiled as if a great weight had been at last lifted from her mind, while her women on either side slowly moved their great fans of yellow ostrich plumes.

A few seconds later, the two cadis who had accompanied the Sheikh advanced, and, taking up the Drum of Nâr, knelt before her.

"Lo! the note of victory soundeth!" she cried. "From this moment none shall rest until the banner of the Ennitra hath been planted on the Fáda of Agadez!" and with her open palms she suddenly struck the drum, and beat a rolling tattoo, that swelled louder and louder, and then gradually died away.

The call to arms caused the wildest enthusiasm, and the final notes of the rude, ancient instrument were drowned by the fierce war-cries that rent the air on every side. All seemed filled with delight at the prospect of the fight, and these shouts were repeated as the Drum of Nâr was beaten in a similar manner by the outlaw Sheikh himself, whose bearded face seemed harder than flint.

The stallions of the six mounted Arabs pawed the ground, impatient as their riders, who, on hearing the sound of the drum, yelled themselves hoarse, throwing back their burnouses and flourishing their rifles high aloft.

"Whomsoever thou shalt fight we will fight, O Ruler of the Desert!" they shouted, and again the cry was taken up by the people, who, amid a scene of intense excitement, handled their knives, swords, and guns, vowing to give no quarter to their enemies, and to make no halt until the Fáda had fallen into their hands.

Zoraida and Hadj Absalam were standing side by side, a strangely incongruous pair—she young, fair, and smiling; he aged and scowling, with merciless brutality portrayed in every line of his sun-tanned, aquiline features. Turning to her, he uttered some words in a low tone, intended for her ear alone. What they were none knew, but she glanced at him, shrugged her shoulders, and, without replying, glanced across at me with a kindly look of recognition.

Yet I dared not to approach her.

Just at that moment a standard was raised aloft, and a green silken banner, embroidered with gold, unfurled, hung over the pair motionless in the heavy, sultry air. The sight of this emblem of war was greeted with renewed shouts of delight, and as Zoraida slowly waved it, there went up on every side deep, fervent declarations of devotion to the Daughter of the Sun.

"Whithersoever thou goest, O Malieah of Beauty! we will go. Thou art still our Bringer of Victory, and we fear not while thou art at our head!" they shouted hoarsely, half mad with eager anticipation.

With queenly air her head bowed slowly in graceful acknowledgment of their compliments, then, raising both arms to heaven, she uttered some words that were lost in the tumult of excitement. The six horsemen drew up before the dais, one of them dismounting, and taking his capacious saddle-bag, held it open, while Zoraida with her own hands placed in it the Drum of Nâr. In a few moments the bag was again upon the animal's back, the tall Arab vaulted into his high-backed saddle, and waited immovable as a statue.

There was a dead silence. At last Hadj Absalam addressed them in a loud voice, saying—

"Speed thee onward, my sons. Halt not until the Drum of Nâr hath sounded its note of victory in the Efigaguen, the Kahir d' Ibn Batouta, and at the well of Enouaggued. Unto our people carry forth our greeting, and tell them that on the tenth day from to-morrow shall we make the dash upon the Fáda, where we shall expect them to aid us in the attack, and to destroy our enemies as were destroyed the tribes of Ad and Thamud. Away! Linger not until thou hast returned unto us with the Drum of Victory."

"Go!" added Zoraida, stretching forth her tiny white hand. "Upon thee be perfect peace, and may Allah, Answerer of thy Supplications, shadow thee with His shadow, and guard thee in thy peril. *Fi amâni-illah!*"

The six sturdy horsemen bowed till their foreheads touched their horses' necks, then, raising loud shouts, they fired their rifles into the air, and, spurring on, dashed through the wildly-excited crowd that opened to let them pass, and in a few minutes were galloping away down the rocky valley, where the misty shadows of sunset had already gathered.

Hadj Absalam's orders had been despatched, and the Ennitra were now working themselves into a frenzy of excitement, preliminary to a mad ride over the ashes of burned homes and the bodies of their enemies, to pillage the richest and most extensive palace in the Great Sahara. Half demented by enthusiasm, each endeavoured to talk more bravely than his fellow, commenting in anticipation of the amount of loot to be obtained from the Sultan's abode. Upon this point I was closely questioned, and, in reply, I gave a brief description of the place. The ceremony of sending forth the Drum of Nâr was over, for Zoraida's women had wrapped her haick about her, and, with a last wistful glance at me, she turned and walked between them back to her pavilion, followed by the great Sheikh and his companions, who, amid the plaudits of the slowly-swaying crowd, bore aloft the green standard under which we were so soon to fight.

Zoraida had gone. Half an hour later, while my companions were repeating their Fâtiha, I stood aside deep in thought. The unquenchable flame of love, I knew, glowed within her heart. Stone to all else, she, forced by some extraordinary circumstance to be the leader of a band of cut-throats, had promised to become my wife. The Ennitra had replaced their faith in her with renewed confidence by reason of her possession of the Crescent, and this she had turned to the best advantage by securing my immunity from molestation. Yet I remembered that, after all, the chances of safety were exceedingly small, and wondered how many of those who were now so ready to murder and plunder would fall under the keen scimitars of the janissaries of the Fáda, and be food for the ever-hungry vultures.

Night fell. The bright white stars shone forth in the clear vault of deep blue with a brilliance that is nowhere seen except in the Great Desert, but through the dark hours the men who had pledged themselves as my friends were busy packing their tents, and at dawn, headed by the green and gold standard, we moved away on the first stage towards the City of the Ahír.

In order to allow time for the other bands of our people to reach Agadez simultaneously with ourselves, we had ten days in which to accomplish a seven days' journey; therefore the first part of our march was at an easy pace, and with everybody buoyant and in excellent spirits, it was not unenjoyable.

Throughout the long day we travelled onward, first down the rocky ravine until we came to a great open, sun-baked plain, devoid of even a blade of herbage, where the way was rough and progress slow, then out into the trackless, stony desert, wherein few, even of the people of Ahír, had ever ventured. Wild, barren, and parched, the broad expanse of uneven stones and patches of sand stretched away as far as the eye could discern, a lone, silent, nature-forsaken land, where not a living thing could exist. Onward over the uneven ground our *méheris* plodded, their spongy feet falling with slow, tedious tread, and our horses stumbling at every step, causing the arms to clank and jingle. Upon a milk-white horse, handsomely caparisoned in gold and purple, Hadj Absalam rode, with keen eye, imperious and commanding, surrounded by his people, to whom his merest gesture was law. Behind him, in litters on the backs of camels, were several women, but the silken curtains of each were drawn to shade them from the sun, therefore I could not distinguish in which Zoraida rode. Around them were a number of faithful horsemen, with rifles across their saddles, while following came a great body of the Ennitra, heavily armed and eager for the attack. My horse, a fine bay thoroughbred, carried me splendidly; nevertheless, the heat was terrific, and throughout the day I suffered greatly from thirst and fatigue. But my companions, careless and light-hearted, discussed on all sides the probabilities of a successful attack, and whiled away the weary, monotonous hours by singing snatches of quaint Arab songs. Thus we marched forward, day after day, over the rugged, waterless wilderness, towards the gilded courts of the Sultan Abd-el-Kerim. Our guns and pistols—many of them ancient flint-locks, with curiously inlaid stocks—were primed, our daggers whetted, and we were all ready for the desperate, bloody struggle into which we must quickly plunge. The Drum of Nâr had gone forth; the Ennitra were rapidly closing in upon the proud and wealthy city.

Spies, who met us in the garb of camel-men, reported that the people of Agadez were continuing their merry-making, in celebration of the formal accession of the young Sultan, and were not dreaming of attack, therefore the way was clear, and a sudden dash would carry us onward, unchallenged, to the Fáda. During the sunniest hours, from noon to *el maghrib*, we usually encamped, making our long, weary journeys over the almost impassable country through the night and early morning; and this having continued for nine days, we at length found ourselves twelve hours' march from the city we intended to plunder. Encamping, we spent six breathless hours, lying hot, panting, and thirsty under what small shade we could improvise; then the order went forth, horses were resaddled, camels, struggling under heavy burdens, regained their feet, and onward we moved again, every eye strained straight before, endeavouring to catch the first glimpse of the square minaret of the Great Mosque which was my goal. In the direction of Agadez the sun sank, and the grey, misty horizon was streaked with lines of blood-red light, Nature's presage, it seemed, of a reign of terror, fire, and sword.

The crowd of stern-faced, hawk-eyed horsemen around me was, for the most part, a motley collection of brutal, villainous-looking Arabs; indeed, from their physiognomy, one could almost imagine that all the criminals of the Algerian cities had formed themselves into a tribe to wage war against their law-abiding compatriots. With coarse jest, low laugh, and murmured imprecation, they spoke of bloodshed and murder with a flippant air, exhibiting always a keen anticipation as to the amount of loot that would fall to their lot, and discussing the probabilities of the women they might capture from the Sultan's harem realising good prices in the slave-markets of the south. Before me was the upright, statuesque figure of the pirate chieftain, and beside him, mounted on a black stallion, with rich gold trappings, was the slight figure of a youth in a dress similar to my own, with white haick, burnouse of palest amaranth silk, and many yards of camels' hair twisted around his head. The rider, whose back was towards me, was unfamiliar, but presently I managed to rein up level with him, and, turning to look, I was amazed to find that the face was that of Zoraida!

Her beautiful countenance was unveiled, and as our eyes met, she nodded and smiled a graceful recognition.

Involuntarily I was prompted to ride up and speak with her, but again remembering her strict injunctions, refrained, and, laughing back to her, spurred onward in front, where the dreaded banner waved lazily in the breath of hot, sand-laden wind. Hiding like any scarred warrior of her tribe, she sat her horse as firmly as if she were part of it, and, heedless of the cloud, of dust raised by those riding on before, or of the constant stumbling of the animal over the rough ground, she seemed the least fatigued of any. Her pale, delicate features, with eyebrows darkened by kohl, were by no means ferocious in the spotless haick that surrounded them, yet it was apparent that she had assumed male attire in order to place herself at the head of these fierce brigands, and that her wistful eyes were constantly turned in my direction, as if wishing to speak, yet not daring to do so.

Once she left Hadj Absalam's side and galloped up to a camel whereon a woman was reclining in a rich, cage-like litter. The occupant drew aside the curtains to speak with her, when I recognised it was Halima. Exchanging a few hurried sentences, they glanced significantly in my direction, by which I knew that I was the object of their conversation, and then Zoraida, with a parting word which seemed like an injunction, spurred back again to the Sheikh's side, while Halima, laughing and waving her hand towards me, drew her curtains again to exclude the hot gusts of whirling sand.

Throughout the evening Zoraida rode onward, smiling with an outward show of happiness, and although I pressed on close to her, she addressed not a word to me. Now and then the Daughter of the Sun would laugh, and the love-look in her eyes told me that her thoughts were constantly of me, and that her silence was enforced. She was leader of the marauders, and her orders were obeyed instantly and faithfully. Hadj Absalam had delivered his authority into her hands, and she had assumed command with the firmness of a military officer, in a manner which showed that it was not the first time that she had occupied that strange position. In galloping, she rode as swiftly and well as any of the bronzed Sons of the Desert, though her hair became unbound and fell in profusion over her shoulders, and she lost one of the tiny heel-less slippers, which, however, was afterwards searched for and recovered by two of her younger cavaliers, one of whom placed her bare foot in it, and received a smile and a word of thanks as reward.

Over sharp rocks and treacherous tufts of hulfa grass, through pebbly ravines and soft sand, into which the horses' hoofs sank deeply at every step, we spurred onward. Zoraida, the beauteous Bringer of Victory, led us to the attack, and of that host none were afraid. From four directions the pirates of the plains were advancing on the City of the Ahír, and all were enthusiastic and confident except myself.

What, I wondered, would be the outcome of this carefully-planned attack on the great Fáda? For Zoraida's safety I trembled. What her fate would be should she chance to fall into the hands of the brutal janissaries, I feared to contemplate. However, though no word was exchanged between us, I was determined to fight by her side, to protect her from her enemies, and dash with this horde of thieves onward to the city in which my one hope was centred.

The Arab had spoken the truth. We had the moon with us, and cared naught for the stars. Zoraida was our light, and we were following her, stout-hearted and strong-armed, prepared to plunder, to murder, to deal death and to spread desolation at every step.

Chapter Thirty Eight
Hadj Absalam's Decree

The attack delivered during the moonlit hours was sharp, decisive, and, being unexpected, was at first little short of a massacre. Yelling with wild, fiendish delight, my companions, Zoraida at their head, swept onward through the gate of Agadez up to the great, gloomy portals of the Fáda, ruthlessly shooting down those who attempted to bar their passage, and engaging in desperate mortal combat with the armed guards, who offered stubborn resistance.

Our success, however, was brief, for our reinforcements had unfortunately not reached us. Recovering quickly from the first shock, the alarm was at once sounded throughout the city. All those capable of bearing arms united to repel us, and as the janissaries in strong bodies poured forth from the Palace gate, the fray soon became fierce and bloody. The Ennitra struggled with desperate courage begotten by the knowledge that they were surrounded by hundreds of the defenders, who would slaughter them and torture those who fell into their hands as prisoners. Knowing not a man would survive if they were defeated, they fought on, madly reckless in their insatiable desire for blood, as with their keen knives they dealt deathblows at those who were defending the gateway, being in turn slashed and maimed by the keen scimitars of the janissaries, until the roads ran with blood, and our horses leaped and stumbled over piles of dead and wounded.

The fight was desperate; the carnage horrible.

On every side men yelled and struggled, while the ill-fated ones fell to earth and died with curses upon their lips. The scene was awful, almost demoniacal, for the shrieks of the vanquished, mingled with the shouts of the victors and the continuous rattle of rifles, drowned the clash of arms.

Amid the desperate conflict I kept as close to Zoraida as possible, though the Ennitra pressed around her, fiercely repelling those who attempted to capture their banner. The Daughter of the Sun, sitting on her sable stallion, with face firm set, gripped in her bejewelled hand a small curved dagger, which from time to time she flourished over her head, urging her outlaw cavaliers to valiant deeds. Time after time her slim, supple figure showed in the very thickest of the mêlée, as with desperate rushes we dashed onward towards the great horse-shoe arch which gave entrance to the Fáda, being, alas! on each occasion met with such strenuous opposition that we were compelled to fall back again, leaving dozens of corpses strewn upon the roadway. Men and horses were hacked in a manner truly horrible by the scimitars of the Sultan's guard, and once or twice Zoraida herself had a narrow escape of death. At moments of extremest peril she behaved in a manner that would have done credit to any trained soldier. Once, as I engaged a well-armed janissary hand to hand in mortal combat, I saw that the guards had broken the ring of fierce warriors who had formed themselves around our standard and dashed into the centre of the group, causing a frightful conflict. Fighting at such close quarters, the long-barrelled guns of the Ennitra were useless, therefore they were compelled to use their knives and swords. Just as, by a lucky cut, I had slashed the right arm of my adversary, I turned to witness a gigantic guard of the harem rush up to Zoraida, brandishing his heavy scimitar, a formidable weapon that I had often burnished and whetted.

"Die, thou accursed son of Eblis!" he shrieked loudly, bringing down his broad, curved blade, that gleamed for a second in the moonbeams; but the fearless leader of the marauders had already become aware of her danger, and, lifting her left hand until it was only a foot from his great brutal countenance, fired her old-fashioned pistol full into his face. The sword fell from his paralysed fingers, and back he staggered next second with half his skull blown away.

Her escape was almost miraculous, yet she betrayed not the slightest trace of fear, although the rust of dust had settled upon the mirror of her beauty. Without a second glance at the body of her slain enemy, she sat her black horse firmly and well, re-primed her pistol, and then fought on with calm courage, heedless of the fact that those whom she led were slowly but surely being swept into eternity by the well-organised opposition they were encountering. Again and again the soldiers of Abd-el-Kerim closed around us in a frantic endeavour to capture the green banner that swayed gloomy and ominous in the brilliant night; but with dogged persistency our men, better armed than their adversaries, fired their rifles with deadly effect, and stood together prepared to fight on desperately until the end. Many were the deeds of cool daring I witnessed during that midnight hour, while men in white burnouses, looking almost ghostly in the deep, enmassed shadows cast by the high walls of the Fáda, struggled with the gorgeously-attired retainers of the Sultan.

Unfortunate wretches, mortally wounded, struggled on till they sank of sheer exhaustion and were trampled to death, and their fellows, some horribly mutilated, with dark, ugly stains upon their burnouses, fought again ere they died, killing their enemies in a frenzy of mad revenge. The encounter grew more desperate every moment. Our hands and faces were besmirched with blood, as larger and more impassable grew the barrier of the slain.

Hadj Absalam had miscalculated the time which must be occupied by the march of our reinforcements, and we had made the assault too early!

Again the heavy gate of the Fáda opened; again there emerged another body of troops. For a moment they halted, then there was a bright, blinding flash, as into our midst a volley was poured, by which a dozen men around me fell from their horses dead. Breathlessly I glanced towards Zoraida, half fearful lest a bullet should strike her, but breathed more freely when I saw her unharmed, still brandishing her knife aloft and shouting words of encouragement to the desperate group of horsemen pressing around her.

"Courage! brothers, courage!" she shouted. "Keep thine enemies at bay, for ere long thou shalt seek revenge within yonder walls. Give no quarter. Let thy strong arms sweep to earth the gilded popinjays of the Sultan!"

"Behold!" cried Amagay, commanding the janissaries, and speaking in a voice that sounded loud above the din of battle. "Lo! the horseman who commandeth the Ennitra seemeth frail, like a woman! What trickery is this? Falter not, fight on! Let not thy scimitars return unto their scabbards until all have fallen!"

Responding to these words, the janissaries made an onward rush that almost overpowered us. With great difficulty, however, we managed to make a stand against it, firing our rifles and slashing at our adversaries in frantic desperation, just managing at length to repulse them sufficiently to prevent our banner from falling into their hands. A serious attack had been made upon Zoraida and Hadj Absalam, but both had struggled with redoubled energy, succeeding in warding off the repeated murderous blows levelled at them.

Those moments were critical ones. Each of us felt that a second rush as powerful as the first would totally annihilate us.

Our fate, indeed, seemed sealed.

Just as our enemies fell back a little, I managed to draw so close to Zoraida that my hand brushed her silken robe. As I reined up, she shouted an order, a dozen rifles rang out, and in a moment the conflict became even more fiercely contested than before. One by one, however, our men dropped their arms and fell from their horses, never to mount again, and I could see that, with the exception of the couple of dozen old men whom we had left on the previous day in charge of the women, camels, and tents, nearly three-fourths of our body had been killed or wounded.

Beside Zoraida I sat in the bright moonbeams, anxiously on the alert. When I saw how critical was our position, I became regardless of her injunctions, and cried—

"It is useless! Let us fly and save ourselves!"

With a strange fire in her beautiful eyes, she turned quickly upon me.

"No," she answered calmly. "Have courage, O Cecil! Dost thou not remember what stake thou hast in the result of this attack?"

Again the rifles of the defenders belched forth their ominous red flashes, as amid the din and rattle a perfect hail of bullets whistled about us; yet she seemed to shed a charmed halo around her, for neither Hadj Absalam nor myself were struck. With teeth firmly set, we struggled on, cutting, slashing, striking death at every blow, amid a scene indescribably weird and ghastly, until each well-delivered volley of the defenders felled dozens of our band to earth, and I knew that the slaughter of my undaunted companions-in-arms would be complete.

The fortune of the fight trembled in the balance. Zoraida's cool, inspiring demeanour and encouraging words stirred the nomadic Ennitra to bold, fearless deeds, and many were the feats of prowess the brigands of the plains in that dark hour accomplished. My life was saved by one of the faithful followers who had assisted Halima and myself to escape. A gigantic, fierce-eyed negro slave of the Fáda had rushed towards me, brandishing his crooked *jambiyah*, and I had fired, missing him. Next moment he closed with me, gripping my throat with long, sinewy fingers, as with a demoniacal, exultant laugh he raised his knife to plunge it deep into my breast, when Halima's slave, fortunately noticing my peril, raised his sword and clave my enemy's skull so swiftly that the warm blood spurted forth over my hands. Without uttering a sound, the dark, evil-visaged brute who intended to kill me staggered and fell back stone dead, while I remained breathless but unharmed.

I gasped a word of thanks to my deliverer, but, shrugging his shoulders, he merely answered, "The Ennitra assist those who fight with them side by side, be they Infidels or Allah's chosen. Thou art our friend and the friend of the Lalla Halima, therefore we are loyal unto thee, and require no thanks for obeying that which is written."

"May Allah honour thee!" I said, fervently thankful, fully realising how narrowly I had once again escaped a violent end.

"And may He be as a lamp shining upon thy path," the man murmured in pious response.

In the desperate onslaught made a few minutes later by the soldiers of the Sultan, now reinforced by a squadron of horsemen who had approached with all speed from the opposite side of the city, Zoraida and I found ourselves together in the thick of the fray. Grappling with their enemies, the Ennitra, with all their bellicose instincts now thoroughly aroused, closed with them in a terrible death-struggle. Each desert-wanderer, determined to sell his life dearly, bade defiance to the great body of janissaries, eunuchs, palace guards, and soldiers, and, armed to the teeth, cut, thrust, and charged, pressing the defenders hard, bearing the brunt of the fight, and showing a bold front in a manner truly astonishing.

With their white drapery flowing in the wind, as they spurred on their horses in repeated efforts to successfully storm the gate of the Fáda, my companions fought like demons. But the defenders held together in solid phalanx, and repulsed us time after time, until many more of our bold, undaunted horsemen lay weltering in their blood.

Again and again Zoraida, whose slim form still showed under the dark standard of the outlaws in the very midst of the desperate conflict, shouted words of encouragement, and each time we swept forward upon the stubborn ranks of the janissaries, only to be ignominiously driven back under a withering fusillade of bullets. Hadj Absalam's gruff voice, raised in desperate imprecation, roared above the din of the fray, but he was unheeded. They obeyed only the commands of the Daughter of the Sun, whom they still implicitly believed would lead them to victory.

In deadly embrace we fought with ferocious strength, grappling our adversaries, and using our knives with horrible fiendishness. Janissaries and eunuchs, slashed and mutilated by the dexterous blows of my dauntless fellow-horsemen, fell groaning to earth, staining the burnouses of the outlaws with their blood; but even then, when slight success aroused redoubled energy within us, any hope of the investment of the Fáda still seemed utterly forlorn.

Suddenly above the noise and tumult there was a loud rumbling, which at first I thought was distant thunder.

"Hearken!" eagerly shouted Zoraida, at that moment only a few feet from me. "Give ear unto me! Lo! it is the rolling of the Drum of Nâr! Fight on! Our brothers are advancing! For evil men Hell, the Worst life; for the righteous the Best Mind, Paradise!"

With a shrill whoop, the Ennitra took up the last sentence as a war-cry, and, with courage strengthened by the knowledge that at last assistance was at hand, dashed forward wildly towards the great arched gateway, many of them being in their reckless onslaught impaled upon the defenders' spears. Then, ere five minutes had passed, with loud, reassuring shouts, mingling with the monotonous thumping of the Drum of Victory, the three bodies of the Ennitra, who, it afterwards appeared, had effected a junction near Tanou-n-Toungaïden, made a vigorous demonstration, by which, in the course of a quarter of an hour, the defenders became hemmed in between two galling fires.

Closely pressed, they were at last, after holding out with dogged resistance until the first flush of dawn, driven back against the gloomy walls of the palace, and there slaughtered without mercy.

The tide of battle turned in favour of the brigands.

There ensued a revolting massacre, from which Zoraida, breathless and panting, turned and shut out its sight by covering her eyes with her delicate hands. The soldiers of the Ahír, finding themselves overpowered by the dreaded band whose vengeance was feared throughout the Soudan, threw down their arms and craved for quarter. But the Ennitra had given rein to their savage bloodthirstiness, and no words from their beautiful leader could avert that fierce, horrible brutality which caused them to be held in dread. Upon their knees proud janissaries of the Sultan Abd-el-Kerim sank in the blood of their comrades, crying hoarsely for mercy, but none was shown them. Dismounted, the men whom Zoraida had rallied and incited to victory threw themselves upon their adversaries, butchering them in cold blood. Murder, mutilation, and torture were rife everywhere in the vicinity of the Fáda, and as the bright streaks of saffron spread in the east, heralding the sun's coming, the massacre was awful.

"Spare the Mesállaje!" cried Zoraida, pointing to the square minaret that loomed dark against the grey of dawn. "Defile not the Great Mosque! The curse of the One of Might rest upon any who dare to enter the holy place with blood upon their hands!"

Quickly the order, shouted aloud, was passed from mouth to mouth, and a few moments later, Zoraida, as she rode swiftly past me, exclaimed—

"With the Mosque free from attack, thou wilt of a surety find the *imam* thou seekest. When it is time I will tell thee;" and away she galloped to where a large force of our people, climbing over the great heap of slain, were battering in the heavy gate of the Fáda, that for centuries had withstood all attack.

At last, by dint of supreme effort, the door was burst open, and with loud, victorious yells, there rushed into the first of the great courts a legion of ferocious brutes, who ruthlessly murdered those who stood in their path. Guards, servants, courtiers, and eunuchs were ferreted from their hiding-places and slaughtered with horrible ferocity, as, headed by Hadj Absalam under his green standard, the thieving hordes swept onward through the luxuriant palace to the Court of the Eunuchs, with which I was so familiar. Then, storming the three great doors of the Sultan's harem, they at last gained that most luxuriant portion of the Fáda.

Zoraida drew back, as if fearing to enter, and for a few seconds stood beside me in the gateway trembling. Summoning courage at last, she allowed herself to be carried on over the bloodstained floors of polished sardonyx and agate into the great arcaded courts, with their columns of marble, plashing fountains, and cool palms. Huddled together in little groups stood the beautiful prisoners of the Sultan, with fear depicted on their handsome faces, as if they had received forewarning of their untimely end. Uttering fiendish yells, the flint-hearted Ennitra, intoxicated by success, bounded towards them, and the awful scenes of loot and massacre that ensued I will not attempt to describe. Suffice it to say that no mercy was shown even to the women. Their jewels were torn from them, fingers on which were valuable rings being unceremoniously hacked off, and their slim white throats and bare breasts were cut and slashed with hellish fiendishness. A few of the more beautiful were chosen by Hadj Absalam to grace his own harem, but the remainder were simply butchered with merciless ruthlessness, the jewels filched from them being flung unceremoniously into a great heap in the centre of the gorgeous Courts of Love, and over it a dozen of the outlaws mounted guard.

The massacre was sickening. Piercing screams of the women as they fell under the knives of their pitiless captors echoed along the great arcades, mingling with the jeers of the outlaws and the hoarse cries of the dying. Blood ran across the polished floors, and, trickling into the fountains, tinged their waters, the walls of marble were bespattered with it, and the once-beautiful Courts of Love were rendered hideous by their piles of mutilated corpses, and became a ghastly Inferno, to be remembered with a fearsome shudder until one's dying day.

Horrified by the terrible sights I had witnessed, I endeavoured to draw back, but with loud shouts the crowd, excited to madness by their work of murder and pillage, made a sudden rush to the Sultan's pavilion, and involuntarily I was carried onward.

"Seek Abd-el-Kerim!" they cried. "Kill him! kill him!" Through the harem-garden, along the edge of the great lake, and on into the Hall of the White Divan they pressed. On entering, we found under the great baldachin of silk and gold the young Sultan, with his Grand Vizier Mukhtar and Amagay, the chief of his eunuchs, on either side, standing erect, regarding our entrance with regal air and unflinching eye. He had drawn his scimitar and was prepared to defend himself.

"What meaneth this intrusion?" he cried, the fierce fire of anger in his face. "Verily hast thou rushed into the Wrath, and the blow of destruction shall descend upon thee!"

"Spare us!" cried Mukhtar, rushing forward, trembling, cringing coward that he was.

"We are thy slaves," added Amagay, throwing away his sword. "Have mercy upon us! Take what thou mayest, but slay us not!"

The fierce, dishevelled band, heedless of all appeal, dashed onward, led by Hadj Absalam. A dozen men rushed forward to dispatch the Sultan, but the latter, wielding his jewelled scimitar, felled the first outlaw who approached, inflicting a mortal wound. Next moment, however, the youthful ruler of the Ahír, pulled unceremoniously off the divan, was struggling powerless in the hands of his ragged conquerors.

For his curses they cared naught, but at a signal from Hadj Absalam, who had in the meantime mounted to the deposed monarch's place, Labakan stepped forward, armed with the executioner's heavy *doka*, which he had just found while searching for plunder.

"Let him die!" exclaimed Hadj Absalam briefly.

"Ah! spare me, O conqueror!" gasped the unhappy youth. "It is written—it is written that the blessings of Allah rest upon the merciful! Spare me!"

But the Sultan, pale and haggard, was quickly forced to his knees upon the polished pavement before his own divan and held with his hands behind his back. Piteous were his appeals, but they softened not his captors' murderous, sanguinolent hearts. The great diamond aigrette was ruthlessly torn from his turban and handed to the robber Sheikh, and then, as the men held him down firmly, Labakan stepped forward, and, swinging the *doka* with both hands, smote off his head at a single blow.

The body, quickly despoiled of its jewels, was kicked aside into a corner, while the head, mounted on a spear, was sent forth into the city in order to strike awe into the hearts of those citizens who refused to submit to the conquerors.

Mukhtar and Amagay were also decapitated in like manner and without ceremony by the villainous Labakan, who, judging from the self-satisfied grin upon his sinister countenance, delighted in the gruesome duties of his self-assumed office. Once he glanced at me and smiled. Doubtless it would have afforded him considerable pleasure to strike off my head by the same means.

In their frenzied thirst for blood, many of my companions, rushing onward, pillaged the Sultan's private apartments and the Treasury. Thence they went to the Hall of Audience.

Here a band of janissaries at first made a desperate stand, but they were eventually butchered, even to the last man.

Through the city wildly yelling bands of the Ennitra were rushing with fire and sword. The hours were spent by them in murder and pillage, in mutilation, in every conceivable kind of nameless atrocity. Into the houses they rushed, penetrating to the apartments of the women, murdering the occupants, and carrying off all that was valuable. Deeds of violence and lawlessness were committed with cruel brutality and heartlessness; women and children were slaughtered before the eyes of husbands and fathers, who in their turn were also murdered in cold blood. Many went down on their knees, supplicating with heads bent to the ground, crying for quarter, and in that attitude were butchered mercilessly by their conquerors. In the open space called the Azarmádarangh between four and five hundred young men and women had by noon been collected to be sold as slaves, and as each hour passed, others were added to the number. Some attempted to escape, and were shot down in consequence, but the majority gave themselves up to their fate, and squatted on the ground silent and morose. The women wept and wailed, but the men made no complaint. They had fought, Fortune had deserted them, and their Sultan's head was being carried around Agadez to the monotonous thumping of the ancient Drum of Nâr. Upon the pinnacles and minarets the great vultures of dirty-greyish plumage with naked necks were awaiting impatiently the feast that the marauders had provided for them, and the captives, noticing them, regarded their presence as an omen that the power of the Sultans of the Ahír had been broken for ever.

In Abd-el-Kerim's pavilion, where I remained, Hadj Absalam, with his banner planted over the great canopy, was seated upon the divan with Zoraida at his side. While the work of plunder was proceeding throughout the Fáda, the apartment was filled to overflowing by a crowd of the less excited of his bloodthirsty band. Labakan having taken his stand on the other side of the chieftain, resting upon his great bloodstained executioner's sword, Hadj Absalam at length commenced an address to his people. But the latter, after he had uttered half a dozen sentences, mainly egotistical of his own prowess, refused him further hearing, crying—

"Let our Daughter of the Sun speak, O Mirror of Virtue! We trusted her and were not afraid. Let her have speech with us!"

"Speak then," he said, annoyed, turning to Zoraida. "May the fear of thy Ruler lie upon thy lips."

Casting a quick inquiring glance at him, she smiled pleasantly upon those around her, saying—

"Lo! thy Sheikh, thy Branch of Honour, hath led thee through these courts of the Fáda—wherefore dost thou not honour him?"

"It was thy voice alone that rallied us when we were failing, and guided us at the critical moment unto a victory great and glorious!" cried one of the warriors, a statement that was hailed with extreme approbation.

Gracefully she bowed in recognition of the compliment, saying, "What I have done hath been in accordance with the promise given unto me. Once again have I led thee to victory, though it be for the last time."

A murmur of dissent went round, and a voice inquired the reason.

"Because," she said,—"Because thou hast conquered the City of the Ahír, therefore thou hast no further need of my services—"

"I have. Thou shalt now become Pearl of my Harem!" Hadj Absalam interrupted, with a scowl of displeasure upon his furrowed face.

This declaration produced a sensation almost electrical, and it seemed that, even though the prospect might be distasteful to them, none dare challenge the autocrat. Zoraida, too, turned pale, clenched her tiny hands, and bit her lips to the blood.

"Brothers," she gasped, her voice faltering, "I, Daughter of the Sun, am thy sister. Oft-times have I risked my life to ensure success in thy forays. Art thou still loyal unto me?"

"We are," they answered, as with one voice.

"Then I fear not mine enemies," she exclaimed, drawing herself up and flinging back her blood—besmirched silken robe with a defiant air. "To-day thou hast broken the power of a great Sultan and beheaded him; thou hast invested the palace that all thought impregnable; thou hast captured many slaves, and thou hast secured plunder almost as valuable as the Treasure of Askiá, which lieth hidden. I led thee hither, but the tenure of my leadership is at an end. Bow now unto the authority of thy Sheikh, and treat me only as one who hath rendered thee a service."

"It is but fitting that, now we have conquered Agadez, thou shouldst become Malieah of the Ahír," Hadj Absalam protested. "I appeal to thee, my people. Do I give voice unto thy wish?" The armed men looked at one another in hesitation. Then one, a big, hulking, half-witted fellow, stepped forward, and, turning back to his companions, exclaimed—

"Is not the beauty of our Daughter of the Sun known throughout the Great Desert; is she not our Lady of Wondrous Beauty, with whom none can compare? Did not the great Sultan, Mulai Hassan, of Fez, offer one hundred bags of gold for her? Why should she not grace our people by becoming the chief wife of our wise and just ruler? She would still retain her power to bring victory unto us, and would at the same time reflect upon us perpetually the light of her beauteous countenance."

Labakan grinned. It was, I felt sure, one of his devilish schemes. "Are any of the houris whom thou hast spared in yonder harem half as beautiful as the Lalla Zoraida?" he asked. "Surely she with the loveliest face should become Queen?"

"Hearken unto me, O my brothers!" Zoraida cried anxiously. "Until this moment thou hast granted me freedom. It is a privilege that as long as I live I will not forego; if thou forcest upon me this marriage, remember that my self-sought death will fall upon thee as a curse, swift and terrible."

"Thy beauty designateth thee as our Sultana!" they answered, influenced by the arguments of the wily Labakan and the others. "Thou must become Queen of the Courts of Love!"

"And is this—is this how thou repayest one who hath acted as a lamp in thy darkness; thy Lode Star that hath led thee unto prosperity?" she cried, with bitterness. "Of a truth herein thou showest—"

"Daughter, thou treatest the generous gift of thy Ruler with contempt," Hadj Absalam roared in anger.

"I utter no contemptuous words," she answered, resolutely calm. "Thou hast conceived a plan to marry me against my will, because of what thou art pleased to call my fair face. Verily, I tell thee that if thou attemptest to force thine hateful favours upon me, my knife here shall score mine own cheeks and render them hideous unto thy sight! Failing that, I—I will kill myself!"

"Bah!" cried the Sheikh, impatiently tugging at his beard. "Thou lovest the white-faced Roumi to whom we have given succour!"

"If he were killed, her objection would be removed," observed Labakan, gesticulating with hands that were smeared and sticky with blood. His cool suggestion was received with mingled approbation and dissent.

"Wouldst thou murder one who hath proved himself thy firm friend?" Zoraida asked, her eye fixed upon the man who had already attempted to assassinate me. Shrugging his shoulders, he showed his even white teeth in a hideous grin, but made no reply.

"Vengeance cometh—vengeance just upon the faithless and those who betray their friends. Their couch shall be in hell!" she continued. "If thou forcest me to sacrifice my life, of a verity wilt thou deliver the Lie unto Truth, and bring upon thee ruin and shame abiding. *Cama tafakal kathâlik tolâ ki!*" ("Such as you will do, so will you find.")

But the fierce, brutal murderers grouped around only laughed. Her strange power over them seemed to have suddenly vanished, for, with her uncovered face handsome in their eyes, there was, alas! a consensus of opinion that she should become the chief wife of their chieftain! What could I do to save her? Nothing. Glancing across at me with a look of mute appeal, she stood silent, her hand upon the hilt of her knife. She seemed deeply agitated, for though her lips moved, no sound escaped them.

Again the half-witted brute who had urged the desirability of the hateful union turned to his companions, asking: "Is it thy desire that the Daughter of the Sun should be exalted and become our Queen of Delights and the Light of our Darkness?"

"Thy words are truly words of wisdom!" his companions cried loudly, with only two or three dissentients. "Our Ruler must take her as his wife."

The cruel face of Hadj Absalam broadened into a benign smile, while Labakan's eyes glittered with murderous craftiness, as, with hands tightly clasped and tears upon her beautiful cheeks, Zoraida made a final desperate appeal—

"A moment ago didst thou vow loyalty unto me, my brothers. Yet even now wilt thou force me into a loveless union that is distasteful—that—that will cause me to seek death by mine own hand! If I have offended, cast me from thee, but wreck not my happiness by an odious marriage! Ever have I been unswervingly loyal unto thee, and He in whose hand is the Kingdom of all Things will assuredly be swift in punishing those who seek my self-destruction. Blessings are the lot of the pure and the merciful. Force this not upon me, O my brothers! Hear and grant this my most fervent supplication!"

There was silence. Fierce words in her defence were upon the tip of my tongue, but—fortunately perhaps—I managed to suppress them.

"It is to-day, peradventure, too early to carry out my generous proposal," Hadj Absalam observed, utterly unmoved by her appeal. "In one moon shall I compel the Lalla Zoraida to become the Pearl of my Harem."

"Thy will be accomplished, O Ruler of exalted merit," they answered. But the woman I loved, hearing his decision, clasped her hands to her temples, murmuring in dismay, "One moon! One moon!" and, taking two or three quick, uneven steps, tottered forward and fell heavily upon her face ere a hand could be outstretched to save her.

A dozen men rushed forth, I among the number. Water was given her quickly, and in obedience to an order from the Sheikh she was carried away, helpless and unconscious, to one of the apartments in the great harem, which, alas! was now strewn with the corpses of its former luxury-loving inmates. I dared not follow, so remained, to hear my companions extolling the wisdom of Hadj Absalam's brutal decision.

Nauseated by the hideous sights of blood that everywhere met my gaze as I wandered through the spacious courts so familiar to me, the afternoon passed heavily. None of my companions, save the wounded, sought their siesta; all were too absorbed in their work of plunder, bringing the treasure they discovered before the Sheikh, who remained seated beneath the royal canopy, so that he might inspect all that was found. Every hole and corner of the spacious Fáda was ransacked, and the pile of gold and silver vessels, jewels, ornaments, and pearl-embroidered robes swelled larger and larger, until it formed a heap that reached almost to the painted ceiling of the pavilion. Backwards and forwards I passed unnoticed, for all were now totally absorbed in their diligent search for articles of value. My only thought was of Zoraida. The decree of the cruel, heartless Sultan of the Sahara had gone forth, endorsed by the decision of the people, and to rescue her from becoming an inmate of the old brigand's harem seemed an impossibility.

An hour after sundown, as I was wandering through the wrecked Court of the Eunuchs, revisiting the scene of those toilsome days of my slavery, a veiled woman approached. Drawing aside her *adjar*, the bright, smiling face of Halima was revealed. The women we had left outside the city prior to the attack had already arrived, for in a few brief words she told me that Zoraida had been placed under her care. Her mistress, who had recovered from her faint, had expressed a desire to see me immediately, therefore she had come in search of me.

"Enter the harem," she said. "Walk down the arcade on the right until thou comest unto the third door. Push it open, and therein wilt thou find our Daughter of the Sun."

I briefly thanked her, and, rearranging her veil, she strolled leisurely away to avoid arousing suspicion. Within ten minutes I was speeding along the arcade, gloomy in the darkening hour, and rendered ghastly by the presence of the mutilated dead. My heart beat as if it would burst its bonds. At the third door I halted, and, pushing it open, passed through a kind of vestibule into a small thickly-carpeted apartment, hung with rich silken hangings, and fragrant with sweet odours that rose from a gold perfuming-pan.

From her soft, luxuriant divan, Zoraida, still in her masculine dress, rose to meet me. She was pale, and her hand trembled, as for a few moments we remained clasped in affectionate embrace, while I kissed her in rapture, with many affectionate declarations of love.

"What must I do?" I asked breathless, at last. "How can I save thee?"

"By performing the mission thou hast promised," she answered, the pressure of her hand tightening upon mine as she gazed into my eyes.

"That I will do most willingly," I said.

"Then lo! here is the Crescent of Glorious Wonders," she said, producing that mysterious object from between the cushions of her divan, "and here also is a letter to Mohammed ben Ishak. Deliver it, and learn the Secret. Then canst thou extricate me from the danger that threateneth."

"But must I be absent from thee long?"

"I know not. Thy mission may perchance occupy thee many days."

"And in the meantime thou mayest be forced to become the wife of that brute, Hadj Absalam!"

"Never!" she cried, setting her teeth. "I will kill myself!"

"Is it imperative that I should be absent from thy side in this the hour of thy peril?" I asked, placing my arm tenderly around her neck and drawing her closer towards me.

A flash of love-light gleamed on her sweet face.

"Yes. Seek the *imam* to-night, ere it be too late. Whatever he telleth thee, investigate at all cost. If thou art successful in obtaining a revelation of the Wondrous Mystery, assuredly thou wilt save me from a fate that I fear worse than the grave."

"Trust me, O Zoraida!" I answered, kissing her fervently, as I took the Crescent and the scrap of paper, concealing them in my clothing. "On leaving thee, I will not halt until I have found the holy man, and have gained from him that knowledge which he alone can give. But what of thee? While I am absent, thou wilt be friendless!"

"Allah, the One Merciful, all things discerneth; to us shall it be as He willeth," she said, slowly raising my hand and pressing my fingers to her lips.

"If thou art, alas! forced to become Queen of this kingdom of murderers! If thou art—"

"I am a follower of the Faith, and place my trust in the Uniter of the Lover and Beloved," she interrupted softly, clasping me in her clinging arms. "By woman's wit I may perchance escape the hateful doom that Hadj Absalam hath devised, under the advice of our enemy, Labakan; therefore let the burdens of my peril be uplifted from thine heart. Seek the director of those who tread the Path, and attend with faith and minuteness unto his instructions."

"The thought that we may be for ever parted must fill me until my return," I said. "But canst thou not fly with me, even now?"

"Alas! no," she answered gloomily. "Escape ere thou hast fathomed the Great Mystery is impossible. I must abide in patience, overshadowed by deadly peril and the dread thought that we may never meet again. But"— and she hesitated—"tell me—answer me with thine own lips one question I would address unto thee."

"What wouldst thou know?"

"Tell me," she said, burying her head upon my breast—"Tell me if thou wilt forgive me for—for the awful massacre that hath to-day been committed?"

"Forgive thee!" I cried, my kisses warming her waxen hands. "Of course I do. Forced to occupy a strange position, thou canst not struggle against thy fate, therefore the horrible butchery is due to neither plot nor strategy of thine, but to the fierce avarice and brutal bloodthirstiness of those who now prove themselves thine enemies."

"Ah! verily thou art generous!" she exclaimed, with tears in her luminous eyes, around which dark rings were showing. "The life of cities, as the life of men, is a vain and uncertain thing, and none knoweth the weal or ill thereof, and none knoweth the end or the way of the end, save only Allah. To thee I entrust my life. Go! seek the key to the Great Mystery, the knife by which my bonds can only be severed. I will fight to preserve mine honour until I die. I am thine until the heavens shall be cloven in sunder, and the stars shall be scattered. May Allah shadow thee in His shadow, and give unto thee strength to perform in faithfulness thy covenant! May He bless and preserve thee, and may He cause thee to drink from the cup of His Prophet, Mohammed, that pleasant draught, after which there is no thirst to all eternity! It is time, O Cecil! Go!"

"Farewell, my one beloved," I said, with a lingering kiss, as her fair head still rested upon my breast. "May the One who sweepeth away darkness guard thee and disappoint not thine hopes! Verily will I set out upon this mission at once, for as steadfastly true thou art unto me, so am I unto thee."

For a long time, as we stood in silence, I rained passionate kisses upon her lips, cold as marble. She trembled, fearing the worst, yet, gathering her strength in a supreme effort to preserve her self-control, she at last pushed me from her with gentle firmness, saying—

"Hasten! Night draweth quickly on, and thou hast but little time to spare. Hourly shall I think of thee until thou returnest with the glad tidings. *Slama!* Allah knoweth the innermost parts of the breasts of men. May His mercy and His bounteous blessing be upon thee!"

"Verily He is Praised and Mighty!" I responded. Then, with a long kiss of farewell, I breathed a few whispered words of passion into her ear, and, promising to return at the earliest moment, I released her supple form from my embrace, and, stumbling blindly out, left her standing, pale, friendless, and alone.

Devoutly-murmured words of a fervent prayer fell upon my ears as I turned from her presence, but I halted not, striding onward—onward in search of the knowledge and elucidation of the Great Mystery, onward to an unknown, undreamed-of bourne.

Chapter Thirty Nine
Mohammed Ben Ishak

That night, while the ferocious horde, half demented by delight, still continued their fell work of massacre and pillage, I slipped through the small arched gate into the courtyard of the Great Mosque.

Outside, in the roadway, corpses thickly strewn showed how desperate had been the conflict. Bodies of men were lying about the streets in hundreds, perhaps thousands, for I could not count—some with not a limb unsevered, some with heads hacked and cross-cut and split lengthwise, some ripped up, not by chance, but with careful precision down and across, disembowelled and dismembered. Indeed, groups of prisoners, tied together with their hands behind their backs, had been riddled with bullets and then hewn in pieces. The sight was awful; but why repeat it in all its painful detail?

The Ennitra had, however, faithfully obeyed Zoraida's injunctions, and the sacred building remained deserted and untouched, although a guard was stationed at the gate to prevent any fugitive from seeking shelter there. In the lurid glare cast by the burning houses to which the firebrand had been applied, I saw how spacious was the open court. A great fountain of black marble, with ancient tiles of white and blue, plashed in the centre, inviting the Faithful to their Wodû; a vine, centuries old, spread its great branches overhead in a leafy canopy, shading worshippers from the sun's scorching rays; while the stones, cracked and broken, the exquisitely dented horse-shoe arches, the battered walls of marble and onyx, all spoke mutely of the many generations who had performed their pious prostrations there. Like sentinels, fig and orange trees stood black against the fire-illumined sky, and as I halted for a moment, the tumult beyond the sacred precincts grew louder, as those whom I had been compelled to call "friends" spread destruction everywhere.

The white façade of the majestic structure presented a most picturesque aspect, with its long arcade of many arches supported by magnificent pillars of marble, while above rose a handsome cupola, surmounted by its golden crescent and its high square minaret, bright with glazed tiles, whence the *mueddin* had for centuries charted his call to prayer.

Kicking off my shoes at the great portal of porphyry, I was about to enter, when my eyes fell upon a stone above, whereon an Arabic inscription had been carved. Translated, it read as follows—

"The virtues of this sanctuary spread themselves abroad
Like the light of the morning, or the brilliancy of the stars.
O ye who are afflicted with great evils, he who will cure them for you
Is the son of science and profound nobility,
ABDERRAHMAN.
745 of Hedjira." (A.D. 1353.)

On entering, all seemed dark and desolate. At the far end of the spacious place a single lamp burned with dull, red glow, and as with bare feet I moved noiselessly over the priceless carpets, my eyes grew accustomed to the semi-obscurity, and I saw how magnificent was the architecture of the lofty interior. Three rows of horse-shoe arches, supported by curiously-hewn columns, divided it into three large halls, the roofs of which were of fine cedar, with wonderful designs and paintings still remaining. From the arches hung ostrich eggs in fringed nets of silk, the walls were covered with inscriptions and arabesques in wood and plaster, while marbles of divers colours formed a dado round the sanctuary, and the glare of fire outside sent bars of ruddy light, through the small *kamarîyas*, or windows, placed high up and ornamented with little pieces of coloured glass. Lamps of enamelled glass, of jasper, of wrought silver and beaten gold hung everywhere, and the niche, or *mirhâb*, indicating the direction of Mecca, before which a solitary worshipper had prostrated himself, was adorned with beautiful mosaics of marble, porphyry, and mother-of-pearl, with sculptured miniature arcades in high relief, framed with a border of good words from the Korân.

Astonished at the vast extent and imposing character of the building, I halted behind the *mimbar*, or pulpit of the *imam*, and, gazing round upon the dimly-lit but magnificent interior, awaited in silence the termination of the single worshipper's prayer. At last, as he rose, slowly lifting his hands aloft in final supplication, I saw he was one of the *hezzabin*. As he turned, I advanced, addressing him, saying—

"May the peace of Allah, who taught the pen, rest upon thee, O Header of the Everlasting Will!"

"And upon thee peace amid the tumult!" he answered.

"I seek the Hadj Mohammed ben Ishak, director of the Faithful," I said. "Canst thou direct me unto him?"

But even as I spoke, the reader of the Korân had detected by my dress that I was one of the hated devastating band, and poured upon me a torrent of reproach and abuse for daring to defile the mosque by my presence. Assuring him that I had the best intentions, and showing him the scrap of paper Zoraida had given me, whereon the *imam's* name was inscribed, I at length appeased him.

"If thou desirest to convey unto the Hadj Mohammed the written message, I will take it," he said reluctantly, at length convinced by the strenuous manner in which I urged the importance of my business with the head of the Mesállaje.

"I am charged to deliver it only into the hands of the *imam* himself," I answered. "Wilt thou not lead me unto him, when I tell thee that the matter concerns the life of one who is his friend?"

Still he hesitated; but further appeal moved him, and, ordering me to remain, he reluctantly passed through a small panelled door, inlaid with ivory and ebony, that led from the *lîwân*, or eastern recess, leaving me alone. Nearly ten anxious minutes went by ere he returned; then, without utterance, he motioned me to follow him. This I did with alacrity, passing through the door, so constructed as to be indistinguishable from the other panels which formed the dado in that portion of the sanctuary, and as it closed behind us noiselessly, I found myself in total darkness. There was a smell of mustiness and decay; but I was prepared for any adventure, for was I not seeking to obtain knowledge of a mysterious and extraordinary secret?

"Let me guide thy footsteps," muttered my companion, and, taking me by the arm, he led me along a narrow passage apparently running parallel with the sanctuary, and constructed in the width of its massive walls. Stumbling along for some distance, we at last turned sharply, where in a small niche there stood a lighted hand-lamp, so placed that its rays remained concealed. Taking it up, he held it before him, and by its yellow, uncertain glimmer we descended a long zig-zag flight of steep, broken steps, deep down into the earth. At the bottom he suddenly drew aside a heavy curtain that hung behind a low arch, and I found myself in a small subterranean chamber, dimly-lit by a brass hanging lamp.

"Lo! the stranger entereth thy presence!" my guide exclaimed, withdrawing almost before my eyes could take in the details of my strange surroundings.

"*Mìn aine jûyi!*" exclaimed a thin, weak voice, and I saw enshrined upon a divan on the opposite side of the apartment a venerable old man of stately presence, his long white beard and portly figure adding materially to the dignity of his bearing.

Returning his greeting, I advanced, noting his thin face, parchment-like skin, and his wasted fingers grasping the black rosary that showed he had made the pilgrimage.

"Know, O Director of those who follow the Right Way, that I bear unto thee a message from Zoraida, who is called the Daughter of the Sun!"

"A message—at last!" he cried, removing his pipe in sudden surprise, as, struggling to his feet, he strode to the door, drew back the curtain, and looked up the stairs, to make certain that the reader of the Korân had actually departed. Quickly returning, with his wizened face full of agitation and his piercing coal-black eyes fixed upon me, he requested me to hand him the letter.

Breaking the seal, he opened the crumpled but precious piece of paper and eagerly devoured the lines of Arabic. As he held it beneath the lamp, I caught a furtive glimpse of it. The scrawled lines had apparently been hastily penned, and beneath there was a dark oval blotch. Straining my eyes, I could just distinguish that it was the impression of a thumb that had been dipped in blood—a seal that could not be imitated!

Without a word, the aged man crossed to an ancient cabinet, inlaid with ivory and silver forming texts from the Korân, and therefrom took a parchment. With trembling hands he unrolled it, and, bringing it to the light, compared it minutely with Zoraida's letter. Upon the parchment was a similar impression, which apparently corresponded to his satisfaction with that on the paper I had brought.

"So thou art the Roumi from beyond the sea upon whom our Lady of Beauty hath gazed with favour?" he exclaimed, turning and surveying me critically after he had carefully put away both documents.

"I am, O Father," I answered. "For many moons have I travelled to seek thee, but have been thwarted in all my efforts until this moment. I am bearer of a precious object, the secret of which thou alone knowest;" and from beneath my gandoura I drew forth the Crescent of Glorious Wonders.

"Verily hast thou acted with faith and fearlessness," he said, taking the piece of metal in his talon-like fingers and seeking the mystic inscription. "Undaunted, thou hast faced many perils in order to fulfil thine oath. Already the report of thy sufferings and thine hardships, and the attempts made upon thy life, hath been conveyed unto me. While thou wert a slave in the Fáda, I knew of thy bondage, and tried to reach and release thee, but without avail. To me the circumstances of the loss and extraordinary recovery of this strangely-shaped phylactery entrusted to thy keeping are no new thing, for while upon thy wanderings thou hast been watched by eyes unseen."

"Didst thou know that I was endeavouring to reach thee?" I asked, amazed. "How didst thou obtain thy knowledge?"

"The Wearer of the Flower knoweth all things he desireth," the aged *imam* answered simply. But his words were full of meaning, for they implied that I had been watched by secret emissaries of the Senousya. Members of this secret brotherhood of Al-Islâm are initiated by the taking of a flower, of which there are fifteen, each being significant of a certain sect.

When two Believers meet as strangers, one will say to the other, "What blossom wearest thou?" a question which is the "Who goes there?" of the affiliation. If the individual to whom the question is addressed has not been initiated into the Senousya, he will reply, "I am no Wearer of the Flower. I am simply the humble servant of Allah."

"The Wearers of the Flower are all-powerful," I said.

"Thou speakest the truth," he answered; piously adding: "Of a surety will the Prophet send his liberator, who will drive the Infidel invaders into the sea. Then will True Believers rise in their millions, and the land of Al-Islâm will be delivered out of the hands of the oppressor. As the locusts devour all green things, so shall the Senousya smite and destroy the Infidels with a strength as irresistible as the falchion of Fate."

"I am one of thine oppressors," I hazarded, smiling.

"No. Thou, although a Roumi, art a respecter of our laws and a friend of our people. At what is written thou hast never scoffed, but hast sought to deliver the fairest woman of Al-Islâm from dangers that have beset her feet."

"Wherein lie those dangers?" I asked anxiously. "In vain have I tried to obtain explanation."

"Unto thee the truth will be revealed in due course. From her own lips wilt thou obtain knowledge," he replied impressively. "Thou lovest her. Some day thou wilt tread the Right Path and believe in Allah, Lord of the Three Worlds. Then shalt thou marry her."

"She hath sent me unto thee because, in Algiers, the Secret of the Crescent was denied me," I said.

"Of that I am aware," he exclaimed. "Already hast thou sought the Unknown and witnessed some of our marvels; but there are others more wondrous that must convince thee. Faith shutteth the seventy doors of evil, and giveth passage over Al-Sirât, the bridge, sharp as a sword and finer than a hair, that stretcheth between hell and Paradise."

"I have faith," I said fervently, remembering the weird things Zoraida had shown me. "Thou knowest the Great Secret, and if thou art so inclined, canst impart unto me knowledge whereby I may rescue the woman I love."

The holy man asked me what peril appeared to surround Zoraida, and in reply I briefly described the scene that had been enacted in the Fáda that day, and told him of Hadj Absalam's declaration of his intention to make her his wife. My words aroused within him the fiercest anger, and as he paced the apartment with feverish steps, he uttered terrible threats against the Sheikh of the despoilers.

"Twice would the Sultan of the Sahara have taken my life, had not Zoraida saved me," I pointed out.

"Allah showeth mercy only to the merciful," he observed, halting suddenly before me. "Cast thine eyes about thee here in Agadez, and gaze upon the frightful ruin wrought to-day by those hell-hounds. Verily are they the sons of Eblis, who walk in the darkness, and to whom all blessings are denied. May their vitals be burned with the fire unquenchable, and may their thirst be slaked with molten metal. Abuser of the salt, and unfaithful Wearer of the Flower, Hadj Absalam seeketh now to crown his many villainies by forcing the Lalla Zoraida, who is pure as the jasmine blossom, to become his wife! *Hâsha!* We shall see! We shall see!"

"She telleth me that I can save her if I discover the Great Secret," I said, with anxious impatience.

"Thou hast not been initiated into the Senousya, neither art thou a True Believer; nevertheless, thou hast kept thy word even at risk of thine own life," he exclaimed, reflectively twisting his rosary between his thin, nervous fingers. The thought of Zoraida's peril seemed to have completely unnerved him.

"Hither have I journeyed from Algiers on purpose to seek explanation of thee," I urged. "Think! the liberty, nay, the life, of one who is as innocent as she is fair is at stake. If thou refusest, I can do nothing. She will become the wife of a man whose fiendish brutality is a by-word and a reproach to the Moslem world. Is it surprising that she hath decided to take her life rather than fall into his polluted hands? Consider, O Reciter of the Prayers—thou who teachest goodwill towards men—reveal unto me, I beseech thee, that which is hidden and the elucidation of which can alone secure the safety of my betrothed."

"But thou art not a True Believer," he protested, shaking his head gravely. "How dare I invoke the Wrath by revealing unto thee the Great Secret, with which I alone of men have been entrusted?"

"Wilt thou not—for Zoraida's sake?" I urged again, growing alarmed at his increasing inclination to preserve the mystery.

"Within this steel there lieth hidden a secret which none know," he said, again examining the Crescent carefully. "Through ages hath it been passed from hand to hand, experiencing many vicissitudes, stranger even than the tales of the story-tellers, or the romances of the Thousand and One Nights, yet its true power hath remained hidden from its various owners, and its secret influence is to all undreamed of."

"How can its power avert Zoraida's peril and give unto her peace?" I inquired anxiously.

"I know not. Peradventure there are minor secrets connected with it of which even I am in ignorance. Yet assuredly must a man believe that there is no God but Allah ere he can rest beneath the tree called Tûba (the tree of happiness), or dwell within the Jannat al Naïm." (The garden of pleasure.)

"Though an Infidel, I respect thy belief profoundly," I said, endeavouring to break down the barrier of his fanatical prejudice. "That I have never reproached a True Believer, impugned his devoutness, or ridiculed that which thou boldest sacred, thou hast already acknowledged. Indeed, I follow many of thy beliefs, and acknowledge the truth of the declaration of thy Khalîf Omar ebn Abd'alaziz, that prayer carrieth us half-way to Allah, fasting bringeth us to the door of His palace, and alms procureth us admission. But not as one who respecteth and honoureth thy people of Al-Islâm seek I the elucidation of the Great Mystery; it is in order that the life of the Lalla Zoraida may be spared, and that she and I may at last become united in wedlock."

The patriarchal head of the old *imam* was bent as he mumbled over his rosary. The words I uttered were intensely in earnest, for Zoraida's final appeal still rang in my ears, and I knew that I had but one short month in which to rescue her from the clutches of the inhuman brute who would snatch her from me for ever.

"Believe," he urged at last. "Turn not to folly, but learn thou the truth, and live in piety; for verily I tell thee that the Holy War is near at hand. Then all of us,—with the exception of the Ennitra, who are the thrice-cursed sons of Eblis,—laying aside all fear and dread, will, guided by the Giver of Strength, strive with one accord against the enemies of the Faith; for Allah the Comforter knoweth that if any man die, he dieth for the truth of the

Faith, for the salvation of his land, for the protection of the tombs and holy cities, and the defence of the Belief. Therefore shall he obtain of Him the bounteous reward in the Jannat al Ferdaws, peopled by the beautiful Hûr al oyûn, that He alone can give."

"I believe in the marvels I have already witnessed," I answered. "I am convinced that thou canst reveal unto me means by which I can release the woman I love from the harem of villainy, ere it be too late. Has she not in her letter requested thee to afford me explanation, in order that I may gain the knowledge for our mutual advantage?"

He hesitated. With his dark, gleaming eyes fixed steadfastly upon me, he remained motionless in deep reflection.

"Darest thou leave this City of the Doomed to go forth in search of what may appear unto thee but the merest phantom?" he asked slowly.

"Zoraida is in deadliest peril," I urged. "Would my absence be of long duration?"

"I cannot answer. Thou art young and reckless. With a stout heart thou mightest obtain knowledge of the truth within short space."

"But within one moon, Zoraida—with whom no woman of Al-Islâm can compare—will be imprisoned in the harem of the conqueror, and she will be irretrievably lost to me!" I urged.

He shrugged his shoulders. "Art thou still undaunted?" he asked. "Art thou still prepared to continue thine efforts to effect her rescue?"

"I am, O Father," I answered fervently. "Tell me, I beseech thee, how to act."

"The medium through which thou canst alone seek to elucidate the Great Mystery hath been hidden from man through many ages," he said in a strange, croaking voice, handling the Crescent of Glorious Wonders as tenderly as if it were a child. "This ancient talisman, which bringeth good fortune and victory to its possessor, containeth a property which is unknown to the wise men of our generation, though when Cleopatra reigned in Egypt the hidden force was well known and freely utilised. To the True Believer this Crescent giveth valour and power over his enemies, besides averting the evil eye, like the hand of Fathma; but profaned by the touch of the Roumi, it assuredly bringeth ruin, disaster, and death. Over our Lalla Zoraida there hangeth a fate that is worse than death, yet that can be averted, provided thou canst fathom that which the wise of successive ages have attempted and failed. She now chargeth me to impart to thee the key of the Wondrous Marvel, the Secret entrusted unto me alone. Verily I declare unto thee, only the deadly peril of the fair woman thou lovest causeth me to unloose my tongue's strings—only the imminent likelihood of her abandonment to that fiend in man's shape induceth me to withdraw the veil."

"Before thee I stand prepared to attempt any task that hath for its reward her escape from the power of the brigand," I said.

"Until now thine heart hath not failed thee. Despair not, for peradventure thou mayest crush those who, while calling themselves her friends, nevertheless seek her destruction," he said encouragingly, stroking his white beard in thought.

"Guide thou my footsteps, O director of men, and I will speed upon the path that leadeth unto truth," I said.

"So be it," he answered, after a pause, waving his thin hand. "Be not sceptical of what strange things thou mayest witness; only believe, and the Way may be opened up unto thee." His small jet-black eyes glittered with a brilliant fire unnatural to one so old, as, placing both his hands upon a portion of the dark wall, he pushed it, revealing a door constructed by a section of the wall itself being made to revolve upon a pivot. Then, pointing to the cavernous darkness beyond, he said in a commanding tone, "Come, follow me!"

Excited at the prospect of ascertaining at last the Great Secret so long promised, I obeyed instantly, and when a few seconds later the piece of the wall slowly swung back into its place, closing with a clang which made it clear that it was of iron painted to resemble stone, I found myself in another passage. The brass lamp, which he had detached from its chain, revealed that the strange corridor was carpeted and hung with rich fabrics, and as we proceeded along, the close air seemed heavy with a sweet, fragrant perfume.

"Fearest thou Azraïl?" he suddenly asked in a deep, mysterious voice, halting for a moment to gaze into my anxious eyes, as if to detect any sign of faltering.

"All men who have dear ones upon earth live in terror of the eternal parting," I said. "Azraïl, inexorable conqueror of the mighty, causeth even Sultans to crave mercy on bended knee. Truly he is the Terrible!"

My aged companion grunted, apparently satisfied with my reply to his abrupt question, for he moved along noiselessly over the thick carpets, and I followed, wondering whither he was leading me, and puzzled over the sentences he continued to mumble to himself over and over again: "The gainsaying of the unbelievers ceaseth not. The two-edged sword is already whetted. Verily shall they writhe their mouths, for their iniquities shall eat away their tongues like a corrosive acid." When we had walked along the curious subway for some distance, we came to a flight of spiral stairs so narrow as to admit of only one person at a time. My guide commenced to ascend, and I followed, filled with curiosity. Upward he went, without a pause, and with footsteps so agile that I was at length compelled to halt to regain breath. He smiled disdainfully at my fatigue, but waited a few moments; then on again he went, higher and still higher, until I felt convinced that we had ascended to the level of the earth. This suspicion was soon afterwards confirmed, for we came to a small door, the heavy latch of which he lifted, and on opening it, I was surprised to find myself in the open space before the palace, at a considerable distance from the courtyard by which I had entered. Gazing round upon the roaring flames that seemed to leap up in every direction, casting a lurid light that revealed the hideousness of the piles of dead about us, and cast long, grotesque shadows over the wide roadway, the old *imam* drew his haick closer to conceal his features, and in a hoarse voice said—

"Come, let us quicken our footsteps, so that thou mayest bear witness, ere it be too late."

Chapter Forty
The Key to the Mystery

Onward we went across the camel market, where a body of the Ennitra were carousing, and, having managed to escape their notice in the deep shadow, we hurriedly traversed several irregularly-built streets, wherein corpses lay thickly, mute witnesses of the frightful massacre; then suddenly we plunged into a narrow, tortuous passage that I remembered I had sped along in my wild scamper for life after fleeing from my taskmasters. The further we went, the nearer we approached the houses that were burning unchecked like veritable furnaces, and as we rounded a bend in the narrow, alley-like thoroughfare, where was situated the well called Shedwánka, and came into full view of the great fire, my guide gave vent to an ejaculation of dismay.

"Behold!" he cried excitedly. "The flames! They are spreading rapidly, and will consume that upon which thine eyes must rest. Let us hasten with all speed!"

This portion of the city seemed deserted, therefore we dashed forward with one accord, the *imam's* nimbleness of foot surprising me. It was well that none of Hadj Absalam's cut-throats detected us, otherwise my guide would no doubt have fallen a victim to their ever-increasing bloodthirstiness. No one had been spared. The whole city had been mercilessly swept with fire and sword.

As we drew nearer, we could see plainly that the great conflagration was spreading in our direction, for the heat and smoke stifled us, and great sparks fell in showers around. Suddenly, however, he halted before the arched door of an ancient house, towards which the flames were rapidly darting. Indeed, only two houses remained uninjured between us and the blazing, roaring mass, and already they were being licked by great tongues of fire.

"Though dangers beset thee, O Roumi, let not fear dwell within thee," my aged companion said, taking a key from the inner pocket of his gandoura and quickly unlocking the heavy door. "Know, O wanderer from beyond seas, thou now goest in with me unto the bower of Al Barzakh, the Presence-chamber of the Marvellous, whence those who enter issue forth changed men!"

"Changed?" I cried, amazed. "Shall I also be changed?"

"A transformation, strange but invisible, is wrought in all who enter here," he croaked, as, breathless and excited, with eyes smarting under the choking volumes of smoke, I stumbled onward after him. Closing the door quickly, he sped across the open patio, into which pieces of ignited wood were falling thickly, and entered another door the arch of which was supported by handsome twisted columns of marble. Through two small apartments, hung with beautiful hangings and furnished with luxurious divans, we passed, until he halted at a door which sprang open at his touch. Evidently it opened by means of a spring, but I sought not explanation, for I held my breath, wondering into what strange chamber I was about to enter. With mumbled words, as he fingered his rosary, Mohammed ben Ishak advanced slowly into the darkness, where a single light in a globe of cut crystal glimmered without illuminating the objects around. As we stepped inside, and the door closed after us automatically, there was a loud, vicious hiss close to me.

I halted, startled, for I knew the sound was that of a serpent, and I feared to tread, lest its deadly fangs should be fastened in my feet.

The old *imam*, droning a strange incantatory chant, advanced to the altar upon which the light was burning, and, turning the wick higher, so that it shed a brighter light, raised both hands piously and called aloud for forgiveness.

Glancing about me in amazement, I found that my surroundings, weird and extraordinary, were almost an exact reproduction of the mysterious subterranean temple to which Zoraida had conducted me in Algiers! The black carpet and hangings reminded me vividly of European funeral palls, while the curious open-work screen, the inlaid *kursy*, or table, of arabesque filigree, and, most remarkable of all, the stone sarcophagus, were all of exactly the same design as those in the mysterious chamber wherein the Crescent of Glorious Wonders had been first revealed unto me.

Amazed, I stood with transfixed gaze and bated breath. There were movements on the carpet, and I became aware of the unpleasant proximity of several snakes. Some coiled themselves and raised their heads, holding them immovable, with their tiny, bead-like eyes riveted upon us, while others darted away, holding themselves on the defensive in darker corners.

A few seconds of silence, and Mohammed ben Ishak turned to me, with hands still uplifted, asking—

"Believest thou that unto Allah belong the hosts of heaven and earth; that Allah is mighty and wise; that unto those who obey the Everlasting Will He showeth mercy?"

"I do," I answered.

"Speak not with thy tongue that which is not in thine heart, for of a surety they who believe not will be chastised with a severe chastisement," he exclaimed solemnly. Then again facing the altar, he cried, "Whoso believeth not in the One Allah and in Mohammed his Prophet, verily shall he be cast into the fire prepared for the unbelievers; but whosoever shall perform that which he hath covenanted, so surely shall he receive great reward, and be admitted to the gardens beneath which rivers flow, to dwell therein for ever. Verily hath a Sura been revealed commanding war against the Workers of Iniquity, and they look towards us with the look of those whom death overshadoweth. Those are they whom Allah hath cursed and hath rendered deaf, and whose eyes He hath blinded. Assuredly have we armed ourselves with an armour invulnerable, and we await the word from the Holy City to rise in our might and sweep from earth the Infidels, in obedience to the law that is written. In that day will the Senousya, whose teeth are as spears, and whose tongues are as sharp swords, fight valiantly and persevere with constancy, for they are the True Believers, who will, ere many moons, rejoice with a great rejoicing."

He paused, prostrating himself, devoutly gabbling a two-bow prayer with many quotations from the Korân, at the same time swaying himself backwards and forwards, throwing his head energetically to and fro till the perspiration streamed down his face. In his paroxysm of religious fervour, he suddenly grasped a serpent and wound it around his head in such a manner that it remained there with its flat head reared in front in the place where an aigrette might have been. Then he arose, and, with the snake still coiled upon him, advanced and held my hands. Instinctively I drew back, for the energy of his devotions had wrought in him a hideous transformation. His cheeks were more sunken, his face seemed but a skull covered by brown, wrinkled skin, and from his wild, wide-open eyes there flashed the terrible fire. With his glittering orbs upon mine, he held me in a grip of steel. Under his searching gaze I flinched, and tried to extricate my hands, but he had pinned me powerless, and so strange was his demeanour that I grew alarmed. He seemed possessed of demon strength; in his hands I was helpless as a child.

I was an Infidel, and he a religious fanatic. Might not this sudden fit of uncontrollable *diablerie* cause him to kill me?

The fiery eyes had fixed themselves searchingly upon me in a manner that seemed to fascinate and draw me closer towards him, causing my strength to fail, and inducing a feeling of languor and helplessness. Setting my teeth, I struggled against it, and, remembering we were in a house that in a few minutes must fall a prey to the flames, demanded release.

But he took no heed. Crying aloud his intentions of leading the Ghuzzat in a merciless campaign against the Infidel invaders, and predicting that the soldiers of the Faith would obtain great spoils, he suddenly released my left hand, but still kept his grip upon the right.

"Thou desirest to learn the Great Secret," he exclaimed. "Thou, the beloved of our Queen of Beauty, art the only person to whom the strange wonders may be revealed. Verily I say unto thee, thou must fight a great fight in regions unknown, exerting a power that I will impart to thee, the secret whereof none can discover."

His eyes seemed to dilate and glow like live coals, while the pain at first caused by the steady pressure upon my wrist was succeeded by a strange tingling sensation, rather pleasant than otherwise. Held in fascination by his glance, every nerve was strained to its utmost tension; then gradually I seemed to sink into a dreamy half-consciousness. With all the self-control I possessed, I strove against the curious delirium into which I was slowly lapsing, but without avail. He held my hand, and with his glaring eyes riveted to mine he seemed gradually to bring me under his thrall by some irresistible magnetic influence. Mingled sensations of delight and repugnance such as I had never before experienced ran through me, and I seemed seized by an indescribable horror of being compelled to perform deeds that in my inner consciousness I regarded as crimes. I felt myself in a state of mind that permitted the creation of hallucinations, for rapidly I saw the weird objects around me distorted into grotesque shapes, sometimes ludicrous, sometimes horrible, with the ever-changing face of Mohammed ben Ishak always the central figure. My limbs felt limp, and I had an inaptitude for any spontaneous action. I was fully conscious of all this, and the inertia alarmed me.

"Verily shalt thou know the Truth that hath so long remained hidden. Thou shalt save the woman thou lovest and who loveth thee so passionately. Behold!" he cried in a loud voice. "Hearken, and likewise let thine eyes bear witness!" and, releasing me, he stepped back to the altar, and, taking a pinch of some white powder, he cast it into the flame of the lamp. Instantly the place was filled by a brilliant light, followed by pungent, suffocating fumes. Then, having repeated this action three times, he drew forth the Wonderful Crescent from his girdle and placed it upon the altar, bowing low in silence.

The strange feeling of half-consciousness faded quickly, and in a few moments I had quite regained my normal state of mind. All had been, I felt convinced, due to over-excitement, combined with the weakness induced by the wound from which I had not yet completely recovered.

"Miserable shall be the abode of the proud!" cried the aged reciter of the daily prayers. "Verily, the Day of the Great Wrath is at hand, when the unbelievers who dwell in darkness shall be driven before the troops of the Senousya. The world shall become paralysed by the awful slaughter of the Christians, who will be cast into hell, therein to dwell for ever. It is written that excellent is the reward of those who work righteousness, and turn not aside from the right path. To Thee who alone canst direct us unto the Behishst of Delights we make supplication, and ask of Thee Thine aid."

Impatiently I awaited the conclusion of his curious prayers, rites, and ceremonies. He seemed to have forgotten the imminent peril in which the house was placed, as with his string of black beads between his skinny fingers, he murmured prayer after prayer, expressing at every breath fervent hope that I might turn from the ways of the Infidels and embrace the Faith.

With a long, final appeal for forgiveness for bestowing the key to the Great Secret upon one who had not been initiated into the mysteries of the Senousya, he turned slowly, and, walking towards the tomb of carved stone, commanded, "Come hither."

As I obeyed, he raised the heavy lid with his hands and cast it aside. Then, peering in, I saw a body. I recognised the face. It was the same man who had been so strangely resuscitated by Zoraida!

Her actions in stabbing the body were repeated by the old *imam* with almost identical sequence, and at length, in response to Mohammed ben Ishak's command, he rose slowly from his tomb, and, stepping forth in his white grave-clothes, advanced in silence to the altar. Taking up two asps that squirmed and writhed under his touch, he knotted them together, heedless of their vicious bites. As he placed them upon the slab of hewn jade that formed the altar, my companion uttered some incantation which was to me unintelligible, and then a few seconds later the ghastly visitant who had risen from the tomb took up the Crescent and with it smote the serpents as they lay. The single blow killed them.

"Assuredly as the *af'á* are in an instant struck dead, so also will the Senousya smite the Infidels and sweep away all evil from our land," Mohammed ben Ishak cried, his voice growing deeper. In the short pause that followed, the weird figure at the altar placed the Crescent upon a great perfuming-pan of gold, afterwards lighting the small brazier of wrought silver beneath. Again my companion, the *imam*, droned his guttural chant, while the white-robed figure, whose back was always turned towards me, sank upon his knees and remained statuesque and motionless.

"Bear witness, O Roumi," cried the aged official of the mosque. "Earnestly I seek permission to impart unto thee that knowledge which thou seekest;" and, taking from a niche in the wall a great golden goblet, filled to the brim with water, he placed it upon the little inlaid table in the centre of the sanctuary. Advancing to the altar, he took from it the crystal lamp and held it over the goblet. In his hand was a lump of yellow wax, and, uttering an incantation in a language unknown to me, save that the words *abarkan* (black), *adhu* (wind), and *thamat't'uth* (woman), I distinguished as being in the Kabyle tongue, he presently melted the wax in the flame, and allowed the liquid drops to fall into the water. Breathless, and with eager eyes, he gazed into the bright goblet, watching each drop as it fell and hardened, until suddenly his contenance relaxed, and he ejaculated—

"Yes! Thou mayest know! The key to the Great Mystery may now be given into thy keeping."

Casting the wax down, he replaced the lamp, for the ceremony was over. By the formation of the drops in the water, he had become convinced that he might, without harm accruing, divulge the secret locked in his heart. On putting the lamp back into its place, he took from the altar a crystal mirror, about a foot square, in a broad frame of solid gold, delicately chased. Placing it in my hands, he said—

"Breathe upon this; then tell me what thou seest."

I dimmed the surface with my breath, as he had commanded, and, lo! in an instant there appeared a picture that entranced me.

"What seest thou?" he inquired.

"There is revealed unto me a landscape, strange and weird," I answered. "By what magic is this effect produced?"

"Describe what is therein revealed," he urged.

"I see the Desert at sunset," I said. "The sky is ablaze, and against it there riseth from the sea of burning sand a single mountain, shaped like a camel's hump. It is far distant, and growing purple in the evening hour, but I can distinguish upon its summit three giant palms. In its side there is apparently a cave."

"And in the foreground?"

"There is a single traveller. He is an old man, who hath fallen from his horse, and while one hand clutcheth at his throat, the other is outstretched towards the mountain. He is in pain," I added; "apparently he is dying of thirst, for birds of prey hover about him, and his eyes have in them the glitter of madness. The picture is beautiful, yet terrible!"

"Good!" he said. "It is finished!" and taking the mirror from me, he returned it to its place. The illusion puzzled me, yet he would not allow me to investigate. At that moment, however, I became aware that the place was filling with a dense smoke, and from beyond the closed door there came a noise as of the roaring and crackling of flames.

The house in which we were was already on fire!

Pointing out the fact to him in alarm, I urged him to tell me at once how to use the Crescent; but he heeded not my words, so absorbed was he, bowing before the mysterious tenant of the grave in pious devotions.

"Tell me," I cried. "For Zoraida's sake, withhold not from me the Secret which thou hast promised, so that I may save her!"

The flames had burst through some panelling behind the altar, and the place was filled with sparks and dense smoke. Just at that instant the statuesque figure turned, raising its hand wildly. For a moment a gleaming knife trembled aloft in the dull glare of the flames, and next second it was buried deep in the breast of Mohammed ben Ishak!

I shrieked, but my companion only laughed a mocking, hideous laugh, and, reeling slightly, stood contemplating the approaching flames quite calmly. The shock seemed to have paralysed him.

"Come, let us fly!" I urged, dashing wildly across to save him. "See, the door is still intact! There is yet time!"

Turning upon me fiercely, he shook me off. It was a terrible moment. I stood transfixed by horror.

"No," he cried, with a strange light in his eyes. "It—it is the blood revenge, the swift vengeance that I dreaded, the punishment I deserve for my sin against the Brotherhood—I—I am a traitor—but I fear not to die—I go—through fire—to the cool waters of Tasnîm!"

"Surely thou wilt not seek thine own destruction, and take thy Secret with thee?" I gasped.

He remained silent; he did not even turn towards the man who had struck the fatal blow. The flames were roaring, and the heat had become so intense that the perspiration in big drops rolled from my face.

"Speak!" I shrieked. "For the sake of the woman whose young life dependeth upon thy word! Be merciful unto her! Tell me what to do!"

But, with a hoarse, defiant laugh, he folded his arms, saying, "I refuse!"

"By Heaven!" I burst out, in sudden anger, "this is no time for dallying words. If thou wilt not, then may the curse of the Daughter of the Sun, whose life thou sacrificest, hang upon thy neck, heavy as a millstone, and may it drag thee down to the place that is prepared for evil doers."

The effect of my words was electrical.

"No! No!" he cried, evidently in as deadly fear of the imprecations of Zoraida as the Ennitra had been. "No! I—I have reconsidered!" he gasped.

As the words left his lips, I saw that the flames had ignited the flowing robes of the man from the tomb, and though he rushed about in paroxysms of intense pain, and at last fell, unconscious, he uttered not a sound! Swiftly, indeed, was he punished for his crime.

"Tell me, quickly!" I cried aloud. "In another moment we shall both be lost. Fly! Let me assist thee. Even now we can escape!" and as I spoke, a tongue of fire singed my hair and burned my eyebrows.

"No!" he shrieked, his voice sounding shrill above the dull roar, as his eyes rolled wildly. Undoubtedly a terrible madness had seized him, and so vigorously did he threaten, rave, and curse, that I felt half inclined to make a desperate dash for life through the door by which we had entered.

Again I clutched him, frantically appealing to him to tell me the secret, and as I did so, the flames leaped past us, and we were both half suffocated by the smoke. Fortunately, I possessed sufficient presence of mind to snatch up the Crescent, and, regardless of the manner in which it blistered my fingers, I wrapped it in my burnouse, crying—

"Impart unto me the Great Secret, I beseech thee! Quickly!"

Reeling, he staggered and fell. The mysterious vengeance of the Senousya had descended upon him, and the life-blood flowed from the ugly wound. In a moment I dropped upon my knees and supported his head, determined that he should not lapse into unconsciousness, and so carry with him to the grave the key to the extraordinary enigma.

In desperation, I shrieked a final appeal to him to fulfil his pledge. Death stared us both in the face, for already had I become seized with a sudden faintness.

It all occurred in a few brief moments.

"Yes," he gasped, wildly and with difficulty, at last. "I—I will save the beauteous Lalla Zoraida. She shall lead the Senousya into—into the holy war, as she hath done the Ennitra. In the great fight every Infidel shall be slain with sharp swords. Yes!—I will tell thee how thou canst save her. Travel with all speed over the Desert to the Oasis of Agram, in the country of the Kanouri, which lieth in the direction of the sunrise. Thence ride onward across the plain of Ndalada, past the town of Dibbela, until thou comest to the Well of Tjigrin, and when thou hast accomplished two days' journey still due eastward from the latter place, past the ruins of a town, thou wilt find a single clump of palms. Then take the Crescent, and—"

His thin lips moved, but no sound came from them. His eyes slowly closed! It was, indeed, a critical moment. My heart sank, for it seemed as though he was no longer aware of the things about him.

"Speak!" I yelled in his ear. "What must I do with the Crescent?"

His eyes opened, but they were dim. In their depths a film was gathering, as life fast ebbed. With a supreme effort, however, he raised his bony hand, pulling down my head until my ear was close against his mouth. Then, struggling to articulate, he whispered hoarsely, and with extreme difficulty—

"Obey my injunctions strictly. Take the Crescent, and—and when thou hast arrived at the spot I have indicated—not before, or thou wilt never gain the Great Secret—*place—it—upon—thy brow*! Then—will—marvels—undreamed of—be revealed. Remember—attempt not to fathom the Mystery until—until thou hast passed the Well of Tjigrin two whole days! May—may Allah—preserve and guard thee, and may thy—"

But his final blessing was never completed, for convulsions shook his frame, and he fell back heavily and breathed his last.

Springing to my feet, I stood for a second. Flames seemed threatening me from every side, but, with a sudden desperate dash, I rushed, half blinded, towards the door, which at that moment was being licked by the darting fire. Then, opening it by raising a curious latch, I fled quickly through the two small apartments, now filled with smoke, out across the patio, finding myself in a few moments standing in the road fainting and unsteady, clutching at a wall for support.

How I accomplished that flight for life I scarcely know. Panting, I stood, unable for a few moments to realise how near I had been to a horrible end. Though my clothes were brown and scorched, my arms blistered, and my hair and beard severely singed, I cared not. Zoraida's future was now in my hands, for at last I had succeeded in obtaining the key by which the Great Mystery might be elucidated—at last I should know the Truth—at last the hidden Secret of the Crescent, the undreamed-of marvel, would be revealed to me!

Chapter Forty One
Through Rose Mists

Mounted on a *méheri*, and alone, I toiled with all speed onward over the glaring, sun-baked Desert, towards the spot indicated by the man from whom I had, at the eleventh hour, wrung the key of the Great Secret.

Had he fooled me? Were not his instructions remarkable; did they not bear suspicion of some ulterior object? Even as I rode along, with face set sternly towards the sunrise, the thought that the dead man had sent me on a bootless errand caused me considerable anxiety. Reviewing his words and actions, I saw how ineffectually he had striven to conceal the bitter prejudice he entertained for unbelievers, how intensely he hated all Christians, and with what eagerness he contemplated the eventual triumph of the Senousya. Such being the case, I reflected, what more natural than he should resolve to retain Zoraida in the ranks of the conspirators, in order that she might lead them to the contemplated victory; what more natural than he should refuse to impart to me the knowledge whereby I might rescue the Daughter of the Sun from the dangers that were fast closing in upon her? Again, by the Ennitra, and in all possibility by the Senousya also, the Wonderful Crescent was believed to be a talisman that gave triumph to its possessor. Was it probable that he would, even though Zoraida had commanded, reveal to me, a Christian, the elucidation of the problem that he had denied to all True Believers?

No. In both word and action the old *imam* had betrayed a firm disinclination to assist me to elucidate the Great Secret, and as I journeyed on day after day, lonely and friendless, in that barren, unfamiliar country, the conviction within me grew stronger that the revelation he had gasped with his last breath was merely a base device to part me from the woman I worshipped.

Yet it was a relief to get away from that doomed city, with its flood of fiendish exultation; to escape from the revolting ebullition of barbarism, and the fiendish glee of my treacherous friends, who were no doubt overwhelming their Daughter of the Sun with attentions that she loathed, like caresses from the ghouls of hell. Even the dead silence of the wilderness was preferable to the din of the hard-fought conflict, with its sickening sequel.

The camel I rode I had found straying at some distance from Agadez, when on the eventful dawn I fled from the city on foot. It was handsomely caparisoned, and, to my delight, I had found that its provision-bags, ornamented in a manner that showed its owner to be a cadi, were packed with necessaries for a long march. In all probability its hapless owner had prepared to fly at the approach of the bandits, but had been murdered when on the point of starting. After a hurried inspection of the bags, satisfying myself that there was a supply of comparatively fresh water in the skin, I concealed the Crescent of Glorious Wonders within a bag of fodder, and, mounting, had started off, without map or plan, upon what, from various appearances, I judged was the caravan route to the well of Tin-dâouen. This surmise fortunately proved correct, for in three days I reached it; then, after halting the night, I discovered a valley full of luxuriant vegetation, with high doum and talha trees and great patches of camomile flowers growing in rich profusion. Continuing through this verdant glen, where antelopes and giraffes disported themselves, I ascended over the rough, rocky ground to a high, barren plateau, and, with my face always to the east, plunged, with a reckless disregard for the consequences, into the great unexplored desert which forms an effectual barrier between the country of the Ahír and that of the Kanouri.

I pushed on with all haste, so that if it proved, as I feared, a fool's errand, I might, by almost ceaseless travel, be enabled to return again to Agadez before the moon had run her course. Armed with a rifle, powder-horn, and crooked dagger that I had taken from the body of an unfortunate janissary, I sped onward through the great lone country. From sundown until dawn I journeyed, resting through the day in what little shade I could devise, then setting forth again, always leaving the setting sun behind, always remembering that each stride of the faithful animal beneath me took me further and further from the woman whose life lay in my hands.

Gradually and irresistibly had I been drawn into a vortex of mystery and treachery, from which I was struggling to extricate myself. Zoraida's piteous appeal rang in my ears; the very thought of her as the wife of that villainous archrebel caused me to grind my teeth. Feeling convinced that the errand I had undertaken must be futile, I was, in my more gloomy moments, sorely tempted to disobey Mohammed ben Ishak's injunctions, and try the effect produced by placing the Crescent of Glorious Wonders upon my brow. Each time, however, the intensely earnest, agonised face of the aged prayer-reciter, as he implored me not to try to fathom the Great Mystery before arrival at the spot indicated, came vividly before me, causing me to stay my impatient hand.

The fatigue of those long anxious nights and blazing days was so terrible, that, on more than one occasion, faintness seized me, and I had a recurrence of those strange hallucinations from which I suffered after Labakan had dealt me the cowardly blow. I seemed at times light-headed, eager and jubilant one hour, despondent and contemplative of suicide the next. But the recollection of the deadly peril of Zoraida, whom I loved with a true and fervent devotion, spurred me onward over shifting sands and treacherous rocks, onward to the place where the dead man had promised the Great Secret should be revealed.

On the seventh day after leaving Agadez, I slept under the palms of the Agram Oasis, filled my water-skin at the well, and, representing myself as a straggler from a trading caravan, begged some food from the camp of the Bedouins of the peaceful Kanouri. It has always struck me as curious how rapidly news travels in the Desert. Already these men had heard rumours of desperate fighting in the city of the Ahír, although it must have been conveyed by way of Tin-Telloust and Bir-ed-Doum, the circuitous route by which caravans travel on account of the wells, and fully one hundred miles further than the straight journey I had accomplished. For several reasons I had deemed it best to feign ignorance, therefore to all my anxious inquirers I represented I had travelled direct from Akoukou without touching Agadez.

Spending one day only with these tent-dwellers, tall, bronzed, handsome, good-natured fellows, I gave them peace, and, with the brilliant sunset once more behind me, rode away through great patches of a poisonous plant my friends called "karugu," and out again upon the plain towards the remote little Arab town of Dibbela, where I arrived two days later, after a somewhat perilous journey across some almost inaccessible rocks which the Arabs call the Tefraska. At dawn on the second day after leaving this place, having travelled due south under the direction of the leader of a caravan conveying ivory and rose oil from the Tsâd to exchange for cotton goods, razors, sword-blades, and pieces of paper with the sign of the three moons, I came upon the Oasis of Tjigrin, rich in herbage, date palms, and clusters of tangled bushes, among which ostriches and gazelles were moving. Here, wearied out, I tethered my *méheri* to a palm tree, and, reflecting that in two days I should know the truth, flung myself down and slept soundly in a dream of quiet ecstasy.

My awakening, however, was sudden, for, feeling myself grasped roughly by the shoulder, my hand instinctively sought my knife, but a loud, hearty laugh caused me to rub my eyes and look up into the sun-tanned, bearded face which shadowed the glare from my eyes.

"*Que diable!*" cried a voice in surprise. "Then I'm not mistaken. It *is* you!"

"*Eh bien! eh bien!* old fellow!" I cried, amazed, jumping to my feet and grasping the rough brown hand that shot from between the folds of the burnouse. "This is indeed a pleasant meeting!"

The man who stood holding the bridle of his milk-white horse was none other than Octave Uzanne, the Spahi who, when we had met on the fatal Meskam Oasis, had told me his life's romance!

"Really, I can scarce believe my eyes," I continued, speaking in French. "I was at Tuggurt when a messenger arrived with the news that Paul Deschanel's column had been cut up and massacred at the Well of Dhaya, near Aïn Souf, by the Ouled Ba' Hammou. I naturally concluded you had also fallen."

"*Sapristi! Je suis un veinard*," he answered in the slang of the Army of Africa, still holding my hand in his hearty grip. Then, with a sigh, he added, with seriousness, "It is, alas! true that our column was enticed into an ambush by the Ennitra, assisted by the Ouled Ba' Hammou, and slaughtered, myself with eight others being the sole survivors. For two months we were held prisoners by Hadj Absalam, until at length I managed to escape and travel back alone to Tuggurt to relate the terrible story. Poor Deschanel! his was indeed a sad end—very sad!"

For a moment he seemed overcome by thoughts of his dead comrades, but in a few seconds he had reassumed his old buoyancy, and, offering me a cigarette, took one himself, and, having lit up, we squatted side by side in the shadow to talk.

"Well, what brings you here, so far from Biskra?" I asked presently, after he had related to me his adventures at the mountain stronghold of the Ennitra, which were almost as exciting as my own.

"Duty," he answered briefly, with a hard look upon his handsome face quite unusual to him.

"You are not alone?" I queried.

"No—not exactly alone," he answered abruptly, without apparently intending to tell me the object for which he had penetrated so far south, for he suddenly exclaimed, "You have not yet told me what sort of life you have been leading among the Bedouins—or why you are here alone."

Briefly I related the story of my capture, my slavery, and my escape, without, however, telling him the real object for which I was working, or mentioning the assault on Agadez.

"You are a born adventurer; I am one by circumstance," he exclaimed, with a good-humoured laugh, when I had concluded. Then he added, "Although my life with the Ennitra was one of terrible drudgery, yet, after all, I would rather have remained with them—had I but known;" and he sighed regretfully.

"Why?" I asked, surprised.

"*She* is here!" he answered meaningly.

"Do you mean Madame de Largentière?" I asked, remembering in that moment how dearly he loved the woman who had been so cruelly snatched from him, and with what self-sacrifice he had buried himself beneath the scarlet drapery of a *homard* of the Desert. "Is *she* in Algeria?" I inquired.

For answer he blew a cloud of smoke slowly from his lips, then from beneath the folds of his burnouse he drew forth a worn but carefully folded copy of the Algiers newspaper, *L'Akhbar*, which he handed to me, saying, "Read the first column."

Opening the limp paper, I noticed it was dated two months before, and on glancing at the column indicated, my eyes fell upon the heading in large type: "The New Governor-General of Algeria: Arrival of Monsieur de Largentière."

Eagerly I read on. The report described the landing and enthusiastic reception of Monsieur de Largentière, who had been appointed Governor-General. The streets had been gaily decorated with Venetian masts and strings of flags, salutes had been fired from the warships in the harbour and from the Kasbah, as the vessel conveying his Excellency from Marseilles had cast anchor, and as the party stepped on shore, the little daughter of the General of Division had presented a bouquet of choice flowers to Madame de Largentière, who, the journal incidentally mentioned, was "well known as one of the most beautiful women in Paris, and a leader of fashion." Algerian society, continued *L'Akhbar*, welcomed her as its queen. No doubt, during the coming season the Governor's palace would be the scene of many a brilliant festivity, and the colony owed a debt of gratitude to the Government for appointing as its representative an official so upright, so experienced, and so genuinely popular. All Algeria, it concluded, extended to the new Governor and his beautiful wife a boundless and heartfelt welcome.

"Well?" I exclaimed, handing back the paper. "You will have an opportunity of seeing her very soon, I suppose?"

"See her? Never!" he answered, with poignant bitterness. "Already I have discovered that she is instituting inquiries about me; that is the reason why I have not sought to return to Biskra. I do not desire the past disinterred;" and he thoughtfully watched the ascending rings of smoke.

"Fate plays us some sorry tricks sometimes. Most probably you will meet her just when you least expect—"

"What?" he cried, interrupting. "Face her? To hold her hand as before—to tell her that her husband, the man whose ring she wears, and over whom the journalists gush and drivel, is—is a murderer! No! No! I never will!"

"But, my dear fellow, is it not your duty to denounce him if you possess absolute proof of his guilt?" I argued.

"My duty? *Bien*" he answered reflectively. "But the denunciation would bring no satisfaction to me—on the contrary, it would kill her."

"You are right," I conceded reluctantly, after a pause. "Your silence and self-denial is the greatest kindness you could show towards her. Indeed, your affection must be very deep-rooted, or your patience would long ago have been exhausted amid this hard life and social ostracism."

"Ah! Heaven knows how well I love her," he said, turning to me with a deep, wistful look. "She loves me too, and the fact that she has sought to find out where I am shows that she thinks sometimes of me. But I mean to keep the resolve I made long ago, for under an assumed name and in the Spahis she will never discover me."

"Now that De Largentière is Governor, he is all-powerful," I observed. "I wonder what he would do if he discovered you, and found out that you held absolute proof of his guilt?"

"Cr-r-r!" he exclaimed, as with a sad smile he drew his finger across his throat. "If he dared not commit the crime himself, he would hire one of the many obliging Arab desperadoes who hang about the fringe of the Desert."

"Yes," I said. "He would, no doubt, make some serious attempt to seal your lips."

"I shall give him no opportunity. As far as I am concerned, he will, for Violet's sake, enjoy his reputation for honesty and uprightness," he declared. Then he added quickly, "But why should we drift to a subject that is to me so painful? The romance of my life has ended. I am a derelict, a piece of human wreckage drifting helplessly upon the sea of despair."

"So am I," I said gloomily. "Only I am struggling to reach a landmark that will direct me to a harbour of refuge."

"I scarcely follow you," he observed, suddenly interested. "That you have some very strong motive for spending your days in these uncivilised regions seems certain, but as you have never exchanged confidences with me, I remain in ignorance. Is it in your case also a woman?"

I nodded an affirmative.

"Tell me about her. Who is she?" he inquired, looking straight into my eyes.

For a few moments I remained silent. Then, returning his steadfast gaze, I answered—

"I love Zoraida!"

"Zoraida!" he cried, starting up. "Surely you don't mean the woman of the Ennitra, known as Daughter of the Sun?"

"The same," I replied. "You may laugh, sneer, tell me I am a dreamer, dazzled by the glitter and splendour of an Eastern court, fascinated by a pair of kohl-darkened eyes and a forehead hung with sequins, but, nevertheless, the fact remains that she and I love each another."

"It seems impossible," he said. "You have actually looked upon her unveiled, and spoken with her, then?"

"Yes. Why?"

"Because it is death to an Infidel to either look upon her countenance or seek to address her. While a prisoner in Hadj Absalam's palace, I heard most extraordinary things regarding her. The terrible story was told me how, on one occasion, three Chasseurs, held captive by the old robber, had, by the purest accident, discovered her passing unveiled from the court of the palace guards into the harem. Amazed at her extraordinary beauty, they stood gazing at her, but those looks of admiration cost them their lives. Their gaze, it was alleged, had polluted her, and within an hour their heads were smote off and their bodies thrown to the dogs."

"Then you have never seen her?"

"No. During the time I was in the hands of the Ennitra, she was absent. Many were the strange rumours I heard about her, however: how she was possessed of almost supernatural power, how she had planned most of the raiding expeditions of Hadj Absalam, how she ruled the fierce band as their Queen, and, attired as a youth, had actually led them successfully against our forces! I can scarcely believe it all, but the palace guards assured me that all they told me was the unexaggerated truth. Six months ago the Government issued a proclamation, offering two rewards of ten thousand francs each for the capture of Hadj Absalam and Zoraida."

"I know what you have heard is the truth, from personal observation," I said quietly. His statement about the reward was, however, startling, and caused me increased uneasiness.

"Tell me all about her," he urged. "How a Christian could succeed in approaching her, judging from all I have heard as to the rigorous manner in which she is guarded, seems absolutely incomprehensible."

"It forms a strange story," I admitted, and then, while he consumed a fresh cigarette, I proceeded to briefly relate the manner in which we became acquainted, and the weird and startling events that followed, suppressing only the fact that Agadez had been occupied by the outlaws. I hesitated to tell him this, because I feared that if a large body of Spahis were in the district, they would at once proceed there, and in all probability capture both the robber Sheikh and Zoraida, to secure the reward. Nevertheless, I explained how I became possessed of the Crescent of Glorious Wonders, of which he had heard rumours, and which he examined with intense interest when I produced it from my forage-bag. Then, after I had replaced it in its hiding-place, I told him of the extraordinary directions the dead *imam* had given me, and that I was on my way to test the truth of his strange statement.

"In two days you will arrive at the spot he has indicated," he observed, after listening to my story with breathless interest. "The mystery is so remarkable, and has so excited my curiosity, that I wish I might be permitted to accompany you in this search for an explanation. Do you object?"

"Not in the least," I answered, laughing. "There is something so uncanny about the whole affair, that your companionship will be most acceptable. When shall we set out?"

"To start now would be unwise," he said, gazing round with practised eye at the Desert, already aglow in the brilliant sunshine, and observing, at a glance, its atmospheric conditions. "Let us eat and idle now, and leave at sunset."

To this arrangement I acquiesced. Then he told me how the Spahis had encamped four hours' march away, that he had strayed from a reconnoitring party, and, having regard to the fact that they were remaining there at least a week and that we should be only four or five days absent, he did not consider it necessary to undertake an eight hours' ride to ask permission of his captain before starting.

"Military regulations are sometimes relaxed in this out-of-the-world spot," he added, laughing. "When they find I'm missing, they will probably search for me; but having now lost myself, why should I return just at present, especially as they are not likely to move on before they find traces of me."

"In what direction are you marching? Towards Agadez?" I inquired anxiously.

"Scarcely," he replied, with a smile. "We have no desire to be annihilated by the Sultan of the Ahír. No. We are travelling due south to Lake Tsâd."

His answer reassured me, and, having prepared and eaten a rather primitive meal, we sought under a tree that dreamy, peaceful repose that desert travellers find so refreshing in an oasis.

An hour before the sun had sunk in its fiery glory of gold and crimson, there was a beautiful mirage of water, rocks, and feathery palms upon the sky, but, as we prepared to depart, it faded from our gaze as rapidly as it had appeared. With the brilliant glow of the dying day behind us, we set forth into an unknown country, Uzanne upon his white Arab stallion, I upon my handsomely-caparisoned camel. Riding down the eastern side of the wooded hill we almost imperceptibly entered the plain, the slope being so gradual. After travelling for some time in the darkening hours along the level ground, we found it was by no means flat, although it usually appeared so in our immediate neighbourhood; yet it had an upward trend, and some distance beyond it rose and fell in long, wavelike swells of sufficient height to hide, at times, even such an object as the range of Gueisiger mountains on our left. On all sides we scanned the fertile plain for any signs of life. A herd of gazelles scampered along in front, but no other living thing seemed near.

When we had been riding about five hours, we detected straight before us, rising from the level of the plain, now sandy and desolate, a long black line, jagged and irregular, which gradually developed, on nearer view in the brilliant moonbeams, into something like a mass of ruins resembling a deserted town.

Evidently we were on the right path, as indicated by Mohammed ben Ishak. In this he certainly had not deceived me. On the outskirts of this desolate pile, lying so far from civilisation, we saw first an old reservoir, edged in with rough-faced blocks of granite. No wall or gate marked the city boundary, nor were the ruined buildings, half buried in drifting sand, conspicuous by their architectural beauty, for square black stones, piled on one another without mortar, formed houses that for size were larger than those in Agadez, but the stony desolation was not relieved by a piece of either wood or metal. Many of the houses seemed in an excellent state of preservation, and all seemed as if the inhabitants had left through a pestilence rather than the ravages of war; time alone, assisted by the wind and tempest, appeared to have dismantled others. There were three mosques, but all were however, in a confused mass of ruins, the cupola of one alone remaining intact, though its crescent that had pointed skyward had rotted and fallen. It was strangely weird riding through that deserted city in the brilliant moonlight, amid grotesque and ghostly shadows. Upon the last-mentioned mosque we discovered a stone, rudely inscribed, in Arabic, with the words, "The building of this holy place was ordered by the Khalîf Othman." This gave us a clue to the age of this half-effaced city, for the Khalîf was all-powerful in Northern Africa in the twenty-seventh year of the Hedjira (A.D. 647), and lived at Sbeitla, once a great city, but now, like this forgotten place, a mere heap of crumbling ruins.

Continuing our weary way, we journeyed straight on between a parallel range of sand dunes, until we came to the open plain again. More stony the country grew, as we proceeded, hour after hour, guided only by the stars, through the barren, desolate land, until we halted at sunrise in the midst of a vast wilderness, where no rising ground relieved the monotony of the rocky level. Eating, resting, and sleeping, we resumed the journey again at sunset, and, throughout the night, pushed onward in eager search of the single clump of palms beneath the shadow of which I was to seek to elucidate the Great Secret.

At last, however, the ground ascended gently, and we saw, away to the south-east, hills rising, peak after peak, as far as the eye could reach. The outlook of rounded hill-tops was varied occasionally by a small plateau, but the landscape was terribly arid and dispiriting. Nevertheless, we plodded still onward in the direction the dead man had indicated, until at length our eager, impatient eyes were rewarded by the sight of a low hill, surmounted by a single clump of about half a dozen palms, their feathery tops looming darkly against the horizon already flushed by the delicate rose-tints of dawn.

We both detected our goal at the same moment, and, with ejaculations of satisfaction, spurred forward excitedly at redoubled pace, breathlessly impatient to put the Crescent of Glorious Wonders to the crucial test.

The spot was actually within sight!

Swiftly we rode over the soft, treacherous sand and great patches of rough stones, our adventurous spirits suddenly stimulated by the anticipation that probably within an hour, the Great Mystery—the secret preserved through so many ages, the knowledge by which alone I could effect Zoraida's rescue—would at last be revealed.

Chapter Forty Two
Vagaries of Vision

Over the rising ground we eagerly sped, halting not till we dismounted beneath the palms. The spot bore no trace of having been visited by travellers; indeed, for the past two days we had not come across a single bone of horse or camel, the country being apparently desolate and unexplored.

Having carefully recalled the old *imam's* dying instructions, Octave and I became both convinced that this must be the place he had indicated. Standing together, we cast our gaze wonderingly around, but saw nothing to relieve the dreary monotony of sand and sky, except far away eastward on the distant horizon, where a great mountain loomed, misty and indistinct, in the purple haze.

"At last the supreme moment has arrived," I said excitedly, drawing the Crescent of Glorious Wonders from the bag in which I had hidden it. "We will put the truth of Mohammed ben Ishak's assertions, to the test."

"How that piece of engraved metal can effect the rescue of Zoraida remains to me a mystery," Octave exclaimed, intensely interested in the strange experiment I was about to make. He had tied his horse to a palm trunk, taken a draught from his water-skin, and now stood with folded arms, intently watching my actions.

Still half dubious as to whether the old *imam* had spoken the truth, I gazed upon the Crescent, tracing its mystic inscription, and vainly endeavouring to decipher it.

"Did the *imam* explain the exact position in which you were to place it upon your head?" asked my friend.

"He told me to let it rest upon my brow," I answered.

"Then you must remove your head-gear."

This I did at once, casting it upon the sand. Then, breathless with excitement, knowing how much depended upon the elucidation of the Great Mystery, I took the strangely-shaped object that had experienced so many vicissitudes, and, while Uzanne riveted his dark, serious eyes upon mine, placed it upon my forehead. Pressing its inner edge against my brow, it fitted tightly, the horns gripping my temples with an unpleasant pressure that caused them to throb violently.

"*Dieu!*" cried Octave, grasping my left hand suddenly. "Tell me—tell me quickly—what ails you?"

I was staggering as one intoxicated. I heard his voice, but it seemed distant, even sepulchral, for when the cold metal came in contact with my brow, I experienced sensations excruciatingly painful. Across the top of my skull and through my temples and eyes sharp pains shot, producing an acute sensitiveness, as though flesh and brain were being torn asunder by sharp hooks. In the first acute spasm of suffering, I cried aloud, causing Uzanne considerable anxiety. For a few moments the agony was intense. The tapering ends of the Crescent pressed into my temples, causing them to shoot in spasms that lancinated every nerve, and I felt myself on the point of fainting under the horrible cruciation.

With a sudden impetuous movement I tried to doff the semicircle of metal, but whether I did not pull it evenly, or whether my head had swollen after I had assumed it, I could not tell. All I knew was, that I could not disengage my head from its tightening grip. Clenching my teeth, I struggled against the nauseating faintness that crept over me, and gradually the sudden pangs decreased, until the maddening racking of my brain was succeeded by a curious tranquillisation that caused me to involuntarily reconcile myself to circumstances.

Octave's presence, and indeed all my immediate surroundings, seemed to fade from my sight, and in their place there was conjured up in the vista down which I seemed to gaze a vision indistinct at first, but gradually becoming more and more vivid. With my face to the east, a feeling of calm pleasure and enchantment overspread me as my vision seemed to extend to treble its normal range.

It was an extraordinary phenomenon.

With my eyes fixed upon the purple mountain fading into a shadowy outline against the clear and brilliant sky, I appeared to gradually approach it. As it grew larger and more distinct, I was enabled to take in the details of the scene, and become enraptured by its charm. The sides of the mountain were clothed by luxuriant foliage and sweet-smelling flowers, and when, in the strange hallucination which had taken possession of me, I approached still nearer, I suddenly experienced a conviction that I had on a previous occasion gazed upon the same scene.

Vainly I tried to recall it. The pressure upon my temples appeared to have crushed and dulled my senses so that any effort to recollect the past was unavailing. My brain seemed electrified by the sudden shock when I had placed the Crescent upon my brow, and now all the past was but a blank, all the present chaotic and incomprehensible. Yet the scene was so familiar, that my inability to recollect where I had before witnessed it was tantalising, and caused me to wonder whether my mind had become unbalanced and the exteriorised image had not been induced by insanity. I dreaded to think it might be so. Yet I now experienced no pain, only a strange, uncontrollable desire to draw nearer. The mountain seemed to act as a magnet, transfixing me, drawing me closer and closer, with a force mystic, but utterly irresistible.

Within me was a violent craving, a sudden longing to search for some unknown person or object concealed there, the truth of which I must at all hazards discover.

Words fell upon my ear; but they were unintelligible. Uzanne was no doubt asking me a question in his eagerness to know what had caused my alarming change of manner, but I heeded not. Swiftly I approached the single mountain rising in its solitary beauty in that vast, lonely land, until suddenly its highest point attracted me, and at last, with an ejaculation of joy, I remembered.

The summit was shaped in the form of a camel's hump, crowned by three palms that looked at that altitude no bigger than the little finger-joint. The centre tree raised its feathery head higher than those of its companions. Yes, it was the same! The scene that my keen vision now gazed upon was a reproduction, exact in every particular, of the picture that had been revealed by the crystal mirror that Mohammed ben Ishak had allowed me to gaze upon!

In the mirror I had been painfully impressed by the figure of a dying man in the immediate foreground, but the presence of death no longer marred the scene. Pushing forward still nearer, over rough, broken ground, without experiencing any physical fatigue, I distinguished straight before me a dark spot in the side of a great wall of grey rock, just at a point where it rose from the plain to form part of the mountain. Presently I could see that it was the low arched entrance to what appeared to be a cave, and as a sudden desire seized me to investigate it, I pressed forward, overwhelmed by a vivid conviction that within that cavern lay an elucidation of the Great Mystery. Eagerly I approached, until I had come within a leopard's leap of the gloomy opening, then suddenly some inexplicable power arrested my progress. Struggling to proceed, I fought desperately with the unseen influence that held me back, determined that even though I risked my life, I must enter that rocky portal and search for the knowledge by which I might rescue Zoraida. Her words of piteous appeal urged me forward, but though I exerted all my strength and will, yet I did not advance a single inch further towards my weird and gloomy goal.

Some strange intuition told me that this cavern was the spot I sought, yet, though again and again I strove to shake off the shackles that had so suddenly been cast about me, all effort was in vain, for an instant later my heart sank in despair as the scene gradually dissolved and receded from my gaze, until the mountain grew so distant as to appear the mere misty outline that I had at first witnessed, and I was rudely aroused from a state of dreamy wonderment by hearing Octave exclaim in alarm—

"*Sapristi*! old fellow, I'm beginning to think you've taken leave of your senses!"

"No," I answered, endeavouring to calm myself. "I—I have witnessed an extraordinary scene."

"Has anything remarkable been revealed?" he anxiously inquired.

"Yes. I have had a strangely vivid day-dream, by which I have been shown the spot whereat to search for the promised explication."

"Where is it?" he asked quickly.

"In a cavern in yonder mountain," I replied, pointing to the horizon.

"In a cavern?" he cried in surprise. "How have you ascertained that?"

I told him of the success of the catoptromancy, of the picture that my breath had produced upon the mirror, and of the exact reproduction which I had just witnessed.

"But do you think the Crescent has produced this remarkable chimera?" he asked.

"Undoubtedly," I replied, releasing my head from it at last, and offering it to him, in order to see whether a similar illusion would be revealed. Removing his head-gear, he allowed me to place it upon his brow in the same position as I had assumed it. I held it there several minutes, and asked whether he experienced either pleasure or pain.

"I feel nothing," he declared at last. Then, with an incredulous smile, he added, "I'm inclined to believe that your remarkable extension of vision is mere imagination. Your nerves are unstrung by thoughts of Zoraida's peril, in combination with the fatigue of your journey."

"But I can describe to you yonder mountain minutely," I said. "The cave is in a high wall of grey granite, and its mouth, once evidently of spacious dimensions, has been rendered small by sand that has drifted up until it has almost choked it. It is semicircular, but seems narrow inside, forming a kind of shallow grotto."

"And what is the general aspect of the mountain side?"

The picture still remained vividly impressed upon my memory, so I had no difficulty in giving him an accurate description of what I had seen.

"*Eh bien*! Let us investigate," he said, evidently amazed at my very detailed word-picture of the place. "Let us see how far you are correct. For ten minutes you've been gazing at it with such a strange, far-off look in your eyes, that I confess I began to be concerned as to your sanity. I have seen a similar look in the eyes of Chasseurs who have fallen victims to sunstroke."

"The mystery is just as inexplicable to myself as it is to you," I answered. "Somehow, however, the contact of the Crescent has created within me a firmly-rooted conviction that we shall discover something in that cavern."

"If we can find the place," he added, laughing good-humouredly.

"Let us try," I said, climbing upon my camel, who had been resting on his knees a few yards away, and causing him to rise. Uzanne, after another pull at his water-skin, sprang upon his horse, and we both commenced to descend again to the sandy plain.

With eyes fixed upon the mountain, rising like an island amid that inhospitable sea of sand, we pressed forward, Uzanne from time to time expressing a hope that we were not seeking a will-o'-the-wisp, and speculating as to what mystery might be concealed within the gloomy opening I had described. The way grew more rough, sand being succeeded by great sharp stones, which played havoc with my camel's feet, causing me to travel but slowly, for my animal's lameness in this vast wilderness might result disastrously. Still we journeyed on, as slowly the great mountain assumed larger proportions, until, after a most tedious course of travel, we found ourselves but a few hundred yards from its base.

The three trees were growing upon the summit as I had seen them in my mental picture, and every detail was the same in reality as I had witnessed it. The ground rose gently, with palmetto and asphodel growing and flourishing among the rocks, but there was no steep cliff of granite— there was no cave!

Uzanne laughed at my abject disappointment.

"My surmise was correct, you see, old fellow," he exclaimed, pulling up for a moment to light a cigarette. "The mysterious cavern only existed in your distorted imagination."

"But how do you account for the fact that I was able to describe the place to you before I had seen it?"

Shrugging his shoulders with the air of the true Parisian, he answered, "There are mysteries that it would be futile to attempt to fathom. That is one."

His reply annoyed me. It seemed that he either doubted me, or attributed my illusion to some trick of my own.

"At least you will accompany me on a ride around the base," I said. "I have not yet abandoned hope."

"Oh, very well," he said, with a reluctance that was apparent. "As you wish. I'm afraid, however, you're in search of a phantom."

The mountain cast a welcome shadow, and as we turned our faces northward and picked our way over the stones, riding was not at all unpleasant. For some time, however, neither of us spoke, but when we had ridden about a quarter of a mile further round the base, I suddenly reined up, and, pointing to a great precipitous cliff of granite that, jutting out before us, rose about a hundred feet from the plain, cried—

"See! The cave! At last! Surely that is more than a phantom?"

My companion shaded his eyes with his hands for a second, then, turning to me, in an awed voice answered—

"Yes! It is indeed a cave, exactly as you have described it! Forgive me for doubting, but the puzzling strangeness of these extraordinary incidents must be my excuse."

"Of course," I answered, too excited for complimentary phrases, and with one accord we both bounded forward, dismounting a few moments later before the strange, mysterious cavern.

Taking our rifles, we both peered into the darkness, which was rendered more impenetrable on account of the brilliance of the day. Breathlessly excited, we stood on the threshold of the natural chamber, the existence of which had been so curiously revealed to me. What mystery lay therein hidden we knew not, and for some moments stood straining our eyes into the dusky gloom. The Crescent of Glorious Wonders had so far revealed the mystery; we had now to explore the cave in search of the Great Secret which Mohammed ben Ishak had promised would be revealed.

"If we are to enter, we shall want a light," Octave said at last, in a voice strained by excitement.

"Around my water-skins are ropes of plaited grass. They will serve as torches," I exclaimed; and, rushing back to where my camel was calmly kneeling, I took my knife and cut the cords away, dividing them into four long strips, two of which I gave my companion. Striking a match, he lit one, and with our rifles slung behind us, we climbed over the great heap of drifted sand and entered the weird and gloomy grotto.

The uncertain light of the torch was scarcely sufficient to illumine our footsteps. The cavern was spacious, the arched roof being formed of bare, jagged rock, but the sand of the Desert, having drifted in, had so closed the entrance that we had to stoop until we had entered some distance, then we went by gradual descent over the mound of soft sand, down some sixteen feet to the floor of the cavern. Here it widened until it was some twenty feet across, then gradually narrowed, as the ground, formed of rocks over which we clambered, shelved gradually down.

Eagerly we gazed on every side, but only saw rough rocks above, beneath, and around us. So dark was it, that I suggested I should ignite a second torch, but Octave would not hear of it, pointing out that we might be in need of them later.

Weirdly our voices echoed, and it was altogether an uncanny place. Penetrating at length to the extreme end, and finding absolutely nothing, we proceeded to make a closer inspection of the sides of the place, for we had now resolved to thoroughly explore it. Eagerly we searched every nook and cranny, expecting every moment to discover something, but being always disappointed. So lofty was the place in one part that the light did not reach the roof, and above us was an impenetrable gloom, into which we vainly strained our eyes.

The dead silence, the intensely dispiriting character of our surroundings, and the unnatural echo of our voices, so impressed us, that we found ourselves conversing in whispers. Indeed, we were awestricken. A great secret—the character of which we knew not—was to be made known to us, and each time we cast our eyes about us, we glanced half in fear that some strange and extraordinary horror, of which we had not even dreamed, would be suddenly revealed.

Having nearly completed our inspection, we were suddenly startled by a curious noise which sounded in the darkness close to us. Halting, we listened breathlessly for some moments.

"Bah! it's only a bird," I said, and we moved on again.

Suddenly, however, my companion, holding the torch higher above his head, and pointing straight before us, started as he shrieked—

"*Dieu*! See! What is that? Shoot! For God's sake, fire!"

So startled was I by his sudden ejaculation, that at first I could see nothing, but, peering in the direction he indicated, I saw in the dusky gloom, about ten yards away, a pair of eyes that in the darkness seemed to emit fire. The eyes moved quickly from side to side, and without a second thought I took my rifle and, aiming full between them, pulled the trigger. The report, deafening in that confined space, was followed by the thud of a falling body, and, rushing up, we discovered that a great panther lay there dead. Our escape had been almost miraculous. The animal had, no doubt, been watching us ever since we entered, and at the very moment when discovered was crouching for a spring. Fortunately, however, my bullet passed through his skull, causing him to leap from the ground and fall in a heap, dead as a stone.

"*Nom d'un tonnerre*! That was a narrow shave! Another instant, and one of us would have been under his claws."

"Yes," I replied. "It was fortunate you noticed him." But we were both too much absorbed in endeavouring to discover the character of the Great Secret to further comment upon the incident.

Resuming our search, ever on the alert lest a similar danger should threaten, we at length found, half concealed behind a projecting rock, a deep recess about four feet square on a level with the ground. Uzanne thrust his flambeau into it, and we were at once surprised to find that the extent of it was not revealed. Briefly we discussed our situation, when my companion exclaimed—

"Well, here goes! I mean to explore this;" and with rifle slung behind, and torch in his hand, he went down upon his knees and crawled into the narrow entry. Following close behind him, with heart beating quickly in anticipation of some startling revelation, I crawled onward through the tunnel-like passage, grazing elbows and knees upon the sharp rocks, heeding nothing in my eagerness to explore the depths of this subterranean grotto. The air was not foul, and we had confidence that the narrow passage was more than a mere recess, but were dismayed a few minutes later, when we came to the end, only to find further progress barred by a wall of rugged rock.

Octave minutely examined the great black stones before him, for the passage was so narrow that I could not pass, and therefore could see but little.

"Strange!" he ejaculated, after he had been carefully examining a long fissure and thrusting his fingers into it. "These stones appear suspiciously as if they have been placed here to block up an entry."

"What causes you to think so?" I inquired.

"Because the stratum runs at a different angle to the rest of the stone. There must be some opening beyond."

"Cannot we force an entrance?" I inquired.

Taking up his rifle, he struck the two great blocks of rock with the butt. A hollow sound was emitted.

"Yes," he said. "We must break down this barrier. But how?"

"Why not blow it up with powder?" I suggested.

"Excellent!" he cried, and forthwith I proceeded to put my suggestion into execution. The only receptacle that we had in which to place the powder, was a large cigarette-case of chased copper, which Zoraida had given me on the last occasion we had met, and though I cherished it as a gift from her, I found myself compelled to sacrifice it. Therefore, filling it from my powder-horn so full that it would not quite close, I bound tightly around it a long piece of wire which Octave chanced to have with him, for the Spahis have capacious pockets, and are in the habit of carrying with them all sorts of odds and ends.

This done, I gave the charge to my companion, who carefully placed it deep into the crevice, emptied the powder-horn into the small fissure, and then with considerable ingenuity constructed a slow match. While he laid a train of powder, we gradually receded until we were about half-way back to the large cave, and then, telling me to continue on and carry his rifle, so that nothing might prevent him from getting out quickly, he ignited the match, and followed me with considerable alacrity. With bated breath we threw ourselves down at some distance from the mouth of the passage, awaiting results.

The moments passed like hours, until suddenly there was a bright flash in the low, rocky recess, and next second a terrific explosion caused the earth to tremble. There were sounds of falling rocks, followed by a volume of thick smoke that belched forth and went past us like a cloud; then all was silent again, and we waited another five minutes to allow the fumes to disperse before again venturing into the narrow tunnel.

Chapter Forty Three
The Great White Diadem

Impatiently we at last crawled forward again, eager to ascertain what our attempt at blasting had effected. Our first impression was that we were worse off than before, as the explosion had hurled great portions of rock along the tunnel, where they now lay nearly blocking it, and in several places we could only advance by squeezing ourselves flat upon our stomachs or struggling sideways between the boulders and the rocky sides of the long recess. Our tedious advance was once or twice almost effectually barred, but each time Octave, whose arms were stronger than I had imagined them, succeeded in pushing back the great pieces of stone sufficiently to allow the passage of our bodies.

"*Épatant!*" cried my companion suddenly, just as he had squeezed himself flat to pass a piece of rock that almost barred our passage completely. "Excellent! The stones that blocked the entrance have been entirely blown away!"

"Hurrah!" I shouted excitedly, struggling along after him. "Can you distinguish anything?"

"Nothing yet," he answered.

A second later I scrambled up close behind him, but, peering forward over his shoulder, I saw only an impenetrable darkness beyond. The torch he now held did not burn as well as the first, shedding only a flickering, uncertain light. Through the breach we had made we crawled together, and as we stumbled on over the rocks that had been displaced by the explosion, we found there was room to stand upright. The flambeau, held high by my companion, revealed only a portion of the gloomy chamber we had opened, but against the rugged walls, that glistened here and there as the rays fell upon them, we saw black, mysterious-looking objects that in the fickle light looked shadowy and indistinct against a background of Stygian darkness. Their sight startled us. Half choked by smoke and dust, we knew not whether there might be another entrance to this pitch-dark cavern, where wonderful stalactites hung glistering from the roof, or what wild animals might be its tenants.

Holding our loaded rifles in readiness, we listened. But the silence, complete as that of the tomb, remained unbroken. Igniting one of the torches I held in my hand, the light became so far increased that we could distinguish we were in a spacious vaulted natural chamber, that bore traces of previous occupation. My feet caught an object on the ground, and, picking it up, I examined it. It was a leathern scabbard curiously ornamented with metal that was black with age. As we advanced, we found that the dark, mysterious objects we had at first noticed were great packages strongly bound in skins. We counted them; there were thirty-seven. Dust, inches thick, was upon them, for they had evidently been borne over the Desert by camels, and lain secreted there many years. What, we wondered, did they contain?

After a brief inspection of the place, we set to work to investigate. Taking our knives, we commenced upon the pack nearest the place we had entered, but so rotten was the leather that our impatient fingers tore it asunder like paper, and the ropes that had once secured it crumbled into dust at our touch. In breathless eagerness we thrust both hands into the openings we had made and drew them forth.

With one accord we uttered loud ejaculations of abject amazement. *Our hands were filled with precious stones!*

We could scarce believe our eyes, each half fearing that our sudden good fortune was but a dream. Yet, nevertheless, in a few moments we were convinced of its reality, for time after time we thrust in our hands and allowed the unset gems to run through our fingers like beans. In our delirium of intense excitement as we tore away the wrappings, the jewels became scattered about the ground, and many were trodden under foot.

Beyond ejaculating expressions of amazement, we could not speak. Dumbfounded, we stood caressing in our hands the newly-discovered treasure, vaguely conscious of its enormous value and of the fact that Fortune had at last, in a most extraordinary manner, bestowed her favour bountifully upon us.

Our wealth was beyond our wildest dreams. We were absolutely bewildered by the sight that met our gaze.

The brilliance of the gems, though somewhat dulled by the dust of ages, held us with fascination. Upon the ground around us they lay heaped in such scattered profusion that we seemed powerless to collect them. There were great diamonds of enormous value that flashed, scintillated, and dazzled us under the uncertain rays of the torches, magnificent emeralds, some almost yellow, others green as the deep sea, white, yellow, and rich blue sapphires, huge purple amethysts, pale, exquisitely-coloured beryls, peerless pink and black pearls larger than any in the Crown Jewels, green, straw-coloured, and blue topazes of enormous size, beautiful topazolites of delicate hues, huge blood-red jacinths, opals marvellous in their iridescent reflection of light, and matchless spinels, turquoises, and other stones of all difference of colour and shade and every degree of translucency.

"Come!" I cried excitedly at last, when speech returned to me; "let us see what the next contains!" and together we tore asunder the wrappings, to discover a similar hoard of unset gems, many of the diamonds being even larger and more magnificent than those we had at first discovered.

Intoxicated by delight, we proceeded to further investigate our newly-discovered wealth, passing on from bale to bale, finding in each a wondrous collection of precious stones of such size and brilliancy, the like of which our eyes had never before encountered.

"Look!" I ejaculated, picking out three enormous diamonds that were lying in a heap upon the floor. "Each single stone will realise a fortune!"

"True," answered Octave gleefully, his eyes glistening with delight. "They are as large as any in the world."

Finding a piece of rotten wood that had originally been placed along the edge of one of the packages, apparently to strengthen it, we utilised it as a flambeau, and, proceeding with our investigations, we found that no fewer than sixteen of the great bales contained nothing but gems, most of which had evidently been hurriedly knocked from their settings in order to be more easily transported.

One pack was nearly filled with treasures that were absolutely priceless from an archaeological point of view, for they were genuine and well-preserved relics of bygone ages. Strangely—engraven zircons, hyacinths, tourmalines, spinels, beryls, all of exquisite hues, delicately carved emeralds, and deep blood-red sards with mystic inscriptions and remarkable designs. Hundreds of Egyptian seals in the form of the scarabaeus, or sacred beetle, curious cylindrical seals in chalcedony, and beautiful Greek scarabs, the engraved intaglio of which in most cases was enclosed in a guilloche or engrailed border. There were also large numbers of finely-engraved ornaments of carnelian, chrysoprase, plasma, bloodstone, jasper, beryl, agate, and onyx, and many seals of thin form, through which the light passed sufficiently to show the engraving by transmitted rays, the stones with this view being mostly cut *en cabochon*.

In another package we discovered, carefully wrapped by themselves in cloths of fine linen—now yellow with age and rotten as tinder—a number of strangely-shaped amulets. Upon many of them were engraved in Arabic gnomic or other sayings, indicating that they were believed to guard the wearer against demons, thieves, and various evils, or regarded as charms for procuring love; while others had on them the names of their possessors, various mottoes, good counsels from the Korân, and even distichs of Arab poetry.

Continuing our search, we came across a great pack of ancient ornaments of gold. Time had in some instances dulled them, but their weight showed their solidity, and the stones set in them were the most magnificent we had ever seen. Rings, bracelets, anklets, necklets, great bands of gold for the arms, earrings, buckles and girdles encrusted with diamonds, emeralds, and sapphires, marvellously-enamelled clasps, jewelled sword-hilts, aigrettes with diamond bases, finely-worked filigree balls of gold, and four magnificent diadems, one of which was set entirely with huge diamonds, that gleamed and flashed with a thousand fires as we held it up, while another was adorned wholly by emeralds. From their delicacy of construction, we judged that their wearers must have been Sultanas. Who, we wondered, were they? Whose harem had their dazzlingly-ornamented figures graced?

From the bottom of this pack I at length drew forth a small oval-shaped casket of tortoise-shell beautifully inlaid with gold devices, around the sides of which was a pious inscription in Arabic. The lid refused to open, therefore I placed it aside, and assisted Octave to further investigate.

On we passed, our amazement becoming more complete every moment, ejaculations of profound surprise and admiration escaping us at almost every breath. In the remaining packs we cursorily inspected, we found a most valuable collection of vessels, goblets, dishes, salvers, urns, and wine-vessels, all of solid gold, each very heavy and exquisitely chased in designs that told their age to be considerably over a thousand years. Some bore hieroglyphics that showed that they had ages before been brought out of Egypt, while upon others were Arabic characters that were easily decipherable. Some indeed were Chaldean, many were Byzantine, while greater portion of the goblets bearing Arabic were profusely set with gems. Fine lamps of chased gold, great heavy ornaments that had once graced the dazzling Courts of Love of some powerful potentate, and beautiful jewelled breastplates we unearthed, together with a large number of shapeless masses of gold, ornaments with the gems still set in them having apparently been ruthlessly melted down in order that they might be the more easily secreted. These rough lumps varied from the size of an orange to that of a man's head, and in several diamonds and other stones were protruding, showing how hurriedly their shape had been altered, and the whole system of careless packing testifying to the fact that they had been brought there with swiftness and secrecy.

"Are we dreaming?" cried my companion in an awed tone, when we had finished examining the contents of the last pack, and relighted another piece of wood we had found. "I cannot yet fully realise the extent of this wonderful discovery!"

"It is indeed amazing," I said, looking around upon the vast hoard of treasure that lay heaped in every direction. "This then is the Great Secret revealed by the Crescent of Glorious Wonders!"

"And a secret worth obtaining," my companion added. "It is yours, for you discovered it. You are indeed a Croesus!"

"Yes, no doubt its value is enormous," I answered. "But in what manner can its recovery effect Zoraida's safety?"

I thought only of her. In my waking hours her fair, wistful face was ever before me; in my dreams she appeared, urging me on to seek the solution of the mystery. I had found an extraordinary and magnificent collection of gems, hundreds of which were unique in the world. They would give me enormous wealth; but would they also bring me happiness? Alas! I feared they would not, for I had not fully solved the problem. I stood silent, thoughtful, and disheartened.

Octave Uzanne roused me. I was thinking little of the piles of gorgeous jewels at my feet; my thoughts were all of her.

"You haven't opened that tortoise-shell box yet, old fellow," he exclaimed. "There might be something in it."

"Ah! I had forgotten!" I answered, suddenly recollecting its existence. Truth to tell, in the excitement of the moment I had thrown it aside, and it lay in a dark corner unheeded. My companion searched for a few moments, found it, and handed it to me.

With trembling hands I tried to wrench off the lid, but it would not budge. No clasp secured it, yet the lid fitted with an exactness that rendered it quite air-tight. Several times I made vain efforts to open it, and at last was compelled to draw my knife, insert the point of the blade, and so wrench it asunder, utterly ruining the lid.

From inside I drew forth a folded piece of skin, dried, yellow and wrinkled with age. So crisp and brittle was it that it almost broke asunder as, on carefully opening it, I found it covered with small Arabic characters closely written in ink that had faded and become brown and dim by time.

Glancing at the bottom, my eyes caught the characters which, more legible than the others, told me its age.

"It is actually over a thousand years old!" I cried. "See! The date is 311 of the Hedjira!" and with Octave holding the torch and eagerly following me, I proceeded to decipher the crabbed and difficult writing, reading it aloud as follows:—

"RECORD OF THE HADJ MOHAMMED ASKIÁ, SULTAN OF THE SÓNGHAY, PEARL OF THE CONCH OF PROPHECY, WHO DESCENDED FROM THE THRONE OF MAGNIFICENCE AND GLORY AFTER MUCH TROUBLE AND AFFLICTION, WHO FROM HIS HEAD REMOVED THE DIADEM OF RESPECT AND FROM HIS BODY THE CLOAK OF HONOUR, WHOSE ROSE-GROVE BECAME A HUT OF GRIEF, WHO WRITETH THESE WORDS IN THE DARK NIGHT OF SEPARATION.

"In the name of Allah, the Merciful, the Clement! Praise is my garment, magnificence is my cloak, grandeur my veil, and all creatures within my kingdom are my men-servants and my maid-servants. O Discoverer of this my Word, know that thou who openest this casket and findest this my treasure, assuredly hast thou learned the secret by the power of the Crescent, the cusp of which is the wondrous Revealer of Secrets and its graven words are as a bright light in the darkness. Before its power men quake in fear, for it bringeth victory over thine enemies and exceeding wealth. By thy belief in the power of the Revealer, thou hast been translated from affliction to the happiness of dignity, and hast been promoted from baseness unto the summit of magnificence; thy mind will be illumined with the light of the interpretation of dreams, and in the storehouse of thine intellect wilt thou deposit the secrets of the treasure of prophecy. Remain ye steadfast, and if thou lovest a woman, be thou not discomforted, for Allah hath predestined blessings, and will bring thine affairs to the desired termination. Upon thee be most abundant salutations and greetings. Those beside whom I fought in battle have deserted me on account of the plague of bloodsuckers. I have descended the throne of dominion and have secreted my treasure, to wander in search of peace. Even though I have presage that I pass in short space from the Mansion of Vexation to the Imperishable Kingdom, yet my memory will only be blotted from the pages of the times to be revived. Happy thou who hast possessed thyself of my camels' packs, for they will guide thee out of the Valley of Confusion, and if thou lovest a woman, easy will be thy path to the tying of the knot of matrimony, and verily will the verdure of the meadow of life be as a cloak unto thee. O my soul, thou hast cramped mine heart; burnt my spirit. I said, I will complain, but thou hast burnt my tongue. Thou art gone, and we gave many promises of meeting, in hopes of which thou hast consumed me as a lamp. I said, I will lament my separation, but within me hast thou burnt that lamentation. I cannot wish evil to anyone, for the good and evil of this world are but transient. Know, O Discoverer of the Treasure, she who is the light of thine eyes will soon invest thee with the ennobling robe of her choice, for I have made thee a confidant of mysteries, and upon thee will the favours of Allah be plentifully showered. If adversities threaten her, give unto her this my record, together with the Great White Diadem, that is of diamonds, and they shall be weapons in her hands by which they who harbour evil designs against her shall fall, while thee and she shall walk in peace beside the limpid brooks, where the waters of good fortune meander into the river of dignity. If the flames of thine enemy's malevolence are kindled against thee, take thee also the Emerald Diadem for thyself, for it shall be an indication of prosperity that shall appear upon thy forehead, and shall astonish and disconcert them. To thee the world shall be pleasant as the face of the woman thou lovest. It is incumbent on thee who hast believed, who hast sought, and who hast found, to live merrily in this brief life during the season of flowers, for this is thy purpose, and life is short. Laugh at the times as the cloud wept, for roses smile because the dawn weeps. Unto one faithful follower, he who is named E'mrân, son of Anûsh, son of Yusuf, who hath been compelled to leave me to travel afar over the Great Desert, have I entrusted the Crescent, to be handed down through generations, and after a thousand years have elapsed, to be given unto one who hath faith in its power, in order that he may solve the Great Mystery. Endeavour not to learn the cause of its secret power, for it is an influence the existence whereof none knoweth in thy generation. Suffice it that thou hast secured the Treasure of the Sultan Askiá; that my hands, long ago crumbled unto dust, have watered the thirsty meadows of thine hopes, and that thou knowest thou wilt hereafter dwell in the meadows of felicity. Remember, O Holder of my Treasure, my commands. May thy feet never cross the threshold of the House of Misery, and may many years elapse ere thou art translated from thy frail abode to the Mansion of Eternity. Enduring and permanent is Allah alone. Peace.

"Written on the fourth of the month Chaoual, 311 of the Hedjira."

"Extraordinary!" ejaculated Octave. "It is a voice from the grave!"

"The will of the most powerful of the Sultans, who has bequeathed to me all his riches," I said, almost stupefied by the stupendous wealth that had been heaped upon me.

Handling the precious document with infinite care, I refolded it and placed it back in its broken box.

"Shall you carry out his commands?" he asked.

"To the letter," I answered; then, looking round, I added, "It seems that, having secreted his treasure here, he walled up the entrance with rocks which he cemented together, thus hermetically sealing this chamber, and so preserving its valuable contents."

"Yes. But the mystic influence of the Crescent of Wonders, and its effect? How do you account for it?"

"It is a mystery which I am commanded not to attempt to solve," I said quietly. "For the present, I am content with what has been revealed;" and, remembering the dead Sultan's instructions, I walked to the heap of gold ornaments and took therefrom the Great White Diadem. It was a magnificent ornament, encrusted with huge and wonderful diamonds of the first water, three exquisitely fine stones, cut in the form of a crescent, forming a centre-piece. After a short search, I drew from the pile of jewels the Emerald Diadem, an ornament of similar shape, but green with flashing gems, the central one, enormous, and of magnificent colour, being fashioned as a star. Dusting both of them lightly with my burnouse, the stones shone with bewildering brilliancy.

To place the Great White Diadem and the parchment record in Zoraida's hands was my first object, and, with that end in view, my companion and I held brief consultation, the result being that, having promised my friend a portion of the treasure, we resolved to take a few of the more remarkable of the jewels, and leave at once, blocking up the entrance after us. As the packages had remained there untouched for a thousand years, it was scarcely likely anyone would find their way to that cavern in the unexplored Desert before we returned, and even if they did, the narrow passage would be barred in such a manner as to be utterly impassable except by blasting.

Therefore, gathering together a number of set and unset gems, rings, bracelets, and seals, we filled our pockets to overflowing, and, wrapping others in a piece of the crumbling leather, we forthwith went back to the narrow entrance, leaving the jewels scattered as they had fallen from the camels' packs. By our united efforts we succeeded in rolling forward great pieces of rock, until the entry was entirely blocked up, and again, at the other end of the tunnel-like passage, we placed a similar barrier.

Then, finding our way up to the surface again, we emerged into the brilliant day, and, after a hasty meal, mounted, and with eager faces turned towards Agadez, we set out hopeful and jubilant, with treasures of great price concealed in our capacious saddle-bags.

Chapter Forty Four
Le Commencement de la Fin

Briefly resting during the blazing noon, we resumed our way speedily across the treacherous sand dunes and rough stones, through the nameless ruined city, until, at dawn of the second day, away on the plain before us, rose the tall palms of Tjigrin.

On reaching the edge of the oasis, Octave took bearings by his pocket compass, and afterwards we continued our way in search of the camp of Spahis, to which it was imperative that he should return. We had arranged that I should rest and obtain supplies from them before continuing my journey alone to Agadez; and that he should, after obtaining leave of absence from his commander, follow me in the guise of a letter-writer. At the City of the Ahír, after I had placed the Great White Diadem and the ancient manuscript in Zoraida's hands, we could then decide the best means by which we could remove the treasure to Algiers. I still kept him in ignorance of the occupation of Agadez by Hadj Absalam, accounting for Zoraida's presence there by the fact that she had performed a pious visit to the tomb of a celebrated marabout in the vicinity. Knowing my friend's eagerness to secure the piratical old chieftain, and feeling that any attempt in that direction would seriously compromise Zoraida, if it did not, indeed, cost her her life, I considered the wisest course was to arouse no suspicion of the truth until he himself discovered the situation. Alone in Agadez, he would be unable to act; whereas if the Spahis obtained the slightest inkling of the whereabouts of the outlaws they had so long and vainly sought, it was certain they would rush to the attack, a proceeding which would no doubt be fatal to all my hopes, having in view the reward offered for Zoraida's capture.

I had grown accustomed to this life of sorrow-dogged wandering—now here, now there—so accustomed to it, indeed, that I did not perceive fatigue. Mirthfully we travelled across the verdant, well-wooded tract, with eyes keenly watchful, until at last, when the sun was setting, tinting the beautiful landscape with exquisite lucent colours, amber and gold with amethystine shadows, we came upon the spot, only to find the camp had been struck. The empty tins that had contained preserved foods, the bones, and the black patches on the sand with blackened embers, told their own tale. The Spahis had resaddled their horses and ridden away, we knew not whither! These flying horsemen of the plains rarely remain at one spot for long, and move with a rapidity that is astounding; yet it puzzled Octave considerably, and certainly appeared to me curious, that they should have left their missing comrade to his fate.

Uzanne, dismounting, examined the ground minutely, picked up some of the discarded tins and peered inside them, turned over the dead embers, and occupied himself for some minutes in inspecting the holes whence the tent-poles had been withdrawn. Then, returning to me, he said—

"They left hurriedly. Rations were flung away half eaten, and in some cases there was not even sufficient time to withdraw the tent-pegs!"

"What could have alarmed them?"

"Most probably they expected an attack by the Kanouri. Before I left, a scout had come in with the news that their fighting men were encamped in force in the valley beyond the rocks of Tefraska. We must endeavour to trace the direction in which they have gone."

The thought flashed across me that each hour I lingered delayed Zoraida's emancipation.

"Why waste time?" I urged. "What is there to prevent you from accompanying me to Agadez? You have not deserted; your comrades have been compelled to desert you!"

At first he was obdurate. It was his duty, he declared, to rejoin his squadron. But presently, after I had persuaded him by every possible argument to continue his companionship, he at last, with much reluctance, consented. Then once again we turned our faces north-west, towards Dibbela. He had grown gloomy and thoughtful, uttering few words, and giving vent to expressions of impatience whenever his jaded horse stumbled or slackened its pace. The cause of this was not far to seek. Our conversation had turned upon Paris and her people. I had been recounting those happy, ever-to-be-remembered days when I lived four storeys up in the Rue St. Séverin; when, careless Bohemian that I was, the sonnets of Musset thrilled me, the quips of Droz convulsed me, the romances of Sue held me breathless, and the pathos of Mürger caused me to weep. An unsuccessful art student, a persistent hanger-on to the skirts of journalism, I lived the life of the Quartier Latin, and though I oft-times trod the Pont Neuf without a sou, yet I was, nevertheless, supremely happy and content.

"Until now, mine has been but a grim fortune," I said. "The money that took me out of the world I loved brought me only unhappiness and discontent. It caused me to become cynical, dissatisfied with my English surroundings, dissatisfied with myself. Even now I gaze back with regret upon those blissful hours of idle gossip over our vermouth and our mazagran; those frugal days of desperate struggle to obtain a foothold in literature, those mad, rollicking *fêtes du nuit*; that pleasant, reckless life, so happily divided between pleasure and toil. How well, too, I recollect those easy-going, laughter-loving children of Bohemia, my boon companions, each of whose purse was ever at the other's command; how vividly their faces and their *bonhomie* come back to me, now that I am, alas! no longer of their world, no longer a denizen of the Quartier where the man is not judged by his coat, and wealth commands no favours."

"You are not ostracised as I am," he blurted out, with much bitterness. "You have riches; you will win the woman you love, and return to Paris, to Brussels, to London, there to live in happiness; while I—*mon Dieu!*—I, professing a religion I do not follow, sailing under false colours, eating kousskouss from a wooden platter, broiling always beneath this merciless sun, shall one day fall, pierced by an Arab's bullet! Bah!—the sooner it is all ended the better."

"Why meet trouble half-way?" I asked, endeavouring to cheer him. "You have come out to this wild land to efface your identity, because if you had remained in Europe you would have been charged with a crime, the sequel of which would have been the lifelong unhappiness of the woman you love. I admit, your future appears dull and hopeless, but why despair? There may be a day when you will be able to return to her without branding her children as those of a murderer."

"Never!"

"*Tout arrive à point à qui sait attendre*," I observed cheerily. "Ah," he replied, smiling sadly, "it is a long and weary waiting. Even while she seeks me, I am compelled to go further afield, in order to conceal my existence."

"I can sympathise with you," I said. "All of us bear our burdens of sorrow."

"What sorrow can possess you?" he retorted. "The woman to whose arms you are now flying will accompany you back to civilisation, there to commence a new life. You will show her our world of spurious tinsel and hollow shams; you will educate her as a child into what we call *les convenances*, teach her what to accept and what to avoid, and she, who to-day is the leader of a band of outlaws, will become an idol of Society. Proud of her beauty, content in her love, you will at last find the perfect peace for which you have been searching, and for which you have risked so much."

"Of you I will make the same prophetic utterances," I answered, laughing. "Your life will not always be darkened by this cloud. It is a passing shadow that will be succeeded by sunshine."

But he only shook his head, sighed, and remained silent.

To the sorrow weighing so heavily upon his brave, generous heart I made no further allusion during the ten days we travelled together, first to the little town of Dibbela,—where he discarded his Spahi's dress for the white burnouse and fillet of camel's hair of the Arab of the plain,—then, spurring over the boundless desert of Ndalada, and through the Agram Oasis, until, in the dazzling glare of a brilliant noon, we passed through a clump of palms, and distinguished, in the far distance, the dome and tall square minaret of the great mosque of Agadez.

Approaching, we gradually discerned the high white walls of the city, with its flat-roofed houses rising tier upon tier upon the hillside, centring round the Mesállaje, while in the background the high strong walls of the palace, wherein Zoraida was incarcerated, awaiting my return, loomed stern and sombre against the cloudless cerulean sky.

But I had elucidated the Great Mystery. I had unearthed the treasure that for a thousand years had lain lost deep down in the earth, and as evidence, in my saddle-bags I bore the two priceless diadems and the scroll traced by the powerful Sultan Askiá himself. Ere long the coronet of diamonds would be in Zoraida's hands; she would open and read the faded record, and the power of the Great White Diadem to release her would then be put to its crucial test. Now that the Secret had been revealed to me in a manner so extraordinary, I doubted nothing. I had implicit confidence in the mystic power of the Diadem, and felt assured that in a few short hours I should hold Zoraida in my arms free, the mysterious trammels that had so long bound her to the Ennitra at last torn asunder.

Suddenly we saw five horsemen galloping out from the deep archway of the city gate towards us. The guard of the Ennitra had evidently discerned us, and, taking us for stragglers unaware of the fall of the young Sultan, were riding forward to capture us.

"They will be disappointed when they meet us," I exclaimed, laughing. "For the present I am under the protection of their Daughter of the Sun, and you, as my servant, are safe also."

"Safe—*safe!*" he cried, a second later, pulling up his horse so quickly that he threw it upon its haunches, and shading his keen, practised eyes with both his hands. "See!—see! Those men who are raising a cloud of sand about them—cannot you recognise them?"

Stopping my camel, I shaded my eyes, and peered eagerly before me. Through the whirling sand raised by their hoofs, and blown by the strong wind before them, I suddenly caught a glimpse of scarlet. Again I fixed my eyes intently upon them, until the sand obscuring them cleared. A second later I was startled, for, to my dismay, I saw that the party consisted of a single Spahi and four Chasseurs d'Afrique!

"What—what does this mean?" I gasped, amazed, with my gaze riveted upon the soldierly figures, sharp cut against the sky, tearing rapidly along in our direction.

"*Que diabe*! It's extraordinary! Come, let us hasten to ascertain the truth;" and, suiting the action to the word, he spurred forward, I following his example.

Ten minutes later we met, and after the Spahi had recognised his comrade, and the Chasseurs had satisfied themselves that I was not an Arab, we learned from them that strange and startling events had occurred in Agadez since I had left it. As they rode back again with us at an easy pace, one of the Chasseurs, who had now sheathed his heavy sabre and lit a cigarette, replying to my hasty questions, explained the situation. With a strong Gascon accent, he said—

"The expedition was carefully planned, and carried out with considerable secrecy. Two months ago, when our squadron was at Tuggurt under Captain Carmier, we heard that the Ennitra were moving towards the Ahír, with the intention, apparently, of attacking Agadez. This news was telegraphed from Biskra to the General of Division at Algiers, who at once decided upon the plan of campaign to be carried out by a punitive expedition. Orders were immediately transmitted to the eastern advanced posts, by which a regiment of Spahis were moved to the Tjigrin Oasis, two regiments of Turcos, three battalions of Zouaves, and three batteries of artillery, with some light machine guns, to Tagama, while we of the Chasseurs—encamped outside Azarara, both of which places are four days' journey south and north respectively from the City of the Ahír. Only the commanding officers knew the object of these movements, and it appears that the plans were so preconcerted that we should combine against the Ennitra just at the moment they marched to the attack of Agadez."

"You failed to arrive early enough to prevent the massacre," I observed.

"Yes, unfortunately. Through some delay in the transmission of an order to the Spahis, several days were lost, and when, at last, two weeks ago, our squadrons effected a junction, and we stole silently at midnight, holding our scabbards until we came before yonder walls, we found the city in the possession of the Ennitra, those of its people who survived reduced to slavery, and Hadj Absalam installed in state in the palace. Swiftly we descended upon the place. Yells and savage cries rent the midnight silence. The crash of the volleyed firing sounded high above the shrieks for quarter. There was indescribable panic in the city, and although through the night the conflict was desperate and the Ennitra fought with that dogged courage that has always made them conspicuous, yet the havoc wrought by our machine guns appalled them from the first. Gaining the city walls at dawn, we stormed the Fáda, and by noon had captured the place, and nearly four hundred of the Ennitra, including Hadj Absalam and the man known as Labakan, were prisoners in our hands."

"And what of Zoraida?" I gasped, with sinking heart.

"You mean, I suppose, the woman, known as Daughter of the Sun? She has been, it is said, leader in most of the marauding expeditions, and on that account a reward was offered by the Government for her capture. It was she who, still in her gorgeous harem dress, rushed out at the first alarm, and led her horde of cut-throats to the defence of the city. Armed with knife and pistol, she plunged with indomitable courage, and with an utter disregard for her life, into the thick of the fight, acting as courageously as any of those wild desert pirates whom she led with such extraordinary tact. Once or twice I caught a glimpse of her as she urged on our yelling and bewildered foe. Report had not lied as to her beauty. Her loveliness was entrancing."

"Where is she now?" I demanded breathlessly.

"I know not, m'sieur," the man answered, shrugging his shoulders.

"But surely you know if she still lives?"

"The bodies of some women were found," he answered carelessly. "It is believed hers was amongst them."

"My God!" I cried brokenly, turning to Octave, who was riding on my left. "It can't be true—*it can't be!*"

"Wait," he said quietly. "Seek Carmier. Perhaps the truth has been hidden from the men."

"M'sieur has asked me a question," observed the Chasseur, raising his eyebrows; "I have replied to the best of my knowledge."

"And Hadj Absalam? What has become of him?" I asked, noticing that we were now passing heaps of human bones, already stripped by the vultures and whitened by the sun.

"We captured him when we entered the palace, and imprisoned him in one of the smaller chambers, under a strong guard. He endeavoured to commit suicide, but was prevented."

I asked no further question. I remembered only the sweet, beautiful face of the brave, fearless woman to whom I owed my life, and who had promised to love me always. How her calm, serious, wistful countenance came up before me! Surely it could not be that I was never to look again into those dark, luminous eyes, so appealing and so true—surely they were not closed for ever in death! Now I had successfully elucidated the mystery that had remained an unsolved problem a thousand years, surely she would not be snatched from me! Yet Zouave guards were resting on their rifles at the gate; in the open space beyond a bugle was sounding, and a word of command shouted in French brought to a halt half a battalion of Turcos in marching order. Agadez was in the possession of the French. Ever extending their territory in the Soudan, they had, while breaking the power of the Ennitra, firmly established themselves at another important advanced post. But at what cost? Alas! at the cost of my happiness!

I was dazed, stupefied. The only idea I could grasp was that all my efforts through long and weary months had been in vain; that I had been unable to save her. Truly, the Omen of the Camel's Hoof was being fulfilled!

Without pausing to gaze upon the half-burned town, I sped onward to the Fáda, where I was told I should probably discover my friend, Captain Carmier. My search did not occupy long, for I found him in the ruined Hall of the Divan, in conversation with General Seignouret, the elderly officer in command of the expedition.

"You! *mon cher* Cecil?" cried the Captain gaily, extending his hand as I advanced. "What brings you here?"

"Cannot you guess?" I answered.

"You told me months ago at Tuggurt that you were journeying here to fulfil some strange promise you had made to a woman. You little expected to find us here before you—eh?" he asked, laughing.

"When I was your guest on my way south, I could not tell you the object of my journey, as I had promised to keep it secret."

"Well, the woman must have been particularly fascinating to have induced you to undertake such a risky journey, especially with Hadj Absalam's band scouring the Desert."

"You will admit, I think, that she was fascinating," I said as quietly as I could. "Her name was Zoraida."

"*Dieu*! Not the woman who is known as Daughter of the Sun?"

"The same. She has promised to become my wife. Take me to her. Let me speak with her," I urged, frantic with impatience.

"Alas! *mon ami*! I regret I cannot," he replied, shaking his head sorrowfully.

"She surely is not dead?"

"No—not dead. She is a prisoner, and, with Hadj Absalam and a man called Labakan, is on her way, under a strong escort, to Algiers."

"To Algiers?" I gasped, dismayed.

"It is unfortunate that she of all women should have fascinated you," observed General Seignouret, who had been standing by, "because her career has been a terrible one. The Ministry in Paris gave orders for her capture months ago, and offered a heavy reward, which my men here have at last won. I have now sent her to Algiers for trial."

"She is innocent. She hated the life; those scenes of bloodshed and horrible barbarities appalled and nauseated her," I cried in passionate protest. "Her strange position had been thrust upon her by sheer ill-fortune. Tell me, for what crimes will she be tried?"

"For outlawry and murder," the General answered abruptly. "And the punishment?"

"Why think more of her?" he suggested, casting away the end of his cigarette. "It is useless to still contemplate marriage, for her freedom is impossible when the punishment for either offence is the guillotine."

"The guillotine?" I cried, in mad despair. "And your men are dragging her onward—onward across the Desert to a cruel, ignominious, and brutal end?"

"Think of the massacre of Deschanel and his brave Spahis, of the many raids whereby unarmed caravans have been looted, and their owners butchered; think of the hundreds of our men who have been ruthlessly murdered or horribly tortured by the fiendish band under the leadership of this pretty savage! It was her presence, her voice, that urged on the Ennitra to the frightful massacre and awful barbarities after this city had fallen into their hands; and again she commanded her people in their desperate defence of the city when we endeavoured to take the place by surprise."

"But I tell you the leadership was forced upon her against her will by those ferocious brutes!" I said warmly. "Ah! you do not know her as well as I."

"We know her quite sufficiently to be aware that her crimes have cost many of our unfortunate comrades their lives, and that the death sentence is the only one that can be passed upon her. The Government are determined the punishment in her case shall be exemplary," the stern old General answered, turning from me to take a dispatch that had just been brought in by a Spahi messenger.

"Come, old fellow," Cannier whispered, taking me kindly by the arm and leading me forth into the once-beautiful harem-garden. "Forget this woman. For her it must certainly be either the *lunette* or *La Nouvelle*. No effort of yours can ever give her freedom. Besides, think of her past; is she, after all, worth troubling about?"

"Worth troubling about? Yes," I answered promptly, turning upon him angrily. "Why should you judge her thus? You only know her by the idle and exaggerated gossip of the camp; yet you believe her to be a bloodthirsty harridan, delighting in scenes of massacre and pillage, a woman who regarded every caravan, every Zouave, and every Chasseur as her lawful and natural prey!"

"No, not a harridan by any means!" he exclaimed. "I admit her beauty and grace is unsurpassed. She is by far the most lovely woman I have ever seen—and I have seen a few beauties in my time at Royat, Etretat, Biarritz, and Trouville."

"I am not discussing her countenance, *mon ami*" I continued, with perhaps undue warmth. "I am asking why you condemn her. Tell me, have the authorities any direct evidence that she has ever been guilty of murder?"

He hesitated, rolling a fresh cigarette thoughtfully.

"Well—no," he answered. "As far as I am aware, there is no specific case upon which they rely."

"Then they intend to transport her to New Caledonia for life, or perhaps even drag her to the guillotine, merely to deter other tribes from defying French rule!" I said, biting my lip.

"*Sapristi*! It is useless to argue with you," he answered quickly. "You are fascinated by her, and, of course, will believe no ill. In your eyes she is simply a paragon of virtue. Therefore, the fewer words we exchange upon the painful topic the better."

"You have declared my inability to save her," I exclaimed with anger, indignant at his prejudice against her and at the thought of her, a prisoner, roughly handled by the uncouth Chasseurs, who even at that moment were hurrying her with all speed over the Desert towards Algiers. "You predict that all my efforts will be in vain; nevertheless, I shall follow, and do my best."

"If you attempt to rescue her from the custody of the escort, you will without doubt get a bullet in your head."

"I need no warnings," I snapped; but further words were cut short by the sudden reappearance of General Seignouret, who, advancing to my friend, exclaimed—

"I must send an urgent dispatch to headquarters at Algiers. Whom do you recommend to carry it?"

"I am starting at once for Algiers," I said; then, turning to Carmier, I urged, "Send Octave Uzanne, the Spahi. He is my friend."

"Uzanne?—Uzanne?" repeated the Captain reflectively. "Ah! I remember, I have heard of him. He was a survivor of Deschanel's detachment, and a valiant fellow. Yes, he shall bear the message."

"In an hour it will be ready," the General said; then, turning, he strode back into the Hall of the Divan, his spurs jingling, and his scabbard trailing over the polished floor that still bore ugly stains of blood.

"So you really intend setting out again on this fool's errand?" Carmier asked, when his General had gone.

"I do. I must—I will save her."

"Bah! Was she not a sorceress, a priestess of that strange secret society the Senousya, of which we can discover nothing; was she not indeed an inmate of Hadj Absalam's harem, a—"

"Nothing you can allege against her can deter me from the strenuous endeavour I am about to make," I interrupted, with firmness. "She shall not be snatched from me, for I love her. Be she innocent or guilty, I will save her!"

But, with a cynical smile, he shrugged his shoulders, and, turning on his heel, walked away.

Chapter Forty Five
The Price of Silence

Along the broad Boulevard de la République the straight double row of gas-lamps that face the sea were already shedding their bright light, as Octave and I drove rapidly, having at last arrived at Algiers. Our toilsome journey over the sun-baked Desert from Agadez had occupied us nearly five weeks, and now, after twenty-four hours in an execrable railway carriage, we had arrived with aching bones, heads wearied, and thoroughly worn out by fatigue.

Both of us were intensely anxious; he bound to deliver his dispatch, yet fearful lest the woman he loved should discover him, and I consumed by grief and despair, but nevertheless determined at all hazards to strive for the release of Zoraida. Inquiries we made at Biskra—the point where we had first touched European civilisation—showed that the prisoners, under a strong guard, had reached there and gone on by train to Algiers, thirteen days before our arrival. I saw, therefore, there was not a moment to lose. Zoraida was in deadliest peril, and I alone remained her friend. Through those long, weary, never-ending weeks, while we had been pressing onward over the glaring, monotonous plains, my thoughts had been constantly of her, and vainly did I endeavour, hour after hour, day and night, to devise some means by which I could effect her liberty. Tortured by gloomy apprehensions of her impending doom, meditating upon the hopelessness of the situation, and utter futility of attempting her release in face of the howling demand of the French colonists for exemplary punishment, I had journeyed onward, not knowing how to act. I had returned to Algiers to be near her, to hear the evidence at her trial, to—ah! I could not bear to contemplate the horrible moment!—to witness sentence passed upon her.

Across the Place du Gouvernement our driver took us swiftly, shouting, as he cleared a way through the crowd of cosmopolitan promenaders, who, while enjoying the refreshing breeze, listened to popular operatic airs performed by the splendid Zouave band. Against the clear, starlit sky, the white dome and square minaret of the Mosque de la Pêcherie stood out in bold relief, familiar objects that recalled vivid recollections of the strange adventures that had occurred to me on the last occasion I had passed under those walls. Reflections were, however, cut short by our sudden stoppage under the clump of palms before the Hotel de la Régence, and very soon we had installed ourselves in the same rooms overlooking the Place that I had previously occupied. While Octave ordered dinner, I walked to a clothier's a few doors away, selected some European habiliments to replace my dirty, ragged Arab garments, and on returning, purchased a copy of the *Dépêche*, which an Arab urchin was crying in a shrill treble. Ascending to the *salle-à-manger*, where my companion awaited me, I sank into a chair, and, opening my paper, glanced at its contents.

A newspaper was of interest, after being so many months cut off from one's own world, as I had been; but almost the first heading which caught my eye was, "The Governor's Reception To-Night;" and, having ascertained that His Excellency was giving a grand ball, I commenced reading an article headed, "The Assassins from the Desert," which, after enumerating the long string of crimes with which Hadj Absalam, Labakan, and Zoraida were to be charged, continued its hysterical denunciation as follows:—

"Too long have the piratical Ennitra been the terror, alike of caravan, village, and advanced post. For many years, indeed, ever since the rebellion, this tribe of freebooters has held sway over the Sahara entirely unchecked, pillaging, massacring, reducing their weaker neighbours to slavery, and attacking our military posts with an audacity and daring that has caused equal surprise on both sides of the Mediterranean. The crowning incident in the startling career of this extraordinary woman—who, if report be true, possesses the *beauté du diable*, and has actually led the marauders on their bloody forays—was the treacherous attack upon the column of Spahis, under Deschanel, at the well of Dhaya, when only nine of the force survived the massacre, all of them being held prisoners. The subsequent desperate assault on Agadez, the fiendish slaughter there, the revolting scenes enacted within the Sultan's palace, all are events fresh in the minds of our readers. Such horrible deeds, openly committed in territory under the rule of France, disgrace the military organisation upon which we pride ourselves, disgrace our *Service des Affaires Indigènes*, disgrace the annals of our colony, and cause all Europe to cry shame upon us. At length, however, the Government has tardily stirred itself; at last it has sent sufficient force in pursuit of this mysterious Queen of the Desert and her bloodthirsty horde; at last they are here, in Algiers, safe in the custody of trusty gaolers. Let justice now be done. Let no false sentiment be aroused on their behalf, merely because Zoraida is a woman. Beauty and sex have too often influenced a jury; but they must not in this case. As leader of the band, she is as guilty as this fierce old Sheikh who is pleased to style himself Sultan of the Sahara, therefore her punishment must be equally severe with his. Her case is unique, and requires exemplary sentence. If, by our present Code, she cannot be sent to the guillotine, then the people of Algeria demand the passing of a special Act. Deportation is no punishment for her many flagitious crimes; she must die."

The waiter brought me *L'Akhbar* and the *Moniteur*, both of which contained strongly-worded articles expressing an almost identical opinion, and all showing how high the feeling ran. Indeed, ere I had been in Algiers an hour, I could plainly see what intense excitement the capture of the prisoners had created, and what eager interest was manifested in their forthcoming trial. All Europeans and colonists were loud in their denunciations of the Ennitra in general, and Zoraida in particular, but the Arabs, who formerly had experienced secret satisfaction at the discomforture of their conquerors, now exchanged glances full of meaning, smoking, stolid, silent, and unmoved. No doubt, the Senousya were holding secret meetings everywhere to discuss the situation, and perhaps, in the *kahouas* at night, when the doors were closed and precautions taken that no unbeliever should overhear, there were whispers of a sinister and threatening character, and the dark-faced men of Al-Islâm clutched at their knives. But, to the world, the followers of the Prophet betrayed no concern. They awaited patiently the signal of the great uprising.

Our almost silent meal concluded, Octave went out to report himself at the military headquarters, and deliver General Seignouret's dispatch, while I ascended to my room and changed my travel-stained rags for the ready-made, ill-fitting suit I had bought. After making a hurried toilet, I stood at the window, hopeless and despondent, gazing out upon the splendid, cloudless night. From the great square below, where ghostly figures in spotless burnouses came and went, where lovers lingered under the deep shadows of the mosque, and Madame sold her journals at the little kiosque lit by a single glimmering candle, there came up a slow, dreamy waltz refrain, borne upon a breath of roses from the flower-stalls beneath the palms. The flashing light of the port swept the sea with its long shaft of white brilliance, a cool, refreshing breeze stirred the palm branches, and a fountain plashing into its marble basin, all combined to produce a tranquil scene, beautiful and entrancing.

But upon me its effect was only discord. Quickly I closed the windows to shut out the music, and looked slowly around the cheerless room. In desperation, I asked myself how I could act, but no solution of the problem came to me. I could only think of my crushing sorrow. The iron had entered my soul.

Slowly the clock in the mosque struck the hour. I counted the strokes. It was ten o'clock.

The bell aroused me. With clenched hands and quick, fevered steps I paced the room in a frenzy of despair. My mind seemed becoming unbalanced again. How true was the prophecy of my dead fellow-traveller, when he warned me that the Omen of the Camel's Hoof was always fatal to love. I had laughed then at his fateful words, but what poignant bitterness their remembrance now brought me!

In my desperation I was seized by a madness, violent and uncontrollable, for with all my hopes shattered and scattered to the winds, only an unbearable burden of grief and woe remained to me.

Zoraida's face was ever-present with me; the calm, beautiful countenance of the pure, honest woman, now being hounded to the scaffold by an indignant populace. I loved her with a true, fervent love; if she died, I told myself that I should no longer care to live. She was the only woman I had ever looked upon with affection, the only woman who had stirred the chords of love within me. I was devoted to her; nay, I idolised her. Surely Fate would not dash from my lips the cup of happiness now, at the very moment when I had discovered riches that would give her every luxury she could desire!

The Great White Diadem, the wonderful ornament concealed in the ragged saddle-bag that lay in the corner of the room, could avail her nothing. Its possession might in some mysterious way have secured her liberty had she been still held in bondage by Hadj Absalam. But alas! she was in a gloomy cell, guarded like a common murderess, night and day, by brutal warders, lest she should attempt to evade the executioner's knife by self-destruction; while I, who loved her so well, though there within sight of her prison, remained powerless to help her, powerless to lift a hand to release her from the clutches of her exultant captors!

Powerless?

I halted. In my despair a thought had flashed across my mind, a suggestion, the sheer madness of which at first stunned me, but which gradually impressed itself upon me as the only means by which I could save her. A bold audacity, a firm determination, and a cool head would be required to accomplish such a master-stroke. Qualms of conscience arose within me, but I calmed them by reflecting that desperate cases demanded violent remedies. Was I strong enough mentally and bodily? I hesitated. Again Zoraida's earnest appeal to me to save her rang in my ears; I could see her pale, tear-stained face, that had haunted me like a vision through so many weary weeks.

Her life lay in my hands. I determined to make the attempt.

Again I threw open the jalousies. The clock in the minaret showed it was half-past ten. Time was passing quickly, and I had not a second to linger. Breathlessly I gathered up the contents of my pockets that lay strewn upon the table, and, seizing my hat, descended the stairs, and quickly made my way across the square, through the crowd of idle promenaders.

Mine was a desperate mission. What its result might be I dreaded to contemplate.

Continuing up a narrow side street, where Arabs were squatting on rush mats calmly smoking and conversing in low, guttural tones, passing the façade of the cathedral, and speeding with hasty steps, I crossed another small square, and at length halted before a great Moorish doorway, guarded by sentries on either side. In answer to my summons, there appeared a French *concierge* in gorgeous livery, who, noticing the cut of my clothes, regarded me with a decidedly supercilious air.

"I desire to see M'sieur le Gouverneur," I said.

"M'sieur de Largentière does not receive," replied the man abruptly; then, as if suspecting me to be a traveller, he added, "If m'sieur wishes to view the palace, he must obtain a card from the aide-de-camp."

"I have no desire to see the palace," I answered. "I wish to see His Excellency himself, privately."

"Impossible, m'sieur. He receives only by appointment," the man said, raising his eyebrows, as with his hand still upon the handle of the great door, he prepared to close it.

"But my business admits of no delay. It is not official, but purely private. I must see him at once. Take my name to him, and say I desire to speak with him upon a matter of the greatest importance;" and, drawing a piece of paper from my pocket, I wrote my name upon it.

After examining the paper, the man reluctantly left me, gruffly telling me to take a seat. The great hall in which I stood was of magnificent proportions, with tesselated pavement and splendid palms. The palace of the representative of the Government—once the residence of Hassen Pacha—is one of the most luxurious in all Algeria, its Oriental magnificence rendering it a show-place where tourists wander, gape, and wonder. Half fearing that His Excellency would refuse me an audience, I remained impatient and excited, yet struggling desperately to preserve an outward calm. Presently the doorkeeper returned with slow, stately stride, and with apparent bad grace, said—

"M'sieur le Gouverneur, although extremely busy, has graciously consented to receive you for a few moments. Walk this way."

Following him to the extreme end of the great hall, he led me down a long, spacious corridor, halting before a silken *portière*, which he drew aside, and, opening a door, invited me to enter. The apartment was half an office, half a library, with a great writing-table littered with papers and official documents; bookcases were on every side, and hanging above the carved mantelshelf was a large portrait in oils of the President of the Republic. The room was thickly carpeted and furnished strictly in European style, while on a side table stood a great bowl of flowers, the tasteful arrangement of which betrayed a woman's superintendence.

Striding up and down, I awaited anxiously the coming of the Governor-General.

At last the handle of the door rattled, and there entered an elderly man, whose closely-cropped, iron-grey hair and pointed moustache gave him a military appearance, and whose thin, tall figure was slightly bent by age. In the lapel of his frock-coat was the button of the Legion of Honour, and as he glanced keenly at me from under his shaggy brows, his face bore a proud, haughty look. He seated himself at the table, and an ill-concealed expression of displeasure crossed his frowning features.

"I must apologise for seeking an interview at this late hour, m'sieur," I began. "But my business is pressing."

"My servant has already told me that," he snapped, toying with a pen and casting another quick glance at me. "And what, pray, is the nature of this—er—business?"

"It is of a strictly private character," I answered, hesitating, exerting all my self-possession.

"Then explain it quickly, m'sieur," he said, turning to look at the clock. "I have guests to-night."

"First I must tell you that I have only this evening arrived from the Desert," I exclaimed, standing before him boldly, my hands behind my back.

"You are English," he growled. "Tourist—eh?"

"No, I'm not a tourist," I replied. "I know the Sahara, perhaps even better than yourself; in fact, I have just returned from Agadez."

"From Agadez?" he exclaimed, suddenly interested. "Then, perhaps, you were with Seignouret when he captured the Sheikh of the Ennitra?"

"No, I arrived later," I said. "But it was not to describe the situation there that I have intruded. I desire to speak to you with regard to Zoraida."

"Zoraida? Zoraida?" he repeated, puzzled. "Ah! of course! the Arab woman taken prisoner with the other scoundrels. Well, what of her?"

"When will she be tried?"

"In two days' time. She has already been examined, and admits all the charges against her."

"Charges! What are the charges?" I demanded.

"Outlawry and murder," he answered, carelessly turning over some papers.

"Then listen, M'sieur le Gouverneur," I said anxiously. "I love her—I—"

"Bah!" he cried in disgust, rising quickly with his hand upon a silver gong. "As I expected—an appeal!"

"Hear me!" I cried. "Before you summon your servants, I warn you that silence will alone secure your own safety!" Standing astride upon the lion's skin spread before the fireplace, he stared at me in alarm.

"What—what do you mean?" he gasped, pale and scared.

"Seat yourself, I beg, and hear me," I said coolly. "Have no fear; I am not an assassin."

"Then how dare you—how dare you threaten—"

"I threaten nothing," I stammered, interrupting. Then firmly I added, "Be seated, and allow me to explain."

Slowly he sank again into his chair in obedience to my command, and I told him briefly that Zoraida had saved my life, that she had become my *fiancée*, and that I intended to effect her liberty.

"You're mad!" he ejaculated at last. "How can this declaration of your intentions to defeat the ends of justice interest me? I'm not governor of the gaol."

"No. But you, M'sieur de Largentière, are Governor-General of Algeria, and in your hands lies the supreme power—the power of life and death."

"Supreme power for what?"

"To effect her escape."

"To connive at the liberty of a person who admits crimes that have from time to time startled the world! Bah! For months, nay, years, our troops have been hunting this band of freebooters, and now at last, when the leaders are in our hands, it is very likely, indeed, that I, of all men, should sign an order for her release!" and he laughed derisively as he twisted his moustache.

"I do not desire you to commit yourself in the eyes of your Government and the public by appending your signature to such a document. Might she not escape—vanish from Algiers, suddenly—eh?"

"Absurd!" he cried impetuously, with flashing eyes. "I must really request you to end this interview. If you have any complaint of your treatment while in Algeria, you had better lodge information with your consul. He will deal with it. I have neither desire nor intention of being bothered over your love-affairs. You request the release of the leader of a robber band. *Ma foi!* you will next try to bribe me with some of the stolen booty!"

"I shall not bribe you, m'sieur," I answered defiantly, with suppressed anger, advancing to the table and bending towards him. "But you will, nevertheless, arrange that Zoraida will obtain her freedom—to-night."

"You must be an imbecile!" he cried. Then, with a sarcastic laugh, he asked, "And how much, pray, do you offer me as a *douceur?*"

"I offer you," I said plainly and distinctly. "I offer you, M'sieur de Largentière, *your own liberty!*" "My own liberty!" he gasped, starting in alarm. "My own liberty? I do not understand."

"Ah, no!" I exclaimed, with a short, harsh laugh. "You do not know me. We are strangers."

"I—I was not aware that I was in your custody, m'sieur," he said, crimson with indignation.

"No," I answered, with a coolness that surprised even myself. "But your life is!"

"You—you come here—to—to demand this woman's liberty under threats of assassination!" he gasped.

"I have a revolver here, it's true," I replied. "But I have no intention of committing murder, even though the life of my *fiancée* is at stake."

"You—you threaten me!—you come here, and—"

"Henri, dear!" a voice called in English. "Why, here you are! I thought you had dressed long ago. Already some of the guests have arrived!" and, turning quickly, I saw a tall, beautiful woman in a marvellous ball toilette. Her face I recognised instantly by the photographs I had seen in London shop-windows. It was Madame de Largentière!

"I—I am coming, dear—coming," he answered hastily, in broken English.

"Then I will wait for you."

"Excuse me, madame," I said; "the business I am just concluding with your husband is of an official and strictly private nature."

"Oh, of course in that case I will leave you alone," she said, with a slight, graceful bow, and, urging the Governor to hasten, she swept out, closing the door after her.

"Well?" he asked when she had gone. "What do you mean by these strange threats? I do not know you, and I've nothing whatever to fear from you."

"As time is of importance to both of us, I may as well speak plainly at once, m'sieur," I said, folding my arms resolutely. "I require Zoraida's release before the dawn."

"Impossible!"

I paused. The moment had arrived when I deemed it expedient to spring the mine upon him.

"Then you will no longer be Governor-General of this colony!" I exclaimed.

"Your words are absolute nonsense. *Diable*! You English are always more or less insane!"

"Do you absolutely refuse to grant her liberty?"

"Most decidedly I do."

"Then listen!" I said determinedly. "Listen, while I bring back to your recollection certain curious facts that, although concealed, are nevertheless not forgotten. You jeer at my discomfiture; you would send a pure, innocent woman to the guillotine, because you fear the consequence of her escape might be your removal from office. Very well. Believe me, you will soon enough be recalled, and sink to a fitting end of ignominy and shame."

"*Dieu*! Your mouth is full of insults."

"Be silent until I have finished; then give me your decision," I continued resolutely. "Not long ago there lived in London a nobleman who had a young and beautiful daughter. She had the misfortune to be an heiress. An aged ex-Minister, a Frenchman, met her, and coveted her gold. He proposed, and was accepted by the nobleman, but there were two barriers to their marriage: firstly, a lover to whom the heiress had already given her heart; and secondly, a cousin who had lived in Paris a long time, and, knowing its seamy side, knew also Mariette Lestrade, a whilom luminary of the Moulin Rouge, who resided in a pretty bijou villa on the edge of the Bois, under the protection of the ex-Minister. The latter, however, was not a man to be easily turned from his purpose, for, strangely enough, the heiress's cousin was found murdered in his chambers in St. James's Street, and—and the alleged murderer—"

"The murderer escaped!" he declared involuntarily, for he had grown pale, and was glaring at me with transfixed, wide-open eyes.

"Yes, quite true, he did escape. He escaped to marry and secure the fortune of the heiress, and—*to become Governor-General of Algeria!*"

"What—what do you allege?" he gasped, jumping to his feet, his face livid. "Do you impute that I—I committed the murder?"

For a moment I regarded him steadily. Under my gaze he flinched, and his hands trembled as if palsied.

"I impute nothing," I answered quietly. "I have already in my possession absolute proof of the identity of the murderer."

"Proof?" he gasped. "What—what do you mean?"

With his eyes fixed upon me, his thin lips quivered as the startling truth dawned suddenly upon him.

"If you desire me to explain, I will," I said. "Violet Hanbury's lover, a compatriot of yours, is believed to have committed the crime."

"It was proved," he declared quickly. "The knife with which the victim was struck was his, and upon the floor was found a gold pencil-case, with his name engraved upon it; besides, he was seen there by the valet. The police have searched for him everywhere, but he has disappeared."

"I now appear in his stead to disprove the terrible charge against him— to bring the assassin to justice."

"If you can," he said, assuming an air of haughty insolence. "Believe me, m'sieur, I shall have but little difficulty."

"And the proof! Of what, pray, does it consist?"

"It is something, the existence of which you little dream."

"Oh!" he cried. "This is infamous!"

"You seek an explanation, therefore I will conceal nothing. When you are before a criminal court, which will be at a date not far distant, M'sieur de Largentière, you will have to explain why the murdered man called on you at Long's Hotel in Bond Street, in the afternoon of the day of the murder."

"He did not call."

"The Court will decide that."

"Bah!—do your worst. I—I am Governor-General of Algeria, and you—you are an unknown alien."

"True, you are on French soil, but there is such a thing as extradition. In a week I shall be in London, and then—"

"What then?" he asked, vainly endeavouring to remain calm.

"I shall place the Criminal Investigation Department at Scotland Yard in possession of such facts that your extradition will be immediately demanded."

"You talk nonsense," he cried impatiently. "Let us end this interview. I—I am really too busy to listen to such empty threats and idle boasts."

"My only boast is that I shall be the means of bringing an assassin to justice," I exclaimed quickly.

"I have not the slightest fear of the consequences of your ridiculous story," he answered, with a sneer. "You are at liberty to act as you think proper. As for this remarkable evidence which you assert is in your possession, well—I do not know its nature, neither do I care."

"Perhaps it will be as well if you are acquainted with its nature," I said. "You declare that Fothergill did not call on you at Long's on that day?"

"Most decidedly I do. I had not seen him for quite a week prior to the tragedy."

"Then would it surprise you very much to know that, an hour after calling on you in Bond Street, he wrote to the man who is now suspected of the crime, telling him the details of that interview—"

"The details?" he echoed, amazed.

"Yes, the details," I repeated. "They were given very minutely regarding Mariette Lestrade and her relations with you, your efforts to preserve your secret, and your threats of violence should he divulge anything to prejudice you in the eyes of Lord Isleworth."

"Absurd. No such letter was ever written."

"It was," I replied, and drawing slowly from my pocket a piece of folded paper, I added, "Its original still exists, and I have a copy here."

"The—the dead man—wrote it?" he gasped, turning ashen pale.

"Yes. It will prove interesting reading at the trial. Glance at it for yourself."

Taking the sheet of paper, he held it to the lamp with trembling fingers. As he eagerly devoured its contents, his eyes seemed starting from his head, so wildly did he glare at it. For several moments he stood, supporting himself by the back of his chair.

"A denunciation from the grave," I said. "It makes your motive plain, and shows your crime was premeditated. When your rival left England, the circumstantial evidence was strongly against him, and though innocent, he was unable to prove an alibi, but that letter will render the discovery of the murderer an easy task."

"You are not my judge!"

"The man accused had no motives for murdering Jack Fothergill—you had."

"Motives do not convict in France, even if they do in England."

"But evidence of the crime does."

"Evidence—I—I—"

Looking steadily for a few moments into his thin face, drawn and haggard, I said at last—

"It is useless to deny your guilt, M'sieur de Largentière. The proof you have in your hand, in combination with the alibi that the man suspected will be able to prove, is quite sufficient to secure your conviction. The punishment for murder is death in my country, as in yours."

"I—I deny it," he said, with a strange, wild look of mingled fear and indignation. "Your so-called proof is mere waste paper. It would not be accepted in evidence."

"I hold a different opinion. Remember the letter was posted and the envelope bears the post-mark. It was written by Fothergill himself, and bears his signature."

"Let me see it."

"No. It may be shown to you when you are before the judge, not until then."

"The accusation is false and infamous!"

"Very well. If you have a perfect answer, you have nothing to fear."

"Nothing—no, nothing!" he repeated quickly, with a hollow laugh.

"Mariette Lestrade also died mysteriously," I said, raising my hand towards him. "Fothergill knew your terrible secret—the secret that she did not succumb to natural causes. You committed the second crime in London *in order to hide the first in Paris!*"

"I—I—" he stammered, but his lips refused to utter further sound.

"I am well aware of the facts, I assure you," I exclaimed. "First, however, let me tell you that I hesitate to place the London police in possession of them on account of the terrible shame and degradation your exposure will cause your wife and children. You who hold the highest office in this colony, who are respected and considered just, upright, and above suspicion, would be convicted of two brutal crimes. What would those who shake your hand at your reception to-night say if they knew their amiable Governor was an assassin?"

"Stop!" he cried hoarsely. "*Dieu!* stop! I—I cannot bear it!"

"It is not for me to heap reproach upon you. You jeered at the suggestion that I could bribe you to allow Zoraida to escape. Do you now refuse the *douceur*?"

"If she escaped mysteriously—what would my *douceur* be?"

"My silence."

"Absolutely?"

"Absolutely."

"And you would give me the original letter written by Fothergill?"

"No. Though I am prepared to take an oath of silence for the sake of your wife and her children, I make one stipulation, namely, that I shall keep that letter."

"Then you will always retain that in order to blackmail me?"

"I shall never blackmail you. Cannot you see that I am driven to this course by sheer desperation? Once Zoraida is safe, you will have nothing whatever to fear from me."

"If—if I could only bury the past completely!" he moaned, gazing wildly around the room. "If only I—I could feel safe!"

"Two courses are open. You must choose between them."

"To-morrow."

"No. To-night. I must have your answer now, immediately. If you refuse, I leave by to-morrow's steamer for England."

There was a long silence, broken only by the low ticking of the marble clock and the distant strains of a waltz from the ball-room. Into his chair the haughty Governor-General of Algeria had sunk, and, resting his elbows upon the table, had buried his thin, pale face in his hands. I had spoken the truth! His terrible secret was in my keeping. Even at that moment I hated myself for promising to shield him from justice; yet I was determined to save Zoraida, cost what it might. Uzanne was in ignorance of my intention to seek the assassin. Would he regard this action as a breach of confidence?

The man before me, whoso reputation as a statesman was world-wide, and whose virtues were extolled in the journals all over Europe, had utterly broken down. He saw that if he connived at Zoraida's escape, such indignation would be heaped upon him that he would be hounded from office; while on the other hand, if he refused, my threat of exposure undoubtedly meant the gallows. He recognised that I was determined, and was completely nonplussed.

"Henri, dear!" cried a voice outside the door. "Have you concluded your business? Do go and dress."

Starting up wildly, he rushed to the door, and, turning the key, stood panting with his back against it.

"Yes, in five minutes—in five minutes I—I shall be at liberty," he answered, with difficulty. Then we both listened, and heard a woman's footsteps receding along the corridor.

"Have you decided?" I asked.

Again he tottered across the room to his chair.

"I—I have," he gasped hoarsely, with bent head.

"What is your decision?"

"That she shall escape. She must leave the country immediately. If the secret that I conspired to set her free ever transpires, my career is doomed. Have you any suggestion to offer as to—as to the manner the flight shall be accomplished?"

"She must be placed on board an English ship," I said. "In the hotel I noticed a placard announcing the calling of the steam pleasure-yacht *Victoria*, and that the vessel will depart for Gibraltar and London at two o'clock to-morrow morning. Would there be any chance of sailing in her?"

"Ah! I had forgotten! That vessel is now lying outside the harbour," he cried suddenly, looking up into my face. "A friend of mine is returning to England in her. He told me yesterday that there were several vacant berths. Seek Stuart Bankhardt, the agent in the Rampe Chasseloup-Laubat, and secure two places. Then go on board and wait."

"Nothing else?"

"No. The captain will be given an explanation, and your *fiancée*, in European dress, will be placed on board before you sail."

Rising quickly, he went over to the telephone and rang the bell. In a few moments the answering bell tinkled, and into the transmitter he shouted—

"Send Jacques to my private room immediately."

Turning again to me, he asked—

"Are you satisfied?"

"If you fulfil your promise."

"I shall," he answered hoarsely. "And you, on your part, swear before Heaven that my—my secret shall never pass your lips?"

"I do."

Grasping my hand quickly with cold, trembling fingers, he gripped it as in a vice, then, bowing stiffly, he said in a low, strained voice—

"*Bon soir, m'sieur. Adieu.*"   .

I murmured some words, expressing a hope that we should never again meet, and a few seconds later strode out and along the marble corridor to the great entrance hall.

Chapter Forty Six
Some Amazing Facts

With eyes eagerly strained in the direction of the harbour, where hundreds of lights shimmered upon the dark, restless waters, I leaned over the taffrail of the steam yacht in anxious expectation. We were anchored some distance outside the harbour, with our bows seaward.

The clock of the mosque had struck half-past one. There was dead silence everywhere, save for the lazy lapping of the waves upon the sides of the steamer, and an occasional distant shout among the shipping inside the breakwater. Moon and stars had become obscured, but ever and anon the revolving light shed its white beams over many miles of shining water, appearing and disappearing with monotonous regularity. From the glass-covered roof of the saloon came a mellow glow of electricity that showed the bearded, rugged face of the solitary British sailor who paced the deck. On the extreme left of the White City, half concealed by the huge breakwater, loomed the great dark walls of Fort Bab Azzoun, wherein Zoraida was incarcerated, and from the shadows of which I expected every moment to see a boat emerge. But though time dragged on, and the escaping steam, increasing in volume, showed that we should soon weigh anchor, I could distinguish nothing. Minutes dragged like days. What if, after all, my efforts failed?

Sailors tramped the deck, orders were shouted from the bridge, ropes were coiled, and a steam-winch whirred with metallic ring. At last the ship's bell tolled. It was two o'clock! -

Still I strained my eyes towards the land, but could detect no moving object. Had the Governor-General deceived me? As each precious moment went by, I began to think he had. From above an order was given, four seamen rushed past me, and in a few moments the anchor was being slowly hauled up. Three long dismal shrieks from the steam siren echoed over the water and among the hills, and just as they died away I heard a distant shout. Dashing headlong to the opposite side of the ship, and peering away into the darkness, my heart gave a bound, for approaching gradually nearer was a boat containing three occupants.

It was hailed by the officer on the bridge, the electric signal rang into the engine-room, and the propeller, that had already begun to revolve, was immediately silent. Quickly the oars dipped, and the two rowers strained every muscle, until at last they drew alongside. A rope was thrown, made fast, and without delay a female figure, enveloped in a long dark travelling-cloak, the hood of which, drawn over her head, concealed her features, was hauled unceremoniously on board.

"Where am I?" I heard her cry in Arabic, alarmed at finding herself standing on deck between two rough sailors, whose language was strange to her.

Advancing quickly, I placed my hand upon her arm, replying in her own tongue—

"Have no fear. I have at last secured thy release. Thou art free! See! already we are on our way to England!"

"Ah!—Ce-cil!" she cried gladly, flinging her arms around my neck, and shedding tears of joy. "I—I thought thou wert lost to me for ever!"

"I made a promise which I have fulfilled," I said, leading her back to the taffrail, where, alone and unobserved, I kissed her fondly, she returning my caresses with a passion that showed how well she loved me. The dress she wore, though fitting her badly, was of a thick, coarse material, well adapted for travelling, but the cloak covered it, and beyond her speech there was nothing about her to show she was a child of the Desert. Her skin was almost as fair as an Englishwoman's, and her bright, luminous eyes had not become dimmed by the weeks of imprisonment, harsh treatment, and mental agony.

As the captain signalled "full steam ahead," and the boat that had brought my idol from the shore was cast off with a shout of farewell, I told her briefly that I was taking her away to my own people, where we should be married and live always in ease and comfort. Locked in each other's arms, I related how I, at the last moment, had learned the key to the Great Secret from Mohammed ben Ishak, and how subsequently I had discovered the wonderful Treasure of Askiá.

"Yes," she said, bowing her head. "I knew of its existence, but dared not break my oath. Forgive me—forgive me!—I am not worthy to be thy wife."

"Why?"

"Because—because I allowed thee to risk thy life when I might have obviated thy danger by confessing all to thee," she answered, her trembling hand grasping my wrist.

"Wilt thou explain everything to me now?" I asked.

"Yes, everything," she said. "I have left my people. The bond between the Senousya and myself is broken, for I go now with thee to the country of the Roumis, and nothing have I to conceal. Ah! thou knowest not the grim tragedy of my life."

"But thou hast given me wealth, and with thee I shall obtain perfect happiness."

"I trust in thee," she said. "I go to thine unknown world with thee, for I know thou lovest me. Now that thou hast given me freedom and a new life, I will relate unto thee the story of my bitter past."

Together we leaned upon the rail, and with the cool sea-breeze fanning our temples, we watched the ever-lengthening line of foam left by the propeller, as the distant, twinkling lights of the city faded in the gloom. The other passengers were below in their berths, and as we stood together unobserved, she explained to me things that I had through so many months regarded as impenetrable mysteries.

"My traducers and my persecutors have always spoken of me as a daughter of the Ennitra," she commenced. "They were mistaken. I was in no way related to any of that fiendish band. My father was Sheikh of the Beni M'zab, and at his death he entrusted to me, his only child, an ancient tablet of wood, together with the Crescent of Glorious Wonders, telling me that for generations these had been in the possession of our family, and that they would lead to an extraordinary discovery; at the same time, causing me to take solemn oath to divulge nothing that he told me. I was held to secrecy by a bond of blood. About one moon after my father's death, our caravan encamped at the palms of El Maessifer, on the border of the Touat Oasis, and at night we were attacked by the Ennitra. The massacre was awful. The majority of our men were slaughtered, our caravan looted, and the women and children, myself included, carried off to Hadj Absalam's palace in the mountains. Already I had learned many feats of magic of the sorcerer of our tribe, and my father had initiated me as a priestess of the Senousya; so with the Crescent and the strangely-carved wooden tablet in my possession, I resolved to try, if possible, to preserve mine honour by declaring myself possessed of miraculous powers. Already had I heard that our enemies the Ennitra were highly superstitious, therefore I strove to impress my captors by performing some simple but astonishing feats of legerdemain. This so impressed the men who held me in bondage, that when we arrived at the palace, they brought me before Hadj Absalam, who himself witnessed some of my feats. He acknowledged himself astounded, and ordered me to be sent to his harem as a portion of the spoils of war."

"To his harem?" I cried, interrupting.

"Yes. An hour later he came to me, and it was then I produced the Crescent of Glorious Wonders, declaring that it bestowed upon its rightful owner good fortune and victory in the field. At once he desired to possess it, but I pointed out that the strange talisman would only bring ill-fortune to one who possessed himself of it forcibly, and at length succeeded in making a compact with him, whereby I should exert its mystic powers on behalf of his tribe, in return for which, he would refrain from taking me to his harem, and treat me as a daughter, and not as a wife. The arrangement was a perfectly equitable one, and proved satisfactory, for a week later, bearing the Crescent, I led an expedition against the Tédjéhé-n'ou-Sidi with such success that we secured nineteen camel-loads of booty, and took one hundred and ninety prisoners. From that moment, though I hated Hadj Absalam and his crafty councillor Labakan, I became their leader and their prophetess. Through the regions of the Tanezrouft, the Ahaggar, and the Tidjoudjelt we rushed with fire and sword, always proving victorious. We were feared on every hand. Against the Spahis, Turcos, and Chasseurs we advanced time after time with the Drum of Nâr—which had been captured from my tribe—spreading terror, panic, and death, until the people, with one accord, acknowledged that I was possessed of power supernatural. I became revered as a prophetess, and earned the appellation of Daughter of the Sun. Meanwhile, from the lips of a soothsayer, Hadj Absalam had learned a romantic, and not altogether unfounded, legend regarding the Crescent, and having obtained a vague suspicion of its mysterious connection with the Treasure of Askiá, offered me my liberty if I could discover the whereabouts of the hidden jewels. Mohammed ben Ishak, who held the key to the mystery, was, however, in Agadez, and though I was striving always to elude the vigilance of my captors, yet I was utterly helpless."

Briefly I told her of the *imam's* tragic death at the hands of the marabout.

"The old tomb-dweller, whom both Mohammed and I could cause to assume cataleptic rigidity at will, and who assisted at the Ramadân seances of the Senousya, was a deaf mute and a fanatic," she observed. "Doubtless he struck the blow, because he considered that by thine introduction to that place—one of the principal sanctuaries of the sect—Mohammed ben Ishak was revealing unto thee, an unbeliever, the secrets he had sworn to preserve." Then, continuing her story, she said: "At last, after the attack on the caravan of the worthy Ali Ben Hafiz, which resulted in thy capture,

I saw thee for the first time and released thee. I confess I loved thee, and was determined to escape and become thy wife. Knowing so little of the manners of the Roumis, I believed that the most secure way in which to cause thee to reciprocate my affection, was to impress thee with an idea of my magical powers. With that object I caused thee to be conducted to Hadj Absalam's house in Algiers, where I took thee below to the subterranean meeting-place of the supreme council of the Senousya, and there showed thee some marvels of magic to mystify thee. The snakes thou sawest were those used in the religious rites of the Aïssáwà, but quite harmless, being kept merely to create an impression of mystical power. I raised from his tomb a marabout,—who, though apparently dead, was only in a cataleptic state,—by an effort of the will, the secret of which was imparted to me by my dead father; and by a feat of magic I caused to be revealed to thee the Crescent of Glorious Wonders, sending thee away to distant Agadez, in order that thou shouldest learn the key of the mystery from the chief *imam*, the only person besides myself who knew of the inscription upon the wooden tablet. He was my father's half-brother, and had left our tribe to devote his life to the administration of the daily prayers in the City of the Sorcerers. At the moment thou hadst left me, Hadj Absalam returned. He had detected thy presence, and in a frenzy of passion struck me down, causing the wound in my side that thou hast already witnessed. While alone with me, thou hadst promised to seek no explanation of any of the mysteries until thou hadst returned to Agadez. In order, therefore, to test thy faith in me, I caused to be sent thee the hand of a dead servant, upon the finger of which I placed my rings with thine. I little dreamed, however, that I was so closely watched, or that Hadj Absalam had ordered Labakan to follow, regain possession of the Crescent, and assassinate thee. After thou hadst left for Agadez, I heard from time to time of thee, until suddenly there came the startling news of thy capture and thy detention within the Fáda. At once I proposed to the Ennitra an attack upon Agadez, pointing out that, owing to the assassination of the Sultan, the country was in a disturbed state. A great council was held, and the prospect of the enormous amount of loot that might be secured caused them to decide upon carrying out my proposal. Little time was lost, although, alas! in the meantime Labakan had followed thee, and secured thy release in order to kill thee. Of the attack, the victory, and the horrible massacre thou art well aware."

"I am. It was frightful."

"Ah! believe me, it was not my fault. True, I suggested the attack, but it was in order to secure thy release, so that thou couldst gain the Great

Secret, and discover the Treasure that would bring me liberty, and wealth unto thee. I had no idea but that thou wert still a slave within the palace, until thy sudden arrival with my waiting-maid Halima at our camp. Then I dared not withdraw, and was compelled to send forth the Drum of Nâr, and lead our fierce band onward into battle. Then, alas! even before we had fully occupied the city, the French troops descended upon us, and after a desperate conflict we fell into their hands."

"Hadj Absalam and Labakan will receive their due reward. They will be hurried to the guillotine," I said.

"None will mourn for them. Both were equally crafty and brutal; incapable of fidelity, even to their firmest friends. They plotted to take thy life; and at the moment they had secured possession of Agadez, Hadj Absalam was prepared to break his compact with me, and compel me to become his wife."

"But thou hast escaped it all," I said cheerily. "In London thou wilt become my wife, and we shall live together always."

"Ah! Cecil, I—I love thee so dearly. I regret nothing, if only thou wilt grant me forgiveness."

"I do forgive thee, dearest," I answered. "Thou hast broken the fetters that have bound thee to Al-Islâm, and, on the threshold of a new life, I wish thee all the happiness that a devoted lover can wish his bride. Thou knowest well how strong is my affection; how utterly I am thine."

She kissed me, holding her lips to mine in a lingering, passionate caress.

"Thou hast not explained to me the Secret of the Crescent," I continued, presently.

"How can I?" she answered, looking away to where the yellow streak of dawn was widening. "I know so little—so very little of it myself."

"But the strange inscription upon it? Hast thou never deciphered it?"

"Yes. It is in the Cufic character, and the words are, 'In the name of Allah, the Compassionate, the Merciful.'"

"And the mystic picture I witnessed on gazing into the mirror of the *imam*. What was it?"

"It was a representation of the death of Askiá, that was already prepared for thee, in order that thou mightest more readily recognise the spot where the Treasure lieth hidden."

"Canst thou not explain the reason of the strange phenomenon induced by the application of the Crescent to my brow?" I inquired.

"The only explanation is rendered here," she replied, drawing from the breast of her dress a small oblong tablet of some dark, hard wood, about six inches long by four wide, worn and polished by age. "See!" and, taking it across to where the light shone through the stained glass roof of the saloon, she added, "Dost thou behold a carved inscription?"

"Yes," I answered, glancing at it eagerly.

"Therein lieth the secret. Mohammed ben Ishak—on whom may the Merciful have mercy!—was well learned in occult things, and it was he who translated it to me, for, as thou seest, it is likewise carved in Cufic. According to his rendering, this writing is a record of the Sultan Askiá, who states hereby that whomsoever believeth in the legend of his hidden treasure a thousand years after his decease, so shall he take the Crescent to the spot—which was indicated to thee by the dead *imam*—and then shall the whereabouts of the concealed jewels be revealed."

"But to what unseen force dost thou attribute its marvellous power of producing an exteriorised image?"

"The inscription further states that so wealthy was the Sultan that he discarded his Great White Diadem, which was of purest gold and diamonds of the first water, and had caused to be constructed a strange semicircle of steel, tempered like a Damascus blade. This emblem of strength he wore upon his head instead of a crown, and it is this which we now know as the Crescent of Glorious Wonders."

"His crown?" I exclaimed, in abject amazement.

"Yes. The inscription telleth us that the steel was treated in such a manner that when placed upon the head of one possessed of a more powerful will than his fellows, it would, in manner most remarkable, retain the thoughts of its wearer, and transfer them to the person who next assumed it. The Crescent was worn by Askiá at the time he concealed his treasure, and though a thousand years have elapsed since that day, yet, by placing it upon thy brow, unto thee there was transmitted the dead Sultan's secret thoughts, which, reproducing the scene in thy mind, have enabled thee to unearth the jewels."

"Extraordinary!" I ejaculated. "But could not another person have learned the clue to the Great Mystery by the same method?"

"No, not unless he knew the spot whereon to stand before he put the Crescent to the test. I myself have secretly tried it, but the cave wherein the Treasure lieth hidden hath never been revealed unto me. Only Mohammed ben Ishak knew in what direction or in what country to seek it. The Crescent was in my possession, and he alone could furnish the key to its secret."

"Wonderful!" I said. "The story is astounding, and would be absolutely beyond belief were it not for the fact that I have already in my cabin below some of the jewels recovered from the dead Sultan's hoard. The transference of thought by means of this crescent of magnetised steel, the horns of which acted as positive and negative poles, must be one of the many marvels which, though known to the ancients, have been lost to us for ages."

I had read much of Dr Luys' extraordinary discoveries regarding hypnotic suggestion, which seemed to deny the existence of free will, for the assertion that the will of one person could be implanted into that of another had been proved over and over again; yet the power to produce this mysterious *rapport* was, I felt certain, a strange and startling development of what the European scientific world now terms magnetism; in fact, nothing less than a confirmation of Dr Burq's metalo-therapeutic theory that for so many years has puzzled the doctors of the Salpêtrière, and to the investigation of which Dr Chareot devoted so much earnest labour.

The love of the marvellous is one of the characteristics of the human race; and contemporary discoveries do not tend to diminish our inclination. Indeed, they extend the limits of the impossible, rendering us more credulous in regard to new ideas. Yet, were not many of the startling phenomena that have recently been discovered at the Charité known in the East ages ago; were not the facts that we believe new and miraculous, common knowledge at that time, and utilised in daily practice?

The absorption of thought by a band of magnetised steel was a startling fact, nevertheless the theory was, as I afterwards found, not an altogether unknown one. In the scientific domain nothing can be declared absolute, and this disclosure, marvellous and incomprehensible as it appeared, was, nevertheless, but a re-discovery of a mystical force which the ancients had accepted without seeking the cause, and the knowledge of which had been lost and forgotten by later generations.

"Is there nothing more thou hast to tell me, Zoraida?" I asked, my arm stealing around her waist, as I drew her towards me.

"Nothing," she answered. "This carved tablet, a portion of the strange heirloom that hath been in my family through so many years, and hath brought thee wealth, I give unto thee. I have no further explanation to make regarding my past—only to tell thee that from the first hour we met, when I was enabled to sever the bonds that held thee to the asp, I have, loved thee;" and as her head pillowed itself upon my breast, I bent, kissing her white brow with fervent devotion.

"Thou art snatched from an ignominious death,—or a fate worse even than the guillotine,—and thou art mine for ever, Zoraida. Thou goest with me to mine own world, a world that to thee will be strange and full of marvels; nevertheless, we shall be happy in each other's love always— always."

Her tiny hand clasped in mine tightened and trembled as she raised her beautiful face.

"I have looked with thoughts of love upon no man but thee, Cecil," she said. "To thee I owe my liberty, my life! Thou art mine own—mine own;" and our lips met, sealing a lifelong compact.

Chapter Forty Seven
Conclusion

The events that followed, although startling, may be briefly related.

On arrival in London, I saw by the newspapers that a most profound sensation had been caused throughout Algeria by Zoraida's escape. In explaining the flight of the beautiful leader of the Ennitra, the published dispatches hinted vaguely at the possibility of a "prominent colonial official" being seriously compromised.

It was apparent that the secret was out!

Breathlessly I opened the papers each morning, and read eagerly of the trial, condemnation, and eventually of the execution of Hadj Absalam and Labakan. But a telegram contained in the *Standard* on the very morning that Zoraida and I were quietly married at St. Paul's, Knightsbridge, was the most sensational of all. It reported that on the previous afternoon Monsieur de Largentière, the Governor-General of Algeria, had been found in his private room shot through the temple by his own hand! A revolver was found beside him, and upon his writing-table there lay a letter begging forgiveness of his wife, and—in the words of the correspondent—"the communication contained a very extraordinary statement," the truth of which was being investigated.

Its purport I easily guessed.

The reason which prompted him to take his life was made plain by Octave Uzanne, who, two months later, called upon me and explained in confidence how, on the day previous to the terrible *dénouement*, he sought an interview with the assassin of Jack Fothergill, asserting that he intended to return to France, and that if he were arrested upon the warrant still out against him, he should denounce him as the murderer. Octave likewise told him of the existence of the victim's letter, by which he meant to prove an *alibi*, and to which I had already referred. This, combined with the revelation made by one of the boatmen he had employed, that he was implicated in

Zoraida's escape, apparently caused him to take his life rather than face the terrible charges against him.

Six months afterwards, Octave and Madame de Largentière were married in Paris, where they still live, in a pretty house in the Avenue des Champs-Elysées. Frequently they are our guests at our Kensington flat;— although Madame Uzanne has never recognised me as the Governor-General's visitor, and is still ignorant of the guilt of her late husband, for she regards his suicide as having been committed during a sudden fit of insanity, brought on by the heavy responsibilities of his office.

As for the Treasure of Askiá, the whole of it has been recovered and sold by a syndicate formed in the City for that purpose. The jewels, the major portion of which, of course, fell to my share, were found to be of enormous value, their size astonishing the dealers, who, in many cases, were at first inclined to reject them as spurious imitations. In Amsterdam and Paris they created a great sensation, and sold for fabulous sums, several of the gems having now been added to the regalia of Queen Victoria and the Sultan of Turkey.

Zoraida, who is now beginning to chatter English fluently, no longer looks askance at our insular manners. Though she has exchanged her *serroual* and zouave for a tailor-made gown, and her little pearl-embroidered skull-cap for a milliner's *confection* of feathers and flowers, yet, happily, our civilisation does not civilise her to feminine foibles. Still an Oriental, she views many of our customs with a horror that oft-times causes me considerable amusement, but she is never so happy as when at evening, in the fitful light thrown by my study fire, she comes to gossip over the teacups in her native Arabic. Seldom, however, she recalls the horrors of those bygone days when she was Queen of the Sahara, and never without a shudder. She is supremely content in her new world, and has left for ever the parched glaring wilderness that once was her home.

In Society she has become popular, and her "at homes" are always crowded. Sometimes, when visiting, she will sing an Arab song, and entertain a small circle of her closest friends by giving them selections of music upon Arab instruments. The intricacies of piano-strumming she has never mastered. On every hand, indeed, my graceful desert-bride receives boundless admiration. There are many beautiful women in London, but it is agreed, I believe, that the countenance of none is more perfect in its symmetry and more pleasing in its expression than that of the Daughter of the Sun.

The Omen of the Camel's Hoof has not, after all, been finally fulfilled, for we live an almost idyllic life of peaceful bliss. My wife's diamonds, which are so often commented upon by the papers, are the same that for a thousand years constituted the magnificence of the Great White Diadem. The little wooden tablet, upon which is inscribed the key to the extraordinary enigma, is preserved in my study; the Crescent of Glorious Wonders, with its mystic geometrical device, is a conspicuous object upon the wall, and over it, suspended by its original thongs of camel's hide, there hangs the worn and battered Drum of Nâr.

They formed my wife's dowry, and, besides demonstrating a remarkable scientific fact, they have brought us sufficient of this world's riches to secure us ease and luxury.

Truly, my lot has fallen in a fair place. At last, in the bright sunshine of Zoraida's affection, the most perfect happiness is mine.